PRACTICAL AESTHETICS

Thinking in the World

Series editors: Jill Bennett and Mary Zournazi

Thinking in the World combines the work of key thinkers to pioneer a new approach to the study of thought. Responding to a pressing need in both academic and wider public contexts to account for thinking as it is experienced in everyday settings, the Reader and Book Series explore our thinking relationship to everything from illness, to built environments, to ecologies, to other forms of life and technology.

Bringing together phenomenology with recent trends in cognitive science and the arts, this unique, field-defining collection illuminates thinking as a practical activity. It interweaves a series of distinctive chapters and commentaries into a compelling whole, constituting a new framework and set of resources for analyzing thinking in real-world situations. Rather than simply thinking *about* the world, the authors examine the ways in which we think *in and with* the world in its physical, material, and social dimensions. A philosophy of thinking in action, it provides a multifaceted but sustained account of neurobiological experience and its inexorable connection to the world.

Other titles in the series:

Thinking in the World, ed. Jill Bennett and Mary Zournazi
An Anthropological Guide to the Art and Philosophy of Mirror Gazing, Lambros Malfouris and Maria Danae Koukouti

PRACTICAL AESTHETICS

Edited by Bernd Herzogenrath

BLOOMSBURY ACADEMIC
LONDON · NEW YORK · OXFORD · NEW DELHI · SYDNEY

BLOOMSBURY ACADEMIC
Bloomsbury Publishing Plc
50 Bedford Square, London, WC1B 3DP, UK
1385 Broadway, New York, NY 10018, USA
29 Earlsfort Terrace, Dublin 2, Ireland

BLOOMSBURY, BLOOMSBURY ACADEMIC and the Diana logo
are trademarks of Bloomsbury Publishing Plc

First published in Great Britain 2021
This paperback edition published in 2022

Copyright © Bernd Herzogenrath and Contributors, 2021

Bernd Herzogenrath has asserted his right under the Copyright, Designs
and Patents Act, 1988, to be identified as Editor of this work.

For legal purposes the Acknowledgments on p. ix constitute an
extension of this copyright page.

Cover design by Charlotte Daniels
Cover image © Getty Images

All rights reserved. No part of this publication may be reproduced or transmitted in any form or by any means, electronic or mechanical, including photocopying, recording, or any information storage or retrieval system, without prior permission in writing from the publishers.

Bloomsbury Publishing Plc does not have any control over, or responsibility for, any third-party websites referred to or in this book. All internet addresses given in this book were correct at the time of going to press. The author and publisher regret any inconvenience caused if addresses have changed or sites have ceased to exist, but can accept no responsibility for any such changes.

A catalogue record for this book is available from the British Library.

Library of Congress Cataloging-in-Publication Data

Names: Herzogenrath, Bernd, 1964- editor.
Title: Practical aesthetics / edited by Bernd Herzogenrath.
Description: London ; New York : Bloomsbury Academic, 2021. | Series: Thinking in the world | Includes bibliographical references and index.
Identifiers: LCCN 2020026387 (print) | LCCN 2020026388 (ebook) | ISBN 9781350116108 (hardback) | ISBN 9781350116115 (ebook) | ISBN 9781350116122 (epub)
Subjects: LCSH: Aesthetics. | Arts–Philosophy.
Classification: LCC BH21 .P73 2021 (print) | LCC BH21 (ebook) | DDC 111/.85–dc23
LC record available at https://lccn.loc.gov/2020026387
LC ebook record available at https://lccn.loc.gov/2020026388

ISBN: HB: 978-1-3501-1610-8
PB: 978-1-3501-8552-4
ePDF: 978-1-3501-1611-5
eBook: 978-1-3501-1612-2

Series: Thinking in the World

Typeset by Deanta Global Publishing Services, Chennai, India

To find out more about our authors and books visit www.bloomsbury.com
and sign up for our newsletters.

CONTENTS

List of Illustration — vii
Acknowledgments — ix

Introduction: Toward a Practical Aesthetics: Thinking *With* Bernd Herzogenrath — 1

1 The Experiment: Between Art and Life Christoph Menke — 25

2 On the Practice of Theory: The Technological Turn of Media Theory and Aesthetic Practice of Media Philosophy Katerina Krtilova — 35

3 Episode Zero: How Empirical Science Discounts Aesthetic Experience, and a Practical Way to Bring It Back Tim Ingold — 45

4 Practical Aesthetics: The Case of BioArt jan jagodzinski — 63

5 Colors without Bodies: Wes Anderson's Drab Ethics Eugenie Brinkema — 73

6 In Lag of Knowledge: The Video Essay as Parapraxis Johannes Binotto — 83

7 Thinking with Film Images in Dawson City: Frozen Time Bill Morrison — 95

8 Lapses, Affects, Supplement: Hiro Murai's Audiovisual Anachronism Tomáš Jirsa — 105

9 Some Notes on Sound Thinking Bernd Herzogenrath — 117

10 Thinking with Sound: Preliminary Thoughts François J. Bonnet — 125

11 In Search of Sacred Space John Luther Adams — 131

12 Thinking in Sound Craig Shepard — 141

13 Music as Sonic Praxis: On the Work of Catherine Christer Hennix Marcus Boon — 149

Contents

14 The Audio Paper as Affective Attunements: Thinking, Producing, and Listening *Sanne Krogh Groth and Kristine Samson* 159

15 Genealogies of Immersive Media and Virtual Reality (VR) as Practical Aesthetic Machines *Michael N. Goddard* 171

16 As *Duo*: Thinking with Dance *Elizabeth Waterhouse* 183

17 The Heart and Other Organs of Darkness in the Year 2019 *Allen C. Shelton* 195

18 Essayistic Imagination as Thinking *With*: Practical Aesthetics and Max Bense's Essay on the Essay *Christoph Ernst* 205

19 Radioactivity and the Typewriter's Breath: Practical Aesthetics in Pound and Olson *Julius Greve* 215

20 Can Practical Aesthetics Change Lives? *Jill Bennett* 227

21 Contaminations: Toward an Empathic Museology *Mieke Bal* 237

22 Thinking with Archival Ordering, or the Politics of Destruction *Ernst van Alphen* 247

List of Contributors 259
Index 267

ILLUSTRATION

Figures

6.1	*The Grand Budapest Hotel* (2014), Dir. Wes Anderson, United States: Fox Searchlight Pictures	77
6.2	*The Grand Budapest Hotel* (2014), Dir. Wes Anderson, United States: Fox Searchlight Pictures	77
6.3	*The Grand Budapest Hotel* (2014), Dir. Wes Anderson, United States: Fox Searchlight Pictures	79
7.1	*Glitched Peyton Place*	87
7.2	*Vertigo Variations, pt. 3*, Directed by B. Kite and Alexander Points-Zollo © Moving Image, 2011. All rights reserved	91
8.1	Film Find B-W photo 023. Courtesy Kathy Jones Gates	96
8.2	Dorothy Davenport in *Barriers of Society* (Universal, 1916)	96
8.3	DAAA Swimming pool—photo credit: Dawson City Museum	97
8.4	*The Christmas Accident* (Edison, 1912)	97
8.5	*Brutality*, directed by D. W. Griffith (Biograph, 1912)	98
8.6	Clifford Thomson, courtesy of the Dawson City Museum	98
8.7	Frederick Trump's Arctic Restaurant, Whitehorse, YT	99
8.8	Pathé Weekly, No. 65, 1914	99
8.9	Alexander Berkman, Pathé's Weekly No. 32, 1914	100
8.10	Film Was Born of an Explosive	100
8.11	*The Butler and the Maid* (Edison, 1912)	101
8.12	Mae Marsh in *Polly of the Circus* (Goldwyn, 1917) 01	101
8.13	*Birth of Flowers* (Pathé, 1920) 02	102
8.14	Florence Fleming Noyes dances in support of the suffragist movement (Pathé Freres, 1914)	102
9.1	*Day Ones ft Novelist & Leikeli47,* Directed by Hiro Murai © Doomsday Entertainment 2016. Vimeo. Screenshot by the author	107
9.2	*Day Ones ft Novelist & Leikeli47,* Directed by Hiro Murai © Doomsday Entertainment 2016. Vimeo. Screenshot by the author	108
9.3	*Day Ones ft Novelist & Leikeli47,* Directed by Hiro Murai © Doomsday Entertainment 2016. Vimeo. Screenshot by the author	112
16.1	"Catalog," Directed by John Whitney Sr., ©John Whitney Sr., 1961 (Held at Academy Film Archive)	176
16.2	"Dancing with the Virtual Dervish: Virtual Bodies," Created by Diane Gromala and Yacov Sharir, CC, Attribution-Non Commercial-NoDerivs	

Illustration

	3.0 United States, 1994 (Virtual Reality event) first "performed" at Banff centre for the Arts, 1994	178
17.1	Regina van Berkel and Jill Johnson Performing William Forsythe's *Duo*	187
17.2	Riley Watts and Brigel Gjoka Performing William Forsythe's *DUO2015*	187
17.3	Image by *Duo2015* Dancer Riley Watts, Superimposing His Body with His Partner Brigel Gjoka's	191
21.1	*Parragirls Past, Present* (viewer in immersive 3D film), 2017. Photo: Saeed Khan/AFP. Parragirls Past, Present. 2017. Immersive 3D Film (Still). Bonney Djuric, Jenny McNally, Lily Hibberd, Volker Kuchelmeister, Alex Davies. Lynne Edmondson Paskovski, Gypsie Hayes, Denise Nicholas Commissioned by: *The Big Anxiety: festival of art+science+people*, Sydney 2017	229
23.1	Marjan Teeuwen, Destroyed House Gaza #1 (2018)	253
23.2	Marjan Teeuwen, Destroyed House Gaza #3 (2018)	254
23.3	Marjan Teeuwen, Destryed House Gaza #6 (2018)	256

Map

1	Courtesy Allen C. Shelton	197
2	Courtesy Allen C. Shelton	203

ACKNOWLEDGMENTS

I would like to express my gratitude to Bloomsbury (in particular Liza Thompson and Lucy Russell) for giving us and me the opportunity to publish this book, and to all those wonderful people that contributed to this volume—it has been a pleasure!

This book is part of the "Thinking in the World" series—thanks to the series' editors for including our volume.

Special thanks go out to Louisa Collenberg, for all the work you've put into this!

I dedicate this book to Janna and Claudia, and to the memory of Frank.

A small part of Bernd Herzogenrath's introduction already appeared as a part of his introduction to *Film as Philosophy*. Ed. Bernd Herzogenrath. Minneapolis: U of Minnesota P, 2017, vii-xv, with kind permission.

Bernd Herzogenrath's chapter already appeared as a part of his introduction to *Sonic Thinking: A Media Philosophical Approach*. Ed. Bernd Herzogenrath. New York/London: Bloomsbury, 2017, 1-22, with kind permission.

All images in Bill Morrison's chapter are printed courtesy of Bill Morrison.

IN SEARCH OF A SACRED SPACE by John Luther Adams

© Taiga Press

Used by Permission

INTRODUCTION
TOWARD A PRACTICAL AESTHETICS
THINKING *WITH*
Bernd Herzogenrath

When in 1750 Alexander Baumgarten published the first part of his *Aesthetica*, he basically reinvented philosophy by defining a new way of how to perceive its objects of inquiry: logical analysis could not cope with the complexity of individual objects. Thus, logic had to be complemented by a nonabstractive way of analysis Baumgarten dubbed *aesthetics*, a theory of sensate thinking. Sensible or aesthetic cognition, "clear-obscure" as it is, is of the utmost importance for "making sense" of the world—the "logic of sense" has to be aligned with the "logic of sensation."

It might be of interest here that Baumgarten's *Aesthetics* (which he considers *both* a science *and* an art: a "science of the lower cognitive faculties" and an "art of beautiful thinking"; see §1 in Baumgarten 2007) opens with a chapter on "heuristics"—which does not denote a clear-cut method (the term "method" in fact denotes a μετά όδός, meta-hodos, a *way afterward*, a retroactive abstraction, a recipe), but is more related to a (nonfinite) inventiveness, an improvisation—and here Baumgarten relates to the αυτοσχεδιασ-ματα (improvisations) of the child that imitates beauty when it sees it, not merely apprehends it (like the adult; see § 57). Thus, what is at stake is not so much the issue of method, but rather the question of art's specific potential for expressing sensible cognition, with aesthetics as an *analogon rationis*, both analogous to and different from rational logics. Aesthetics thus counts as a defense of the Sensual as the Nonrepresentational, and this is not only evident in the content of thinking, but also in new forms of presentation, in which figures of thought reveal themselves.

The second part of Baumgarten's *Aesthetica*, though never published, was to be called *Aesthetica practica*—"practical aesthetics." And although it is safe to say that Baumgarten here wanted to show practical examples of his theory, I would rather pick up the thread of heuristics and improvisation, and would like to speculate on aesthetics as a science-art that mimics and imitates beauty and art in its performance, that is a "practical aesthetics" not as an "aesthetic practice," but an approach that takes aesthetics' double signification as both science *and* art serious and performs it from the perspective of the philosopher, not the artist—it takes the practice of the artwork not as its object of analysis, but as its own modus operandi: not thinking *about* art according to external (mostly rational, propositional) categories that more often than not follow the logic of the "written word," but thinking *with* art, thinking *with* images, thinking *with* sound, and so on.

The term "practical aesthetics" has of course been used before. Gesa Ziemer, who in *Verletzbare Orte* proposes a similar project, singles out Deleuze and Blumenberg as two "thinkers with art." She relates her idea of "practical aesthetics" to the architect Gottfried Semper, while I think that already Baumgarten points into a similar direction (Ziemer 2008)—as I mentioned, the term itself is his own. And of course, there is Jill Bennett's book *Practical Aesthetics. Events, Affect and Art after 9/11* (Bennett 2012). But while Ziemer is mainly relating this concept to artistic (or arts-based) research, Bennett calls for "an aesthetics informed by and derived from practical, real world encounters" (Bennett 2012: 2). Bennett's influential book is clearly indebted to Jacques Ranciere's idea of *aisthesis*, as perception and experience, whereas this book is rather about the more old-fashioned idea of philosophical aesthetics as "judgment of art," but under a new perspective. While Bennett deals with "affect" and its relation to a wider political and social field, pointing at an almost-"therapeutic" dimension of art (in particular as a—or in its—response to the 9/11 trauma), the concept of "practical aesthetics" guiding this collection is much more small scale: it is rather about a change in perspective and judgment on art—aesthetics in the philosophical sense—that might be welcomed (and is already approaching), an approach that is as theoretical as it is practical. This concept of practical aesthetics will have some aspects in common with both approaches, but will follow a different path.

In their book *A Thousand Plateaus*, Deleuze and Guattari argue for the importance of the artisan, "We will therefore define the artisan as one who is determined in such a way as to follow a flow of matter . . . it is a question of surrendering to the wood, then following where it leads by connecting operations to a materiality, instead of imposing a form upon matter" (Deleuze and Guattari 1987: 409–10). This quote praises the artisan in contrast to the artist, who does not work *with* the material, following its direction, but imposes his thought (and his form) on an otherwise stupid matter. If we take this idea one level further, a practical aesthetics, as I conceive it, requires a researcher who thinks with and through the artwork, not about it (in the sense of imposing external concepts on it).

According to Gilles Deleuze, one of the philosophers who, I argue, was instrumental in the notion of thinking *with* art:

> [t]he theory of cinema does not bear on the cinema, but on the concepts of the cinema, which are no less practical, effective or existent than cinema itself. . . . Cinema's concepts are not given in cinema. And yet they are cinema's concepts, not theories about cinema. . . . Cinema itself is a new practice of images and signs, whose theory philosophy must produce as conceptual practice. (Deleuze 1989: 280)

For Deleuze, art cannot be contained by making it conform to preexistent categories and concepts, explanations, and, thus, "judgments" that are brought to it from the outside. For Deleuze, the most important question is if—and in how far—art addresses life, how its creativity liberates vitality and processuality (of affects, of thought), or if it is rather a blockage to these forces, containing the free play of vitality and making it "play by the rules" of any given institution, language system, or "organization." Art thus is evaluated by the way it either enhances or reduces our powers to act, and it does so by affecting us in a particular manner. Art—as well as life—is a process of production and creation, and by that very characteristic involved in the bringing forth of "newness," which by definition is what evades "normative criteria": the indeterminable processes of both life and art can only be evaluated by and on their own terms, by features that are immanent to these processes themselves, but not by explanatory logics external to them. What is at stake here is not representation, but presentation—practical aesthetics is not the theorization of the sensual, but the inquiring and accompanying production of sensuality—or sensual thinking. Philosophy here does not morph into art, but proceeds in a playful proximity to art. To do philosophy in the way of a practical aesthetics is "to fabricate concepts in resonance and interference with the arts" (Rajchman 2000: 115), to facilitate an encounter "in which both art and thought come alive and discover their resonances with one another" (Rajchman 2000: 115).

"Do not count upon thought to ensure the relative necessity of what it thinks. Rather, count upon the contingency of an encounter with that which forces thought to rise up and educate the absolute necessity of an act of thought or a passion to think" (Deleuze 1994: 139). Deleuze distinguishes between two strategies of knowing, of thinking, of making sense. The one is what we might call (re)cognition, which simply relies on matching our experience with our culturally acquired knowledge, ideology, habits, and beliefs. It only confirms our expectations, what we already know, and this lack of friction does not allow for real thinking. This other strategy is what Deleuze calls an encounter.

An encounter challenges our habitual ways of experiencing and perceiving the world. It creates a fundamental break with our strategies how to conceive the world. Making or perceiving art is an encounter that opens up possible worlds, and it is "the object in question" that determines the strategies with which you "make sense."

As Deleuze specifies in one of his seminars, "Between a philosophical concept, a painted line and a musical sonorous bloc, resonances emerge, very, very strange correspondences that one shouldn't even theorize, I think, and which I would prefer to call 'affective' . . . these are privileged moments" (Deleuze 1983).[1] These moments privilege an affect where thought and sensation merge into a very specific way of "doing thinking" *beyond* representation and categorization—here, "traditional [rational] thinking" faces its own shortcomings. This is why, for Deleuze (and Guattari), "[p]hilosophy needs a nonphilosophy that comprehends it; it needs a nonphilosophical comprehension just as art needs nonart and science needs nonscience" (Deleuze and Guattari 1994: 218), in order to focus on the ways in which art, philosophy, and science ask the same kinds of questions and relate to each other's "findings," as it were. In that respect, whereas science involves the creation of functions, of a propositional mapping of the world, art involves the creation of blocs of sensation (or affects and percepts), and philosophy involves the invention of concepts. Yet, since "sciences, arts, and philosophies are all equally creative" (Deleuze and Guattari 1994: 5), it might be fruitful, as Deleuze proposes, "to pose the question of echoes and resonances between them" (Deleuze 1995: 123).

Practical Aesthetics

Film Philosophy

During the last ten to fifteen years, the convergence of Film Studies and Philosophy has become the recent "big thing," with a community growing fast, and on a global scale. However, under the heading of "Film Philosophy," different approaches have found an umbrella term—mainly an American tradition, represented by scholars such as Noel Carroll, Thomas Wartenberg, a.o., and a German line, with researchers such as Martin Seel, Gertrud Koch, and others. Both these approaches relate film to philosophical questions (ethics, justice, aesthetics, anthropology, etc.), but leave the disciplinary boundaries intact—film may illustrate philosophical problems, but these problems "belong" to the field of (academic) philosophy proper.

However, there is an alternative tradition in which philosophy takes film as a serious field of philosophical engagement: beginning with Henri Bergson this contestation culminated in recent decades in the approaches of the film philosophies of Stanley Cavell and Gilles Deleuze, who argued for an appreciation of film *as* philosophy. How can this relationship between film and philosophy be thought anew? Can philosophy renew our concepts of film as art and/or as a medium? And vice versa: Can film change our understanding of philosophy as a scholarly practice and endeavor? Should both concepts of "film" and "philosophy" be reconsidered once we dare their encounter? Regarding the recent ubiquity of neuroscience in the humanities, a new perspective opens which puts a focus on the process of thinking itself: What is thought and where does it occur? Examining the philosophical status of film, this project thus situates it within a greater context: Is there something like cinematic thought? And if cinema can be a medium of thought, how does it relate to philosophical enquiries or to scientific analyses of this process? Can those disciplines benefit from each other?

This chapter argues that the two questions "what is film?" (as a slight rephrasing of Bazin's question *What is Cinema*?) and "what is philosophy?" (as Deleuze and Guattari have asked) are intimately intertwined—also in a very pragmatic and institutional way. When Roger Odin, one of the pioneers of "institutionalized" Film Studies in France, was called to office in the early 1980s, he was faced with the fact that the field of Film Studies as a discipline did not (yet) exist. But, far from despairing, Odin rather felt confirmed in his belief that film and cinema are not suitable objects for an academic discipline. By that he did not mean to discredit cinema as an object not worthy of academic analysis—on the contrary, Odin's firm belief was that cinema opens up a whole field of research, with a whole range of disciplines contributing. While Odin was taking Gilbert Cohen-Séat's "Institut de filmologie" as a model, which was an interdisciplinary institute par excellence, he found that his own institute was still miles away from that ideal. But nevertheless: it can be stated that the amount of film scholars worldwide that have a degree in another subject (Odin himself is a linguist by training)—be it one of the National Philologies, Art History, Musicology, or Philosophy—is overwhelming. So, also institution-wise, an interdisciplinary approach to film (including philosophical expertise) is not only desired, but fact.[2]

In the 1980s, cognitive film studies discovered the brain for the analysis of film. Against the "Grand Theories" of psychoanalytic and (post)structuralist theory, they employed the findings of cognitive psychology for explaining the processes in the spectator's mind to "make meaning," seeing the understanding of film as a rational and cognitive endeavor that applies scientific "theories of perception, information processing, hypothesis-building, and interpretation" (Currie 2004: 106). At that time, the dominant strand in neuroscience was the field of "computation," which took the computer as its model: the brain here was essentially seen as an input/output machine of representation.

Approximately at the same time, Gilles Deleuze, in the "new image of thought" he developed (among others) in his two cinema books, also utilizes the concept of the brain, with implicit and explicit references, on the one hand, to Henri Bergson and, on the other hand, to a more constructivist brand of neurosciences in the wake of Maturana, Varela, and Changeux, seeing both film and brain as agencies of the "creation of worlds"—"the Brain is the Screen" (see Flaxman 2000). Certainly, the brain that cognitive film studies, neuroscience, and Deleuze talk about is not the same "object/concept" in these discourses. Recent developments in cognitive neuroscience into the so-called 4EA-cognitivism that considers the brain as embodied, enacted, extended, embedded, and affective might however create new insights into the encounters of brains and screens. Here, in contrast to classical computation, and even in contrast to "connectionism," which is more advanced than computation in so far that it involves a far more complex (and a-centered) dynamics, thinking finally does not take place inside our skull (only) anymore, but "out of our heads" (to quote the title of Alva Noë's book 2009).

Yet one of the main difficulties that impede a smooth and simple marriage of film studies, (Deleuzian) philosophy, and the neurosciences is the fact that the brain in question is in fact many brains. Not only do the concepts of the brain between these various disciplines differ, Deleuze himself uses the brain in different guises. First, on a very general level, he traces the motif or metaphor of the brain in movies by Alain Resnais and Stanley Kubrick. Far more important in the context of our interest however are Deleuze's references to the philosophy of Henri Bergson and his "new conception" of the brain—Bergson "introduced a profound element of transformation: the brain was now only an interval [écart], a void, nothing but a void, between a stimulation and a response" (Deleuze 1989: 211). In a universe that consists, as Bergson has it, of images in motion that all react on one another, the subject (and the brain) functions as "centers of indetermination" (Bergson 1991: 36), in which the direct cause/effect or stimulus/response reaction is slowed down. This idea of the brain as a center of indetermination is supported by findings in neurosciences that focus on the brain as "an uncertain system" (Deleuze 1989: 211), as rhizomatic neural networks. Deleuze is here referring to Jean-Pierre Changeux's *Neuronal Man: The Biology of Mind* and Steven Rose's *The Conscious Brain* (which also refers to Delisle Burns's *The Uncertain Nervous System*): what it boils down to, for Deleuze, is that

> [w]e can consider the brain as a relatively undifferentiated mass and ask what circuits, what kinds of circuit, the movement-image or time-image traces out, or invent, because the circuits aren't there to begin with . . . the brain's the hidden side of all circuits, and these can allow the most basic conditioned reflexes to

prevail, as well as leaving room for more creative tracings, less "probable" links. The brain's a spatio-temporal volume: it's up to art to trace through it the new paths open to us today. You might see continuities and false continuities as cinematic synapses—you get different links, and different circuits, in Godard and Resnais, for example. The overall importance or significance of cinema seems to me to depend on this sort of problem. (Deleuze 1995: 60–1)

One of the most decisive questions that emerges in the wake of thinking the interrelation between media—and here, more specifically, film—and thought is related to the respective status of "philosophy." As we have seen, there seems to be a great divide between analytic and continental "schools of thought." A possible answer is best summarized by the Cavell-inspired words of Stephen Mulhall:

I do not look at these films as handy or popular illustrations of views and arguments properly developed by philosophers; I see them rather as themselves reflecting on and evaluating such views and arguments, as thinking seriously and systematically about them in just the ways that philosophers do. Such films are not philosophy's raw material, nor a source for its ornamentation; they are philosophical exercises, philosophy in action–film as philosophizing. (Mulhall 2008: 4)

In this claim, films themselves are seen as capable of doing a unique kind of philosophical work (even though Mulhall's characterization of films philosophizing "in just the ways that philosophers do" might still be in need of some qualification). Thus, the question is, "What kind of knowledge (affects and percepts themselves giving rise to concepts) does the medium film generate qua medium?"

Ultimately, the question "what is film philosophy?" might better be restated as "where is film philosophy?" Does it reside in the institutionalized version of (academic) philosophy ("proper"), or might it also be said to be inherent to film itself? An important qualification has to be made here: the question of "what is philosophy" has to be addressed again at this point, because the different relations of film and philosophy also owe a lot to the definition of the philosophical. If the rubric of film as philosophy claims that films or cinema can do philosophy, this does not mean the institutionalized version of academic philosophy, that is, the production of propositional knowledge but rather what Deleuze and Guattari call the "creation of concepts" (Deleuze and Guattari 1994: 5). This entails a definition of philosophy that goes beyond its traditional territorialization, one that is extensional, forming assemblages rather than propositions, what—again—Deleuze has called "the new image of thought."[3]

Following this approach, the terms "philosophy" and "thinking" do not necessarily refer to rational propositions and/or a purely neural activity, though. Thinking is not just a representation of the world as "it is"—as Deleuze puts it, "[s]omething in the world forces us to think. This something is an object not of recognition, but a fundamental *encounter*" (Deleuze 1994: 139). While the idea of "thinking as (re-)cognition" is based on the verification of ideologies, of precollected knowledge, customs, and articles of faith, the notion of "thinking as an encounter" shatters our epistemological and experiential habits; it produces a break in our "normal," habitual perspective of the world and enables the possibility to approach alternative points of view and means of thought and to question our common practices. Thus, film-thought is philosophical since it offers its own genuine cinematic reflections about the world. According to Deleuze, these are especially new looks at concepts of images, time, space, and movement (concepts that are grounded in the peculiarity of the medium as a stream of "moving images").

In an interview with Raymond Bellour and François Ewald, Deleuze stated, "I've never been worried about going beyond metaphysics or any death of philosophy. The function of philosophy, still thoroughly relevant, is to create concepts" (Deleuze 1995: 136). This affirmative function of philosophy is also a call to transdisciplinarity, so that even when Deleuze was working on "painting and cinema: images, on the face of it . . . [he] was writing philosophy books" (137). In defense of Deleuze against Sokal/Bricmont's attempt to control and regulate the limits of the disciplinary fields, Paul Harris points out that Deleuze's work in contrast shows "how productive it is to work with and think through material from others and other fields . . . , working with ideas cooked up in geology and geography, zoology and ornithology, archeology and paleontology, and even mathematics and physics" (Harris 2010: 24–5). The philosophical practice of "creating concepts," as a creation of "newness" as well, necessitates, according to Deleuze, that philosophy enters into manifold relations with arts and sciences, since philosophy "creates and expounds its concepts only in relation to what it can grasp of scientific functions and artistic constructions. . . . Philosophy cannot be undertaken independently of science or art" (Deleuze 1994: xvi). It is these resonances and exchanges between philosophy, science, and art that make philosophy "creative," not reflective. These relations—from the perspective of philosophy—are vital for reasons internal to philosophy itself, that is, vital for the creation of "concepts," and—from the perspective of Film Philosophy—in resonance with the percepts and affective logics and modalities of art in general, and film in particular.

This approach attempts to bring film studies and philosophy into a productive dialogue without assigning the role of a dominant and all-encompassing referee to one of these disciplines. Rather, it is about relating the diverse entry points—the many colors of the spectrum—toward each other in a fertile manner in order to establish, ultimately, a media philosophy that puts the status, the role, and the function of the medium—here, film—into a new perspective: no longer are the representational techniques of the medium at the center of inquiry but rather its ability to "think" and to assume an active role in processes of thought, in finding alternative and differentiating point(s) of view.

If we take this a step further, relating this approach to the whole range of media (production), but also take a step back, and see what this approach basically means, we begin to see the seeds of a new "media philosophy"—not talking *about* media by way of "philosophy proper," but by realizing the "philosophical qualities and impacts" of the medium: it all starts from the assumption that our memory, perception, and thinking are not just a given, as with a body—and weightless, immaterial logics, reason, or internal process that takes place behind the walls of our skull and is purely mental—there is always a "material basis." As Nietzsche already claimed, "*our* writing equipment takes

Practical Aesthetics

part in the forming of *our* thoughts." From here, we can derive the media-philosophical insight that media (help us) think (differently). Media thus reveal themselves as the body (or, better: different bodies) of thought. It is important to note that these "bodies" are not "retroactive" to those thoughts that they "materialize," just like the telescope is not retroactive to the discovery of planets—media are coextensive to the thoughts they "allow." Media Philosophy is an event, even a praxis—but *of* the media *themselves*. It takes place *through* and *in* the media in question—and this in turn opens up the question, "Could this philosophy be described only by translating it into the human 'master-medium': philosophical writing-thinking. . .?"

The Audiovisual Essay

One way to deal with this problem of "media change" is a form of aesthetic presentation that stays within the realm of the art form or medium it reflects on, thereby using the very modus operandi that somehow defines that very art form/medium—in this case: film.[4]

Question: Does film analysis have to exist in the form of words alone, words in written or spoken language, as conventionally published in books and journals, or as verbally delivered in lecture halls, or on a DVD audio commentary? Might one not perform a thinking *with* film with the very tools of the cinema itself—with images and sound, that is? Hence the audiovisual essay—and I like the term "audiovisual essay" much better than other terms such as "Videographic or Digital Criticism," because it both keeps the provisional and the experimental character of the "form of the essay" intact, as Adorno described it, and it also makes a point of the "relational character," or the montage, that is characteristic of the audiovisual essay as well:

> The essay . . . incorporates the anti-systematic impulse into its own way of proceeding and introduces concepts unceremoniously, "immediately," just as it receives them. They are made more precise through their relationship to one another. (Adorno 1991: 12)

Thus, even if there are academic audiovisual essays that present a combination of written commentary and film, as well as sound clips, a more radical version of the audiovisual essay—"truer" to the idea of practical aesthetics, that is—consists in the form of a creative montage and juxtaposition of images, sequences of preexisting film works that "realize" a filmic idea, a film-thought, so to speak.

In his 1919 dissertation on *Der Begriff der Kunstkritik in der deutschen Romantik* (The Concept of Art-Criticism in German Romanticism), Walter Benjamin describes one of the key notions of the Romantics' aesthetic as follows:

> Thus, criticism is, as it were, an experiment on the artwork, one through which the latter's own reflection is awakened, through which it is brought to consciousness and to knowledge of itself. (Benjamin 1996: 151)

The work of art—according to Benjamin—thus already contains its own criticism, a knowledge of its own which, if we follow Deleuze, is not (yet) conceptual or, rather, propositional. Again, Adorno points at the form of the essay to accomplish exactly this (and essay here, I argue, does not only refer to the written essay—it is rather a certain form, or a way of doing thinking that is hinted at):

> The essay approaches the logic of music, that stringent and yet aconceptual art of transition, in order to appropriate for verbal language something it forfeited under the domination of discursive logic . . . it coordinates elements instead of subordinating them, and only the essence of its content, not the manner in which it is presented, is commensurable with logical criteria . . . the essay is more dynamic than traditional thought by virtue of the tension between the presentation and the matter presented. But at the same time, as a constructed juxtaposition of elements, it is more static. Its affinity with the image lies solely in this, except that the staticness of the essay is one in which relationships of tension have been brought, as it were, to a standstill. (Adorno 1991: 22)

Today, there are quite some approaches to different arts that work on that brink between art and science, "sensible cognition" and proposition, aesthetic knowledge and rational knowledge, while thinking *with* art (or the artistic material) rather than *about* it. New forms of aesthetic research and presentation, such as media philosophy, the audiovisual essay, the audio paper, artistic research, and so on, are no longer only a topic or an object of study, but a medium of medi(t)ation; aesthetic modes of representation are increasingly being incorporated into critical academic practice, with the role of the aesthetic for "thought" coming to matter more directly than mere discussions of the aesthetic in whatever discipline hitherto could envision. What is at stake is not to explain and interpret, but to "appropriate the artistic forms we encounter" (Felski 2015: 176). The question here is no longer about what kinds of critical methodologies we adopt to understand works of art, but about how we think *with* works of art—how they both shape our understanding and experience of the world, and also how they serve as "partners in crime" to our thought. If a practical aesthetics performs a thinking with images, with sounds, and so on, such a non-writerly, non-propositional thinking pushes a strictly representational and logocentric reflection to its limits.[5] And if what we have is a companion, then that relation is not one of hierarchy, subservience, or distance, but is instead a relation predicated on an attraction that cannot be explained in terms of absolute identity. To have a partner or companion is to be with someone whose sensibility one shares, but in ways that are not identical, or else it would result in an entropic deadlock.

Practical aesthetics cannot be reduced to a common singular practice. It is a mobile and disparate set of practices; as a dynamic approach, it takes art not as an object of (external) analysis, but as a subject with a knowledge in its own right, creating a co-composing "conceptual interference pattern" (Manning and Massumi 2014: viii) between theory and practice. A "practical aesthetics," thus understood, can be described as thinking *with* art, and *with* media, in order to find new ways to create worlds and thus to perceive and experience the world in different ways.

Practical aesthetics, as outlined in the chapters that follow, is a multilayered issue: on the one hand, there are artists thinking WITH the material, not about it, going along with what the material they are working with provides, and not attempting to make it "succumb" to their own will. Then there are analyses of the way artists think with their material; and finally, a practical aesthetics refers to the way researchers, academics, philosophers themselves comment on/analyze artistic works from a new perspective—not by making it adhere to external principles (thinking ABOUT), but to the artworks' internal principles. These chapters are offering possible ways how to engage in a practical aesthetics—not as a method, but as a heuristics. Not only does every artform/genre have its own parameters that determine a thinking with, but also every single work, and every single reading does so as well—practical aesthetics, as we understand it, is not (and will never be) a "unified field" or "unified theory."

* * *

Christoph Menke
The Experiment: Between Art and Life

Every work of art is an experiment: it is an experiment in art, an attempt to see whether one can make art in this way, whether it can be made in this way, and whether it can be made at all. Every work of art is an experiment, because every work of art starts from nothing—an artwork that does not start from nothing is not an artwork at all, for the zero state of the artwork's inception is the aesthetic state. Every work of art is an experiment, because it tests the possibility to create a work from the state of aesthetic freedom.

However, every work of art is not only an experiment of art; it is also an experiment of life. Those who make a work of art and those who experience a work of art are aesthetically active, but they practice this activity in their lives. Whoever makes a work of art and whoever experiences a work of art is confronted with the question of how she wants to and can live with it and after it. She is confronted with the question of what place she wants to and can give the aesthetic activity in her life—and whether the aesthetic activity can in fact be limited to this place, that is, what the aesthetic activity she performs does with (or to) her.

Every work of art is an experiment because it asks for the possibility of art, and every work of art is an experiment because as an object of aesthetic activity it asks for the possibility of living with art.

Katerina Krtilova
On the Practice of Theory:
The Technological Turn of Media Theory and Aesthetic Practice
of Media Philosophy

Digitalization has become not only an important topic in the humanities but also a challenge to their methods. Questioning the positivist turn to technology in digital humanities, the chapter proposes to rethink media theory, confronting its focus on the role of techniques in culture in Kittlerian media theory with the "revolutionary practice" (Jacques Derrida) of a new philosophy as a transformation of the "method of thinking" (Vilém Flusser). Media philosophy can, in this sense, be characterized as a revision of theoretical reflection detached from its media, writing as well as image or computation, but not determined by these media; media philosophy reflects that it is not just as an effect of media as technologies. Connecting the shift between media theory and media philosophy to the problematization of literary theory in the 1980s, turning (in) *Against Theory* to practical methods of analysis, this chapter turns the attention to the "blind spot" of the arguments in the debates in 1980s and today's technological ends of theory: the practice of theory. It suggests to criticize the convergence of theory and practice in technological practice stressing the nonpractical effectivity of doing theory based on aesthetic practice, "thinking as a performative art" (D. N. Rodowick). Following Martin Heidegger's critique of techno-science a "medial" theory—linked to but not determined by media practices— can unsettle the distinction between theory and practice and thus not presuppose a certain technological practice and logic, but question the very notion of practice and find new ways to practice theory.

Tim Ingold
Episode Zero:
How Empirical Science Discounts Aesthetic Experience, and a Practical Way to Bring It Back

Empirical aesthetics seeks an objective, experimentally based and scientific explanation of how human beings respond to art. Its roots lie in late nineteenth-century Germany, in the psychophysics of Gustav Fechner, who was the first to turn aesthetics from a way of studying objects (as proposed by Immanuel Kant) into an object of study in its own right. Ingold's argument in this chapter is that this move effectively discounts the lived reality of aesthetic experience. Drawing on recent work in the field, Ingold offers a critical review of the way empirical aesthetics models what it calls the "aesthetic episode." This begins when a viewer stands before a work of art and ends with a judgment of the work, on a scale of preference, and an emotional response to the viewing experience. In between lie stages of perceptual analysis, implicit memory recognition, explicit classification, cognitive mastering, and evaluation. The movement from stage to stage is said to involve a gradual shift from "bottom-up" to "top-down" information processing, the former governed by hardwired neural mechanisms, the latter by higher-order and increasingly self-conscious cognition. Fundamentally, however, empirical aesthetics sees the encounter with the work of art as a problem-solving exercise, and it is the satisfaction of solving the problem, rather than the work itself, that underpins the response. The idea of problem-solving, however, implies that a solution is already at hand in the work, and merely waiting to be found. Were that the case, then the time devoted to finding it would be entirely accessory to the work itself. It could in principle be reduced to zero. Ingold argues, to the contrary, that the work of art is distinguished from a puzzle precisely in that, like life, it is a problem without a solution. Time, then, is intrinsic to the work, just as it is to life. Following the pragmatic philosophy of John Dewey, Ingold suggests that to view a work of art is to relive the process of its creation. This is not processing in the transitive sense, converting inputs to outputs, but in the intransitive sense of carrying on, as in breathing in and out. Distinguishing between these two senses of processing, he contends that a practical aesthetics cannot align with the episodic but must always cut a way through, improvising a passage. In this journey, works of art are not items of baggage but travel companions. Ingold concludes that what empirical aesthetics really gives us, under the guise of experimental science, is a form of market research entirely consistent with the commodification of experience characteristic of advanced capitalism.

jan jagodzinski
Practical Aesthetics: The Case of BioArt

Practical aesthetics, as an "apprenticeship" in signs as Gilles Deleuze argues, presents a practical problem common to all art practice. It means capturing forces that are life "itself." It is not a matter of reproducing, representing, or inventing forms. The challenge, in the visual arts is to render visible what is invisible, while in music it is to render nonsonorous forces sonorous. One of the most distinguishing features of contemporary art has been the overcoming of the separation between art and science, a relationship that was much more intimate during the period known as the Renaissance; some have called this an age of radical Enlightenment with the shift toward bioengineering and biogenetics. This renewed interface has been made possible since the advent of computerized and digitalized technologies that began roughly in the mid-twentieth century. The last two decades, especially with the turn toward installation art, have brought technology (engineering), experimental science, and art together in much more evident ways than had previously been realized. jagodzinski explores the recent artistic development referred to as bioart where science and art come together in a unique way to answer to this problematic of practical aesthetics. Following Deleuze, he maintains that bioartists have become the new "symptomologists" of the age. What is extraordinary is that "life" has become the "new" material. Bioartists introduce us to new affective and perceptive states that had never before been experienced. There are affirmations of lifeworlds that present for our species, perhaps for the first time, an insight as to the profound relationships we have with the word-as-it-is, enabling the wonders of technology to mediate, transverse, and make possible relationships with the organic and inorganic life that has remained hereto silent and without agential voice. Bioartists produce new sensations by using scientific insights into the material life as lived—in this case this includes understanding the entire genetic biome of various bacterial strains, being able to experiment with genetic sequences of plants of every variety, and speculating on the complex ecologies of species in their specific environments that remain invisible, not only to the human eye such as bacteria, but to processes that are never static, but dynamic in their movement.

Eugenie Brinkema
Colors without Bodies: Wes Anderson's Drab Ethics

The starting point for this chapter is the question of how the problem of color might make certain impersonal relations thinkable. Radical formalism—the concept Brinkema proposes in *The Forms of the Affects* to regard shape, line, light, color, and so on as the very grounds for a speculative thinking of the as-yet-unthought dimensions of ethical and affective life—enables a rereading of color aesthetics, one that moves away from discourses of the ornamental or beautiful (let alone the sentimental or excessive) and eschews claims for color's bond to metaphoricity (what loans *something else* its theoretical significance) to argue instead for a thinking with color as a way of speculatively reckoning with a problem of violence. Her argument focuses on Wes Anderson's *The Grand Budapest Hotel*, in particular the film's juxtaposition of a pastel palette that dominates the formal language of the film and the spoken insistence that the black costumes of the cruel death squads are so very "drab." Brinkema asks the question: What might it mean to take color not as a symbolic register, nor merely as an aesthetic curiosity or as an authorial palette or signature, but rather as a form of formal aesthetic thinking of the ethical? This chapter explores the notion of drabness as a field in which color has yet to take form and this comes to name an immanent potential for violence. The strict etymology of the word *drab* suggest both dirt and muddiness, but also that which has yet to take on sufficient saturation in the realm of the visible. Brinkema's argument is that the formal language of the film uses color to think through an ethics of violence that is uniquely articulated through aesthetic concepts of drabness, hue, saturation, palette, and is not available on a narrative or representational level. Color force, rather, takes on the burden of a critique of force autonomous of the twee narrative structure.

Johannes Binotto
In Lag of Knowledge: The Video Essay as Parapraxis

The video essay as a form of film studies which does not only think about cinema but which is working with film excerpts as tools of their own analysis has seen widespread success and proliferation in recent years. Instead of providing a survey on the long and rapidly evolving history of the video essay, this chapter focuses on one specific aspect of the form which is all the easier overlooked as video essays and their practitioners become more professional. Namely, this chapter is interested in how digital technology not only facilitates the engagement with cinema but also produces new forms of interference. Furthermore, it wants to outline how accidents like data corruption and digital lag can serve an analytical function. Binotto argues that disruptions of digital media can be recognized as critical encounters instead of accidents that need to be circumvented. He thus proposes a video essayistic practice which thinks not only with the film but also with the new viewing and formatting technologies of film and, more specifically, with the uncontrolled and contingent side effects of those technologies. The term "Binotto" proposes for these productive contingencies of technology, as well as for our critical engagement with these contingencies, which is "parapraxis." Understanding the video essay as parapraxis is not only revelatory in regard to its engagement with film and film history, but also allows for a radical rereading of psychoanalytic and media theory and sheds new light onto (para-)practical aesthetics and its epistemological implications in general.

Bill Morrison
Thinking with Film Images in *Dawson City*: Frozen Time

Morrison's particular "hand-writing" and style of filmmaking consists in his very idiosyncratic way of using the filmic material, the material carrier—the celluloid strip—as a prime factor in his art, the way that this material disintegrates, decays, and thus renders a very special and affective quality of the scenes filmed. In his film *Dawson City: Frozen Time*, Morrison's modus operandi was directed by the material found in the Dawson City Film Collection, a treasure of 533 silent films, including newsreels and feature films of all types, dating from the 1910s and 1920s. Most were thought to be totally lost and marked by immense water damage. Bill Morrison invites us to view his work through the lens of practical aesthetics, a method of "thinking with images."

Tomáš Jirsa
Lapses, Affects, Supplement: Hiro Murai's Audiovisual Anachronism

Following the premise of this volume to its paradoxical conclusion—that thinking *with* aesthetic forms involves thinking *without* them—this chapter probes a theoretical force of music video produced by its anachronistic audiovisual gestures, performative mechanisms, and affective work of forms. Since the music video dissolves the boundaries between its moving images, sounds, and lyrics, short-circuiting and merging them into one audiovisual movement, to think with the music video invites moving away from the alleged substantiality of its visual and sonic constituents, and, instead, considering them as forms just taking shape, hybrid configurations at work that are both aesthetically and epistemically generative. Reading the formal effects of anger and violence as unfolded throughout the ironic reenactment of the American Revolutionary War on the nocturnal periphery of a deserted parking lot in the music video *Day Ones* (2016), directed by Hiro Murai for the trap music producer Baauer, Jirsa argues that the way the music video thinks with history is performative and grounded in a creative betrayal of the past, undermining representation of a historical experience in favor of its affective performance. Merging the hip-hop suburban reality of the twenty-first century with an eighteenth-century war by means of pseudo-historical details, obsolete props, and antiquated objects, Murai's transhistorical strategy opens up an avenue for *anachronistic audiovisual thinking*, which recasts the past through contemporary images and music while reshaping the present through the images of the past, arriving at a point where history makes sense only through temporal paradoxes, failures, and lapses. Driven by the principle of anachronism, *Day Ones* switches from the Barthesian reality effect, whose main function is to connote the category of the real, to what might be dubbed the "unreality effect" which uses evocations of the past only to exhaust and empty their historical core in favor of actualizing and unfolding their contemporary affective potential. As a result, the audiovisual thinking of the video is in line with its dominant perspective of anger and dark atmosphere that operate both through peculiar lapses brought about by the violent camera movements, aggressive zooming, and claustrophobic mise-en-scène and through the sinister beats, irregular rhythms that peak and collapse, and the ferocious rapping voices. Not only does Murai's video uncover the contemporary affective force within the canonical past while reading contemporary violence in an anachronistically deconstructive way, but it also makes their mutual short-circuiting operate within their audiovisual forms. Suggesting that such a creative betrayal of the past is always already incorporated into the supplementary structure of the music video—which enacts the visual potential of the preexisting music and lyrics, and, in turn, transforms them—Jirsa proposes a concept of the *audiovisual supplement* which takes seriously the double bind of the visual addition and substitution, thus complementing some of the recent voices in the emerging music video turn.

Bernd Herzogenrath
Some Notes on Sound Thinking

Taking its cue from observations by Edgar Varèse, John Cage, and other "sound thinkers," this chapter suggests that "sound thinking" does not only imply "thinking of (or with) sound," but also "healthy thinking," or, as Deleuze puts it: a thinking that rightfully earns its name—a thinking that does not derive its parameters/concepts from an exterior "verified knowledge" (Deleuze calls this "recognition") in order to adapt the object of investigation to these parameters, but rather a thinking that develops its very concepts from the examination of the object of investigation (Deleuze calls this "encounter"): here—a thinking *with* and *by means of* sound, not a thinking *about* sound, which eventually does not deal with the question what music *is*, but rather what music *can become*. And from this vantage point, research and art, theory and practice, are coextensive.

François Bonnet
Thinking with Sound: Preliminary Thoughts

What can it mean—to think with sound? To try to attempt a preliminary answer, it seems necessary to question once again the nature of sound, or, more precisely, to affirm its absence of nature, of essence. It is also essential to question the link between language and sensitivity, to differentiate the audible from the sonic, precisely in the light of language. Because thinking with sound is not thinking about sound, let alone trying to make it speak. Thus, it's something else. But, then, would it be talking "about" sound? But how to formulate what resists the formula, what is not said, but simply "sounds"? Perhaps, then, it is also necessary to examine the very idea of thinking, and stop substituting it for an area strictly dominated by logos. Can thinking with sound, thinking outside of language, therefore, be assimilated to a practice? And if so, what name could be given to such a practice? By a hazardous route, the following hypothesis is addressed in this chapter: thinking with sound would be like making music. But it is, then, a music reinvented, a music redefined or reexposed, precisely in the light of this very idea: that of a music after having done with language, a music that drifts through the harshest of areas, through territories of untamed sensitivity. Music that draws its inspiration from sound and no longer from language.

John Luther Adams
In Search of Sacred Space

In his personal contribution, American Composer and Pulitzer Prize Winner John Luther Adams reflects on his way of making sense of the world through thinking with sounds. In his piece, Adams talks about his indebtedness as a composer to the Alaskan landscape—both physical and mental, a journey through actual places and cultural heritages. As if his compositions emerge from an actual sense of place, new harmonic colors give depth to the sonic landscapes Adams creates. The natural world is an inexhaustible source of inspiration and music. So for Adams, his sonic landscapes relate to spiritual spaces and almost become prayers.

Craig Shepard
Thinking in Sound

Christian Wolff tells a story about when John Cage came to visit him in the 1970s: "He described the difficulties of making the orchestra piece Apartment House 1776—the chance procedures hadn't worked out quite right, the sound was too thick, he had to start all over again." This says to me that Cage had a sense of the sound of the piece beyond the construction of the chance procedures.

The physician Dr. Alfred Tomatis recognized that the sense of hearing functions through vibrating the ear drum. The ear drum is activated by vibrations coming through the air as well as vibrations conducted through the bones. As these vibrations work directly on the body, the experience of sound relies on the felt sense. The rewards of listening to our inner voice without the masking effects of language are immediate. We all have a kind of knowing that comes to us from our inner voice. We may think of it as intuition, or call it a hunch or a feeling in the bones. In fact, it is the bone conduction that brings this voice to us.

Felt sense is not linguistic or logical; sometimes language can describe experience. As we learn to notice the felt sense, we can learn to rely on it. In the beginning, this is often trial and error. As a composer begins to develop the felt, intuitive sense with sound, he or she begins to get in tune with the music which resonates with them. Shepard's chapter describes his creative work as direct experience in sound, and a practice of relying on intuition.

Marcus Boon
Music as Sonic Praxis: On the Work of Catherine Christer Hennix

Swedish-born musician and composer Catherine Christer Hennix has produced works in a variety of media, including sound, light, theater, and so on. She has always insisted that her work should not be considered art, invoking religious, mathematical, therapeutic, and psychoanalytic models and goals for her practice. Particular soundworks take various trajectories toward the revealing of a sonic or vibrational ontology—this revealing is beyond discourse, and its success is measured by experience at the phenomenological level. At the same time, it is formal, in that Hennix seeks to account in a rigorous way for what occurs. It is also therefore in principle repeatable. In this chapter, Boon explores the ways in which Hennix's work emerges from a thinking through of the mathematical problem of the continuum, and the possibilities of a modal ontology, derived from Hennix's work and the recent work by Fernando Zalamea on the continuum and topos theory. Modes offer a way to understand the ways in which practice in general is shaped by attunement to the demands of the real.

Sanne Krogh Groth and Kristine Samson
The Audio Paper as Affective Attunements: Thinking, Producing, and Listening

With the recent project and publication "Fluid Sounds" (2015–16), the authors suggested a new format of academic publication named "Audio Papers." The present chapter wishes to develop the audio paper format as a reflective movement in which philosophical, aesthetic, and practical attributes are considered.

As suggested in Groth and Samson, 2016, the audio paper is an aesthetic academic practice working with auditory, aesthetic, and affective production of sensation and knowing. Following Deleuze's depiction of affects as "blocs of sensations" (Deleuze 1994: 123), the audio paper is here suggested as an experimental encounter between the "blocs of sensations" in art with a propositional mapping of concepts found in philosophy and science.

In the present chapter, Groth and Samson wish to develop an argument from their audio paper manifesto, that "the aesthetic, material aspects of the audio paper produce affects and sensations" (Groth and Samson 2016). Such production of affective distributions of the sensible enables the producer and the listener to participate in an affective attunement. Following Massumi and Manning's adaption of Sterne's notion of "relational attunement" as emergent or affective attunement (Manning and Massumi 2014: 217), they here find a knowledge practice that allows an attunement that opens up linear knowledge toward a singular event. Such affective composition allows for heterogeneous sensations to coexist in which the thinker, producer, and listener are folded together in the temporal materiality of sound.

As such, the audio paper is a practical and relational encounter between bodies (thinking, audio production, listening) and their mutual capacity to affect and to be affected (see also Deleuze 1988). It is an encounter that, among others, relates to the materiality of sound, the intensity and polyrhythms in dramaturgy or the enactments of environmental sounds (see Groth and Samson 2016). Affects are not divisible in themselves, but consist as affective tonalities that open up toward timely affective attunements in (a) the process of production in which the academic producer engages with the sound material and its aesthetics, and in (b) in the attunements of the listener.

Through such *affective attunements*, the chapter suggests that the audio paper gives rise to thinking, producing, and listening through temporality and sonic material.

Practical Aesthetics

Michael N. Goddard
Genealogies of Immersive Media and Virtual Reality (VR) as Practical Aesthetic Machines

When virtual reality "first" appeared on the scene in the 1990s, its philosophical, and even metaphysical, potentials were not lost on several authors whether they perceived them in largely dystopian terms (see Kroker 1993) or naively affirmative ones (see Rheingold 1991). Perhaps the author who most intimately connected virtual reality and philosophy was Michael Heim, whose work *The Metaphysics of Virtual Reality* (1993) situated technologies of the virtual as ontological machineries, enabling the practical design of modes of experience that philosophers had hitherto only been able to imagine; to paraphrase Marx, where philosophy had only been able to describe the world, virtual reality designers were making new worlds of ontogenetic experience available to their users. Of course, virtual reality is only the last of a long line of technologies of the virtual in the twentieth century, passing through all the technological innovations of cinema, stereoscopy, 3D, and other immersive media whose deeper history dates back to panoramas, Viewmasters, and other devices, and further to such philosophical machineries as Plato's cave.[6] More specifically, virtual reality emerges out of an intersection between audiovisual moving images and sounds and computing that began as early as the 1960s, as so many varieties of what Gene Youngblood called "Expanded Cinema" (1970). This chapter will explore these genealogies of virtual immersive technologies as modes of practical aesthetics, enabling concrete experiences of perceptual transformation and metamorphosis, a becoming other to oneself and one's habits of perceiving and being in the world. It will argue that rather than the transcendence often attributed to these experiences in the 1990s that immersive technologies of the virtual open up space of pure immanence and becoming which may exceed habitual lived bodies, but only by creating a new body without organs, a "new flesh" of technologically remediated pure immanence. As such, it will draw on Deleuzian concepts of the virtual, as well as taking a media-archaeological approach to the nonlinear development of virtual and immersive technologies drawing on the work of Siegfried Zielinski and Jussi Parikka.

Elizabeth Waterhouse
As Duo: Thinking with Dance

Based upon a life as a dancer and extensive research of the duet practice of dancers performing William Forsythe's choreography *Duo* from 1996 to present, this chapter addresses thinking *with* dance, asking the following questions: What aesthetic theory emerges from the example of *Duo*? What ways do practical aesthetics of dance contribute to the broader field of aesthetic theory? When, or can, such theoretical contributions be relevant to both scholars and dancers? And how, using what methods, would thinking *with* dance become inscribed?

Without sealing any of these questions with final answers, the author presents a case study as a raw proposition for how this might go forward: poetically evoking the choreography of *Duo* for the reader. The performance-translation is, as revealed in the footnotes, based on extensive learning from the artists, including the ethnographic process of writing "thick description" about fieldwork experience: attending performances, interviewing the artists, reviewing archival material, and even dancing with the dancers (Geertz 1973). Looking at the performance plurally, Waterhouse creates a composite "reading" across events in the history of *Duo*, linking her own and multiple artists' perspectives.

Forsythe is a well-known choreographer prominent in the field of contemporary European dance. In the short duet *Duo*, performed by either two men or women, the dancers move in and out of synchrony, breathing movement audibly. The choreography of *Duo* echoes a history of ballet steps and is defined by a specific sequence and interpretation practice. The dancers create time and space between their bodies, pushing and playing with the sequence as it unfolds. Dancing together, *Duo* is a journey through ethical time-space. It is a process of a common-ing and creating time between the dancers and the audience.

One term Waterhouse uses to convey to these dynamics is borrowed from philosopher Alfred North Whitehead, *concrescence*, which "presupposes the notions 'creativity,' 'many,' 'one,' 'identity' and 'diversity.'" (Whitehead 1985: 21). Concrescence embodies "growing together," suggesting the artwork as a complex unity in process (1967: 236). It is this main idea, modeled in *Duo* and in Waterhouse's research of *Duo*, that the author puts forth for thinking *with* dance. More generally, performances like *Duo* encourage scholars to move beyond thinking of art—as object-bound, finished, and a pure expression of the author—to thinking more fluidly and multiperspectivally. Choreography is not only an ephemeral but in fact an enduring process, historical and situated in a sociocultural field. Such a view rifts with earlier modernist aesthetics, enforcing the timeless and autonomous nature of art. Drawing from process philosophy, Waterhouse explores the working hypothesis of art as *pluralistic creative process*.

Allen C. Shelton
The Heart and Other Organs of Darkness in the Year 2019

At a point in his chapter, Shelton conceives Joseph Conrad's novel *The Heart of Darkness* to act like a bathysphere that allowed him to dive into himself. Behind this image is Roland Barthes's reading of the mythical Greek ship the Argos that was constantly being rebuilt piece by piece until nothing remained the same besides the name. Likewise, Conrad's image and Shelton's bathysphere are a composite of other pieces—*Vertigo*, *Blue Velvet*, Benjamin, Taussig, the music that was on Shelton's turntable as he was writing, and his own melancholia, to name some, and that the author of the chapter and the narrator/character inside the same text are composites suspended between fiction and the lived world. Writing and thinking from this place is often described as fictocritical, a place where the poetic and the historical blend. The Argentine Luis Borges describes this in his essay "Partial Enchantment of the Quixote." He finds an unease, a kind of vertigo, when the reader finds that the author appears as a character inside their own narrative looking back to the outside of the text, which is tantamount to a map so complete it contains the map itself. This unease is based on the realization that they, the author and the reader, can be as fictitious as the characters inside the account. This is vertigo. This is the other dark heart and the object of Shelton's chapter.

Christoph Ernst
Essayistic Imagination as Thinking *With*: Practical Aesthetics and Max Bense's Essay on the Essay

As a form of "thinking with," a practical aesthetic exposes an independent epistemic quality of sensual perception. Intertwined with a reflection on art and aesthetic experience, various authors in the twentieth century have moved this perspective in a media-aesthetic context. "Thinking with," for which sensual perception is of particular importance, is always "thinking with media." The text links this perspective with a specific aesthetic context, the reflection on the epistemological potential of essayist thought and writing. Using Max Bense's theory of the essay in his text "The Essay and its Prose"—one of the key texts in the discussion of an "essayistic" way of thinking and writing in the twentieth century—as an example, it is shown to what extent Bense provides a "proto-theoretical" perceptual dimension of thinking. In a discussion of Bense's arguments, it becomes clear that Bense explicates an independent aspect of "practical aesthetics" through the concept of an "essayistic imagination." A practical concept of imagination, in which imagination comes into play as an epistemic achievement indistinguishable from perception, is crucial for the argument of practical aesthetics. Understood against the backdrop of a "practical aesthetic," it becomes clear that Bense conceptualizes "thinking with" as a translation between practices of perception and practices of thinking which takes place in an "essayistic experiment." Thus, Bense makes an independent contribution to an understanding of practical aesthetics as a form of media aesthetics.

Julius Greve
Radioactivity and the Typewriter's Breath: Practical Aesthetics in Pound and Olson

Julius Greve's chapter inquires into the ways in which poetry and poetics amount to what may be called a *practical aesthetics*, along the lines of Alexander Baumgarten's multivolume project *Aesthetica* and its contemporary heirs. In this respect, the following questions are sufficiently broad, yet, in the context of the primary texts at hand, aptly specific, at the same time: How to think the relation between doing (*praxis*), making (*poiesis*), and sensing (*aisthesis*)? How is thinking (*theoria*) to be reconceived along the lines of a firmly practical approach to the realm of literary activity, in general, and to that of poetry, in particular? Along these lines, in what sense can we describe poetry as a *material* expression of thought?

This chapter traces the adamantly practice-oriented strands of thought in Ezra Pound's and Charles Olson's work. It does so, first, by tracing the prehistory of the contemporary turn to, or rather continuous fascination with, the aesthetic, in order to then demarcate the complicated tension between practice and technique in the writings of both poets. Second, the chapter scrutinizes the pragmatic lineage of Pound and Olson by looking at how their poetry stakes out specific conceptions of material practice and the significance of human technology (*technê*) for poetry, discerning the main assumptions of Pound's essay fragment "Pragmatic Aesthetics" (c. 1940–3) vis-à-vis Olson's manifesto "Projective Verse" (1950) and "Human Universe" (1951). Emphasizing the thematic intersections of history, philosophy, and scientific method in the idiosyncratic styles of both poets, respectively, the chapter will examine the conditions of possibility for thinking their poetics as individual attempts at *a pragmatic "science of the human" by poetic means*—one of the multiple types of what could be named a *"thinking with* X." As Greve's argument demonstrates, the particular practice that is key for both poets is the media-specific form—that is to say, technique—of ventriloquism: in Pound's case, a radio-inspired treatment of cultural influence, in Olson's work, a form of articulation that peculiarly summons what Greve conceives of as "the breath of the typewriter."

Jill Bennett
Can Practical Aesthetics Change Lives?

This chapter examines practical aesthetics as an empirical program, enacted through collaborative art and design processes with the goal of transforming mental health and well-being. Building on Bennett's 2012 book *Practical Aesthetics*, it draws on theoretical analysis of the politics of sensory-affective experience but proposes a "bottom-up" approach to thinking with, and working with, lived experience in relation to trauma and marginalized subjectivity. It examines the tension between applied, goal-oriented arts-health practice and radical aesthetics, asking how and where (beyond academic and disciplinary frameworks) we can generate a broadly accessible practical aesthetics that makes possible new forms of lived experience.

Mieke Bal
Contaminations: Toward an Empathic Museology

In this chapter, Bal seeks to articulate ways in which art can propose a deeper, more creative reflection on violence and its assault on human subjectivity (trauma). Given the current state of the world, this seems an urgent task for art, with its access to the imagination that can help think up hitherto unknown possibilities. Theoretically as well as practically, she concentrates this question on the way theatricality can be deployed for museological presentations. The practical goal is to solicit a form of "contamination" that makes visitors vulnerable to, and thereby understanding of, the traumatic states of others. Bal is interested in how images can help articulate and embody *thought*. Images can perform an equivalent of speech acts; they can respond ("speak back") to the look cast onto them, and that they can entice viewers to theorize, think, and feel all at once. They are *performative*. With the title of this chapter, Bal seeks to draw attention to the fluidity between domains, including differences. A socially productive contamination can be forcefully explored around the topic of the social recognition and acceptance of traumatic life, because this is where a change in attitude is necessary, and can be solicited and assessed. The deployment of theatricality for museological innovation is a fitting means to that end.

Practical Aesthetics

In this chapter, Bal exposes a current collaborative research project. The starting hypothesis is that theatricality ("live") can be usefully transformed into forms of museal display that get closer to the visitors and thus turn "live" into "life." This is a project of artistic research, integrating creation and analysis; our case study is the transformation of a historical masterpiece, Miguel de Cervantes's *Don Quixote*. Rather than an "adaptation," the work we aim to make is a response, a mode of turning a historical object into an interlocutor with suggestions for today's world. Collaboration is one crucial aspect of this project, and Bal would venture to affirm that it is indispensable, and makes for a spontaneous interdisciplinarity. The work with actors, as she has been able to understand before, contributes insights that, in light of artistic research, are quite simply inherent in the actors' art. Between theater studies and pedagogy, there is already quite a history (e.g., Brazil). Literary analysis and video installation bring us to intermediality. If aesthetics, conceived as a sensuous interaction between artwork and spectator, is to have practical sense, it, too, must collaborate with both makers and spectators.

Ernst van Alphen
Thinking with Archival Ordering, or the Politics of Destruction

Marjan Teeuwen's interventions in discarded houses look like further destructions of houses that are already in the process of being destroyed. The projects of this artist are then not acts of creation, but acts of destruction, or rather creation is seen as a form of destruction. But paradoxically, her interventions in ruined houses create order and structure into chaos. Her creation of beauty and harmony out of chaos and destruction is, however, not an end in itself. It embodies the ordering activity of memory. This ordering activity is even intensified in her photographic practice. The photographs she takes of these destroyed houses are much more than documentation of temporary installations. Making use of how linear perspective in the photographic image imposes a very specific order on space, she intensifies that ordering quality of the photographic image. Her temporary installations, and next the photographic images she makes of these installations, help us to understand how the temporality of trauma distinguishes itself from the temporality of memory, and it contributes to the transformation of trauma into memory. It is only by thinking *with* her interventions and photographs that this transformation takes place, because her work is not about it, it is not a representation of memory and trauma. It is IN the aesthetic act of ordering and structuring that the transformation takes place.

Notes

1. My translation: "Alors je dirais que le concept philosophique n'est pas seulement source d'opinion quelconque, il est source de transmission très particulière, ou entre un concept philosophique, une ligne picturale, un bloc sonore musical, s'établissent des correspondances, des correspondances très très curieuses, que à mon avis il ne faut même pas théoriser, que je préférerais appeler l'affectif en général . . . . Là c'est des moments privilégiés" (Deleuze 1983).

2. I am very grateful to Vinzenz Hediger for this information.
3. With a nod to Arthur Danto, Robber Sinnerbrink has shown this tightrope act as an oscillation between the philosophical "disenfranchisement" of film and its "re-enfranchising." See Sinnerbrink (2010 and 2011).
4. And although Johannes Binotto will reflect on the audiovisual essay (or, the video essay) later in this volume, let me just already take this format as an example.
5. This is not to say that practical research is not to be accomplished in writing—far from it, only the writing in question would be one that does not necessarily follow the strict confines of the so-called academic writing. It would be a writing that "is tainted" by literary and experimental modes of writing, a writing that does not judge, confine, or define, but a writing that—like art—is "a tool for blazing *life lines*" *(Deleuze and Guattari 1987: 187).* See e.g. my "Et in Academia Ego: Affect and Academic Writing" (Herzogenrath 2019: 216–34).
6. This deep time of audiovisual media has been traced by Siegfried Zielinski in Zielinski (2006), *Deep Time of the Media: Towards and Archaeology of Hearing and Seeing by Technical Means,* trans. Gloria Custance, Cambridge, Massachusetts, London: MIT Press.

References

Adorno, T. W. (1991), "The Essay as Form," in R. Tiedemann (ed.), trans. Shierry Weber Nicholson, *Notes to Literature,* vol. I, 3–23, New York: Columbia University Press.

Baumgarten, A. G. (2007), *Ästhetik/Aesthetica,* vol. 1, ed. D. Mirbach, trans. D. Mirbach, Hamburg: Felix Meiner Verlag.

Benjamin, W. (1996), "The Concept of Criticism in German Romanticism," in M. Bullock and M. W. Jennings (eds.), *Selected Writings, vol. 1, 1913–1926,* 116–200, Harvard: The Belknap Press of Harvard University Press.

Bennett, J. (2012), *Practical Aesthetics. Events, Affect and Art after 9/11,* London and New York: Tauris.

Bergson, H. (1991), *Matter and Memory,* trans. N. M. Paul and W. S. Palmer, New York: Zone Books.

Currie, G. (2004), "Cognitivism," in T. Miller and R. Stam (eds.), *A Companion to Film Theory,* Oxford: Blackwell.

Deleuze, G. (1983), "Cinéma cours 22," *Cours Vincennes – St Denis: le plan,* November 2, 1983. Available online: http://www2.univ-paris8.fr/deleuze/article.php3?id_article=124 (accessed April 11, 2019).

Deleuze, G. (1989), *Cinema 2. The Time-Image,* trans. H. Tomlinson and R. Galeta, London: Athlone Press.

Deleuze, G. (1994), *Difference and Repetition,* trans. P. Patton, New York: Columbia University Press.

Deleuze, G. (1995), *Negotiations 1972–1990,* trans. M. Joughin, New York: Columbia University Press.

Deleuze, G., and F. Guattari (1987), *A Thousand Plateaus,* trans. B. Massumi, Minneapolis: University of Minnesota Press.

Deleuze, G., and F. Guattari (1994), *What Is Philosophy?,* trans. H. Tomlinson and G. Burchill, New York: Columbia University Press.

Felski, R. (2015), *The Limits of Critique,* Chicago and London: The University of Chicago Press.

Flaxman, G. (ed.) (2000), *The Brain Is the Screen. Deleuze and the Philosophy of Cinema,* Minneapolis: University of Minnesota Press.

Practical Aesthetics

Geertz, C. (1973), *The Interpretation of Cultures*, New York: Basic Books.

Harris, P. A. (2010), "Deleuze's Cinematic Universe of Light: A Cosmic Plane of Luminance," *SubStance*, 39 (1): 115–24.

Herzogenrath, B. (2019), "Et in Academia Ego: Affect and Academic Writing," in E. van Alphen and T. Jirsa (eds.), *How to Do Things with Affects. Affective Triggers in Aesthetic Forms and Cultural Practices*, 216–34, Leiden and Boston: Brill/Rodopi.

Kroker, A. (1993), *Spasm: Virtual Reality, Android Music and Electric Flesh*, New York: St. Martin's Press.

Manning, E., and B. Massumi (2014), *Thought in the Act: Passages in the Ecology of Experience*, Minneapolis: University of Minnesota Press.

Mulhall, S. (2008), *On Film*, London: Routledge.

Noë, A. (2009), *Out of Our Heads. Why You Are Not Your Brain, and Other Lessons from the Biology of Consciousness*, New York: Hill and Wang.

Rajchman, J. (2000), *The Deleuze Connections*, Cambridge: MIT Press.

Rheingold, H. (1991), *Virtual Reality*, New York: Touchstone.

Sinnerbrink, R. (2010), "Disenfranchising Film? On the Analytic-Cognitivist Turn in Film Theory," in J. Reynolds, J. Chase, J. Williams, and E. Mares (eds.), *Postanalytic and Metacontinental: Crossing Philosophical Divides*, 173–89, London and New York: Continuum.

Sinnerbrink, R. (2011), "Re-Enfranchising Film: Towards a Romatic Film-Philosophy," in H. Carel and G. Tuck (eds), *New Takes in Film-Philosophy*, 25–47, Basingstoke: Palgrave MacMillan.

Whitehead, A. N. (1985), *Process And Reality*, corrected edition by D. R. Griffin and D. W. Sherburne, New York: The Free Press.

Ziemer, G. (2008), *Verletzbare Orte. Entwurf einer praktischen Ästhetik*, Zürich: Diaphanes.

CHAPTER 1
THE EXPERIMENT
BETWEEN ART AND LIFE*
Christoph Menke

Every work of art is an experiment: it is an experiment in art, an attempt to see whether one can create art in such a way—if in fact one can *create* it at all. Every artwork is an experiment because every artwork starts from nothing. An artwork that does not start from nothing, but rather takes art to be assured and a given, is no artwork at all. For the zero state of the artwork's inception is the aesthetic state, the state of aesthetic freedom. Every artwork is an experiment because it tests the possibility of art. It tests the possibility of creating something, a work, *out of* the state of aesthetic freedom. Because this possibility is in equal measure an impossibility—for the aesthetic state is a state of form-lessness and therefore of work-lessness—the existence, that is, the bringing-into-being of the artwork is fundamentally uncertain. The artwork is in its essence an experiment because nothing can have guaranteed its having become real.

But every work of art is not only an experiment in art; it is also an experiment in life. Those who make works of art and those who experience them, those who begin composing, playing, singing, writing, or painting, and those who listen to them, watch them, and follow them are thus aesthetically active, but they put this aesthetic activity into practice in their lives. Those who create and those who experience artworks are faced with the question of how to live with and according to these works. They are faced with the question of what place in life they want to or can give to aesthetic activity—and of whether this activity can be confined to that place. They are faced, that is, with the question of what the aesthetic activity they (re-)perform does to them. Every artwork is an experiment because it interrogates the possibility of art, and every artwork is an experiment because, as an object of aesthetic activities carried out in someone's life, it interrogates the possibility of living with or according to art.

In the following I will first determine the experimental character of art (Section 2.1) and then pose the question of living with art (Section 2.2). Both of these steps will be guided—though without interpreting them—by thoughts of Nietzsche's: the first by his radicalization of Kant's aesthetics, the second by his interpretation of Wagner's music.

---

*Revised translation by Stephen Haswell Todd.

2.1. Art

The concept of the "experiment" is a cognitive concept. The experiment is a mode of experiencing, as it aims at knowledge: one conducts an experiment in order to find out what a thing is like and how it behaves. At the same time, the concept of "experiment" is a practical concept. The experiment is a mode of action: to experiment is to create constellations, situations, and arrangements in which something then takes place. The experimenter creates something and exposes herself to an event. The experiment shows that in order to know something, one must do something. The experiment connects receptivity with activity; indeed, it *binds* receptivity *to* activity.

This binding of receptivity to activity is the topic of the (mini-)theory of scientific experimentation that Kant sketches in the preface to the second edition of the *Critique of Pure Reason*. Kant's objective is to provide evidence for his anti-empiricist theory of empirical experience (here meaning: experience that cognizes, determines objects): the scientific experiment is meant to reveal what empirical experience is. More precisely: it is meant to make evident (before this is extensively carried out in what follows) that the relation to reality which makes an experience "empirical" *cannot* mean—as empiricism according to Kant would have it—that one "must be content to be pulled along, as it were, by its thread [i.e., of nature]" (Kant 1999: B XIII). To grasp reality does not mean to be ruled by reality. If this were the case and hence if empiricism were right, our experiences—and, by extension, science—would allow us only to attain "accidental observations, made according to no previously designed plan," and not to grasp their relation to each other under "a necessary law, which is after all what reason seeks and requires" (Ibid.). The experiment is to show why that is not the case. Insight into the specific way in which the scientific experiment organizes experience is thus intended to provide a general model of experience which is capable of avoiding the consequence of empiricism, namely the dispersion of experience into coincidental and unconnected moments.

The scientific experiment demonstrates this in that it organizes experience as a subjectively controlled process:

> Reason, in order to be taught by nature, must approach nature with its principles in one hand, according to which alone the agreement among appearances can count as laws, and, in the other hand, the experiments thought out in accordance with these principles—yet in order to be instructed by nature not like a pupil, who has recited to him whatever the teacher wants to say, but like an appointed judge who compels witnesses to answer the questions he puts to them. (Kant 1999: B XIII)

Here, as he so often does, Kant finds a legal metaphor to elucidate his point: like a judge, law in hand, a scientific experimenter registers reproduced events in a prescribed form. This is what it is, according to Kant, to do an experiment: to take the testimony of witnesses and put it into a form in which it can be subsumed under the law. The receptivity of experience thus either takes place under the conditions of the law—or it leads to no experience at all, but rather produces something merely coincidental, without meaning: noise. The fact that empirical experience takes place according to the law means furthermore nothing other than that it reveals itself, in the scientific experiment, to be an activity of the subject, in spite of or precisely in its receptivity; for the subject is nothing other than the instance of the law, which in the experiment proves to be the form, the innermost principle of experience. According to Kant, the scientific experiment is thus the act of exposing oneself receptively to an event in such a way as can establish the guiding role of subjective laws; receptivity is here a stage in the legislative activity of the subject or, better, a means of consummating this activity. The scientific experiment thus proves for empirical experience the truth of the Vicoanian formula, according to which "reason has insight only into what it itself produces according to its own design" (Kant 1999: B XIII).

Whatever one may think of Kant's theory of the experiment with regard to scientific practice,[1] it does help to understand what place the concept of experiment occupies in the theory of art. For just as the scientific experiment can be called the "technology"[2] of empirical experience, the artistic experiment is the technology of aesthetic experience: In the artistic experiment, aesthetic experience is revealed in its truth, just like empirical experience in the scientific experiment. However, precisely in this, the artistic experiment shows that in aesthetic experience the receptivity of the senses and the legislative activity of the subject stand in an entirely different, even opposite, relation to each other than that which Kant finds in empirical experience: the artistic experiment does not test the ability of reason to bring forth insights "according to its own design" (Kant), but rather the aesthetic ability of the subject to exceed itself, to "surrender" its "individuality" (Nietzsche 1999: 43).

Kant sees this difference between aesthetic and empirical experience in the fact that in aesthetic experience, the criterion for the success of empirical experience, that is, the subsumptive relationship between the law and sensuous receptivity, is suspended. This is for Kant the basic determination of aesthetic *freedom*—of aesthetic experience *as* freedom: nothing in it enforces satisfying the form of the law. In the aesthetic state, the receptive ability—the imagination—is free, because it is not led from without by the laws or the concepts of the understanding: "since the [aesthetic] freedom of the imagination consists precisely in the fact that it schematizes without a concept" (Kant 2000: B 146). The fundamental determination, which was developed in aesthetics following Baumgarten and which Kant here reformulates, defines the "aesthetic" as the freedom of the sensuous from the law-giving power of the rational.

In his understanding of aesthetic freedom, Kant again lets himself be guided by a juridical metaphor: "lawfulness without laws" (Kant 2000: B 69). That is to say, according to Kant, imagination in its aesthetic freedom follows, without any external compulsion—*of its own accord*—the formal prescriptions of the law. Kleist's *The Broken Jug* puts this assumption to the test. It shows that when the judge loses control over the witnesses, they begin to talk disregarding any law, their discourse dissolving into formlessness. The aesthetic liberation of the witness leads, according to Kleist's insight, not to an unconstrained "harmony" (Kant) of the subject with the form of the law, but to the very dissolution of the law and hence of the subject that Kant had decried as the consequence of empiricism. The aesthetic trial of experience, if one still wishes to call it that (for nothing is experienced here), which is not led in its receptivity by the law, can also no longer be understood as the subject's self-determined activity, as a bringing-forth "according to its own design": without law there is no self-determination, no subjectivity, no (self-)conscious activity. The aesthetic freedom of the imagination is thus precisely the state which Plato described as "enthusiasm" and Nietzsche, following Plato, as "intoxication." As the free play of the imagination, aesthetic experience is unconscious. The free play of the imagination is a subject's activity, which however is not guided *by* the subject: not the realization of a capacity, but the unfolding of a force.[3]

This explains why art is an experiment and why it is in the opposite sense of Kant's concept of the experiment in science. As science is the technology of empirical experience, art is the technology of aesthetic experience. For art too is a self-conscious, planned activity (or because art is *also* such an activity): an activity pursued upon the basis of knowledge. The aim of art as a self-conscious activity or technique is to bring forth forms, forms of representation as representations of forms: the forms of life. This is the *poetical* definition of art as technology. Radically distinct from this is the aesthetic understanding of art. Aesthetically understood, the activity of art passes all the way through the freedom of the imagination: it is a bringing-forth of forms *from* and *through* the freedom of the imagination. The imagination is free because it is without form. The freedom of the imagination is the infinite play of creating, dissolving, transforming and recreating forms. This play brings forth no works (of art), because it brings forth nothing that is not dissolved in the same act. The aesthetic technology of art thus consists in bringing forth forms from formlessness. This is the experiment which the activity of art must constantly conduct anew: in the process of formation, it must expose itself to that which in turn exposes and questions its telos, that is, its form. The artistic experiment is always, if and as long as art is the technology of the aesthetic, an experiment in the breaking of form—but not by another, new form; rather, by no form at all, by formlessness or nonform as the grounding of form.

According to Kant, the scientific experiment should ensure and simultaneously prove and guarantee that even in empirical experience, which is essentially receptive, "reason has insight only into what it itself produces according to its own design"—that reason in empirical experience is and remains productive according to its own laws. The experiments of art, in contrast, reveal the collapse of precisely this certainty, which the scientific experiment is supposed to supply. Any artwork is an experiment because its accomplishment depends on this collapse. This is the radical new meaning which art aesthetically understood, art as a technology of aesthetic experience, lends to the concept of the experiment. The artistic experiment is an act of bringing forth that is subject to the loss of itself in the lawlessness of the imagination: the experiment of form-giving out of the freedom of formlessness, the experiment of an act out of the loss of the ability to act.

2.2. Life

If there can be no art, no making and experiencing of artworks, without "surrender of individuality by the entry into a strange nature" (Nietzsche 1999: 43); if on the other hand we can at the same time only lead our lives as "individuals," as self-sustaining and self-governing subjects—how then can we live in the face of the experience of art and its experiment in aesthetic freedom? In the wake of the experience of art and its experiment, life itself becomes an experiment. Life becomes an experiment because it sees itself confronted with an insoluble problem: the "problem" of "*finding the culture for our music*" (Nietzsche 1988: VII, 426, emphasis in the original), that is, the problem of finding or inventing a culture, a form of life which does justice to the fact, gleaned from the experience of art, that form proceeds from the surrender of one's self to the freedom of formlessness.

This is Tannhäuser's problem. The problem Tannhäuser attempts to solve is the problem of how he can live *as* a singer, how he can sing *and* live. What Nietzsche said about Wagner applies to Tannhäuser as well: "It is only in order to provide his art with a place in this world that we see him busy and active" (Nietzsche 1988: VII, 767). According to Nietzsche, Tannhäuser (like, later, Wagner himself) fails to solve this problem. Much more important, however, is the fact that he dares to take it on—as well as what he does with it and what he learns by doing what he does. Tannhäuser learns that he must set out to solve the problem of how he can live as a singer twice—and in two opposite ways. And that neither of the two ways of life he attempts can lead to a solution, but that each therefore refers him back to the other, opposite way.

Let us begin, though, at the beginning of the opera. *Tannhäuser* begins in medias res, with a sudden act: the sudden *termination* of an experiment. The attempt that Tannhäuser had made, story and background of which only gradually, by way of allusions, become clear, is the most radical one imaginable. It is the attempt to live an entirely different life—a life so different that it is no longer even clear whether this is the life of a human being or of a god. The opera begins with Tannhäuser's violent termination of this experiment due to his realization that he is only human, that he cannot live in that way.

Tannhäuser's abortive experiment consists in the attempt to live entirely in the love of Venus. Later on, at the "singers' contest" in the Wartburg with which Wagner reenacts (and repeals) the Platonic Symposium, it will become clear just what love means here: love is the power of longing which is not limited by any aim or measure, a longing that is not for something which satisfies it, but is rather infinite—indefinite. The love of Venus is excess: the excess of a love which cannot be fulfilled by any other, work, form, idea, but exceeds and reclaims for itself everything which it brings forth.

Tannhäuser gained access to this excessive love by his very singing about it. That's how he won this love and entered its realm. Above all, however, this excessive love was already the "source," the ground of his singing: "Your sweet charms," Tannhäuser sings to Venus—and he is to repeat these words at the singers' contest—"are the source of all beauty, and every fair wonder springs from you" (Wagner 2008, I.2 and II.4[4]). Whenever Tannhäuser sings, no matter what he sings about, he sings *out of* love—out of its unlimited enthusiasm and force. Tannhäuser sang his way to life in the Venusberg: this was the way of life that followed directly from his singing, for it was its—aesthetic-erotic—condition.

As a way of life, however, this state is at the same time "too much." "*Zu viel! Zu viel!*" are the first words Tannhäuser sings. The allure of Venus is "unbounded," and the "enjoyment" of her love is unbearable. To remain in her realm means "only to become a slave"; to flee it is to regain "freedom." Here, Tannhäuser understands "freedom" as the possibility of acting, and he understands "action" as strife and struggle (Wagner 2008, I.2). There can only be action where, instead of the excess of the One, a state of "change" or alternation prevails between the One and the Other, between pleasure and pain. For alternation means difference, sequence, and moderation. In alternation, the extremes are no longer "unbounded," but merely large or small; no longer immoderate, but measured—elements of a world in which the sky is clear and blue, the meadows fresh and green, birdsong sweet, and the sound of bells familiar. The human world to which Tannhäuser wishes to escape from the excessive world of love is a world of manageable order and healthily measured sensuousness.

In this human world of which Tannhäuser sings only one thing is missing: he who sings of it, and thus the singing which dreams up this world. For Tannhäuser's first words in the opera—his "Too much! Too much!"—describe not only what he experiences, but also *how* he sings: hastily, breathlessly, on the verge of overexertion. Tannhäuser's own singing is "too much" for him. Because he can only sing out of love, because the "sweet charms" of Venus are the "source" of his singing, Tannhäuser carries Venus, whom he desires to leave—he carries this excess *within himself*. For this reason, his singing immediately carries him back out of the humanely "beautiful world," into which he had fled in order to be free: he *sings* his way out of it. He need only begin to sing in order to lose it—to be hurled straight out of it. Tannhäuser's song in the singers' contest is quite literally a provocation: a demand for his exclusion by the others, who—according to Tannhäuser's scornful judgment—can be called "singers" only in an inferior and, in fact, an entirely different sense. To them, Tannhäuser the singer is a sinner, a blasphemer (Wagner 2008: II.4), because he questions the very basis of the human world. He disputes its fundamental distinction between good and evil. For in contrast to his competitors in the singers' contest, the love which *he* praises is not the love *of* the good. Tannhäuser's sin is the sin of asserting the innocence of a love that cares not for the opposition "good and evil"—the sin of the absence of sin.

Tannhäuser's first experiment consists in moving into the Venusberg—an attempt to give himself over completely to the excessive power of love. This attempt fails as soon as Tannhäuser, in this "other state," recalls in a dream the prior state of his human existence: the experiment with super-human love could only succeed under the—bestial—condition of complete, dreamless forgetting. Tannhäuser's second experiment consists in returning from this other state to the human world of moderate order and normative distinctions. This experiment of returning fails because Tannhäuser remains a singer and because he knows that his singing is predicated upon the excessive enthusiasm of love: without this excess there can be no art. It is his singing and nothing else which leads Tannhäuser from one world to the other and then once more out of this one. For Tannhäuser's song has its source in the love of Venus; when he sings he *is* already with her. But when he sings, he already dreams himself away from her again. His singing exceeds the source from which it flows—it is form and measure and thus the opposite of love.[5] In his singing, Tannhäuser attempts to cross from one world into the other, only to wish to return once again from this one to the first.

But what justifies to speak here of an "experiment"? Is this precisely what Tannhäuser, whom Wagner puts through a "series of ecstatic states" (Nietzsche 1988: VII, 759) to which he is helplessly subject, is *not*—the "epitome of a youngster" (Nietzsche), but for this exact reason not an experimenter? The only reason to speak of Tannhäuser's "experiments" consists, according to the discussion so far, in the fact that both ways of living—in the Venusberg and at the Wartburg—prove impossible for Tannhäuser to realize, and in the fact that we observe this. *We* say that Tannhäuser merely "attempts" to live, first in the Venusberg and then in the Wartburg, because we know in advance that he fails. Just as we say of somebody who fails to perform an action that he merely attempted it: that is, did not succeed in performing. It is the failure that retroactively makes the action into a—mere—attempt. But for precisely this reason, it is an attempt only for the observer. So it is not Tannhäuser who experiments with how he can live as an artist, but rather Wagner's opera that conducts an experiment *with* him. To talk of an "experiment" or an "attempt" presupposes the difference of internal and external, between an act's performance and its observation. The performer of the action simply acts. It is an experiment only for someone who observed him. The experiment is a category, indeed a *privilege*, of the observer.

Or is there a more radical, a performative concept of the experiment—the concept of an experiment in which act and observation, the act's performer and its observer, come together—or, in other words, the concept of a *self*-experiment? Can the performer of the act himself view his action as an experiment, perform it experimentally? If so, then that which makes the act an experiment for its observer would have to apply to the agent as well: awareness of the fact that its success is an open question. In acting, this is usually not, and cannot be, the case. We speak of an action only in cases where there is an ability to perform the action, and hence where success is not an open question but rather in principle guaranteed. *During* the performance of an action and *for* the performer of it, success is the normal outcome—for conceptual, not just empirical reasons. So acting can only become an experiment for the agent when the normalcy of success is shattered. But since the normalcy of success defines action, to see and perform it as an experiment means nothing less than putting into question the possibility of acting itself. The question which someone who performs an act experimentally asks herself, which she must be prepared to ask herself, is not just: Can I act successfully in this manner? Will these steps lead me to my aim? But rather: Can I act at all? Am I—still—an agent? To act experimentally, to conduct an experiment on oneself, is to act without knowing whether one can act—to act in the obscurity of not-knowing.

However, this not-knowing, this ignorance about one's ability to act, and therefore about the act's success, is at the same time a knowledge of knowledge, a higher knowledge:

the knowledge, or more precisely the experience, that the action which thereby becomes an experiment is subject to an opposing force which undermines it and calls it into question. Action as an experiment is acting in the awareness of its opposite. The radical experiment with oneself is likewise only possible and it is only needed where the ability to act is faced with an opposing force that works against it and puts into question its exercise, and thus the success of the act—making it an open question which can only be answered by the performance itself.

With this, we can say what would make Tannhäuser's double life, in the Venusberg and in the Wartburg, an "experiment" in the full sense of the word—an experiment in a life with or according to art, conducted not by the opera and thus by us with Tannhäuser, but rather by Tannhäuser himself, with himself in his own life: Tannhäuser would have to realize both his entry into the Venusberg and his return to the Wartburg in the awareness of the opposite, the opposing force of the respective other—of the Wartburg when entering the Venusberg and of the Venusberg when returning to the Wartburg—*at the very moment in which he performs these acts.*

Read in this way, Tannhäuser's flight from the Venusberg and his self-provoked banishment from the Wartburg are not an expression of stubbornness, but of truthfulness. Moreover, of artistic or aesthetic truthfulness; since Tannhäuser gains the insight that he can no longer live here—in the Venusberg or in the Wartburg—from the experience of his singing. It follows from the fact he can no longer *sing* here. The measure by which he judges the divergent ways of life of the Venusberg and of the Wartburg is whether they have a *place* for his singing. Tannhäuser, after all, learns from his singing something about himself that has consequence for his life: because he can only sing out of unlimited love, he wishes to live in this love; because his singing brings forth a form, he wishes to live in an ordered, human world. Tannhäuser breaks with both the worlds in which he lives by stating a truth about them that he learned in the aesthetic experience of his song: the truth about the excess of love, that it cannot be lived and that he can only become its "slave"—because he will be unable to act; and the truth about the order of society, that it is just as unlivable and that there he is only a "servant"—because there he cannot love. The aesthetic truth about both is servitude. Tannhäuser's break with both worlds is grounded in this truth. But his singing not only lets him experience what is lacking to both worlds; his singing is simultaneously the act of his liberation. In singing, Tannhäuser succeeds in freeing himself—his singing is a successful act. It is in fact the *only* act in which he succeeds, albeit only for a moment. Tannhäuser's artistic act of singing succeeds because he carries it out as an experiment: as acting in the awareness of the opposing force. In singing, *he himself* (i.e., not Wagner, the opera, and we alongside) makes the attempt to create a new form out of the "source" of limitless love and enthusiasm or, conversely, to bring forth anew the "order" of human speech out of the experience of enthusiasm.

In the experiment of reading Tannhäuser's life as a self-experiment, we can thus ascribe to him the eminent virtue which Nietzsche detected in Wagner during the brief phase of his admiration. It consists in the way in which Wagner succeeded in performing "the drama of his life":

His nature appears in a fearful way simplified, torn apart into two drives or spheres. Below there rages the precipitate current of a vehement will which as it were strives to reach up to the light through every runway, cave and crevice, and desires power. Only a force wholly pure and free could direct this will on to the pathway to the good and benevolent; had it been united with a narrow spirit, such an unbridled tyrannical will could have become a fatality; and a way out into the open, into air and sunlight, was in any event bound to be found soon. (Nietzsche 1997: 201)[6]

The greatness of Wagner, according to Nietzsche, lies in *how* he found this way: not through self-negation but through self-assertion—in such a way, that is, that "the two sides of his nature remained faithful to each other, that out of free and unselfish love, the creative, ingenuous, and brilliant side kept loyally abreast of the dark, the intractable, and the tyrannical side" (Nietzsche 1997: 203). The loyalty to oneself of which Nietzsche speaks is not to one's own identity, is no confirmation of one's own way of being, one's own nature or destiny, but is loyalty to the opposing force one bears within. Such self-loyalty is the precondition for self-experimentation. To experiment with oneself means to be loyal to the force which, in one's actions, works against one's ability and thus makes the accomplishment of one's actions into a radically open question—and precisely thereby possible.

Tannhäuser exercises this loyalty to the opposing force within him, in his singing. Only in that way *can* he sing: in the awareness of his inability to do so, hence in ignorance of success, in the trial. In his life, he is unable to do it. He finds no place for his singing, he knows no way of life that corresponds to it. To his loyalty to himself in the experiments of art corresponds no practice in life. Instead, Tannhäuser speaks from the start of "penance and reconciliation," through which he will find peace. The aesthetic experiment is suppressed by religious hope: "My salvation lies in Mary" (Wagner 2008: I.2).

Notes

1. As Hans-Jörg Rheinberger has emphasized, the scientific experiment is a system for the "production of differences" (Rheinberger1997: 224)—not for the re-production of the law.
2. In the sense of Martin Heidegger: "Technology [*Die Technik*] is a way of revealing. . . . It is the realm of revealing, i.e., of truth" (Heidegger 1993: 12).
3. For some details, see Menke 2012.
4. All translations from Wagner in the following by Stephen Haswell Todd.
5. This is true of the Venusberg in general—insofar as it is artistic practice. The stage directions for the Paris version of the opera read: "By way of gestures of inspired drunkenness, the Bacchantes urge on the lovers to ever greater excess. Intoxicated, they throw themselves into passionate embraces. Satyrs and fauns appear from out of the rocks and drive themselves into a frenzy. Here, in the midst of the outbreak of madness, the three Graces arise, horrified. They attempt to rein in and to banish the revelers. Powerless, they are fearful of being caught up themselves in the motion: they appeal to the sleeping Cupids, shake them awake, chase

them into the air. Rising like a flock of birds, the Cupids take up the entire space of the cavern as if in battle formation, and rain arrows down upon the mayhem in the deep. The wounded, seized with overpowering longings, sink back from the mad dance into exhaustion" (Wagner 2008: I.1). Its doubling into intoxicated frenzy and classical grace is inherent to the Venusberg as the realm of art.

6. Baudelaire (1995) describes the same doubling in *Tannhäuser*.

References

Baudelaire, C. (1995), "Richard Wagner and Tannhäuser in Paris," in C. Baudelaire, *The Painter of Modern Life and Other Essays*, ed. and trans. J. Mayne, London: Phaidon.
Heidegger, M. (1993), "The Question Concerning Technology," trans. W. Lovitt, in M. Heidegger, *Basic Writings*, ed. D. Farell Krell, San Francisco: Harper.
Kant, I. (1999), *The Critique of Pure Reason*, ed. and trans. P. Guyer and A. W. Wood, Cambridge: Cambridge University Press.
Kant, I. (2000), *Critique of the Power of Judgment*, ed. P. Guyer, trans. P. Guyer and E. Matthews, Cambridge, UK: Cambridge University Press.
Menke, C. (2012), *Force. A Fundamental Concept of Aesthetic Anthropology*, New York: Fordham University Press.
Nietzsche, F. (1988), *Kritische Studienausgabe*, ed. G. Colli and M. Montinari, Munich, Berlin, and New York: Deutscher Taschenbuch Verlag, de Gruyter. All excerpts are translated from German by Christoph Menke.
Nietzsche, F. (1997), *Richard Wagner in Bayreuth*, in F. Nietzsche, *Untimely Meditations*, trans. R.J. Hollingdale, ed. Daniel Breazeale, Cambridge, UK: Cambridge University Press.
Nietzsche, F. (1999), *The Birth of Tragedy and Other Writings*, trans. R. Speiers, ed. R. Geuss and R. Speiers, Cambridge, UK: Cambridge University Press.
Rheinberger, H.-J. (1997), *Toward a History of Epistemic Things: Synthesizing Proteins in the Test Tube*, Stanford: Stanford University Press.
Wagner, R. (2008), *Tannhäuser und der Sängerkrieg auf der Wartburg*, ed. K. Pahlen and R. König, Mainz: Schott. All excerpts are translated from German by Christoph Menke.

CHAPTER 2
ON THE PRACTICE OF THEORY
THE TECHNOLOGICAL TURN OF MEDIA THEORY AND AESTHETIC PRACTICE OF MEDIA PHILOSOPHY
Katerina Krtilova

The End of Theory

If today we can detect a new *practice turn* in the humanities, it is not in the form of new theories or philosophies of practice, but rather changing practices of the humanities—an "upheaval on the level of the method" (Galloway, Thacker and Wark 2014: 4). In contrast to the exposed "battlefield" of practice turns, the "experimental systems" (Rheinberger 1998) of the sciences which turn the attention to the materiality and mediality of (theoretical) knowledge, the "laboratories" of the humanities with their discursive practices (Foucault 1970) remained a "grey zone" between theory and practice. The use of digital technologies not only changes practices of reading, writing, archiving, searching, analyzing, commenting, and so on in the humanities but also allows to explore completely new research practices in "digital humanities." Digital humanities not only pursue a theoretical discussion of the role of digital technology in the humanities but also introduce new *technologies* of research. Experimenting with new techniques of analyzing texts might not intervene in "old" methods—hermeneutics, semiotics, historical analysis, and so on—at all, or might be a first step toward a fundamental change in the practice of the humanities.

Theory can be replaced by algorithms—as Chris Anderson claimed in his article "The End of Theory: The Data Deluge Makes Scientific Method Obsolete," published in 2008. "We can stop looking for models. We can analyze the data without hypotheses about what it might show. We can throw the numbers into the biggest computing clusters the world has ever seen and let statistical algorithms find patterns where science cannot" (Anderson 2008).

Following Beatrice Fazi's response to Anderson—discussing "The Ends of Media Theory" (Fazi 2017: 107–21)—I want to stress that it is exactly this way of *thinking technology*, in fact replacing thinking with technology, which asks for media philosophy; a media theory that *problematizes* the ways technology intervenes in, constitutes or shapes methods of the humanities. Fazi opposes Anderson's "With enough data, the numbers speak for themselves" (Anderson 2008) connecting media theory or media philosophy to Critical Theory of the Frankfurt School and their rejection of positivism. Andersen's conclusion "It's time to ask: What can science learn from Google?" (ibid.) is almost too easy to dismiss as it is clearly not just numbers, but Google speaking. "Google

Practical Aesthetics

views society as a network of value-producing agents . . . ; is it, then, the role of university English departments also to propose that society is a network of value-proposing agents?" (Galloway 2014: 126). Alexander Galloway's critique of positivist expediency in the humanities makes the case for questioning knowledge, rather than just subjecting it to "technological innovation." "Having inherited the computer, are we obligated to think with it?" (ibid.).

I want to propose that we can take this critique of (not only) Andersen's technological positivism a step further, into the heart of media theory: to Friedrich Kittler's dictum "media determine our situation" (Kittler 1999: xxxix) on the one hand and turning away from media theory to media philosophy on the other hand, criticizing the "media apriori" or "technological apriori" (Krämer 2003: 79–90; Mersch 2010: 191–208) and proposing an alternative: to "practice thinking as a performative art" (Rodowick 2019: 40).

A New Method of Thinking

Kittler's media, and more precisely technical "apriori," which he has proposed at the dawn of the computer age, in the early 1980s, undermined the understanding of culture as the sphere of ideas, articulations of the human mind or spirit (*Geist*). Concepts, theories, philosophies, and ideologies are effects of technical operations of storing, processing, and transmitting information, of writing, reading, calculating, measuring, visualizing, and so on. Kittler criticizes that the humanities (*Geisteswissenschaften*) have not paid attention to the material-technical, nonsignificant part of cultural and social processes, leaving technology as a blind spot of the anthropological, hermeneutic, or phenomenological perspective (Kittler's favourite "media-ignorant" approaches). "Media, then, are (at) the end of theory because in practice they were already there to begin with," as Geoffrey Winthrop-Young points out in his preface to Kittler's *Grammophone, Film, Typewriter* (1999: xx), "Media are the alpha and omega of theory. If media do indeed 'determine our situation,' then they no doubt also determine, and hence configure, our intellectual operations." This idea corresponds with Andersen's approach up to the point that computers can detect patterns no one was even looking for, could not even imagine—they are not exclusively instruments or projections of human imagination, will, or capacities. Unlike Andersen however, Kittler was well aware of his own theoretical gesture, "casting the human spirit out of the Humanities,"[1] introducing a technical approach into the realm of hermeneutics. (Kittler was trained as a literary scholar.) He was able to prove his argument, radically changing the method of the study of cultural practices: transforming the interpretation of texts into describing various "cultural techniques" (Siegert 2015; Krämer and Bredekamp 2013) in the context of media history or media archaeology—including technical description, excluding "meaning."

In its beginning, German media theory thus performs a technological turn, yet also questions it. Before the philosophical twist of media theory, around the turn of the twentieth century, Vilém Flusser, considered one of the pioneers of media theory, had already in the 1980s both embraced Kittler's media apriori and undermined it. Flusser states in one of his last interviews from 1991 that with new technologies "a new philosophy" arises, "by itself," "not just because the topics change, but also and above all the method of thinking" (Flusser 2003: 7, my translation). At first glance, Flusser's new method of thinking seems to converge with the project of "digital humanities"—not only in practical experiments with new media. For example, in 1987 the German edition of his book, *Writing: Does Writing Have a Future* (*Die Schrift. Hat Schreiben Zukunft?*) (Flusser 2011) was released also on a floppy disk, the author instructing readers to continue, rewrite, or delete the text. Close to Kittler, Flusser argued that computers produce new knowledge and moreover "new realities" their (human) users can't even think of. "Thinking itself proves to be a knot in a calculated network" (Flusser 1998: 21, my translation). However, in his statement quoted earlier the importance of the "new *philosophy*" comes into focus. In contrast to Kittler, Flusser stresses that he is above all interested in the "revolution in thinking" (*Umbruch im Denken*)—which is not just an effect of the new medium in the kittlerian sense, but a reflexive turn which is at the same time performed and "detected" in thinking (thinking)—and that there is an active and passive aspect of the "revolution" or, in a different translation, "upheaval." Proposing a new philosophy, Flusser *performs* a revolution in the thinking of thinking turning the attention to new media that allow to think in a new way—especially "technical images."[2] At the same time, this "revolution" is so to speak imposed on thinking. New technologies *force* to think in a different way—thinking that was shaped by writing "decomposes" (Flusser [1993] 1995: 16). The revolutionary action is interleaved with losing control, losing the sovereignty over one's own thinking of thinking, which Flusser invokes with the cartesian tradition of philosophy as a method of reflection based on the certainty of "I think therefore I am," purifying thinking of any external elements or influences. Crossing this method Flusser proposes: "Thinking before articulation is only a virtuality, which is to say nothing. It is realized through the gesture. Strictly speaking, there is no thinking before making a gesture. . . . To have unwritten ideas really means to have nothing" (Flusser 2014: 24).

Flusser suggests a new philosophy in a precarious position "in between" the "universe of texts" which still essentially shapes our thinking, and the new "universe of computing" we are about to "jump into" (Flusser [1993] 1995: 16), leaving writing behind. This leap into the new universe *is* the revolution in thinking that happens "by itself"—in Flusser's writing. In this performative dimension, Flusser parts ways with his own "media determinism": we *can* abandon philosophy, leaving thinking to computers, thinking in the sense of a "combinatory game using number-like symbols," which according to Flusser can be fully mechanized (Flusser 2000: 32)—but there is also the possibility of not losing the freedom to think in a different way—paradoxically letting go of the full control of thought and action.

There Are No Media or the Revolutionary Practice of Media Theory

"Theory only makes sense as an attitude; otherwise, the generalization of the very concept of 'theory' is pointless" (Bal and Boers 1994: 8). In accordance with Mieke Bal's point, turning attention to "doing theory" or "theoretical practice," media philosophy might be considered a "revolutionary practice" (Derrida 2019: 11), questioning theory by introducing a new practice of philosophy. Thus, taking up Flusser's revolutionary gesture I want to focus on the media turn in terms of not only a technological shift, which changes cultural, social, economic, or political practices and forces theory to adapt to these changes, but also the shift *in* theoretical practice.

Opposed to "positivist" tendencies of more or less radical technical determinisms—stressing the *fact* of new technologies changing culture and society—philosophical approaches in German media theory introduced a "negative" turn,[3] articulated already in 1999 in Lorenz Engell and Joseph Vogl's "first media theoretical axiom," stating that "that there are no media" (Engell and Vogl 1999: 10). This well-known (alleged) "axiom" in German media theory does not really work as an axiom—although the text continues with several suggestions on how to describe "media"—but rather marks a specific theoretical gesture that refuses to provide any "positive" definition of the subject matter of media theory: media. Defending this unorthodox move Engell concludes in a polemic from 2011: "*Medienwissenschaft* [German Media Studies][4] can declare anything a medium (and deny everything this denomination)" (Engell 2011: 119, my translation); with every new "medium" it "reinvents itself" (ibid.).[5]

Dismissed by some media theorists like Knut Hickethier as a rhetorical strategy of "metaphorical mystifications" and nonacademic "pseudo-theories" (Hickethier [2003] 2010: 381, my translation) this kind of media theory radically questions what theory and an "academic" approach means or else how (academic) theory can be done. As such, nothing is "substantially" a medium (Engell and Vogl 1999: 10). That is the point of the "first axiom," not computers, not books, not a library, nor a piece of paper, they can all *become* media. Paper becomes a medium, used to write a letter, a bill, to print a text or to make fire, determining certain cultural practices—a specific kind of (two-dimensional) notation, certain types of images, methods of accounting, administrative procedures, and so on—and opening up new possibilities—of communication, archiving, aesthetic practice etc. The way in which writing, archiving, visualizing or calculating turn out to be "media practices," "work" as media—in the dialectic of determination and possibility or transparency and opacity, differentiating "medium" and "form" and other models of mediality[6]—is part of "becoming a medium" (Vogl 2001: 115). Becoming a medium is both a media practice (which can be observed as a phenomenon "out there" so to speak) and brought forth or "made visible" thanks to a certain theoretical perspective, developing a concept of medium or mediality. With every new definition of a "medium," media theory "discovers" new media, but at the same time every media practice discovers a new way of (theoretical) reflection, new ways to think with/in writing or calculation or images or moving images (Herzogenrath 2017). The objects of *Medienwissenschaft* "are at the same time its own tools, which constitute and determine its practice" (Engell 2011: 119, my translation). Engell's media theory/media philosophy is thus not "applied" to film(s). He proposes theoretical/philosophical figures developed with/in film—following, above all, Gilles Deleuze's philosophy.[7]

There is no meta-perspective, as stressed in Flusser's "revolution in thinking," the perspective can change with every medium, with every new aspect of *mediality*. Vogl's example of the telescope becoming a medium is thus a change of perspective in a literal as much as metaphorical sense: you can see different things and see the world with different eyes—what seeing and observing (as scientific practice) means changes.

The Technological Turn of Theory

The practice of a media philosophy and its accompanying media practices are intertwined. This is in Hickethier's view clearly an "illegitimate" theoretical practice which makes it impossible to define objects and methods—obscuring instead of "clarifying facts" (Hickethier [2003] 2010: 381). The even more serious consequence, however, might be that media philosophy also *does* something else than expected of theory.

Theory doesn't do anything, that is the starting point of Steven Knapp and Walter Benn Michael's *Against Theory* argument: they criticize not only "wrong" theory, as Hickethier does, but "the founding gesture of all theoretical argument" which is "a position outside practice" (1985: 26), "theory is nothing else but the attempt to escape practice" (ibid., 30). Their argument however takes the opposite direction of unsettling theory turning to the practice of theory. They turn practice *against* theory, assuming practice is given in actual fact, self-evident, "self-sufficient and all-encompassing" (Crewe 1985: 54) independent of theory. Their argument presupposes a distinction between theory and practice which allows us to address "theory" in the first place—in a *theoretical* argument. Knapp and Michaels identify a number of methods of literary studies like narratology or stylistics as "essentially empirical" (1985: 11)—thus, in his response not only Jonathan Crewe points to Knapp and Michaels's theoretical moves and the rather arbitrary distinction between "theory" and "practice." The practice Knapp and Michaels exclude is precisely the one crossing the theory/practice distinction: practical interventions in theory, which can be called programmatic in media philosophy, based on "practical disruptions rather than theoretical coherence" (Goppelsröder 2010: 100, my translation). In line with Paul de Man (a "pro-theory" protagonist of the initial *Against Theory* debate /de Man 1982/) and Mieke Bal, Fabian Goppelsröder draws on the "media-reflexive" practice of the study of literature: of course, its objects are at the same time its tools, writing (literary) theory a (literary) writing practice, writing in/about writing.

Beyond the intertwining of literature and theory (of literature), there is a further spin of the media practice of theory that escapes the practical turn of *Against Theory* underlying Stanley Fish's critique of Noam Chomsky's theory of language as an example of an obsolete theory. Fish criticizes that Chomsky turns away from "empirical activity" (meaning the behavior of a particular linguistic community) to follow the dictate of "an abiding and general rationality" trying to find rules which are in principle "formalizable" and "can be programmed on a computer" (Fish 1985: 108). For Fish, practice proves Chomsky wrong: it doesn't work. Around thirty years later, artificial intelligence will generate perfectly reasonable sentences and texts, dialogues or translations—not based on a chomskian model, but the actual use of language: programs analyze huge amounts of texts and utterances written/spoken by human users "learning" to construct meaningful sentences and texts. These data are based on actual practice, but processed mechanically, "function in the manner of a 'mechanical computation'" (ibid., 109). I don't want to make the case for a kittlerian techno-determinism, but adapt Kittler's view to point to the convergence of theory and technology: Chomsky's theory is perfectly close to empirical regularities of the behavior of a particular community stressed by Fish—if it is understood to include the practice of computing. Practice as described by Fish—the behavior of a linguistic community—is today inextricably tied to digital technologies (and has always been tied to some kind of technology, following Kittler). Thus, practice is always already analyzed, the analysis—algorithms that allow or predetermine certain actions, collecting and evaluating data with or without the knowledge of the users and so on—is an intrinsic part of practice. Fish's approach to practice as something theory can turn to or overlook is challenged not only by new technological forms of practice, but more so by the uncanny link between technology and theory outlined by Martin Heidegger as characteristic of modern technology. Theory does not only provide models which can be applied by technologies, but approaching reality as something that can be modeled in theory in the first place—developed in the "cybernetic hypothesis" (Galloway 2014)—is essentially *techno-logical*. According to Heidegger, science[8] provides a "theory of the real" (Heidegger 1977a: 157) which turns out to be a paradoxical practice: exactly in establishing a distance from its object and withdrawing from practice, not interacting with the world, theory manipulates reality (thus turned into "objects" that are "at disposal"). "For after all science as theory is surely 'theoretical.' It spurns any refining of the real. It stakes everything on grasping the real purely" (ibid., 167). Looking closer at this *practice* of theory as observing (*Be-trachten*), it turns out to be "an observing that strives after is a refining of the real that does encroach uncannily upon it. . . . challenges forth the real specifically through aiming its objectness. Science sets upon the real" (ibid.). Theory seizes the real, strives (trachten), which means, "to manipulate, to work over or refine (*bearbeiten*). To strive after something means: to work one's way toward something, to pursue it, to entrap it in order to secure it. Accordingly, theory as *Betrachtung* (observation) would be an entrapping and securing refining of the real" (ibid.). Technology is thus for Heidegger not applied scientific knowledge— aka "objective" knowledge—but the other way around, modern science is essentially a technology. It relies on *calculability* as predictability, an approach that is prone to process (*bearbeiten*) everything—and inversely there *are* only things or facts that can be processed in a particular way. This kind of thinking—in the universe of computation, the "algorithmic rationality" (Mersch 2017)—applies both to theory and to practice; it governs thinking and doing or rather producing.

In contrast to a pragmatic reading of Heidegger, stressing that thinking is embedded in practices, part of being-in-the-world,[9] I want to turn the attention to his notion of thinking (*Denken*) as a practice radically different from the "theory of the real": the *Vollzug* (performance) of thinking which Heidegger also describes as a *Sprung* (leap) in/ of thinking.

Thinking before the Distinction of Theory and Practice

Thinking can be as effective as technology while not being "practical" in the sense of an "objective" manipulation—it can transform "what there is" (in Heidegger's terms) in a different way than technology. This is the point of Derrida's reflections on *Theory and Practice* in his seminar in 1976–7 mentioned before: philosophy as revolutionary practice transforms practice. Drawing on Karl Marx' *11 Thesis* on Ludwig Feuerbach, especially the famous 11th: "Philosophers have only *interpreted* the world, in various ways; what is important is to *change* it" (1970: 123), Derrida stresses the performative dimension—"the practical imperative or imperative performative" (2019: 9) of this thesis: it is marked not by "a theoretical determination but a determination that is itself practical, and practico-revolutionary" (ibid., 10). This revolutionary practice is not practice in the pragmatic sense, a "practice whose meaning everybody already understood" (ibid., 11), but a new practice of philosophy (and not a philosophy of practice).

Heidegger offers also a further hint as to how to understand the practice or rather performance of thinking. In "The Letter on Humanism," he characterizes thinking as "neither theoretical nor practical. It comes to pass [ereignet sich] before this distinction" (1998: 272). As we have seen, the practice of theory always slips away presupposing a distinction of theory and practice, predefining theory in relation to practice and vice versa. The practice of theory is the practice of drawing this distinction—neither "practical" nor "theoretical." Trying to think the practice or rather performance of theory attempts to think before the distinction of "theory" and "practice," in order to open up the possibilities of doing "theory," not presupposing practice (knowing what practice is, giving a "positive" account of practice), but rather "inventing" it. "Such thinking is, insofar as it is," as Heidegger continues the sentence quoted earlier: Thinking is there, not just as an effect of a practice.

Thinking derived from technological operations in kittlerian media theory—in which thinking or reflection comes down to recursive operations—fails to acknowledge the possibility to think a technological practice of thinking in a non-technological way (as demanded by Heidegger /1977b: 20/), thus *performing* a different kind of thinking. Thinking, as such, is different than merely enacting a "theory of the real." The shift from media theory to media philosophy is tied to this different practice of thinking, which "may also be considered a practice of change and invention, . . . of creating new styles of thought, ... Call this philosophy as experimentation" (Rodowick 2015: 69). Following Hannah Arendt, Rodowick considers this a kind of "effective" thinking (yet not "practical"), constitutive for the humanities: thinking as an "impracticable" practice, without "practical results" (Rodowick 2019: 45). "There is no measure of thinking apart from the act or performance of thinking itself" (ibid. xx).

In his "negative media philosophy," Dieter Mersch specifies media practices as aesthetic practices[10]—not as practices referred to by theory (in an "objective," scientific approach), but which I would call (in this context) reflexive practices before the theory/practice distinction: not separating the theoretical "step back" from practice—describing, conceptualizing, analyzing practices, relations, processes—and writing, composing and decomposing, shaping, dissolving, turning (and crossing out these descriptions, concepts, metaphors, designations as already part of theoretical language). Flusser's gestures as gestures of thinking, not as a "theory of gestures" (which Flusser proposes, contradicting himself) are an attempt of an "aesthetic theory" of this kind.

Not dealing with artistic practices "out there," as presupposed practices (defined as "art"), or an "object of aesthetic experience," Kathrin Busch points out the role of art in Heidegger's, Deleuze's, or Derrida's philosophies. Artistic practice affects them as "a change in thinking. Art is not an object of philosophical reflection but rather sets the stage for a different kind of thinking, performed alongside and through/by means of art" (Busch 2016: 12, my translation). Media philosophy does in this sense not refer to artistic practices, describing, interpreting, analyzing them; it *is* an "aesthetic theory." As Mersch and Busch stress the importance of artistic practice, I want to stress the importance of philosophy as "a performative art" (Rodowick 2019: xx). As an impracticable practice, philosophy changes practice, drawing and constantly shifting the line between theory and practice.

Theory can be replaced by technology, we could say, realizing Heidegger's *Ge-stell* (enframing)—science converging with technology, a technical logic governing thinking and being (or, in this context, *doing*)—but, at the same time, thinking (in Heidegger's sense) is not determined by its media, but rather refracted by them, in the philosophical practice of media theory.

Notes

1. A free translation of *Die Austreibung des Geistes aus den Geisteswissenschaften* (Kittler 1980).
2. Thinking in technical images combines calculation and imagination, overcoming the "linear discourse." See Krtilova 2015.
3. Dieter Mersch develops his media philosophy explicitly as a "negative media theory" (2013)—I am using this notion in a broader sense, including different kinds of questioning (media) theory.
4. German Medienwissenschaft—literally "Media Science"—is a specific discipline distinct from Anglo-American Media Studies; therefore, I am using the German term.
5. German media philosophers like Engell, Mersch, and Krämer use frequently "media theory" and "media philosophy" as synonyms—due to the specific notion of theory outlined earlier. D.N. Rodowick links a notion of theory corresponding with Engell's to a shift from theory to philosophy, suggesting that one task of theory is to make us aware "that we are constantly creating out objects, or at least the forms of their intelligibility and value" (2015: 298).
6. For an overview of different positions in German media philosophy, see Stefan Münker and Alexander Roesler's volume *Was ist ein Medium?* (2008).
7. Corresponding with the idea of "film as philosophy," as suggested by Bernd Herzogenrath (2017).
8. As German Humanities are called literally "Sciences of the Mind" (*Geisteswissenschaften*), or "Sciences of Culture" (*Kulturwissenschaften*), science as *Wissenschaft* applies in Heidegger's "Science and Reflection" both to Physics and Literature.

9. In the "Question Concerning Technology," Heidegger suggests a turn to the Greek notion of *techne* and *poiesis*, a "bringing forth" in contrast to manipulating something which is at disposal (1977b: 3–35).
10. This is close to Heidegger's turn to art (and, especially, poetry) as way to reflect language not in a theoretical, "objective" way, but in a passive mode of thinking always already receptive to and shaped by language discovering its traces in thinking (Mersch 2013).

References

Andersen, C. (2008), "The End of Theory: The Data Deluge Makes Scientific Method Obsolete," in *Wired*, June 23. Available online: https://www.wired.com/2008/06/pb-theory/ (accessed January 10, 2019).
Bal, M., and I. E. Boers (1994), "Preface," in M. Bal and I. E. Boers (eds.), *The Point of Theory. Practices of Cultural Analysis*, New York: Continuum.
Bal, M. (1994), "Scared to Death," in M. Bal and I. E. Boers (eds.), *The Point of Theory. Practices of Cultural Analysis*, 32–47, New York: Continuum.
Busch, K. (2016), "wissen anders denken," in K. Busch (ed.), *anderes wissen*, 11–33, Paderborn: Fink.
Crewe, J. (1985), "Toward Uncritical Practice," in W. J. T. Mitchell (ed.), *Against Theory. Literary Studies and the New Pragmatism*, 53–64, Chicago: University of Chicago Press.
de Man, P. (1982), "Resistance to Theory," *Yale French Studies*, 63: 3–20.
Derrida, J. (2019), *Theory and Practice*, trans. D. Wills, Chicago: The University of Chicago Press.
Engell, L. (2011), "Medien waren: möglich. Eine Polemik," in C. Pias (ed.), *Was waren Medien?*, 103–28, Zurich: Diaphanes.
Engell, L., and J. Vogl (1999), "Vorwort," in C. Pias et al. (eds.), *Kursbuch Medienkultur*, 8–12, Stuttgart: DVA.
Fazi, B. (2017), "The Ends of Media Theory," *Media Theory*, 1 (1): 107–21.
Fish, S. (1985), "Consequences," in W. J. T. Mitchell (ed.), *Against Theory. Literary Studies and the New Pragmatism*, 106–31, Chicago: University of Chicago Press.
Flusser, V. ([1993] 1995), "Lob der Oberflächlichkeit," in *Lob der Oberflächlichkeit. Für eine Phänomenologie der Medien*, 9–59, Mannheim: Bollmann.
Flusser, V. (2000), *Towards a Philosophy of Photography*, London: Reaktion Books.
Flusser, V. (2003), "Gespräch mit Florian Rötzer in München 1991," in N. Röller and S. Wagnermaier (eds.), *absolute Vilém Flusser*, Freiburg: orange-press.
Flusser, V. (2011), *Writing. Does Writing Have a Future?*, Minneapolis: University of Minnesota Press.
Flusser, V. (2014), "The Gesture of Writing," in *Gestures*, Minneapolis: University of Minnesota Press.
Flusser, V. (1998), *Vom Subjekt zum Projekt. Menschwerdung*, Frankfurt/Main: Fischer.
Foucault, M. (1970), *The Order of Things. An Archeology of the Human Sciences*, New York: Pantheon Books (Random House).
Galloway, A. (2014), "Cybernetic Hypothesis," *Differences*, 25 (1): 107–31.
Galloway, A., E. Thacker, and M. Wark (2014), "Introduction: Execrable Media," in *Excommunication. Three Inquiries in Media and Mediation*, 1–24, Chicago and London: University of Chicago Press.
Goppelsröder, F. (2010), "Irritation als Methode? Vom störenden und versammelndem Philosophieren," in M. Rautzenberg and A. Wolfsteiner (eds.), *Hide and Seek. Das Spiel von Transparenz und Opazität*, 97–108, München: Fink.

Practical Aesthetics

Herzogenrath, B. (2017), "Film and/as Philosophy. An Elective Affinity?," in B. Herzogenrath (ed.), *Film as Philosophy*, vii–xxv, Minneapolis: University of Minnesota Press.

Heidegger, M. (1977a), "Science and Reflection," trans. W. Lovitt, in M. Heidegger (ed.), *The Question Concerning Technology and Other Essays*, 155–82, New York: Harper & Row.

Heidegger, M. (1977b), "The Question Concerning Technology," trans. W. Lovitt, in M. Heidegger (ed.), *The Question Concerning Technology and Other Essays*, 3–35, New York: Harper & Row.

Heidegger, M. (1998), "Letter on 'Humanism,'" trans. F. A. Capuzzi, in M. Heidegger (ed.), *Pathmarks*, 239–76, Cambridge: Cambridge University Press.

Hickethier, K. ([2003] 2010), *Einführung in die Medienwissenschaft*, Stuttgart: Metzler.

Kittler, F., (ed.) (1980), *Die Austreibung des Geistes aus den Geisteswissenschaften*, Paderborn, Wien, München and Zürich: Schöningh.

Kittler, F. (1999), *Grammophone, Film, Typewriter*, trans. G. Winthrop-Young, Stanford: Stanford University Press.

Knapp, S. and W. B. Michaels (1985), "Against Theory," in W. J. T. Mitchell (ed.), *Against Theory. Literary Studies and the New Pragmatism*, 11–30, Chicago: University of Chicago Press.

Krämer, S. (2003), "Erfüllen Medien eine Konstitutionsleistung? Thesen über die Rolle medientheoretischer Erwägungen beim Philosophieren," in S. Münker, A. Roesler, and M. Sandbothe (eds.), *Medienphilosophie. Beiträge zur Klärung eines Begriffs*, 78–90, Frankfurt/Main: Fischer.

Krämer, S. and H. Bredekamp (2013), "Culture, Technology, Cultural Techniques – Moving Beyond Text," *Theory, Culture & Society*, 30 (6): 20–9.

Krtilova, K. (2015), "Medienreflexiv. Zur Genese eines Verfahrens zwischen Martin Heidegger und Vilém Flusser," *Internationales Jahrbuch für Medienphilosophie*, 1: 95–118.

Marx, K. and F. Engels (1970), *The German Ideology*, New York: International Publishers.

Mersch, D. (2010), "Meta/Dia. Zwei unterschiedliche Zugänge zum Medialen," *Zeitschrift für Medien- und Kulturforschung*, 10 (2): 85–208.

Mersch, D. (2013), "Introduction to a Negative Theory of Media," trans. Mauricio Liesen, *MATRIZes* 7 (1): 207–22.

Mersch, D. (2017), "Digital Criticism. For a Critique of 'Algorithmic Reason,'" trans. M. Turnbull, *Diaphanes* 3, December 10. Available online: https://diaphanes.de/titel/digital-criticism-5313 (accessed April 5, 2019).

Münker, S., and A. Roesler (2008), *Was ist ein Medium?*, Frankfurt/Main: Suhrkamp 2008.

Rheinberger, H.-J. (1998), "Experimental Systems, Graphematic Spaces," in T. Lenoir (ed.), *Inscribing Science: Scientific Texts and the Materiality of Communication*, 285–303, Stanford: Stanford University Press.

Rodowick, D. N. (2014), *Elegy for Theory*, Cambridge: Harvard University Press.

Rodowick, D. N. (2015), *Philosophy's Artful Conversation*, Cambridge: Harvard University Press.

Rodowick, D. N. (2019), "Hannah Arendts Denkungsart," *Internationales Jahrbuch für Medienphilosophie*, 5: 39–57.

Siegert, B. (2015), *Cultural Techniques. Grids, Filters, Doors and Other Articulations of the Real*, New York: Fordham University Press.

Vogl, J. (2001), "Medien-Werden. Galileis Fernrohr," *Mediale Historiographien*, 1: 115–23.

Winthrop-Young, G. (1999), "Translator's Introduction," in F. Kittler (ed.), *Grammophone, Film, Typewriter*, xi–xxxiii, trans. G. Winthrop-Young, Stanford: Stanford University Press.

CHAPTER 3
EPISODE ZERO
HOW EMPIRICAL SCIENCE DISCOUNTS AESTHETIC EXPERIENCE, AND A PRACTICAL WAY TO BRING IT BACK
Tim Ingold

I recently attended an interdisciplinary conference, including evolutionary biologists, ethologists, sociocultural anthropologists, evolutionary psychologists, neuropsychologists, and philosophers, tasked with investigating "the biological mechanisms that underlie symbol making and the perception and appreciation of beauty."[1] At the conference, I was introduced to some of the cutting-edge research now underway in the field known as empirical aesthetics. Lavishly funded, and founded on the principles of cognitive science, this research claims to unpack the mechanisms by which the mind, operating by way of various regions of the brain, is alleged to convert the inputs of sensation emanating, say, from a work of art into outputs such as emotional reactions and aesthetic judgments. Every such input-output conversion, we were told, amounts to an "aesthetic episode."

I was appalled by what I heard. It was as if I had entered a dystopic world wherein living, breathing human beings had been cloned by disembodied mind-brains, their eyes and ears having been co-opted as sensory ports into which objects of art can be plugged and their information downloaded, for processing and conversion into products calculated to provide immediate gratification for the mind-brains' witless hosts. This struck me as not just bizarre, but a willful and perverse corruption of the aesthetic imperative at the heart of art and experience. In the heat of my outrage, however, I was unable to articulate my objections with any coherence. Not only did I make myself unpopular at the conference, with my uncontrolled outburst; I was also left feeling deeply unsatisfied with myself. To make up for it, I resolved—at some future opportunity—to undertake a more careful study and critique of empirical aesthetics in order that I could explain, to myself and others, why art and experience, if they are to be taken seriously, call for an approach to aesthetics that is practical rather than empirical. This chapter is the result.

I

Allow me to begin with a brief reminiscence that will help to set the scene. A few weeks ago, during a trip to the southwestern tip of the British Isles, in the county of Cornwall, my wife and I had the opportunity to visit the seaside town of St. Ives, which has been a mecca for artists ever since the sculptor Barbara Hepworth made her home there in the 1950s. A quarter of a century ago, in 1993, a branch of the Tate Gallery was established in the town, to celebrate its artistic tradition, and we were keen to visit it. Our visit was memorable in many ways: for getting soaked in torrential rain on the way there, for the loveliness of the new building, for the way the light streamed in through the windows of the café, opening to a view over the sea, when the sun eventually burst through, for the struggle I had with reading the captions for the works on display, having forgotten my spectacles in the pocket of my raincoat now confined to a baggage locker, and for our walk on the sandy beach between the gallery and the sea in brilliant sunshine that had suddenly and miraculously replaced the thunderous clouds of only a couple of hours before.

Then, of course, there were the works themselves, which we had ostensibly come to see. More, of course, caught our attention than I could possibly list here, but I would like to mention one that, for me especially, remained a highlight of the visit. It was the painting *Thermal* (1960), by Peter Lanyon. A native of Cornwall, Lanyon was one of a group of painters active in St. Ives in the postwar years. He had started with landscapes, but later developed a passion for gliding. This soon came to dominate his painting as well, in which he began to cover the canvas with swathes of paint much as the skies in which he would fly are filled with swirling expanses of air. These expanses are moved by powerful forces of convection, which can not only afford lift to the glider but also obstruct its movements, almost as if it were hitting a brick wall. A sky that looks empty and featureless to a spectator on the ground becomes, in the experience of the glider pilot, something more like the roaring ocean for the mariner. And this is what Lanyon had painted in *Thermal*, one of the most powerful of his glider compositions. Perhaps it was a premonition. Only four years later, Lanyon died from injuries sustained in a gliding accident.

Why did this work, above all others, mark my memory of the gallery? The immediate reason is that I had seen it before, a few years previously, on a visit to the Courtauld Institute in London. It happened that the Institute was staging a temporary exhibition devoted to Lanyon's work.[2] Knowing nothing about it, I decided to take a look, and was intrigued by what I saw. I thought no more of it, however, until three months later, during a flight from London to Chicago. I was writing an essay to accompany a major installation by the artist Tomás Saraceno, who has pioneered solar-powered balloon flight as part of an ambitious vision for a future epoch envisaged as the *Aerocene*.[3] Balloons and gliders have in common that they ride the air currents, as birds also do, rather than forcefully drilling through them like missiles powered by an external energy source. It occurred to me, as a passenger on board a transatlantic airliner, that the plane was more analogous to a missile than a bird, and that sat inside the fuselage, strapped to my seat, the one thing I definitely was *not* doing was flying (Ingold 2017). And it was at this moment that Lanyon's glider paintings came back to mind. Of these paintings, *Thermal* was the most evocative, and I brought it into my essay to show how the air, in Lanyon's own words, "is a very definite world of activity as complex and demanding as the sea."[4]

That's why, when I came across it again some three years later, in the gallery at St. Ives, it felt like greeting an old friend. "So nice to see you again," I wanted to say, "and what a coincidence! I had been thinking about you. Let me introduce my wife, I don't think you have met." So it was that this meeting, along with the soaking in the rain, the sunlit café, the mislaid spectacles, and the walk on the beach, became part of the story of our visit to St. Ives. What is more, neither in my memory nor in the way I tell them do these incidents stand apart from one another. Each, rather, lends a certain color to all the others. With this in mind, let me now come back to the matter at hand. Suppose that I were an aficionado of empirical aesthetics, what would I make of it all? Prior to venturing an answer, I'll need to sketch in some of the background to the history of aesthetics, as a subject of study, before going on to show how it was subsequently converted into its empirical object. This, in turn, will lay the foundations for my critique.

II

The notion of *aesthesis*, referring to the nature and quality of sensory perception, has been around since classical Greece. But its co-option to denote the field of inquiry now known as aesthetics is generally attributed to the eighteenth-century philosopher Alexander Baumgarten.[5] In the very first sentence of his *Aesthetica*, published in 1750, Baumgarten defined his subject as "the science of sensitive cognition." That there was a need for such a science stemmed from his conviction that there is more to thinking than the work of intellect. It is not that Baumgarten was against intellection; on the contrary it was for him the highest faculty of cognition. Yet it has, as its complement, a lower faculty that operates not with concepts but with sensations. Both faculties strive for perfection, but for the one it is the perfection of logic, for the other the perfection of beauty. If logic is the art of thinking intellectually, by means of concepts, aesthetics—according to Baumgarten—is the art of thinking beautifully (*ars pulchre cogitandi*), by means of the senses (Beiser 2009: 132).

Aesthetica was a somewhat fragmentary work. Although a second volume was published in 1758, with Baumgarten's premature death in 1762 his overall philosophical project lay largely unfinished. There is no knowing how he might have developed it. The subsequent reception of the work owed much to both the advocacy and the criticism directed from the pen of Immanuel Kant. Key to Kant's view, advanced in his *Critique of Judgement* of 1790, was that no properly aesthetic judgment can be made that is not from a position of pure disinterest. Can beauty be so judged? It may give us pleasure, but if pleasure is to be combined with disinterest, then it cannot be laced with desire, or with any will to possess. Pleasure without desire, for Kant, is the basis for judgments of taste, or at least for those judgments deemed to be "pure." Beauty, then, is a matter of taste. And since taste falls outside the realms of cognition, an aesthetics that strives for beauty cannot find a place within the science of cognition. In essence, this was the point on which Kant took issue with Baumgarten who, as an avowed rationalist, believed that it could (Beiser 2009: 133–4).

Practical Aesthetics

It is hardly necessary to venture into the dense thickets of eighteenth-century German philosophy to realize that there is a difference between the art of thinking beautifully and judging the beauty of art. Thinking beautifully, for Baumgarten, was an art of skillful composition, working with the materials of feeling. But it was also an art of attention, in so far as there can be no feeling without a kind of sensory coupling, in perception and action, between the thinker and those aspects of the world with which he or she is preoccupied. In this conjoining of composition with attention lies the work of imagination. Beauty lay primarily in the imagining, rather than in any products to which it might yield. Baumgarten was particularly interested in poetry, for which the materials are words whose very sounds evoke their own resonances. Indeed, much of his *Aesthetica* is a kind of manual for poets, laying down rules for beautiful writing. But he could just as well have been talking about music or painting. With Kant, however, there is a shift of emphasis from process to product. The imaginative work is over and done; its object already present: the question is, how to judge it? This shift had fateful consequences from which the philosophy of aesthetics has yet to recover.

For reasons that will become apparent as we proceed, I am more with Baumgarten than with Kant. I am for process over product, more for feeling than its objects. Yet the idea of "sensible cognition"—of thinking with feeling—at the heart of Baumgarten's program, still leaves us with a conundrum. For how can a mind feel if it knows only by way of the deliverances of the senses, of what they yield to thought? Or to put the question in reverse: How can feelings, born of sensory commerce with the world, be enrolled into the cognitive operations of a mind confined to the interior space of its own deliberations? How can they register as anything other than abstractions, mere husks of sentience, appearances without substance, or—in a word—as representations? A mind that is free to mingle with the world can hardly be expected, at one and the same time, to remain dispassionately on the sidelines. Is aesthetics asking the impossible, for the mind to do both things at once: both to stir in the fluxes of sensory experience and to offer its considered assessments like judge and jury at a beauty contest?

III

One way to set about answering questions such as these is to treat the mind itself as an object of investigation. In the 1870s, principally in Germany and the United States, a new science of experimental psychology was proposed to do just that. And one of the first fields of mental activity to attract its attention was aesthetics. What had begun as an artful way of thinking—and had subsequently morphed into a way of thinking about art—became, in the hands of scientific psychology, an object of empirical study in its own right. With this, empirical aesthetics was born, not as the study of art, but as the study of how minds *respond* to art. The acknowledged founder of the field, Gustav Theodor Fechner, had started out as a physicist but was driven by his conviction of the unity of the physical and spiritual worlds to inquire into the relation between physical stimuli and the sensory responses they induced. Having coined the term "psychophysics" to describe his approach, Fechner went on to apply it to the domain of aesthetic sensation, notably in his *Introduction to Aesthetics*, published in 1876.[6]

There are two kinds of response, Fechner surmised, to objects of art. One kind is direct, the other associative. The direct response is immediate and is triggered by properties intrinsic to the object such as its color or its symmetry. The associative response depends on the way the observer might place it among other things, or ideas, that occupy his or her attention. A work that is overtly representational is bound to call to mind a host of other images linked to the memory of what is represented. Such associations, grounded in the specificity of experience, are liable to override and obscure the more direct, visceral response evoked by the object itself. For this reason, Fechner advised the student of empirical aesthetics to concentrate on the perception of objects stripped of any representational content or functional significance, namely those that could be regarded as purely ornamental. The study of responses to ornament, he thought, could take us closer to an appreciation of the universal in aesthetic responsiveness (Westphal-Fitch and Fitch 2015: 388–9).

As we shall see, this duality between the visceral, working from the "bottom up," and the contextual, working from the "top down"—the one opening to universals of mental functioning, the other to their cultural and historical inflections—still reverberates in contemporary studies. Its persistence suggests that more is at stake than matters of research strategy. At stake, indeed, is the very possibility of a science of aesthetics. As happened in so many other areas of empirically based, experimental science—among them, technology and biology—so too in the foundation of empirical aesthetics, the principles integral to a field of study, its concepts and theory, were transferred onto the object of study itself, whence they were supposed to generate observable results.[7] Thus, technology, once the study of technique, came to denote the operational principles already embedded in technical objects; biology, once the study of living organisms, was reconfigured as an interior program directing their morphology and behavior. And in psychology the same inversion happened. The mind, once a congress of thinking and feeling, was turned into a mechanism that neither knows nor feels, but of which thoughts and feelings are the terminal products. As a branch of psychology, empirical aesthetics is concerned with the workings of this mechanism, insofar as it responds to stimuli of exceptional intensity—above all, those triggered by encounters with objects classified as "art."

In short, the "aesthetics" in empirical aesthetics has nothing to do with the artfulness of thinking of its practitioners, or with the beauty of what they study. It is entirely to do with the measurement of observable responses to sensory stimuli. Indeed, any empirical science that pretends to have converted aesthetics from a study of objects into an object of study has necessarily to be purified of all aesthetic elements, lest its claim to objectivity be compromised. Thinking with feeling, or sensible cognition, can play no part whatever in its modus operandi. The things that science observes, and seeks to explain, should stay on their side of the fence and not start telling scientists how to observe, let alone participate in their own explanation! A by-product of this purification, however, is that aesthetic experience, no longer buoyed up in the imaginative movements of attention and composition, is deposited as a kind of precipitate. Ways of knowing and feeling are reduced to repositories of inarticulate thoughts and raw emotions. In effect, the logic of empirical science drives a filtration process by which conceptually explicit propositions rise to the top, and inchoate feelings sink to the bottom, of an imaginary column of consciousness which is often—especially in the language of neuroscience—mapped to a stratified conception of the brain, with its cortical and subcortical regions.

It is no wonder, then, that a psychology looking for primal aesthetic drives, common to all humans, should gravitate in its interests toward the lower end of the scale (Westphal-Fitch and Fitch 2015). Nor does it come as any surprise that critics of scientific reductionism should seek its complement in a humanistic approach that attends to matters of interpretation—to the decipherment of aspects of style and meaning sensitive to variations of historical and cultural context (Currie 2003). Its interests rise to the top. Advocates of the so-called "psycho-historical" approach never cease to remind us of the need to bridge the gap between the "two cultures," of the sciences and the humanities, here represented by empirical and neuro-aesthetics on the one hand, and art history and criticism on the other (Bullot and Reber 2013). Each drives the other's cause. What use is there, however, in bridging academic cultures if all the water flows underneath? On the bridge, with one foot on each bank, the human mind is pictured as a compound of two parts: one part brain, one part art critic. But streaming between the two banks, respectively of mechanism and interpretation, is precisely what we are after, namely human aesthetic experience.

IV

Returning to the conference from which my story began: among those who spoke for empirical aesthetics was one of its leading advocates, the psychologist Helmut Leder. I began my inquiries, therefore, by reading an authoritative outline of the approach, coauthored by Leder and his colleagues Benno Belke, Andries Oeberst, and Dorothee Augustin. Their aim, they say, is quite simply "to explain why people are attracted by art" (Leder et al. 2004: 489). To do this, they construct a model of what they call an "aesthetic experience." In a reassessment of the model, which Leder published a decade later with coauthor Marcos Nadal (Leder and Nadal 2014), the aesthetic experience is rebranded as an "aesthetic episode," and it was in these terms that Leder referred to it in his conference address. The episode begins with a viewer, such as myself, standing before an object of aesthetic interest, such as an artwork. It ends with two things: an evaluative judgment and an emotional reaction. Between beginning and end, or input and output, a great deal of processing is supposed to go on in the viewer's head, some of it automatic, some of it under deliberate or conscious control. Diagrammatically, the aesthetic episode is depicted in the form of a box, with inputs to the left and outputs to the right. Inside the box are a number of smaller boxes, each depicting a particular cognitive operation, and sequentially linked by way of arrows. Some arrows point only one way, others point both ways, but with various possibilities for feedback (Leder et al. 2004: 492).[8]

Let us, then, begin at the beginning, with the input. For Leder and his team, the input for their model is a work of art. Certain questions immediately arise. For surely, aesthetic experience—whatever it may be—does not come only from encounters with things that happen, for sundry curatorial and institutional reasons, to be classified as artworks. Light streaming through windows is not an artwork, nor is the sun bursting through clouds, yet both can be profoundly moving. Conversely, artworks can have countless other-than-aesthetic resonances: they may, for example, carry an explicit political message or appeal to environmental concerns. Acknowledging the problem, Leder and Nadal narrow down their interest to "the aesthetic appreciation of art," as distinct both from non-aesthetic kinds of art appreciation, and from the aesthetic appreciation of nonart. It lies, in other words, at the area of intersection of art and aesthetics (Leder and Nadal 2014: 445). Even with this qualification, however, all manner of contextual factors can affect the way an object already classified as art is experienced. For example, viewers accustomed to the idea that an object of art should be unique, bearing the hallmark of individual genius, are predisposed to respond more positively to an original than to a copy. They want to see the real thing, and a copy—even if perfectly executed—is not the same, as it upsets their understanding of the work's causal history (Bullot and Reber 2013: 132). The same goes if the original is seen not directly but remotely, by way of its projection on a screen. Either way, whatever feelings are evoked by the work itself, taken on its own merits, will likely be tinged with disappointment (Leder and Nadal 2014: 453–4).

How, then, can the aesthetic responses specifically attributable to a work of art be separated out from the effects of all this contextual noise? Experimental science typically proceeds by removing the site of investigation from real-world settings, such as the street or the gallery, to the simulated environment of the laboratory. Artificially isolated from extraneous influences, so far as is practicably possible, the work can be viewed under strictly controlled conditions. Indeed, one reason for the recent advances in empirical aesthetics reported by Leder and Nadal is technological, for it is now possible, under laboratory conditions, "to present and to manipulate high-quality stimuli on computer screens for well-controlled durations" (Leder and Nadal 2014: 444). You can even put your subjects inside an fMRI scanner and get them to look at reproductions of artworks, while having their brains examined (Kirk et al. 2009)! Yet laboratory controls are not neutral, and they can have their own effects on the viewing experience. It is not only that people prefer the real thing to screen images; they also much prefer the gallery to the laboratory as a place for viewing art.

Studies have indeed confirmed that viewers tend to spend more time before artworks in the gallery than in the lab, as well as showing greater interest in them (Brieber et al. 2014). As Leder and Nadal (2014: 454) are forced to admit, the laboratory context, in which most research in empirical aesthetics is carried out, can attenuate the experience of art. No one wants to spend longer in the laboratory than they have to, least of all cocooned inside a brain-scanning machine. Then there's the question of mood, or what psychologists call "affective state." If you are otherwise in a bad mood—that is, in a "negative affective state"—then this might depress what might otherwise be a positive experience of art. In one study, by psychologists Vladimir J. Konečni and Dianne Sargent-Pollock (1977), subjects were deliberately subjected to "treatments" that made them either angry or happy. Anger was induced by an unpleasant sound they could not control, happiness by the reward of a small sum of money. Their state of arousal, whether positive or negative, as measured by skin conductance, was then correlated with their responses to Renaissance and twentieth-century paintings. If they were angry, they preferred Renaissance art; but if they were happy, they preferred the art of the twentieth century. But if they were neither positively nor negatively aroused, they were quite indifferent to both!

As these results suggest, what counts as input to the aesthetic episode, and what count as contextual factors qualifying that input, depend on the model, not on the actual situation as it is encountered by the subjects of experiments. An experiment designed to test reactions to artworks under laboratory conditions could just as well turn out to test reactions to laboratory treatments under conditions ameliorated by the presence of artworks. Let us pass over this indeterminacy for the moment, however, and move on to the next phase. This is the part of the model inside the box and consists of what Leder and his colleagues call "processing mechanisms" (Pelowski et al. 2016: 2), which act on the informational input from the artwork so as eventually to deliver certain attitudinal and behavioral outputs. On its way, the received information passes through a sequence of stages. These are perceptual analysis, implicit memory recognition, explicit classification, cognitive mastering, and evaluation. In what follows, I shall briefly review each of these in turn. First, however, a few words are needed on the general approach of cognitive science to vision.

V

There is a common belief, writes Semir Zeki, a leading figure in visual neurobiology, "that one sees with the eye rather than with the cerebral cortex" (Zeki 1998: 77). But this belief, he insists, is erroneous. The eyes see nothing; they are but passive receptors stimulated by the continually changing flux of incident radiation. It is the brain that actively sees, and it does so by first distilling from the flux only what is necessary to identify the constant properties of the objects seen, extracting such features as line, contour, symmetry, and color, and then matching these properties against a record, stored in memory, of all the objects it has seen before. In this way the brain manages to create the illusion that what we see is actually present, as such, in the physical world, when in fact it is but an image that the brain has constructed for us by fitting together the raw material of sensation, reduced to its bare essentials, with the knowledge it already possesses, based on past experience. In the stratified language of neuroscience, this involves a combination of "bottom-up" and "top-down" processing, the first deploying hardwired mechanisms, built into the brain at birth, the second bringing to bear higher cognitive faculties, of attention, association, and imagery, by which the brain makes an informed guess of what might be "out there." Every percept, then, is in the nature of a hypothesis and in visual perception the brain continually tests these hypotheses against the data of experience without, however, ever reaching complete certainty about what it sees.[9]

Broadly speaking, this is the approach that Leder and his team bring to the question of what happens when we observe a work of art. It begins with the "bottom-up" stage of perceptual analysis. This occurs in the instant that the image of an artwork is flashed before the viewer's eyes. At this moment the brain extracts salient features from the visual stimulus, including contrast, pattern complexity, color, symmetry, grouping, and order. The process is extremely rapid, automatic, and apparently effortless, and it quickly leads on to the next stage, of implicit memory recognition. This is the first step in matching identifiable features with the record of things previously encountered. It is implicit because its results can affect subsequent stages of aesthetic processing without ever reaching the level of consciousness. Recognition may rest on familiarity, prototypicality or "peak-shift." Familiarity comes from simple repetition of the stimulus, as when the same image is flashed up over and over again. With prototypicality, the object or image is recognized as a representative of a class. With peak shift, object recognition is enhanced through the artificial magnification of core features (Leder et al. 2004: 494–7).

The apparent parallel between what the brain does, in perceptual analysis and memory recognition, and what art is alleged to do, in extracting the essence of things and bringing out their most salient characteristics, has not gone unnoticed. For Zeki, the artist is the very personification of a brain: whatever the artist does, the brain does also, not because the artist *has* a brain but because he, or she, *is* one (Zeki 1998: 76–8). Could the appeal of art, he asks, lie precisely in the way it mimics or extends the operations of the visual brain? Could part of the pleasure in viewing, say, a painting stem from its gratification and reinforcement of the brain's natural drive to get to the bottom of what the painting represents? One might even say, with neuroscientist Vilayanur Ramachandran and philosopher William Hirstein, that the very purpose of representational art is to "titillate the visual areas of the brain," playing above all on their susceptibility to peak shift, by exaggerating the essential characteristics of the things represented in order to activate more powerfully the neural mechanisms that would otherwise be triggered in the presence of the things themselves. "All art," they say, "is caricature" (Ramachandran and Hirstein 1999: 17–18).

After implicit memory recognition, the next stage is explicit classification. With this, we begin to cross the Rubicon from neuroscience to art history, for classification is about identifying a work in terms of content and style. This does not, in itself, require any prior knowledge or expertise on the part of the viewer: even so-called "naïve" observers can tell the difference between one style of painting and another—between, say, baroque and rococo—and perhaps derive some satisfaction from being able to do so (Hasenfus et al. 1983; Leder et al. 2004: 497). Nor does the identification need to be put into words. Indeed, the ability to discriminate between styles appears to be common to a range of animal species that lack anything approaching human verbal competence. In one of the strangest experiments to be reported in the literature, a team of behavioral scientists in Japan trained pigeons to discriminate between the styles of Monet and Picasso. Correct answers were rewarded with access to a feeder containing hemp seeds. Once trained, the pigeons could even distinguish between paintings by the two artists they had never seen before (Watanabe, Sakamoto, and Wakita 1995). We can safely assume that the birds were motivated by a desire for the reward they received on picking the right answer, rather than by any feeling for the art itself. The question is whether it should be any different for a human brain-turned-critic.

Acknowledging that not all discrimination need be put into words, Leder and his team nevertheless place stylistic processing in the box of explicit classification, on the grounds that it is, in principle, verbally explicable (Leder et al. 2004: 497–8). And with explication, they argue, comes expertise. With the growth of expertise, knowledge of the artist, of the technique employed, of the historical significance of the work, and the context in which it was made, all become part of the content. They confer an added value. Thus, Monet's celebrated painting *La Garre St Lazarre* is not just a picture of a railway station with steam engines. It is a Monet, and an exemplar of Impressionism! Art criticism trades in values such as this. And it is in the final stages, of cognitive mastering and evaluation, that the balance between the two parts of the human mind—the brain and the critic—finally pivots toward the latter. Top-down interpretation, based on prior knowledge, semantic association, and personal taste, trumps the neural machinery of bottom-up processing. Rather than following one another sequentially, however, evaluation and cognitive mastery are supposed to proceed in tandem, the one guiding the other by continually measuring its success (Leder et al. 2004: 499–500).

From the perspective of empirical aesthetics, the encounter with a work of art is fundamentally an exercise in problem-solving. Modern art is said to present problems of exceptional difficulty, due to the plethora of its styles and the obscurity of its meanings (Leder et al. 2004: 499). It is nevertheless assumed that every problem already contains its solution, hidden inside the work. Perhaps the artist deliberately put it there; perhaps it crept in of its own accord. Regardless of how it got there, the task of the viewer is to find it—to ascertain what the work means, what it represents, and to what school or movement it owes its conception. Following the cognitive model of visual processing outlined at the start of this section, the answers are supposed to be found through the successive construction of hypotheses and their testing against the data of experience. Getting them right undoubtedly brings a sense of satisfaction. In the language of neuroscience, it activates rewarding centers in the brain. According to Ramachandran and Hirstein (1999: 33), it is nothing less than a "law of aesthetic experience" that solving perceptual problems is self-rewarding. Perhaps, as Leder and his team suggest, "the self-rewarding character of art processing . . . explains why perceivers continue to perceive art" (Leder et al. 2004: 500). They are like contestants in a quiz show, competing for the title of mastermind. Once hooked, they become addicted. It is doubtful, however, whether the rewards of winning the competition have anything more to do with the feeling for art than did hemp seeds for the pigeons which managed to tell a Monet from a Picasso.

VI

Finding the solution brings closure to the aesthetic episode. The work is now understood, cognitively mastered, leaving a glow of satisfaction induced by the feeling, not of the work itself, but of having cracked it and decoded its contents. With that, viewers can put the work behind them and move on to the next. Introducing his essay of 1912 *On the Spiritual in Art*, the painter Wassily Kandinsky wrote despairingly of visitors to the gallery who—catalog in hand—would parade from picture to picture, identifying each one as by this artist, of that school, painted in such-and-such a year, and representing this or that person, landscape, or object. "And then they leave," Kandinsky observes, "just as rich or poor as when they came in, immediately absorbed once again by their own interests, which have nothing whatever to do with art. Why ever did they go?" (Kandinsky 1982: 130). They went, of course, to see the pictures, and so that they could say they had seen them. But the life in each work—an entire life with its torments and doubts, its moments of ecstasy and insight, the life that cries out to be heard—completely passes them by.

The aesthetic episode is exemplary of Kandinsky's caricature of the visitor experience. It begins with its inputs and ends with its outputs. Every episode begins, as we have seen, at the point when the viewer sets eyes upon the work—eyes which relay its visual input to the brain. The outputs, according to Leder and his team, are twofold: aesthetic judgments and aesthetic emotions. The judgment is no more of the work itself, however, than is the emotion triggered by it. The claim, rather, is that both judgment and emotion depend on the relative ease of processing through the immediately preceding stages of cognitive mastery and evaluation (Leder et al. 2004: 503). One can be happy or pleased with the result, when it is felt to have gone well, or annoyed and frustrated when it has not—when, for example, efforts to solve the work have led nowhere, so that the episode cannot be satisfactorily closed. The aesthetic judgment, in short, is in the nature of a self-assessment, a rating of the mind's success in critically evaluating the work at hand. And the aesthetic emotion is kindled not by the work but by the rewards of successful processing, or conversely by the penalty of failure. Judgment and emotion, however, are not necessarily connected. One can solve a problem without enjoying it: indeed, the Leder team suggests that the superiority of experts over naïve perceivers lies precisely in their being better able to distance the work of critical evaluation from feelings of pleasure or displeasure (Leder et al. 2004: 502). They are ruled, as we might say colloquially, by their heads rather than their hearts.

At what point, then, does the episode end? It ends, presumably, when the problem posed by the work has been solved. In terms of the model, this is the point at which the processing of visual information yields up to its outputs. But how can we tell when, or whether, this point has been reached? A study from the Metropolitan Museum of Art in New York, conducted by Jeffrey and Lisa Smith, found that the mean time for perceiving artworks was 27.2 seconds (Smith and Smith 2001). Another, from a temporary exhibition of paintings by the artist Gerhard Richter, found averages per picture of between 25.7 and 41.0 seconds (Carbon 2017). But measurements of this kind tell us little. Viewers who have successfully identified a picture, and already classified its style and content, might choose to linger in its presence, perhaps even to breathe its atmosphere. Or to the contrary, they might give up on their attempts at mastery and evaluation, and move on to another work, perhaps in frustration, before reaching any kind of conclusion.

In laboratory studies, viewers have been artificially exposed to images of artworks for controlled durations, of three seconds or less, much shorter than what would be usual in the gallery. The idea is that by incrementally reducing presentation times, it might be possible to isolate early processing stages and estimate their durations. In an experiment conducted by Leder and his colleagues (Augustin et al. 2008), subjects were tasked with spotting differences of style and content between images flashed up for periods of between 10 and 3,000 microseconds. The experimenters were careful to exclude anyone who reported having been educated in the arts or art history, who might perhaps have had an unfair advantage, knowing the answers in advance! Even for those who did not, however, they were able to show that content differences could be identified with astonishing speed, even within the minimal 10 ms margin, but that stylistic identification needed up to 50 ms. Other studies have suggested processing times of between 300 and 600 ms.

This temporal attenuation, though in itself remarkable, is possible only because the work of art is understood as a problem that contains its solution. It is, in this sense, a puzzle. As we know from virtuosi with the Rubik's cube, or with the crossword, the time it takes to solve a puzzle can be progressively reduced to the point of virtual instantaneity. It is an approach to zero. In theory, since the result is already given, finding it requires no time at all. The work of art, however, is not a puzzle. In making it the artist has joined in his or her own thinking and feeling, for an indefinite period, with the materials of the work, which gradually takes shape or form in the process of their going along together. This is the work of time, and the time of work. "To the artist who creates a picture by drawing it from the depths of his soul," as philosopher Henri Bergson observed long ago, "time is no longer an accessory; it is not an interval that may be lengthened or shortened without the content being altered. The duration . . . is part and parcel of his work" (Bergson 1911: 359). Without time, the work would be empty.

But nor is time an accessory to the viewer. In his essay of 1934, *Art as Experience*, John Dewey insisted that to perceive a work of art, "a beholder must create his own experience." Moreover, "this creation must include relations comparable to those which the original producer underwent" (Dewey 1987: 60).[10] In Dewey's pragmatic philosophy, an experience undergone is also actively done. The beholder surrenders to the work, as the artist to the materials of which it is made, not passively but actively: "we must summon energy and pitch it at a responsive key in order to take in" (ibid.: 59). Thus understood, experience is not—and cannot be—episodic. Neither can it be contained within a temporal interval, however long or short, nor can one interval follow the next like beads on a string, each separate from those preceding and following. For experience actively undergone always takes in what is past, even as it gives out into that which is to come. It does not begin here, and end there, but continually turns endings into beginnings, digesting the former as it extrudes into the latter. Dewey (1987: 62) compared it to breathing in and out, and like breathing, it is essential to the continuity of life.

VII

Shifting the register from inputs and outputs to breathing in and out involves more than a change of idiom, for it entails a quite different sense of process. For empirical aesthetics, as we have seen, it is axiomatic that encounters with art involve processing of information by the mind-brain. The verb "to process" is here understood in a transitive sense, commonly employed in the field of computing, where it means to operate on a corpus of data by way of a program. Neuroscientists disposed to model the brain as a massively complex computer have adopted the idea of processing in much the same vein. Breathing, however, is part of a life process, and key to this process is that far from effecting a conversion from input to output, it keeps on going, continually overtaking itself. Or to return to an earlier analogy, it does not, like a bridge, afford transport from one river bank to another, but rather flows with the water between. Life processes in an intransitive sense, not carrying *across* from one state to another, but carrying *along*. This is to regard processing, as I have stated elsewhere, "not . . . as a step-by-step refinement or repackaging of sensory data already received, but rather as the unfolding of the whole system of relations constituted by the multi-sensory involvement of the perceiver in his or her environment" (Ingold 2000: 18).

In this intransitive sense of processing lie the foundations of an approach to aesthetics that, following the lead of Dewey, is practical rather than empirical. It starts from the premise that art, in its making as in its experience, is a process of life. It carries on. Neither the making of a work, nor the experience of it, is ever truly finished. This does not mean that it is half-finished, as if the process had been interrupted and prevented from reaching a final conclusion. With art as with life, the process is not heading to a conclusion but always issuing into fresh beginning. In it, as the philosopher Merleau-Ponty once put it, lies the "continued birth" of our vision (Merleau-Ponty 1964: 168). Even if the work appears complete as it is hung in the gallery, and is carefully curated to keep it so, it nevertheless lives on in the imaginations of those who come to see it and who create for themselves an experience comparable to that of its original making—just as a piece of music lives on in its performances, or a story in its tellings. Even Leder and Nadal, in their retrospective review, admit that "long extension in time" may be precisely what makes an experience aesthetic—meaning that it is in the very nature of the aesthetic episode that an extended period needs to be devoted to "perception-cognition-emotion interactions" (Leder and Nadal 2014: 449). Whole episodes, they say, may take place over different time scales and interact in complex ways. Nevertheless, the transitive sense of processing and its episodic character imply a movement toward closure. For practical aesthetics, to the contrary, what is fundamental to the experience of art is that it affords an opening.

The work of art is a problem. But unlike the puzzle, it does not already contain its own solution. Problems of this kind, like the life to which they belong, do not close in on their solutions but open to further generation, variation, and metamorphosis.[11] They are less cognitive than affective; they call on us not to be the masters of art but to submit to it—not to put art in its place but to go along with it and to attend. For art, if it is to carry on—if it is to undergo the continued birth on which its vitality and renewal depend—must ever escape the clutches of identification, classification, and evaluation that would fain pin it down. With art we cannot put the work behind us, or close the episode, thinking that once understood and interpreted, it need trouble us no further. The work carries on as life does; it stays with us, as we stay with it. To borrow a phrase from theorist Donna Haraway, we *stay with the trouble* (Haraway 2016). And together we move on, never further from a beginning or closer to an end, feeling our way as we go and improvising a passage. On the journey, works of art are our travel companions, not the contents of our baggage.

A practical aesthetics, then, that attends to living art and thinks by way of it, cannot align with the episodic but rather cuts a way through, in real time, like the river between its banks.[12] It is the work of a mind that, far from projecting fantasies of its own making from its prison within the head, reaches along the lines of its sensory participation into an ever-forming world. While visual neuroscience adheres doggedly to the view that the mind completes a world picture by adding its own share, dredged from the sediments of memory, to the deliverances of the senses (Kandel 2016: 20–1), experience teaches us otherwise, namely that perception is the achievement, not of a mind in a body, but of a whole being in a world, moving around in, and exploring, what it affords. This being has eyes to see, ears to hear, and skin to feel—eyes, ears, and skin which are not just passive receptors for sensory data to be sent to the brain for processing, but organs of a perceptual system tuned to picking up information that specifies the properties of the environment. Information is present in the structure of ambient light, sound, and pressure, it is not transmitted over a channel from outside to inside. As the psychologist James Gibson put it in his pioneering work on the ecology of visual perception, "there is no sender outside the head and no receiver inside the head" (Gibson 1986: 64). There is a being, alive and present to a world.

VIII

Many years ago, the anthropologist Claude Lévi-Strauss reminded the delegates at a conference that seated among them was an "uninvited guest" who—unbeknown to them—had all along been quietly directing their deliberations. That guest, he said, was the *human mind* (Lévi-Strauss 1968: 71). Could it be that I, too, had brought with me an uninvited guest to the Tate Gallery at St. Ives? Invisibly stowed inside my head, like a homunculus, it would have had no ticket and paid no fee for admission. Yet what a useful guest it would have been! For once in the gallery, it could have done all the work for me. For painting after painting, I would have only had to stand there, placing my eyes squarely before each canvas to ensure an adequate scan. The mind could then get to work on the visual input, starting from the bottom with basic brain functions and then working up to the top with more complex cognitive operations, until, perhaps only a fraction of a second later, it would issue a receipt that would have not only told me what I had seen but also provided it with a neurally certified preference rating.

This scenario might sound fanciful, but it is not far removed from what, according to empirical aesthetics, happens in reality. Picture the scene. After having viewed many other works in the gallery, I eventually find myself standing before Peter Lanyon's *Thermal*. My mind, quickly recognizing that I have seen it once before, calls up the relevant contextual data—it was in the exhibition at the Courtauld. This feeds directly into implicit memory integration, adding a level of domain-specific expertise that piques interest levels. Out comes an evaluation that is highly positive. It puts words into my mouth. Turning to my wife, I explain: "You see, this is a painting by Peter Lanyon, one of the school of artists working in post-war St. Ives. Lanyon was a keen glider pilot, and in *Thermal* he depicts the pilot's feeling for air." To be able to pronounce on the matter with such authority gives me a warm glow inside, a sense that even though other works have proved hard to comprehend, I am at least the master of this one. And the glow colors my appreciation of the work. I'll definitely give it a high preference score, maybe I should even purchase a reproduction in the gallery shop!

But wait. As I linger before the picture, a shadow falls across my eyes. Doubt creeps in, unsettling my composure. The air around stirs, tingling the skin with its cool draught. Suddenly, there's a great blast and I am swirling in the elements. It is as though the walls of the gallery had tumbled and the turbulent weather outside had permeated the space. At the same moment, the picture dissolves. Canvas melts into air. I cannot see it clearly: I am, as you will recall, without my spectacles and things are out of focus. Yet it seems to me that a figure emerges from the mist. Could it be the shade of Lanyon himself? Hark, it speaks, with tones of admonishment and despair. "*Why are you here?* Were my life and death for nothing? Can you not feel for yourself the air, the violence, the sheer force of the elements? This is what it means to be alive, this is what I died for. I cannot explain it; I cannot describe it. But this *is* it." As I cast my eyes again toward the painting, I find that I am already there inside it—inside the movement of its generation. I feel the wind blowing through, the rush of air that had once both swept the hand of the painter in the throes of composition and borne him aloft in his craft. This, I realize, is not painting of or about the wind; it is wind-painting, and I am flying in it, my mind churning in the very same currents that animate the artist's immortal soul. It is churning still, as I write these lines.

Then I remember the art of Saraceno, an art that literally transports us into an aerial milieu, carried along on a balloon. Is this not an aesthetic experience, every bit as powerful as being bathed in sunlight streaming through the windows, or watching the sparkling breakers on the shore and listening to the roar and hiss of their surge and ebb? In a commentary on Saraceno's work, literary theorist Eva Horn urges us to recover the phenomenological dimension of inhabiting the air, of breathing it, and feeling it. It is a matter of developing an *aesthesis of air*, of exploring "new and different forms of *being in the air together*" (Horn 2017: 26). This is not about understanding or judging works of art, let alone about transforming them into objects. Nor is it a matter of putting work on show, or turning aesthetic performance into a spectacle, designed to engender a response among those who pay to see it. Were the aim of art to stage a life, to re-present it as drama, then the work itself would be devoid of feeling—it would be but a vehicle for its evocation, calculated to produce an effect. Art would be reduced to advertisement.

Practical Aesthetics

This kind of aestheticization of the real, as philosopher Gernot Böhme has observed, is an endemic feature of societies in the advanced phases of capitalism (Böhme 2017: 20). Under such an economic regime, experience becomes the acquisition of "experiences." Ways of being and going along together, in which the viewer is enrolled as co-producer in the ongoing life of the work, become objects of consumption, or commodities, appealing to individual wants. Ways of seeing become sights, ways of hearing sounds, ways of feeling impressions. Sights, sounds, and impressions, plugged readymade into the mind-brain, are strategically targeted to convey subliminal messages and to elicit specific behavioral and attitudinal responses in an audience who are now no longer co-producers but consumers. This is the logic of advertising. What the advertising industry needs, and what empirical aesthetics offers, is a theory of consumer behavior underpinned by the economic logic of advanced capitalism. Dressed up in the apparel of science is a highly sophisticated and slightly sinister form of market research. Far from affording a window into aesthetic experience, empirical aesthetics effectively reduces it to zero.

Notes

1. The international workshop *The symbolic animal: evolution and neuroethology of aesthetics* was held at the Ettore Majorana Foundation and Centre for Scientific Culture, Erice, Sicily, October 15–19, 2016. I am grateful to the organizers of the workshop, and especially to Vittorio Gallese, for inviting me to participate, and to the Foundation for financing my visit. I also thank the European Research Council (Advanced Grant 323677 KFI, 2013–18) for the funding which supported the research on which this essay is based.
2. The exhibition, entitled *Soaring Flight: Peter Lanyon's Gliding Paintings*, was held at the Courtauld Gallery from October 15, 2015, to January 17, 2016.
3. See https://aerocene.org/, accessed May 26, 2019.
4. Quoted from the Tate Gallery display caption, see http://www.tate.org.uk/art/artworks/lanyon-thermal-t00375, accessed February 29, 2016.
5. For the following account of Baumgarten's philosophy of aesthetics, I rely heavily on the authority of Beiser (2009).
6. A useful summary of Fechner's approach, from self-professed advocates, is in Westphal-Fitch and Fitch (2015).
7. Objectivism, as sociologist Pierre Bourdieu puts it, requires that the observer, taking up a "sovereign point of view," should stand back, "transferring into the object the principles of his relation to the object" (Bourdieu 1977: 96).
8. This box-and-arrow design is common to most efforts to visualize models of art engagement in the cognitive sciences. These are reviewed in Pelowski et al. (2016).
9. Perhaps the classic statement of this view comes from visual psychologist Richard Gregory. "If all perceiving of objects requires some guessing," Gregory writes, "we may think of sensory stimulation as providing *data* for *hypotheses* concerning the state of the external world" (Gregory 1973: 61–2, original emphases). Cognitive neuroscientist Chris Frith concurs, concluding that "perception of the world is a fantasy that coincides with reality," a fantasy that arises when "our brains discover what is out there in the world by constructing models and making predictions" (Frith 2007: 111, 138). In the same vein, neuroscientist Eric

R Kandel asserts that "our brain takes the incomplete information about the outside world that it receives from our eyes and makes it complete" (Kandel 2016: 20). All such assertions, be it noted, rest not on the evidence of neuroscience but on largely implicit metaphysical assumptions that these and countless other authors bring to the task of analyzing it.

10. Leder et al. (2004: 499) cite the first of these consecutive sentences from Dewey, but not the second, thus twisting his meaning to support their own position. For them, "creating an experience" doesn't mean reliving the processes of a work's origination but processing the results from its conclusion.

11. What we say of art, here, matches what philosopher Gilles Deleuze, along with his collaborator Félix Guattari, say of "minor science," by which they mean a science "of becoming and heterogeneity, as opposed to the stable, the eternal, the identical, the constant." Such a science, they say, is comprised of problems rather than theorems. "Whereas the theorem belongs to the rational order, the problem is affective and inseparable from the metamorphoses, generations and creations within science itself" (Deleuze and Guattari 2004: 398–9).

12. Educational philosopher Jan Masschelein describes the art of walking in precisely these terms, as "a kind of cutting the road through" (Masschelein 2010: 278).

References

Augustin, M. D., H. Leder, F. Hutzler, and C.-C. Carbon (2008), "Style Follows Content: On the Microgenesis of Art Perception," *Acta Psychologica*, 128: 127–38.

Beiser, F. C. (2009), *Diotima's Children: German Aesthetic Rationalism from Leibniz to Lessing*, Oxford: Oxford University Press.

Bergson, H. (1911), *Creative Evolution*, trans. A. Mitchell, London: Macmillan.

Böhme, G. (2017), *Critique of Aesthetic Capitalism*, trans. E. Jephcott, Milano: Mimesis International.

Bourdieu, P. (1977), *Outline of a Theory of Practice*, trans. R. Nice, Cambridge, UK: Cambridge University Press.

Brieber, D., M. Nadal, H. Leder, and R. Rosenberg (2014), "Art in Time and Space: Context Modulates the Relation between Art Experience and Viewing Time," *PLOS ONE*, 9(6): e99019. Available online: doi:10.1371/journal.pone.0099019 (accessed June 8, 2019).

Bullot, N. J. and R. Reber (2013), "The Artful Mind Meets Art History: Toward a Psycho-historical Framework for the Science of Art Appreciation," *Behavioral and Brain Sciences*, 36: 123–80.

Carbon, C.-C. (2017), "Art Perception in the Museum: How We Spend Time and Space in Art Exhibitions," *i-Perception* 8 (1). Available online: https://journals.sagepub.com/doi/full/10.1177/2041669517694184 (accessed June 8, 2019).

Currie, G. (2003), "Aesthetics and Cognitive Science," in J. Levinson (ed.), *The Oxford Handbook of Aesthetics*, 706–21, Oxford: Oxford University Press.

Deleuze, G. and F. Guattari (2004), *A Thousand Plateaus: Capitalism and Schizophrenia*, trans. B. Massumi, London: Continuum.

Dewey, J. (1987), "Art as Experience," in J. A. Boydston (ed.), *John Dewey: The Later Works, 1925–1953, Vol. 10: 1934*, Carbondale, IL: Southern Illinois University Press.

Frith, C. (2007), *Making Up the Mind: How the Brain Creates Our Mental World*, Oxford: Blackwell.

Gibson, J. J. (1986), *The Ecological Approach to Visual Perception*, Hillsdale, NJ: Lawrence Erlbaum.

Practical Aesthetics

Gregory, R. L. (1973), "The Confounded Eye," in R. L. Gregory and E. H. Gombrich (eds.), *Illusion in Nature and Art*, 49–95, New York: Scribners.

Haraway, D. (2016), *Staying with the Trouble: Making Kin in the Chthulucene*, Durham, NC: Duke University Press.

Hasenfus, N., C. Martindale and D. Birnbaum (1983), "Psychological Reality of Cross-media Artistic Styles," *Journal of Experimental Psychology*, 9(6): 841–63.

Horn, E. (2017), "Aesthetics of the Air: Tomás Saraceno's Aerocene," in T. Saraceno (ed.), *Aerocene*, 18–30, Milano: Skira Editore.

Ingold, T. (2000), *The Perception of the Environment: Essays on Livelihood, Dwelling and Skill*, London: Routledge.

Ingold, T. (2017), "On Flight," in T. Saraceno (ed.), *Aerocene*, 132–9. Milano: Skira Editore.

Kandel, E. R. (2016), *Reductionism in Art and Brain Science: Bridging the Two Cultures*, New York: Columbia University Press.

Kandinsky, W. (1982), *Kandinsky: Complete Writings on Art, Volume I (1901–1921)*, ed. K. C. Lindsay and P. Vergo, London: Faber & Faber.

Kirk, U., M. Skov, O. J. Hulme, M. S. Christensen, and S. Zeki (2009), "Modulation of Aesthetic Value by Semantic Context: An fMRI Study," *NeuroImage*, 44: 1125–32.

Konečni, V. J. and D. Sargent-Pollock (1977), "Arousal, Positive and Negative Affect, and Preference for Renaissance and 20th Century Paintings," *Motivation and Emotion*, 1: 75–93.

Leder, H., B. Belke, A. Oeberst, and D. Augustin (2004), "A Model of Aesthetic Appreciation and Aesthetic Judgements," *British Journal of Psychology*, 95: 489–508.

Leder, H. and M. Nadal, (2014), "Ten Years of a Model of Aesthetic Appreciation and Aesthetic Judgments: The Aesthetic Episode – Developments and Challenges in Empirical Aesthetics," *British Journal of Psychology*, 105: 443–64.

Lévi-Strauss, C. (1968), *Structural Anthropology*, Harmondsworth: Penguin.

Masschelein, J. (2010), "The Idea of Critical E-ducational Research – E-ducating the Gaze and Inviting to Go Walking," in I. Gur-Ze'ev (ed.), *The Possibility/Impossibility of a New Critical Language of Education*, 275–91, Rotterdam: Sense Publishers.

Merleau-Ponty, M. (1964), "Eye and Mind," trans. C. Dallery, in J. M. Edie (ed.), *The Primacy of Perception, and Other Essays on Phenomenological Psychology, the Philosophy of Art, History and Politics*, 159–90, Evanston, IL: Northwestern University Press.

Pelowski, M., P. S. Markey, J. O. Lauring, and H. Leder (2016), "Visualizing the Impact of Art: An Update and Comparison of Current Psychological Models of Art Experience," *Frontiers in Human Neuroscience*, 10: 160. Available online: doi: 10.3389/fnhum.2016.00160 (accessed June 9, 2019).

Ramachandran, V. and W. Hirstein (1999), "The Science of Art: A Neurological Theory of Aesthetic Experience," *Journal of Consciousness Studies*, 6: 15–51.

Smith, J. K. and L. Smith (2001), "Spending Time on Art," *Empirical Studies of the Arts*, 19 (2): 229–36.

Watanabe, S., J. Sakamoto, and M. Wakita (1995), "Pigeons' Discrimination of Paintings by Monet and Picasso," *Journal of the Experimental Analysis of Behavior*, 63 (2): 165–74.

Westphal-Fitch, G. and W. T. Fitch (2015), "Towards a Comparative Approach to Empirical Aesthetics," in J. P. Huston, M. Nadal, F. Mora, L. F. Agnati, and C. J. Cela Conde (eds.), *Art, Aesthetics and the Brain*, 385–402. Oxford: Oxford University Press.

Zeki, S. (1998), "Art and the Brain," *Daedalus*, 127 (2): 71–103.

CHAPTER 4
PRACTICAL AESTHETICS
THE CASE OF BIOART
jan jagodzinski

One of the most distinguishing features of contemporary art has been the overcoming of the separation between art and science, a relationship that was much more intimate during the period known as the Renaissance. The contemporary change has led some to call this a Radical Enlightenment (Gare 2014). This renewed interface has been made possible since the advent of computerized and digitalized technologies that began roughly in the mid-twentieth century, which was then supplemented by the biological sciences, accelerated especially by the field of genetics prompted by the Human Genome Project that ended in 2003. The twenty-first century eventually came to be known as the biotech century (Rifkin 1999).

The last two decades, especially with the turn toward installation art, has brought technology (engineering), experimental science and art together in much more evident ways than had previously been realized. The proliferation of Modernist movements at the turn of the twentieth century always were scientifically informed as "mechanization took command" (Giedion 1948), yet this relationship remained in separate disciplinary spheres, especially with the charge of scientism as the century wore on. Art & design remained both separate and conjoined by an ampersand presenting the tensions related to subject and object, "life as art" and "art as life," a relationship that Marcel Duchamp ironically exposed with his ready-mades. This exposure of the "false" division been art and design has led to the contemporary speculative projections initiated by what can be called "cosmic artists and artisans" (Deleuze and Guattari 1987) who have overcome what is essentially a Kantian aesthetic dualism, necessitated, by and large, by the crisis of the Earth's ecology, currently called the Anthropocene.

Before presenting the way bioart has profoundly exposed this problematic, the historical overcoming of the Kantian dualism in aesthetics can be briefly reviewed, as philosophers such as Gilles Deleuze (1990) have paved the way where a "practical aesthetic" orientation has emerged, overcoming what was a hylomorphic position where form was imposed on "passive" nature. As is well known, the Kantian aesthetic position presents the apotheosis of modernism where epistemology is forwarded at the expense of ontology; in other words, the faculties of understanding, reason, and imagination via a transcendental synthesis provide the certainty of what we know of the lived phenomenal world, whereas the noumenal world, the world-as-it-is for-itself is beyond our comprehension; we are left with speculation. Given this paradigm, Kantian and post-Kantian aesthetics present a double meaning, a dualism, which is always in tension. On the one hand, there is a "theory" of art where we are able to reflect on our experiences with different material forms of expression. The arts in this regard provide a "sensible cognition" or a "logic of sense" that address a historically changing paradigm of structural "objective" or representational principles and elements in the way various arts are composed and organized, shaping and solidifying the identity of things and ourselves in relation to them. However, there is also a more general theory of sensibility that is the fundamental ground for subjective experience. On this side of the ledger we have a "logic of sensation" that seems to be at odds with the "logic of sense"; there is an "encounter" with phenomena that occur below the level of consciousness (cognition); an encounter with affects and percepts (or "signs") that "belong" to the world-in-itself that express themselves and affect us emotionally as our relation with the world changes, thereby changing our subjective identities as well. Kant's *Critique of Pure Reason* (1781) developed the objective analysis of a transcendental aesthetic and then in 1790 in his *Aesthetic Judgment*, through the aesthetic categories of the beautiful and the sublime, Kant theorized bodily intensities of affect based on the "distance" of the impact of sensible experience so that the body is not entirely overwhelmed. Beauty and sublimity, as limits, are "still" phenomenologically experienced as the encounter is in a subject's control. A threshold has not been stepped over. Kant reserved threshold experiences of sublime beauty, space-times of undecidability and indiscernabiltiy, time that is out-of-joint, as the disruptive and at times unbearable rupture of identity in the way the world is being perceived takes place: for instance, the "shock" when the first atom bomb exploded, traumatizing J. Robert Oppenheimer and company to forward a new axiology given the changed global ontology. Or, the beautifully sublime, ecstatic pleasure that is felt in certain spiritual experiences that are overwhelming such as conversion experiences, near-death experiences, and the like. With bioart, as we shall see, we are faced again with a changed ontology given the biotech revolution.

An aesthetic dualism is a persistent stance that dwells on subjectivity, in its psychological, psychoanalytic, and philosophical dispositions; what is central to art, it is maintained, is exploring the emotions and representing the world of perceptions. In Lacanian psychoanalysis, artworks are misrecognized representations of the unconscious; in neuropsychology, art represents the neuronal laws of the brain (Zeki 1999). For phenomenology (e.g., Maurice Merleau-Ponty), art is the representational intentionality of subjective experience. Across the board, the arts as representation, reference, or reproduction become an appendix of subjective thought or expression, *and not the genetic production of thought and subjectivity, which changes the axis toward practical aesthetics.* Such a position is challenged and supplanted by reversing the Kantian aesthetic dualism: for Deleuze (1994), art does not represent, but expands and creates the world we experience through sensations. Art and identity do not form a harmonious accord; rather, they offer a fundamental rift or dissension. The fundamental subjective acts of thinking, feeling, hearing, and seeing are not to be presupposed (especially by clichés, stereotypes, habits, all forms of a "dogmatic image of thought"), but disrupted so that we become subjectivated through art. There is a nonhuman element of thought at play given that the definition of "human" is always conditioned representationally. The nonhuman element always draws from an "outside," that is, from the forces of the world (nature) as it is in-itself. It is through such a process that subjectivity, which is to say its *dissolution* into something "else" becomes possible. There is always an infinite "becoming" through a practical aesthetic, which makes this possible through an affirmation of life.

This practical aesthetic always requires an "*encounter*"; as Deleuze (1994) would say, "Something in the world forces us to think" (139). We are struck by "signs" that existentially grip us beyond what the body can remember or what can be imagined as the realm of the "unthought" is reached. The differential or contradictory element of sensation of the "sign" presents a "difference" (and not "diversity" as diversity itself is already "shaped" by differences such as temperature, pressure, levels of potentiality, intensity, etc.). Forces are orders of difference, which Deleuze refers to as pure physical elements that condition the "given." A genesis must take place, as there are no *a priori* transcendental conditions of possibility as in the Kantian system.

Practical aesthetics is therefore an "apprenticeship" in signs (Deleuze 2000), while the practical problem common to all art practice becomes capturing forces that is life "itself." It is not a matter of reproducing, representing, or inventing forms. The challenge in the visual arts is to render visible what is invisible, while in music it is to render nonsonorous forces sonorous. "Is this not the definition of the *percept itself*—to make perceptible the imperceptible forces that populate the world, affect us, and make us become" (Deleuze and Guattari 1994: 182, emphasis added). By going beyond recognition and representation, art becomes an experimental apprenticeship in the forces of sensation (forces of sensation being percepts and affects). Part of this process is an apprenticeship in learning that is not defined by a given established epistemology, methodology, or truth. An experimental poetics is called for. It is an encounter with a "problematic" that raises or forces a "faculty" to go beyond its recognition and representation: to a "level of its transcendent exercise" as Deleuze (1994: 165) would say. The production of sensations through art goes beyond any representation or any already-established organization of given conditions. In this way, there is no fine arts system per se: there are only "very diverse problems whose solutions are found in the heterogeneous arts" (Deleuze and Guattari 1987: 300).

Learning for the creative person (artist) involves a "relation between a sign and its response (an encounter with the Other)" (Deleuze 1994: 22). Signs, as symptoms, exert "forces" on us. As *external* phenomena, they *affect* us below the level of consciousness. They are not apparitions or appearances of a given phenomenon; they spark our creative (artistic) process to produce potentially a new fabulation. A sign presents an unknown, and it has no distinct meaning; how it is used, discovered, interpreted is more at issue. Becoming sensitive to the signs emitted by the material is crucial for learning so as to be "with" the material. Every artist recognizes this. Artists work in series primarily because the practical aesthetics that they are involved in require what Deleuze referred to as a "passive synthesis of time" rather than an active synthesis of present moments; this is to say that encounters with signs, with forces of the world-in-itself that force us to think, respond, and do, "happen" at a time which we cannot anticipate, necessarily prepare for, nor ever predict. The event "is always and at the same time something which has just happened and something about to happen, never something which is happening" (Deleuze 1990: 63). The event starts the problematic upon a contemplative reflection; it starts the series of repetitions to explore its effects so that a "world" begins to emerge.

Deleuze saw artists as the symptomologists of the age, that is, "reading signs" that open the problematics of the current world. To be sensitive to signs, that is, to be open to new sensitivities of the world is to affirm the infinite pluralism of "a life." Such "life" is not individual, and it is not life that has us dependent on being; rather, it refers to life which carries with it events and singularities that are then actualized as subject and objects (Deleuze 2001). "A Life" points to the pragmatics of aesthetics; it is always "in process." The artist who taps into such life, in this sense, sees "more than meets the eye," and hears "more" than just sounds that enter the ears. Artists create "worlds" that have never been experienced before. So, when Deleuze and Guattari (1994) say: "Art wants to create the finite that restores the infinite" (197), they are addressing A Life, which is impersonal, an infinite force to which an artist responds to and captures in an act of creation, which is then actualized in spectators as perceptions and affections. Art is a "being in sensation" that exists in-itself. It is an organized bundle of forces that "contain" such impersonal life, which can be released when encountered. In this way, art exposes us to relations of forces outside our subjective being, which (at the same time) become immanent as a genetic force of our subjective lifeworld, possibly changing our subjectivity as we merge "with" the art.

Practical artistic processes require facing problems that are immanent to the materials and techniques when producing and presenting sensations; art cannot be subjugated to a philosophical concept or a scientific function. Artworks remain singular. It is not a question to present thinking *about* art, but rather to think *with* it. However, the principles for the composition of art are the same as the genetic principles for the sensations it presents. Hence, works of art become that which call for the creation of concepts that correspond to the sensations presented. Most often genres or –isms attempt to encapsulate a broader problematic (e.g., Surrealism, Cubism, Expressionism, etc.). Art as a practical thought exposes us to the question of the origin of the being of the sensible; that is, the conditions for what can be sensed. The encounter of intensive or differential forces in art is what expands the limits of what can be sensed. One's subjectivity is opened up. Hence, a "pedagogy of the senses" becomes possible.

The Case of Bioart

Bioartists have become the new symptomologists of the age. What is extraordinary is that "life" has become the "new" material. They introduce us to new affective and perceptive states that had never before been experienced. There are affirmations of lifeworlds that present for our species, perhaps for the first time, an insight as to the profound relationships we have with the word-as-it-is, enabling the wonders of technology to mediate, transverse, and make possible relationships with the organic and inorganic life that has remained hereto silent and without agential voice. For practical aesthetics, where thinking with art is crucial, the functionality of science presents new challenges as it is essential to harness technologies that enable new relations to emerge through interactive artistic installations. The bioartist produces new sensations by using scientific insights into the material life as lived—in this case, this includes understanding the entire genetic biome of various bacterial strains, being able to experiment with genetic sequences of plants of every variety, and speculating on the complex ecologies of species in their specific environments that remain invisible, not only to the human eye such as bacteria, but also to processes that are never static, but dynamic in their movement.

Bioart provides a rather new grasp of art as the production of what Deleuze and Guattari (1987) called a Body without Organs (BwO). This is a virtual domain that frees sensation from an actual, that is, an already-established organization. The virtual refers to the transcendental production—a creative field that conditions the domain of actual recognition or identification of what is currently thought to be the represented world. The virtual is not unreal or imaginary; it is rather relational in the sense that an actual state or organization always presupposes the production of a relational possibility. In this sense, the production of a Body without Organs in art is a dissolution of the actual understanding of what a body is. Yet, it is also a virtual engagement of producing a new bodily relationship, opening up new ways of becoming, and expanding our grasp of "A Life," as Deleuze (2001) puts it. The Body without Organs is a practical aesthetic that frees up the concept of the body; there is a dismantling of the self through experimentation, the forceful production of new possibilities of subjective sensibility. "It is not at all a notion or a concept but a practice, *a set of practices*" (Deleuze and Guattari 1987: 149–50, added emphasis).

Human portraiture and the organization of the human body is perhaps the most obstinate, iconic, and representationally clichéd problematic in art. To create and find opening to forces of sensation that are still to be sensed in this domain require that the artist must overcome the already-established subjectivized ideas of sensibility and bodily habits, no small task. Deleuze (2003) wrote a remarkable examination on the way Francis Bacon's paintings dwelled on the "figurative forces"; that is, the "figural" or "diagram" that undergirds, or makes possible the representation of the figure in the first place: the lines, smudges, bush strokes. The "figural" (a development first formulated by François Lyotard (2011) and liberally borrowed by Deleuze) refers to the "body of sensation" that goes beyond representation by exploring pure differential relations of force immanent to the composition. It is an attempt to paint pure "sensation"—what is intensely figurative. The comparison and contrast between Edvard Munch's well-known iconic *The Scream* and Bacon's *Study after Velazquez's Portrait of Pope Innocent X* is an exemplary case that moves away from Munch's more libidinal representation. The violence of the sensation that produces the scream is isolated as an intensive force. As a portrait, it renders visible the invisible forces of the body's becoming-scream. "The entire body escapes through the screaming mouth," writes Deleuze (2003: 20). There is a direct encounter with the invisible intensive forces of sensation directly in and with the material.

While Bacon shows us another "world" of the body, presenting us with a Body without Organs that is violently startling, shocking the nerves, there is a new form of bioart that radicalizes these forces in yet another unexpected way by exposing viewers to the invisibility of the biome that each of us carry in a peculiarly singular way. Representation targets and organizes what is "human" through an entire range of signifiers that position the social body in specific contexts and in specific ways via gender, sex, race, ethnicity, age, skin color, blood type, disability, and mental acuity. Such a list can go on to now include one's apparent genetic makeup via various commercial lab "services" that "test" your DNA to determine the hybridity of one's genetic ancestry, once again organizing diversity in terms of representation. Although these ancestry tests are highly questionable and bioethically suspect in their results, they continue to be taken seriously by both test-makers and a gullible public (Charmaine et al. 2010). There are a number of bioartists who began the processes of making a new BwO that pushes past Bacon's "probe heads" and contortions of bodily flesh/meat by understanding life to be symbiotically relational and malleable in yet unknown ways. This particular swath of bioartists began to explore the bioengineering paradigm of genetic research that had received such a high profile at the turn of the twenty-first century. Biomedia and biotechniques came together for artistic exploration.

In 1999, Sabrina Raff's performance *Breath Cultures* asked audiences who entered the gallery to breathe inside petri dishes that contained nutrient media. The microorganisms that grew she called "biological fingerprints" that were then pictured under a microscope as "Biological Portraits" of each person's unique microbiome. No two microbiomes were identical but presented singularities of differences. Each petri dish, as a laboratory grown culture, presents a biotechnology that makes visible the invisibility of breath where identity in its diversity cannot easily be neatly codified into new forms of biometrics such as identity recognition via voice, vein pattern recognition in the retina, facial thermograms, or facial feature recognition. Breath, as our "modified" air, shows us that it carries its own force. A new appreciation is found as "breath" becomes alive, a "semi-living" thing; "semi-living," a term developed by the Tissue Culture and Art Project, generally known as TC&A (Catts and Zurr 2011), refers to the recognition that it is through biotechnological means that bacterial cultures are kept "alive." The entwinement of life-death is very much at the center of such bioart, to the point where TC&A has a "killing" ritual at the end of each installation where tissues are put to death by touching them as they can no longer be kept alive. This problematic refers not only to "tissue cultures" but also to bioart that involves larger organisms. The paradigm example here is Mark Dion's installation *Neukon Vivarium* (2006), a "dead" 18-meter Western hemlock that fell outside of Seattle in 1996. Dion's team moved the tree into a specially constructed greenhouse as part of Seattle Art Museum's sculpture garden, its ecology kept on life-support system through advanced technologies. The gap between life and death characterized as a form of suspended-animated "sleep" presents us with the wonderment of life-as-it-is, what Deleuze again called immanent pure life, or "A Life." Dion's installation is an exemplar of practical aesthetics that explores the various bioprocesses that are in play in the tree's ecology. It forwards the problematic that surrounds all "semi-living" beings as well as synthetically created organisms, and that is the question of *termination*. It refers to a moment of "deterritorialization," or disorganization, which inevitably morphs into a new phase of development that is yet to come.

An extension of Raff's new BwO was Joana Ricou's *Other Selves: An Artist's Study of the Human Microbiome* performed in 2015. Ricou swabs her head, face, and hands, as well as objects in her environment, and then has these microbes incubate and grow in petri dishes. From the outcome, individual bacteria colonies and samples of fungi are then harvested and grown separately in liquid agar. A culture-palette of colors is created that are used as paint using traditional brushes for a series of portraits. Sonja Bäumel performed the apotheosis of exploring the body's biome in 2009 called *Oversized Petri Dish*, part of a series of works called *(In)visible Membrane Project*. Collaborating with the Wageningen University laboratory in the Netherlands, she grew an image of her own body's skin bacteria in a large petri dish. Her invisible skin bacteria became visible, documented over a forty-four-day period. This experiment was expanded in 2012 with another project called *Expanded Self*. Again, using an oversized gigantic petri dish as her canvas, the bacteria living on her body was colored and imprinted on agar. This living and growing "clone" of Bäumel's body was documented via photographs and video on the seventh day. The coexistence of human and nonhuman agential selves as a diverse ecosystem became evident; the human being is a changing superorganism.

Bio-sculptural art consists of living or semi-living materials such as blood, cells, and tissues to create forms that are kept alive via incubators. Aside from TC&A, Marc Quinn's self-portrait, *Self*, is cast with 4.5 liters of his own frozen blood. This casting of his head is immersed in frozen silicon and kept refrigerated, a system on life support. Every five years, beginning in 1991, a new "blood sculpture" is produced charting the passage of time, yet raising the question of immortality as his head can be forever preserved. Gina Czarnecki and John Hunt's *Heirloom* (2016) grow skin portraits of their daughters' cells onto traditionally produced glass casts of their faces, which are coated with a growth medium as well as preventing contamination. When the cell growth is that of a thin tissue paper, the layer is removed, preserved, and displayed. These framed "portraits" are made of a person's own biological materials. The claim is that these methods could offer possible facial reconstruction and cosmetic modification. The projection is that biobanks of stored information about the 3-D structure of the face—along with the youthful skin cells—could provide a facial "heirloom" for anyone.

There are other manifestations of "identity" via the information sciences such as Justin Cooper's *Transformers* and *Trap, Self-portrait*, and the self-portrait by Patrice Caire: *Cyberhead . . . Am I Really Existing*—an MRI full-body scan that enable audiences to take a virtual tour through her brain. But perhaps the oddest is Charlotte Javis's *Ergo Sum* (2012), which is bio-wetware work. Jarvis creates a "second self" through stem cell technology: a collage of synthesized body parts all grown outside her body, and all of which were genetically identical to her. The stem cells were kept alive in incubators in the gallery space. Javis donated her blood, urine, and skin biopsy to a laboratory at the Leiden University Medical Center (Amsterdam). Heart cells, brain cells, and blood vessel cells were chosen (beating heart, thinking brain, and flowing blood) to metaphorically form a second "Charlotte." This is a body identity outside her existing body raising again similar ethical issues as to who owns "it/her" since the "bits" of Jarvis are "technically" her corpse. The incubator that keeps the other "Charlotte" alive was designed as a medicine cabinet and an altarpiece, a combination of personalized medicine (being able to grow parts of yourself on demand) and the catholic idea of transubstantiation (the transformation of one organic matter into the body parts of a person). Her "pieces" can be stored indefinitely making them "immortal," again questioning the entwinement of life and death.

Identity and surveillance are a problematic that has received wide attention by bioarts, given the plethora of DNA commercial kits that are available to "identify" your genetic inheritance. Who owns your DNA? The Chicago-based bioartist Heather Dewey-Hagborg is able to 3-D print faces based on the DNA sampling she finds on gum and cigarette butts and hair follicles. The masks that are produced are a startling look-alike of the actual person as Heather Dewey-Hagborg's own experiment shows. Ironically, like many bioartistic tactics, Heather Dewey-Hagborg has marketed a spray to mask one's DNA. The ethics of the question of regulations surrounding human tissue donorship has received wide attention (Czarnecki 2012). *Face Lab*, located in Liverpool's John Moore's University, is capable of reconstructing facial images of historical figures who have long since passed away from their skull and bone remains alone. These bioart experiments have a way of dissipating what are conventional understandings of representational identity. The symbiotic relationships and exchanges with invisible ecologies reveal dimensions of life that otherwise would simply allude our awareness of them.

While what I have presented is just a small trip of the iceberg known as bioart, it is perhaps important to end with the recognition of the new BwO of transhumanism that has proven to be extremely controversial. It presents perhaps the greatest challenge to practical aesthetics as it asks us to recognize the power of art and science together as genetic engineering that can virtually change the course of evolution through genetic modification of our species being; in other words, transhumanism is "practical" for it charts the change to the human genome in ways that can modify our species to cope, perhaps, with the changes that the Anthropocene has already foreseen, like the projection of humans having gills as in the science fiction film *Waterworld*. Chinese geneticist He Jiankui has already modified the human genome (CRISPR babies) as of November 25, 2018. It seems improbable that such medical experimentation will stop despite the protests from the geneticists around the world as the line has already been crossed.

Transhuman bioart has begun to explore this scenario, presenting us with a BwO that seems sci-fictive. This would also include bioart like Julia Reodica's *hymNext Hymen Project*, whose "designer hymens" are sculptures made from her own vaginal cells utilizing a form of regenerative tissue engineering. Natasha Vita More's *Primo Posthuman* projects the future of a trans-technological body, and Micha Cárdenas is engaged in trans-body transformations, investigating how technologies can extend and morph the human body. Perhaps one of the most extreme examples here is the *Fellatio Modification Project*, where Kuang-Yi Ku, a Taiwanese dentist, modifies the structure of the mouth using tissue engineering to enhance the physical pleasure of having oral sex with gay people, an obvious example of pharmaco-pornography (Chen and Lin 2017), as is the Pandrogeny Project (1993–2009), where Genesis and Lady Jaye underwent body modification to resemble one another, identifying themselves as a single pandrogynous being named "Beyer P-Orridge."

The transhuman side of bioart concentrates what bioengineering can do for us, the premise being that the profound embodiment of materiality as presented by blood, skin, wounds, penetrations, and body fluids of all kinds presents us with the enigma as to "what a body can do." Encoding, recoding, and decoding the body, the informatic protocol used in regenerative medicine provides bioartists with all kinds of potentialities (like Strelac's third ear); yet, this direction is more in terms of the transhumanist flights of the imaginary, questionable when its affects seem to reinforce humanist values of a world-only-for-us. Eugene Thacker (2004) usefully refers to this as "biomedia" and has attempted to develop an appropriate "biophilosophy" (Thacker 2008) rather than a philosophy of biology for the ethical and political challenges that our species faces given that the Anthropocene has already happened, but we do not yet know it. All this is to say that the transhuman presents the challenge to practical aesthetics as the twenty-first century wears on as an ecological crisis.

References

Catts, O. and I. Zurr (eds.) (2011), *Partial Life*, London: Open Humanities Press.
Charmaine, D. R., J. Novembre, S. M. Fullerton, D. B. Goldstein, J. C. Long, M. J. Bamshad, and A. G. Clark (2010), "Inferring Genetic Ancestry: Opportunities, Challenges, and Implications," *The American Journal of Human Genetics*, 86: 661–73.
Chen, H.-H., and L. Pei-Ying (2017), "Post-Human Affects and the Biopolitics of Eroticism: Emerging Bio-Art Movements in Taiwan," *Technoetic Arts: A Journal of Speculative Research*, 15 (3): 317–23.
Czarnecki, G. (2012), *Art and Ethics Advisory Panel*. Chaired by S. Poulter. Available online: https://vimeo.com/43719685 (accessed May 27, 2019).
Deleuze, Gilles (1990), *Logic of Sense*, trans. M. Lester and C. Stivale, ed. C. Boundas, New York: Columbia University Press.
Deleuze, G. (1994), *Difference and Repetition*, trans. P. Patton, New York: Columbia University Press.
Deleuze, G. (2000), *Proust and Signs: The Complete Text*, trans. R. Howard, Minneapolis: University of Minnesota Press.
Deleuze, G. (2001), *Pure Immanence: Essays on A Life*, trans. A. Boyman, New York: Zone Books.
Deleuze, G. (2003), *Francis Bacon: The Logic of Sense*, trans. D.W. Smith, London: Continuum.
Deleuze, G., and F. Guattari (1987), *Thousand Plateaus: Capitalism and Schizophrenia, Vol. 2*, trans. B. Massumi, Minneapolis: Minnesota University Press.
Deleuze, G. and F. Guattari (1994), *What Is Philosophy?* trans. H. Tomlinson and G. Burchell, New York: Columbia University Press.
Gare, A. (2014), "Deep Ecology, the Radical Enlightenment, and Ecological Civilization," *The Trumpeter*, 30 (2): 184–205.
Giedion, S. (1948), *Mechanization Takes Command: A Contribution to Anonymous History*, New York: Oxford University Press.
Lyotard, F. (2011), *Discourse, Figure*, trans. A. Hudek and M. Lydon, Minneapolis and London: Minnesota University Press.

Practical Aesthetics

Rifkin, J. (1999), *The Biotech Century: Harnessing the Gene and Remaking the World*, New York: Penguin Putnam, Inc.

Thacker, E. (2004), *Biomedia*, Minneapolis: University of Minnesota Press.

Thacker, E. (2008), "Biophilosophy for the 21st Century," in M. Kroker and A. Kroker (eds.), *Critical Digital Studies: A Reader*, 132–42, Toronto: University of Toronto Press.

Zeki, S. (1999), *Inner Vision: An Exploration of Art and the Brain*, Oxford: Oxford University Press.

CHAPTER 5
COLORS WITHOUT BODIES
WES ANDERSON'S DRAB ETHICS
Eugenie Brinkema

An uncontroversial claim (to be shaded later): in his aestheticism and mannerism; inventive use of color; long tracking and symmetrical, planimetric tableau shots; and meticulous construction of mise-en-scène and soundscapes, Wes Anderson is one of the great cinematic stylists working today. But critical regard for the director is remarkably split: lauded or derided under the mantle of nearly every sensibility or structure of feeling deployed to describe the contemporary landscape—postmodern pastiche, irony, post-irony, the new sincerity, the new [whimsy, quirky, cute] cinema, the New American smart film, or post-death-of-the-author auteurism—critical praise for Anderson's films turns on his collector's aesthetic, antiquated cinematic techniques, and stylistic excess, while critical loathing generally points to the very same attributes. As goes one summary of the condemnations: "Critics say that Anderson's fastidiousness is his downfall, that the fussiness of his vision restricts his actors. They see his films as Fabergé eggs, beautiful but manufactured and empty" (Marshall 2014: 246).

What makes Anderson particularly vulnerable to critical distaste is his relationship to violence. His films are marked by a tension between beautiful, if manufactured, surfaces and disturbing cruelties and maltreated children; broken families and the exquisitely lonely; vicious mutilations, nonchalant injuries, and indifferent deaths; depression and suicide; or, as in the case of *The Grand Budapest Hotel* (2014), the totality of twentieth-century European catastrophe and trauma given metonymic form in the film via death squads emblazoned with the initials ZZ—evoking what Badiou dubs in *The Century* "the site of apocalyptic events . . . the crimes of Stalinist communism and the crimes of Nazism. . . . This century is an accursed century. The principal parameters for thinking it are the extermination camps, the gas chambers, massacres, tortures and organized state crime" (2007: 2). The omnipresence of this evental potency of violence in Anderson's films has led to intensely negative evaluations like that of Eileen Jones, who declares that Anderson "candy-coats a world of casual nastiness in bright colors and hummable tunes, and death in his films makes no mark, it just functions as a design element, a dash of dark pigment that sets off the bright colors to better advantage" (2014).

As a result, even among those who would defend Anderson, his style's relationship to suffering requires an overt accounting for, usually effected by converting form into a responsible engagement with those ethically disturbing aspects of his film's narratives. Donna Kornhaber, for example, reconciles interpretive bellwethers by putting aesthetics to work as itself a matter of shared feeling: "There is along the axis of collection a kind of unity and reduplication between content and form within Anderson's filmmaking, one that offers a means of understanding his visual style not from the stance of cold stylistic removal but as a manner of deep thematic engagement in the cinematic worlds he calls into being, one that seeks to offer sympathy for an act in solidarity with the characters who suffer there" (2017: 10). Likewise, Kim Wilkins writes that "his film worlds are more than affectation or pure aestheticism: their artifice performs both narrative and thematic functions. These film worlds mobilize irony and artificiality to mediate sincere emotional and psychological concerns" (2018: 152). Both defenses play out familiar topologies of critical commitment: instead of cold removal, Kornhaber promises "deep" engagement, while Wilkins insists on something "more" than affectation or pure aestheticism. In other words, even those who would praise Anderson's formal inventiveness insist that aesthetic form has "real" (as in more-than-mere and as in deeper, higher, closer) concerns at play—or, in Wilkins's insistence that his work is not "pure aestheticism," an unstated avowal of an *impure* aestheticism that vouches for a purity of emotional sincerity (that latter word one that hides its etymological debt to notions of the clean, the sound, the uninjured, any one of which we might want to read and thereby hold accountable). Taking a broader view, we can say that Anderson's films restage the fundamental and old fight at the heart of the question of formalism, or rather, how you feel about his films has much to do with how you feel about formalism: either agreeing with those who accuse it of abandoning the world, as in Fredric Jameson's promissory offering of a "literary or cultural criticism which seeks to avoid imprisonment in the windless closure of the formalisms" (1981: 42), or defending the self-showing formal language for its sincere showing of a philosophical seriousness taken as prior and exterior to the cinematic object—justifying aesthetic attention by presuming the legitimacy of notions such as sympathy or solidarity as the ground of ethics, holding form ransom until it proves its appropriate utility.

If Anderson's films are the perfect testing ground for complaints against formalism, my argument will be that both those who would dismiss his stylistics as empty form and those who would defend his formalism for its non-empty utility for a conversion to an external framework of ethical or political meaning make a common mistake of failing to treat his form *radically* enough, as rooting *The Grand Budapest Hotel*'s rigorous engagement with ethics and politics and history as problems, themselves, of form, specifically the way in which that film attests to a thinking of the scale of historical loss that is diagrammatic, impersonal, multiple, and marked by difference. Radical formalism, given due seriousness, disimplicates the sense that criticism must choose one of the two paradigmatic interpretations of Anderson: as empty aesthete or as thinker despite his aesthetic language. Instead, we might shorthand this as: it is nothing but the form of his works that is doing the thinking. In relation to the conceit of this collection, *practical aesthetics* requires beginning with the understanding that it is the realm of aesthetic form that is thinking with, speculating on, unfolding the as-yet unthought questions, problems, and aporias of historical trauma. This requires taking seriously what form attests to in its own right, in particular in its most apparent aspects: in autonomous problems of color and of light. A speculative relation to catastrophes of unimaginable scale does not require accounting for form, defending form, or moving past form; it requires putting more of our faith in form. For one thing that form can do is attest to a concept of suffering, shock, and loss that contains many *nuances*.

There are two privileged structures in *The Grand Budapest Hotel*: the general form of repetition with minor difference and the general form of nesting. The latter is complex and the following is a gloss, but briefly: nesting accounts for the hypotactic narrative structure. It begins in the present at a cemetery, in which a young girl visits the memorial of a dead author (modeled after the early twentieth-century Austrian novelist Stefan Zweig), sits, and reads his book *The Grand Budapest Hotel* (and the film takes place in the real-time duration of her reading), moving from his author's photo on the back cover into a 1985 frame in which the author explains how he came to hear the story that comprises that work, flashing back to a 1968 conversation between the author as a younger man and the elderly proprietor of the titular hotel, during which they dine together and that man, Zero Moustafa, recounts his life in 1932 as a young refugee and lobby boy in the hotel under the mentorship of a legendary hotel concierge named Gustave H. with whom he forms an intimate friendship and whose death bequeaths a fortune to Zero. Each nesting is also a triple framing: a historical and a narratological one, and also an aspectual, cinematically-specific one. The standard 1.85 aspect ratio is used for the present day, a letterboxed version for the 1980s, widescreen for the 1960s portion, and the 4x3 industry standard (the "Academy ratio") for the 1930s. The film's use of nesting and shifting aspects accounts for its theory of memory and its co-implicated theory of ruins in numerous ways including this salient one: save for the reading girl, everyone we meet in the film is dead, and this overwhelming thanatographic attestation will be important in the analysis to come. The film is set in a fictional former empire, Zubrowka (a stand in for the Czech lands), in which there is an invented war, collapsing the First World War and the Second World War, pointing to the Nazi invasion, but also pointing ahead to the suffering of the Czechs under the Soviets. In other words, there is a broad interest in the *generality* of history's hurts, the *scale* of millions dying, the *totality* of variable modes of human suffering accumulated by century's end.

The other general form, that of repetition with minor difference, governs the film's chromatic palettes and spatial grids, but also bears on two nearly identical scenes on a train that set in place aesthetic problems of color and light in explicit relation to force. The first scene takes place twenty minutes into the film; the second, four minutes from the end. They are mirror inversions and elemental conversions of each other: in the first, leaning into the frame from the left, Gustave asks, "Why are we stopping at a barley field?" as the train pauses next to an expanse; text gives the date as "19 October, Closing of the Frontier." In the repetition of the scenario, Zero leans in from the right, asking the same question but adding "again," and the text now reads, "17 November, Start of the Lutz Blitz." The first sequence, in which border patrols attempt to arrest Zero for a lack of papers, concludes when he and Gustave are given a reprieve from violence through the timely intervention of a soldier who recalls Gustave's kindness to him in childhood; at his promise of no further disturbance and the soldiers' departure, Gustave says to a shaken Zero, "You see, there are still faint glimmers of civilization left in this barbaric slaughterhouse that was once known as humanity. Indeed, that's what we provide in our own modest, humble, insignificant . . . oh fuck it." The two scenes are formally symmetrical but ethically nonreciprocal because the second time brings with it two differences: at the sight of the death squad tableau in the barley field, Gustave declares, "I find these black uniforms very drab"; and the result of the encounter is not evaded violence and an ironic dismissal of civility, but arrived violence and a reassertion of civility. In the narrative block in which an elderly Zero recounts this story, to the author's question of what happened to Gustave, Zero resignedly says, "In the end? They shot him." The resulting ethical judgment turns on Zero's accompanying insistence: "There are still faint glimmers of civilization left in this barbaric slaughterhouse that was once known as humanity. He was one of them."

Any strict repetition of two scenarios invites comparison. While the first train scene ends as comedy, the second concludes as tragedy, inverting Marx's famous lines in *Eighteenth Brumaire*. More precisely, the first time ends in irony and cynicism (all that is at stake in the "oh fuck it"), while the second de-ironizes irony and concludes with a positive declaration of sincerity: insisting on the possibility of a concept of civility in Gustave's defense of, and ultimately sacrifice for, Zero. Or, rather, the second scene does not insist on the concept of civility—when Zero pronounces a *faint glimmer* of civilization left in humanity's slaughterhouse, this is an avowal of an ethics of civility bound to *percept* and not to *concept* at all. That question of percept and not concept likewise appears with the supplement, the aspect that does not repeat across the two sequences: Gustave's aesthetic judgment that greets the appearance of the death squads—his "I find these black uniforms very drab." It is neither civility nor death squads that should interest us; our primary concern (in the sense of ordinality and prerogative) must be with *glimmer* and with *drab*: with qualities of light and color.

The two train scenes repeat a formula, which is to say they take on and share a common and visible shape. Each begins with an interrogatory aimed at a change in movement, "Why are we stopping at a barley field?" Before it is anything else, the barley field is a clearing, a visible expanse of earth marked by a flooding of the distant space with light, the free, clear open space for light to play against which the constraint of the train and its diegetic mise en abyme frame is set as different. Before they are encounters with military force, state brutality, and death squads, these two scenes are meditations on the autonomy and vitality of illuminated landscape. The barley field gives the play of *lux* as the give and expanse of the world beyond and outside the train, set in stark contrast to a symmetrical window in a vertical aspect ratio, opposite the aperture in the train and visible behind the passengers. This interior window is a gridded frame delimiting an opaque field, one showing a constraint and restriction of light with no depth behind it, the alternations of montage introducing a difference between this and the light into which the world recedes. Light as the extensibility of illumination is thus set against light given shape, edge, structure, limit, form.

These scenes are not meditations on light (as metaphysics or metaphor) or color (as symbol) so much as meditations on and encounters with questions of degrees of *difference* in relation to light and color: the drabness Gustave finds of the black

Colors Without Bodies

Figure 6.1 *The Grand Budapest Hotel* (2014), Dir. Wes Anderson, United States: Fox Searchlight Pictures.
Screenshot by Eugenie Brinkema

Figure 6.2 *The Grand Budapest Hotel* (2014), Dir. Wes Anderson, United States: Fox Searchlight Pictures.
Screenshot by Eugenie Brinkema

uniforms; the glimmer refused to civilization in the first encounter and reattributed to Gustave's sacrifice in the latter. For all that Anderson is taken to be a master aesthete of world-building palettes (as in the exhaustive "Wes Anderson Colour Palettes" Tumblr page), drabness is not a problem of the palette, and in fact it takes an oblique relationship to color altogether. On the one hand, "drabness" is a positive color, referring to the undyed color of material like hemp, linen, or wool; the *Oxford English Dictionary*'s etymological tracing of the term notes that from naming the positive color of undyed cloth, it "gradually became an adjective of color," referring to a "dull light-brown or yellowish-brown." On the other hand, drabness names a lack of specificity in color—it is a symptomatic confusion that history cannot agree on whether it points to dull light-brown or a luminousless gray. In many languages, the words for drab and gray are the same; the 1869 *A Dictionary of Dyeing* insists, "Drab is a kind of gray" (199). Perhaps brown, perhaps gray, drab is also taken to mean plain, unsaturated, not luminous (a quality applicable to any color); but it can also mean *not a color at all* but its possibility, its not-yetness, referring to what is "wanting brightness or color," emphasizing not the positive chromatic attributes of undyed cloth, but the fact of having failed to take on color at all. This parallel sense of drab as in what lacks color makes it simultaneously a positive—if shineless and unsaturated—color and, in naming a hueless state of what has yet to take on color, it renders drab the negative ontology of the chromatic.

Gustave's pronouncement bonds together both senses of drab: as a quality of things, but also that which judges something to be lacking in chromatic intensity. However, there is no drabness in itself as essence or substantive; rather, this avowal of a black uniform marked by drabness is made within a cinematic episteme of black-and-white film stock. As a result, there is an inconstancy of tone in the color field of the death squad uniforms: against the rich continuous expanse of unmarked black in Gustave and Zero's jackets, signaling the perceptually unavailable presence of color on the level of textile, the shots of the death squad textiles present patches of unevenness (difference, modulation, variability). Drab, applied to the black of the uniforms, appears as gray; the only perceptually absolute black in the image is that of Gustave and Zero's jackets, which disaffirm being black on the level of material precisely because they are not drab in this visual regime. (And indeed from previous appearances, we know them to be a vibrant purple.) Put another way: it is the formal aspects of the black-and-white film stock that visually interpret Gustave's claim for drabness. This sequence is not a narrative climax in which an illustration of innocence and brutality confront each other so much a *formal climax* in which cinematic form interprets the qualities and intensities of light—in which form is offering a reading of qualities and intensities of form. The radical impersonality of drab and glimmer stands to offer an irreducibly aesthetic relation to the political violence that stains both sequences.

The negative motor of drabness (that it is indistinct and uncertain, that it marks having yet to take on color) positively attests to something else. This is most visible in a claim made by Benjamin, one of the great theorists of gray. In his 1925 essay on Naples, written with Asja Lacis, they pronounce of the city "In reality it is gray" (165). But this gray has a particular aesthetic power: in its chromatic deficiency, it brings line to the forefront. Of Naples's grayness, "anyone who is blind to forms sees little here" (165). Gray is form-revealing: its negative qualities make form visible, unconceal it as *all there is*. In drabness, there is the inexhaustible potentiality of what has yet to take on color (that *yet* marking the tonality of possibility) and the infinite unconcealment of the possibility of form, what gray or drab or huelessness brings forth. Gustave's pronouncement, "I find these black uniforms very drab" is an aesthetic judgment—a claim for regarding the

Figure 6.3 *The Grand Budapest Hotel* (2014), Dir. Wes Anderson, United States: Fox Searchlight Pictures.
Screenshot by Eugenie Brinkema

uniforms as forms. Not to offer an ethical-political judgment on historical force but to offer an aesthetic reckoning with historical force as nothing but form.

Benjamin and Lacis insist that those unconcerned with form will behold very little in Naples. We might say: they will see only a glimmer. If drabness is the infinite potentiality of color, what has yet to take on sufficient hue but thereby reveals form, *glimmer* also takes a complex relation to light. Just as drab is simultaneously a dull brown and a dull gray—or it is no color at all, but the state of the undyed and uncolored—glimmer means both "to shine brightly" with attendant notions of visibility and unconcealment (its fourteenth-century usage) and "to give a faint or intermittent light," "a feeble or wavering light; a tremulous play of reflected light," to send forth a weak, dim, and scattered light—its dominant sense by the fifteenth century. Glimmer thus comes to name both a self-showing brightness and the unsteadiness of light such that glimmer is always nearly not there at all (as in the nested qualifications of *The Comedy of Errors*, "My wasting lamps have yet some fading glimmer left"—wasting, yet, some, fading, and glimmer multiply attesting to illumination's barelyness that nevertheless is not absent). As a reading of light, glimmer has a fundamental *qualification* attached to it: in the sense of a hedge or limitation, but also in an emphasis on *qualities*. Glimmer is not the vibrancy of an attestation, glimmer is the imperfection of light (as transitory, unsteady, notional); it is always the last glimmer of hope that marks a caesura before some form of finitude.

The two words—drab and glimmer—resonate with each other, but also within each other, an insufficiency of luminosity, and an unsteadiness of its dispersion. They name, each of them, a vulnerability in the potency of light and a rhythmic unfolding of that potency's modulation and differing by degrees. And so, the speculative claim: If the question of historical force and catastrophe and loss is given in a formal register, as a problem of aesthetic qualities and intensities, then only a resolute formalism can account for how the film navigates this terrain—not through allegorizing *a priori* ethical or political claims but in taking seriously the film's formal language as a showing of drabness, glimmer, saturation, as degrees of difference in light. This is resolutely opposed to a taking of illumination as metaphor for a legible state of feeling: as in one reading that avows, "The hotel is bursting with colour in its heyday.... But the colour fades as the war approaches.... Like Zero, the hotel never recovers from the war; in 1968, it is as decrepit beige, orange and sickly pale blue as Zero is sad" (2014: 249). Such a reading takes saturations as stable, fixed representations of affective states of being instead of treating changes in chromatic aspects as what positively shows nuances in the quality of light.

Drabness is the unvibrancy of a chromatic attestation having taken on sufficient color; glimmer is the unvitality of a brilliance having taken on the steadiness of light. If drab is a quality of things that reveals nothing but the potential for form, glimmer is a quality of light that reveals nothing but a difference: Glimmer names the minimal difference between the presence and absence of light itself. And it is the minimal difference that concerns us here, whether between the presence and absence of light, or the presence and radical absence of civility, a minimal mark, that is, of the possibility of a perceptible form of differentiation. This question of differentiation is a fundamental one with which any reading of the film's relation to historical trauma must grapple, in particular in the way *The Grand Budapest Hotel* navigates the figure of Zero, whose presence as a refugee whose village was burned and family murdered and displaced opens up wounded European history to include the register of loss from the Levant.

Attending to qualities of light negates the grounds for the alternative presented earlier: either condemning a formal exercise as failing to generate a speculative relation to the ethical or instrumentalizing form as demonstrating a prior conception of the ethical. Instead, *The Grand Budapest Hotel* is aesthetically proposing a general account of historical trauma that itself is a formalism—an effort to think violence as a structure that contains differences, degrees, nuances, one that places together (without mediating, synthesizing, scaling, or hierarchizing) Agatha's death, Zero's infant's child's death, his father's death, his family's execution, his village's burning, the total violence engendering refuge in Europe, the violence of the First World War, the violence of the Second World War, the death squads, Gustave's execution, Madame D's murder by her own children, and the assorted tortures and cruelties and beheadings of minor characters in the film in plot points this essay has failed to yet mention. The critical question is whether the film is indifferent to the historical specificity of these different losses (the question of form's relation to content always a question of whether textual form is adequate to context) or whether one can positively theorize difference without returning it to a logic of the same, without presuming all speak to an ineffable in-commonness. How to let each (every) loss retain their quality of being different?

One answer can be gleaned from the intervention Deleuze makes in his 1956 essay "The Conception of Difference in Bergson," in which he offers a theory of difference that he will revisit a decade later in *Difference and Repetition*. Here, Deleuze reads Bergson's account in *The Creative Mind* of how to develop concepts, in which his privileged example is the case of the concept "color." How do we determine what colors have in common? Bergson says there are two ways: either we start with a color, say purple, efface its purpleness, and then do the same negating process to other colors, to blue, to orange, until we have arrived at and extracted the abstract notion of color in itself, emptied of any specific content in a singular concept referring to multiple objects by containing and subsuming them. In Deleuze's reading of this option, "We are left with a concept which is a genre, and many objects for one concept" (54). That's the first way (and, of course, the first way is never the right way in Deleuze). The second way to arrive at the concept of color is to start with a continuum and pass the rainbow through a "convergent lens that concentrates them on the same point: what we have then is 'pure white light,' the very light that 'makes the differences come out between the shades'" (54). Deleuze reads this as a case in which "the different colors are no longer objects under a concept, but nuances or degrees of the concept itself. Degrees of difference itself, and not differences of degree. The relation is no longer one of subsumption, but one of participation" (54). The concept is no longer a genre (or a generality) but a universal and concrete thing. What the formal language of *The Grand Budapest Hotel* bears out is not the content of difference but the quality and intensity of nuances or degrees in order to make present the aesthetic *force* of difference. Historical trauma is not a unifying or totalizing concept; every instance of violence and trauma is a manifestation of a process of differentiation, moving past thinking degrees of violence (and critical hierarchies that pose the question of which trauma best gives the concept of the twentieth century) to instead regard nuances or degrees *within* the concept as co-participants in history.

Anderson's film is not uninterested in a serious engagement with the traumas that run through the film, but nor should we instrumentalize the aesthetic as offering an abstract *genre* of "historical violence or trauma." Rather, *Grand Budapest*'s formal language unsettles any claim for a genre (or generality) that would adequately contain the inexhaustibility of nuances and degrees. Instead of a concept of formalism premised on negation (what ignores the world, what is indifferent to history, what fails to speak to ethical seriousness), formalism is revealed to be an aesthetic attestation of difference as a question of action. Claims for the film as "form for form's sake" do not, therefore, go far enough: what the text's navigation of color and light does is perform the *irreducibility* of form to any (every) serious thinking of the objects of critique: Anderson's is a case of *form for everything's sake*. If *Grand Budapest* is an aesthetic exercise, it is so in the strictest sense: the aesthetic keeps busy and does not wait to come about, is not a demonstration of a prior claim but is itself an active and generative and practical operation of thought—indeed, the best one we have to make sense of the form of history: a grand accumulation of degrees of loss.

References

Badiou, A. (2007), *The Century*, trans. A. Toscano, Cambridge, UK: Polity Press.
Benjamin, W. and A. Lacis (1978), "Naples," in P. Demetz (ed.), *Reflections: Essays, Aphorisms, Autobiographical Writings*, trans. E. Jephcott, 163–73, New York: Schocken Books.

Deleuze, G. (1999), "Bergson's Conception of Difference," trans. M. McMahon, in J. Mullarkey (ed.), *The New Bergson*, 42–65, Manchester: Manchester University Press.
The Grand Budapest Hotel (2014), [Film] Dir. Wes Anderson, USA: Fox Searchlight Pictures.
Jameson, F. (1981), *The Political Unconscious*, Ithaca: Cornell University Press.
Jones, E. (2014), "Wes Anderson and the Old Regime," *Jacobin*, March 2014. Available online: https://www.jacobinmag.com/2014/03/wes-anderson-and-the-old-regime/ (accessed December 20, 2018).
Kornhaber, D. (2017), *Wes Anderson*, Champaign, IL: University of Illinois Press.
Marshall, L. (2014), "Wes Anderson's Fabulous Fancy," *Queen's Quarterly*, 121 (2) (Summer): 242–51.
O'Neill, C. (1869), *A Dictionary of Dyeing and Calico Printing*, Philadelphia, PA: Henry Carey Baird.
Wilkins, K. (2018), "Assembled Worlds: Intertextuality and Sincerity in the Films of Wes Anderson," *Texas Studies in Literature and Language*, 60 (2) (Summer): 151–73.

CHAPTER 6
IN LAG OF KNOWLEDGE
THE VIDEO ESSAY AS PARAPRAXIS
Johannes Binotto

In the preface to the enlarged version of *The World Viewed*, Stanley Cavell points out a banal yet fundamental predicament of his philosophical engagement with film, namely the fact that "in speaking of a moment or sequence from a film we, as we might put it, cannot *quote* the thing we are speaking of" (1979: ix). The advent of digital film formats and the fact that editing software, once reserved for professional filmmakers, has now become easily accessible to every owner of a computer seem to have solved Cavell's problem. Film, once famously described by Raymond Bellour as an ultimately "unattainable text" (2000: 21–7), has become, thanks to digital formats, more at hand than ever before. The success and extreme proliferation, in recent years, of the genre of the video essay (or videographic essay or audiovisual essay)[1] is a result of this new "attainability" of the filmic text which allows for an engagement with cinema in which the object of study has finally become quotable. Instead of being a mere object for analysis which needs to be translated into (and is thus continuously missed by) the written text, the video essay uses film as the very tool of its own analysis. Rather than thinking *about*, the video essay is thinking *with* film, and is thus a prime example for what a "practical aesthetics" of film in the digital age could mean.

As a booming strand of film studies video essays have become part of academic research as well as film criticism or expression of personal cinephilia. They are found as "Special Features" on DVD editions and as additional content on film streaming platforms. They are collected in specialized YouTube and Vimeo channels and featured in film magazines, exclusively devoted to this format, like *[In-]Transition* or *The Cine-Files*.

It would, however, be a mistake to take the contemporary video essay as a new phenomenon only. Rather, it is also a continuation and reemergence of essayistic film practices already extensively deployed by filmmakers such as Agnès Varda, Jean-Luc Godard, and Harun Farocki and can be traced further back to surrealist avant-garde cinema in the 1930s or Dziga Vertov's radical investigations of the medium in the 1920s. What is new is how broadly popular the form has become, since digitalization has not only facilitated the access to film history and its artifacts but has also made the transition from consumer to producer easier: the smartphones in our pockets serve as portable movie screens and double as film cameras, making potential directors out of us all.

I will not attempt a survey on the rapidly evolving history (or rather: histories) of the audiovisual essay and its manifold theoretical implications, since they have already been

Practical Aesthetics

outlined much more thoroughly by other scholars (cf. Baptista 2016; Grizzaffi 2017; Pantenburg 2019) and in particular by the extensive work of film theorist and video essayist Catherine Grant in her numerous video essays and publications on the subject, collected in her blog *Film Studies for Free* and on her Vimeo channel *Audiovisualcy. An Online Forum for Videographic Film Studies*.

Instead, I aim to focus on one particular aspect in video essayistic practice which seems more crucial to me, while video essays have become more professional due to better digital equipment. Namely, I am interested in what new forms of disruptions and frustrations the new technologies confront us with when looking at films and how these disruptions can serve as critical practices in the video essay. In contrast to the common assumption that digital devices increase and facilitate our consumption of audiovisual content, I would argue that while providing broader access to film and film history they also install new and intricate forms of interference or "unattainability" which are worth being analyzed. Picking up on Catherine Grant's discussion of the different "affordances" of digital technology for video essayistic practice (2014), I would claim that—rather paradoxically—some of its most interesting offerings are precisely the ways in which digital technology makes film viewing not easier but more difficult.

Dealing with Lag

It has happened to all of us: we are streaming a sports game, we are watching the latest episode of our favorite drama series on our iPad, and we are getting to the grand finale, the players are approaching the finish line—and then, all of a sudden, the image comes to a halt. The ball is suspended in mid-air, the lips of the two protagonists cannot meet. The effect, commonly referred to as "lag" (or "buffering") is as ubiquitous as it is annoying. Caused by slow connection speed which hinders the stream of digital content to catch up with our consumption of it, the moving images comes to a sudden halt. Similarly, a corrupted file or a software error can suddenly turn the movie classic we are so fond of into an unrecognizable pulp of glittering pixels. What could be more infuriating to the cinephile's eye? Yet at the same time and totally by accident, these moments of irritating interruption produce their own form of beauty. As the novelist Tom McCarthy pointed out: "[A]ll these blocks of color and movement collaging in every which arrangement—it becomes this really avant-garde piece of visual art. The interruption is a wonderful moment and it's not nothing, it's something much more interesting than the other thing" (2014: 55).

My question is thus: Can moments like these be taken as the starting point for an analysis of film? And could the video essay be a form not only to think *with* film but also to think *with* these new tools that we use and get interrupted by when watching and analyzing film today? "Our writing tools are also working on our thoughts," Friedrich Nietzsche famously wrote in one of his typewriter letters (2003: 18). Meant as expressing his own frustration over the unreliability of the often dysfunctional machine, the aphorism has since become a "leitmotif" for media theory after Friedrich

Kittler (cf. 1999: xxxi). Picking up on Nietzsche (and Kittler), I argue that the video essay may render this interaction *with* and interruption *by* the working tools of film viewing visible by dealing with interferences such as "lag" no longer as accidents which are foreign to film experience but as productive new encounters with cinema and its history.

In *Death 24x a Second*, Laura Mulvey already outlined the potential of practices like pause and interruption for film analysis in her concept of "delayed viewing"—a practice that is deeply intertwined with the change in film formatting. As Mulvey argues, the possibility to stop a film when watched on a DVD satisfies a desire of the movie audience, turning them from passive into "possessive" spectators (2006: 161–80). The cinematic experience, once elusive and ephemeral due to its particular technological dispositive which was controlled by the operator in theater, is now in the hands of the viewer. With digital formats, every spectator becomes operator, able to stop, rewind, replay, slow down, or speed up the film at his or her own discretion.

What makes Mulvey's concept so fascinating is that it encompasses both the fetishistic pleasure *in* and the destructive annihilation *of* cinematic experience. The ability to replay certain scenes from a film holds the promise of prolonged and supposedly inexhaustible enjoyment. At the same time however, the very practice of stopping, repeating, and delaying a film puts into question its very properties: a paused film is no longer a film. The act of fetishistic inspection is at the same time an aggressive dissection which literally stops the moving image dead. In accordance with this ambivalence, delayed viewing brings to our attention something that is undeniably part of the actual film while at the same time invisible when watched as intended, as a moving image. D. H. Miller, in his *Hidden Hitchcock* for example, uses delayed viewing in order to unearth details planted in films by Alfred Hitchcock that could never be seen in cinema but which only become visible when clicking through the films on your computer frame by frame. Miller calls this practice a "too-close viewing" (2016: 4)—a term that already points out how problematic and questionable its findings might be.

All the same, precisely because delayed viewing is an excessive strategy which renders the "normal" movie consumption impossible, it can serve a critical function. As Mulvey points out, ideologies at play, for example, in Classical Hollywood become subverted simply by slowing the films down:

> The smooth linearity and forward movement of the story become jagged and uneven, undermining the male protagonist's command over the action. The process of identification, usually kept in place by the relation between plot and character, suspense and transcendence, loses its hold over the spectator. And the loss of ego and self-consciousness that has been, for so long, one of the pleasures of the movies gives way to an alert scrutiny and scanning of the screen, lying in wait, as it were, to capture a favorite or hitherto unseen detail. With the weakening of narrative and its effects, the aesthetic of the film begins to become "feminized," with the shift in spectatorial power relations dwelling on pose, stillness, lighting and the choreography of character and camera. (2006: 165)

Practical Aesthetics

Inviting Contingence

Delayed viewing as critical practice with its potential to subvert normative readings of films can be seen at use in large numbers of video essays, and it is not surprising that Laura Mulvey's concept (alongside Raymond Bellours notion of the "unattainable text") has served as a starting point for theorizing the genre (cf. Baptista 2016: 11; Grizzaffi 2017: 32–5).

However, I would propose to go even further and include even more contingent forms of delay as critical tools. As Mary Ann Doane has argued, in Mulvey's delayed viewing "there is something very determined and controlled about this 'individual' access to contingency" (Doane 2007: 23). As Doane points out, pausing and slowing down of DVDs has in fact already become an "institutionally authorized form of contemporary spectatorship" (23). In contrast to this, she is far more interested in "unstructured and unanticipated" moments of contingency "outside of or beyond that of the shot, the editing, the narrative of the film" but which are nonetheless "certainly a part of the experience of a film" (18). Doane mentions in particular the experimental films by Bill Morrison with their chronicling of the deterioration and destruction of nitrate film stock and how Morrison's films turn those very material changes—which are no longer controlled nor intended by any human actor—into an artistic investigation of the film medium per se (cf. Herzogenrath 2018).

But while Doane seems to reserve such encounters with contingency only to the analogue film material and sees the digital as mostly "antithetical to . . . the fascination with contingency" (20), I would rather extend her argument onto phenomena that are even more unstable and can be attributed to the film even less as corpus but which result from the new viewing technologies themselves. As I would argue, it is precisely in phenomena like "lag" that we encounter events of contingency which are even less fixed (and thus even less controllable) than the deteriorations of analogue film material but which are nonetheless inscribing themselves into our film experience. But at the same time the status of these disruptions and deformations in relation to the "original" film are even more unclear.

We can easily imagine how a cinephile might cherish a particular worn-out analogue film copy of, let's say, Douglas Sirk's *All That Heaven Allows* for its faded colors or intricate scratches. And although such a copy would not be considered as reference for a restoration of the film in question, it would undoubtedly be granted cinematic value. It is however certainly much more unlikely that we would have similar acceptance for a corrupted digital version of that film which is highly pixelated, glitched, and disfigured by lag effects. Accidents like these are also less "shareable" with other viewers because they are not materially part of the distorted movie—in contrast to the marks on analogue film strip—but result from an individual interaction between data, software, and hardware and that can therefore never be fully reproduced. Digital distortions occurring only within a series of translations and remediations (film stock being scanned and turned into digital data, which then gets copied, compressed, streamed, and played back) thus seem to have nothing to do with the "original" film.[2] Nonetheless, as I would argue,

In Lag of Knowledge

it is precisely because these distorted film images lag/lack authority they can become surprisingly revealing.

Illegitimate Offspring

As I was recently rewatching the 1957 melodrama *Peyton Place*, the image at one point, due to an interruption in the stream of digital data, stuttered and disintegrated into blocks of pixels. It was a scene in which Constance MacKenzie—one of the main characters and played by the film's star Lana Turner—just got up from her desk in order to greet her housekeeper, Nellie. Instead of a glamorous star body, my device showed Lana Turner as split into two ghosts, one with parts of her body already disappearing, while the other, even more uncannily, only consisted in dress, legs, and arms with an empty spot where the face would have been. Luckily, I reacted quickly enough to at least capture a screenshot of this fleeting and irretrievable moment (Figure 7.1).

It struck me how this image, inadvertently, serves as a metaphor for so many of the film's concerns. The digital lag produced what Walter Benjamin describes as a dialectical *Denkbild*: "when thought comes to a standstill in a constellation saturated with tensions, there appears the dialectical image" (Benjamin 1999: 475).

As I have outlined in a different context, the narrative of Grace Metalious's scandalous 1956 novel *Peyton Place* about infidelity and illegitimacy in a conservative New England town is mirrored by a sprawling, transmedial production history: Metalious's manuscript was thoroughly censured, edited, and revised in order to become a best seller, which then was adapted into a blockbuster movie, which then led to Metalious writing a sequel, which in turn was made into a second movie, all of which eventually led to the series *Peyton Place* (the first soap opera smash hit on American television in 1964). However, each of these transmedial reformulations and revisions of the *Peyton Place* narrative enacts on the level of production, via screenwriting and casting decisions, mise-en-scène,

Figure 7.1 *Glitched Peyton Place*,
Photograph by the Author.

Practical Aesthetics

and advertising campaigns those very acts of hypocrisy, silencing, and abuse that the original story tells about. If the central question of Metalious's novel is that of bastardy and illegitimacy, it is also the central question for the different adaptations, which are not only illegitimately rewriting the author's original text but which themselves put her authority as writer into question (cf. Binotto 2016).

Repetition, translation, transformation, transmediation, reproduction, procreation, embodiment, disfigurement, dismemberment, destruction, and deconstruction—all those practices and the question of their (il)legitimacy are found perfectly incapsulated in this lagging image on my iPad. Taken from a film about a novel about bastardy, this image itself, as the product of an illegitimate accident, begs the question: What gave birth to that?

Working Poor

Pixelated and degraded, the scene from *Peyton Place* as was presented to me by my digital device is also an exemplary case of what the video artist and theorist Hito Steyerl calls a "poor image":

> The poor image is an illicit fifth-generation bastard of an original image. Its genealogy is dubious. Its filenames are deliberately misspelled. It often defies patrimony, national culture, or indeed copyright. It is passed on as a lure, a decoy, an index, or as a reminder of its former visual self. It mocks the promises of digital technology. Not only is it often degraded to the point of being just a hurried blur, one even doubts whether it could be called an image at all. (Steyerl 2009)

However, the poor image as an "illicit bastard" not only raises the question of genealogy illegitimacy again, but also links this with questions of class struggle. As Steyerl writes, the poor image must also be seen as a "lumpen proletarian in the class society of appearance," which makes visible the production and exploitation within capitalist mass culture of which the poor image is both product and waste.

Keeping that in mind, it strikes me even more that exactly in this scene from *Peyton Place*, right after the lag occurred, the character of the housekeeper Nellie in answer to her employer's question why she didn't stay at home utters the following line: "Work keeps my mind off of things." All of a sudden, this simple sentence (which in the context of the film's plot is hinting at Nellie's distress over having found out about the abuse of her daughter) is now revealed to be highly overdetermined: Inadvertently, it becomes a contradictory but curiously apt metatheoretical comment on what just occurred on my iPad: If the film streaming had worked as usual, I wouldn't have minded the scene and this particular sentence. But also: The way it worked my device kept my mind off of things we normally focus on like plot or character. Instead, it brought to my attention the work itself: the functions and dysfunctions of the very technology we use.

"Work keeps my mind off of things"—so the lagged film told me—could ultimately be the slogan of a practical aesthetics of film, a practice that does not already know beforehand what "things" it wants to prove but which is open for unexpected encounters found in the process of "work" itself.

Para-Practice, Para-Site

Such a practical aesthetics—which I have just tried not only to describe but also to perform—puts the accident and the lag/lack of knowledge at its center. As a name for this particular form of an accidental practical aesthetics, I propose the Freudian term of *Fehlleistung*—parapraxis. But while parapraxis is normally (and also by Freud) thought of as an inner conflict between the subject's conscious intention and the unconscious, I would take the term in a both more pragmatic and literal but thus also in a more radical sense. Parapraxis is to be located "beyond" or "beside" it (as the prefix "para-" already suggests) instead of within the subject. Following Jacques Lacan's claim for an "ex-sistence" of the unconscious, with which he means that unconscious processes have less to do with supposedly inner motives but rather with external (media) practices such as language (cf. Lacan 2002: 6), so too "parapraxis" must be seen at work in those technological practices with which we engage. And picking up on Félix Guattari's concept of a machine-unconscious (cf. Guattari 1984: 111–19), I argue that not only slips of tongue but also the parapraxes of technical objects and devices, the slips, blips, beeps, and lags of microphones, typewriters, cameras, projectors, and computers make us encounter the unconscious (cf. Binotto 2018).

I understand the video essay as a preeminent field of parapraxis inasmuch as it does not try to contain or exhaust film by analyzing its contents but instead by opening it up to those distortions that supposedly have nothing to do with it and that seem to come from outside as interferences. Parapraxis is thus also a parasitic practice in the sense that Michel Serres used the term. As Serres elaborates in his discussion of the "parasite" what lies at the center of all media and technology is not the undeviated transfer of information but distortion: "No canal without noise" (Serres 1982: 79). Accordingly, the parasite is not simply an external intruder which lives off of the host but rather an agent of the host's evolution (184). Similarly, the video essay as a parasite of cinema lives off of film history but also revolutionizes it, by exposing cinema to new forms of interference. The video essay thus eventually can be seen also as a para-site, a different scene of film, a new site for making and watching films differently.

Against Certain Tendencies

There seems to be a certain tendency in the contemporary video essay (to borrow the famous phrasing of François Truffaut's polemic against French cinema)—a tendency toward the polished and the smooth, toward the elegant, and the easily scrollable (cf. Lee

2017). And this tendency is not restricted to one of the two major modes of the video essay as they have been distinguished by Christian Keathley (2011) as the "explanatory mode" and the "poetic mode." Not only the explanatory video essays with their focus on traditional interpretative practices are prone to being reductive (cf. López and Martin 2017) but also the essays in the "poetic mode." Particularly, when "poetic" means that these videos are primarily invested in a celebration of the beauty of cinematic images (perhaps most extremely exemplified in the format of the supercut), they often feel like they rather gloss over than really engage with film.

In addition to Keathleys's distinction between the poetic and the explanatory, I would thus propose a third mode, the mode of parapraxis. It is important to note that the parapraxis mode, for that matter, is located neither in-between nor in clear distance to both the poetic and the explanatory modes but rather crosses the two in accidental and uncontrollable ways.

Pam Cook's video essay *Timeless* on Wong Kar-wai's *In the Mood for Love* may serve as an example for that. Looking forward to using the beautiful imagery of the film for her argument, Cook soon felt frustrated by the poor quality of the digital clips she had to use. However, as she relates in the accompanying text to her essay (and as the essay itself proves), she eventually saw in those very degradations of the digital images a potential: "My sense of loss provoked me to reflect on the affective resonance of image deterioration and its potential as a conduit for memory and nostalgia. . . . the aesthetic of imperfection draws attention to videography's micro-scale, cut-and-paste mode of production and situates it outside, sometimes in opposition to, mainstream digital output and the aspiration to hyperrealism" (Cook 2014).

In the lack *of* and *in* those images Cook accidentally but much more profoundly encountered the "lag" of time and memory, which is central not only to Wong Kar-wai's film but also to the engagement with this film and to the videographer's practice per se.

Something similar could be said about the highly compressed, stuttering, and jerking clips from Allan Dwan's *Heidi* in Catherine Grant's video essay *Mechanised Flights* as they undercut our enjoyment of the children's classic and its star Shirley Temple but instead force us into acknowledging the disturbing ambiguities that were always already present within the film but which also arose from the film's digital afterlife, as well as from our own troubled and changing relationship to said film.

To me, one of the most striking examples of such a parapractical video essay which *thinks with* the accidental coincidences of digital technology is still B. Kite's and Alexander Points-Zollo's three-part *Vertigo Variations*. Abstaining (at least for the most part) from the film's imagery, so fetishized by cinephiles, this video essay shows instead a *Vertigo* as one has never experienced it before: blurred, fractured, pixelated, and disappearing in clouds of digital noise with an unstable soundtrack (Figure 7.2). But in these abrasive, jarringly poor sounds and images, produced by a parapractical use of digital tools, an incredible richness of new encounters can be found. A supposedly all-too-familiar film alongside an assumed all-too-functional technology becomes a new site, a para-site of thinking with film. One could yet bemoan that such an experimental approach still feels obliged to revisit such an over-fetishized film and is thus still holding to classical

Figure 7.2 *Vertigo Variations, pt. 3*, Directed by B. Kite and Alexander Points-Zollo © Moving Image, 2011. All rights reserved.

auteurism, instead of looking at a far-less appreciated and noncanonized film like *Peyton Place*. Furthermore and perhaps more fundamentally, one can criticize that most digital distortions in the *Vertigo Variations* are of course no longer merely accidental but must be controlled in order to result into an actual video essay. Defects are eventually turned into effects and thus domesticated. Accidental artifact quickly becomes commodity (cf. Menkman 2011: 46–58).

This predicament, however, is the predicament of a parapractial aesthetics per se: Parapraxis cannot become a method to be taught and followed, but is far more a question of attitude. It means to be open to the occurrence, to be willing to work *with* instead of needing to prevent the accident. Parapraxis will thus also never become a tendency within the genre of the video essay, due to tendencies by definition being about foreseeable developments. In parapraxis, we all must remain, by necessity, amateurs, mere practitioners instead of professionals—with our minds kept off of things by the work itself, in constant lag of knowledge.

Notes

1. Regarding terminology, Cristina Álvarez López and Adrian Martin have suggested that "audiovisual essay" is to be preferred over "video essay" because, firstly, the former acknowledges the decisive role of sound and, secondly, because video is an anachronistic format (2014). I would nonetheless hold on to term "video," because of the digital format's close relation to electronic video signal, particularly to its aspects of instability, processuality, and reflexivity as discussed by Yvonne Spielmann (2008). Furthermore, I like that it suggests a connection between contemporary video essay practice and the radical investigations in the visual by video artists such as Shigeko Kubota, Dara Birnbaum, or Steina and Woody Vasulka.
2. In contrast to that, Barbara Klinger in her research on the "aftermarket" of cinema convincingly argued that the different (transmedial) reissues of a film (including pan-and-

scan TV versions or VHS-tapes) must be read not as mutilations but as legitimate texts which foreground an "inherent changeability of the film body" per se (2013: 27).

References

All That Heaven Allows (1955), [Film] Dir. Douglas Sirk, USA: Universal Pictures.
Álvarez López, C. and A. Martin (2014), "Introduction to the Audiovisual Essay: A Child of Two Mothers," *Necsus: European Journal of Media Studies*, Autumn 2014. Available online: http://www.necsus-ejms.org/introduction- audiovisual-essay-child-two-mothers/ (accessed March 30, 2019).
Álvarez López, C. and A. Martin (2017), "Writing in Images and Sounds," *Sidney Review of Books*, February 2017. Available online: https://sydneyreviewofbooks.com/writing-in-images-and-sounds/ (accessed March 30, 2019).
Baptista, T. (2016), "Lessons in Looking: The Digital Audiovisual Essay," PhD Thesis, Film and Screen Media, Birkbeck, University of London.
Bellour, R. (2000), *The Analysis of Film*, ed. C. Penley, Bloomington, IN: Indiana University Press.
Benjamin, W. (1999), *The Arcades Project*, ed. R. Tiedmann, trans. H. Eiland and K. McLaughlin, Cambridge, MA and London: Harvard University Press.
Binotto, J. (2016), "Continuing Peyton Place: Das Melodrama und seine Bastarde," in I. Ritzer and P. W. Schulze (eds.), *Transmediale Genre-Passagen. Interdisziplinäre Perspektiven*, 269–88, Wiesbaden: Springer.
Binotto, J. (2018), "Übertragungsstörungen. Pschoanalyse als Tontechnik," *Journal für Psychoanalyse*, (59): 88–111.
Cavell, S. (1979), *The World Viewed. Reflections on the Ontology of Film*, enlarged edn, Cambridge, MA: Harvard University Press.
Cook, P. (2014), "Dancing with Pixels. Digital Artefacts, Memory and the Beauty of Loss," *The Cine-Files*, (7). Available online: http://www.thecine-files.com/cook/ (accessed March 30, 2019).
Doane, M. A. (2007), "Imaging Contigency: An Interview with Mary Ann Doane," *Parallax*, (45): 16–25.
Grant, C. (2012), "Film and Moving Image Studies: Re-Born Digital? Some Participant Observations," *Frames Cinema Journal*, (1). Available online: http://framescinemajournal.com/article/re-born-digital/ (accessed March 30, 2019).
Grizzaffi, C. (2017), *I film attraverso i film. Dal "testo introvabile" ai video essay*, Milano: Mimesis Edizionio.
Guattari, F. (1984), *Molecular Revolution: Psychiatry and Politics*, London: Penguin.
Heidi (1937), [Film] Dir. Allan Dwan, USA: 20th Century Fox.
Herzogenrath, B., (ed.) (2018), *The Films of Bill Morrison. Aesthetics of the Archive*, Amsterdam: Amsterdam University Press.
In the Mood for Love (2000), [Film] Dir. Wong Kar-Wai, HKG: Block 2 Pictures.
Keathley, C. (2011), "La caméra-stylo: Notes on Video Criticism and Cinephilia, " in A. Clayton and A. Klevan (eds.), *The Language and Style of Film Criticism*, 176–91, London, New York: Routledge.
Kittler, F. (1999), *Gramophone, Film, Typewriter*, trans. G. Winthrop-Young and M. Wutz, Stanford: Stanford University Press.
Klinger, B. (2013), "Cinema and Immortality: Hollywood Classics in an Intermediated World," *SPELL Cultures in Conflict / Conflicting Cultures*, (29): 17–29.
Lacan, J. (2002), *Écrits. The First Complete Edition in English*, trans. B. Fink, New York and London: Norton.

Lee, K. B. (2017), "The Cinematic Power of the Individual. Video-Interview with Kevin B. Lee", *filmexplorer* (Oktober). Available online: https://www.filmexplorer.ch/forum/room-for-discussion-digital-criticism-of-moving-images/the-cinematic-power-of-the-individual-kevin-b-lee/ (accessed March 30, 2019).

McCarthy, T. (2014), *Recessional – or, The Time of the Hammer*, Berlin and Zurich: Diaphanes.

Mechanised Flights: Memories of HEIDI (2014), [Video Essay] Dir. Catherine Grant, UK. https://vimeo.com/86428511 (accessed May 21, 2019).

Menkman, R. (2011), *The Glitch Moment(um)*, Amsterdam: Network Notebooks.

Miller, D. H. (2016), *Hidden Hitchcock*, Chicago and London: Chicago University Press.

Mulvey, L. (2006), *Death 24x a Second: Stillness and the Moving Image*, London: Reaktion Books.

Nietzsche, F. (2003), *Schreibmaschinentexte. Vollständige Edition*. ed. Stephan Günzel and Rüdiger Schmidt-Grépály, Weimar: Bauhaus Universität.

Pantenburg, V. (2019), "Videographic Film Studies," in M. Hagener and V. Pantenburg (eds.), *Handbuch Filmanalyse*, Wiesbaden: Springer.

Peyton Place (1957), [Film] Dir. Mark Robson, USA: 20th Century Fox.

Serres, M. (1982), *The Parasite*, trans. L. R. Schehr, Baltimore and London: John Hopkins University Press.

Spielmann, Y. (2008), *Video: The Reflexive Medium*, Cambridge, MA: MIT Press.

Steyerl, H. (2009), "In Defense of the Poor Image," *e-flux Journal* (10). Available online: https://www.e-flux.com/journal/10/61362/in-defense-of-the-poor-image/ (accessed March 30, 2019).

Timeless (2014), [Video Essay] Dir. Pam Cook, UK. https://vimeo.com/108562747 (accessed May 21, 2019).

Vertigo (1958), [Film] Dir. Alfred Hitchcock, USA: Paramount Pictures.

Vertigo Variations, pt.1–3 (2011) Dir. B. Kite and Alexander Points-Zollo, USA. http://www.movingimagesource.us/articles/vertigo-variations-pt-1-20110921 (accessed May 21, 2019).

CHAPTER 7
THINKING WITH FILM IMAGES IN DAWSON CITY: FROZEN TIME
Bill Morrison

A central hypothesis to my work is that Film is—quite literally—Social Memory. When we lose filmic record, we lose the memory that these things occurred.

An enormous amount of film was shot throughout the twentieth century. We are destined to lose most of it, and it will be quickly forgotten.

There was a story that was often repeated in archival film circles at the end of the 1970s and throughout the 1980s. It was about a collection of old films that had been discovered by a construction crew in the Yukon in 1978. The films had been in a buried in a defunct swimming pool and yet were still intact, having been preserved in the permafrost for forty-nine years.

When I first heard of this story as an art student in the late 1980s, it was a story that was in "circulation" among people interested in film. Now, thirty years later, I have found that no one younger than me had ever heard of this story, and most of the people who had heard it are older film people, with some connection to archival film or to Dawson City. Sam Kula, head of the audiovisual division of the National Archives of Canada, wrote an article about the discovery.[1] But there was no book or movie about the collection, and a collective amnesia was taking the story away from us. Some years later, I set out to make *Dawson City: Frozen Time*, a film that would endeavor to tell the story of this collection. While working on the film, I overheard an archivist telling a news team about the collection of films that had been discovered under a bowling alley in Alaska. Time was already eroding the story, even among those of us who did remember it.

Hundreds of film reels had been buried in this swimming pool as landfill in 1929. Yet no sooner were they buried, they were forgotten. A newspaper account from 1938 reports that "it appears that the former swimming tank had been used in the distant past as a depository for discarded movie film."[2] At that time, the films had only been buried ten years. They had begun to leech out of the ice after a fire had destroyed the recreation center that sat above them. Some of the films found their way up through the frozen tundra, and would push through the ice that covered it as an improved skating rink. There the children who knew what it was would light it on fire and they would burn like roman candles on the frozen surface, instantly vanishing in a violent plume of flame and noxious fumes. The older children would pass the knowledge of this ignitable trick on to the younger children, who in turn would pass it on to others, until the films stopped surfacing.

Practical Aesthetics

Figure 8.1 Film Find B-W photo 023. Courtesy Kathy Jones Gates.

Figure 8.2 Dorothy Davenport in *Barriers Of Society* (Universal, 1916).

As the physical embodiments of social memory, film has the power to resurface, where it may be remembered, reexamined, and recontextualized. When the films were first screened in Dawson in the 1910s and 1920s, they were already several years out of date, due to the circuitous distribution what would eventually bring them to a remote outpost. Storing the flammable nitrate prints was seen as a potential safety hazard in a town already susceptible to fires. By 1929, the sound projection equipment rendered silent films irrelevant worldwide. While it would be several more years before "talkies" reached Dawson, the films that were disposed of in 1929 were quickly forgotten.

Unlike almost any other archaeological discovery, the Dawson City Film Find is blessed with a first-person account by the man who actually buried the films in the swimming pool. CBC Bank manager's Clifford Thomson's letter to the Klondike Korner of August 15, 1978, outlines what happened to the films once they reached Dawson and how they came to be buried in the swimming pool. In part, this became my script,

Thinking with Film Images in Dawson City

Figure 8.3 DAAA Swimming pool—photo credit: Dawson City Museum.

Figure 8.4 *The Christmas Accident* (Edison, 1912).

as I set out to tell the story of how these films came to be buried and rediscovered in Dawson City. As I delved into the collection, this history expanded to include the origin of Cinema, the Gold Rush, and the rapid rise and long decline of Dawson throughout the twentieth century.

I quickly saw this peculiar tale as a synopsis of the American Experience in fast forward: the displacement of the indigenous people carried out on the dream of the individual striking it rich on his own, which gave way to the corporatization and mechanized harvesting of resources, and the exploitation of the workers and destruction of the environment, which eventually killed the town off, all within a couple generations. Which is why the inclusion of the Trump story is not only timely, but incredibly

Practical Aesthetics

Figure 8.5 *Brutality*, directed by D. W. Griffith (Biograph, 1912).

Figure 8.6 Clifford Thomson, courtesy of the Dawson City Museum.

compelling. It was on the dreams of the Gold Rush stampeders that the current US corporate autocracy was built.

One thing I was struck by was how the early news films championed the worker and those who fought corporate greed. Anarchists and labor leaders were profiled as fearless warriors, especially in the Pathé News. I was shocked to find actual footage shot during

Thinking with Film Images in Dawson City

Figure 8.7 Frederick Trump's Arctic Restaurant, Whitehorse, YT.

Figure 8.8 Pathé Weekly, No. 65, 1914.

the Colorado Coalfield War of 1913–14, leading up to the Ludlow Massacre of 1914 (Pathé Weekly 65, 1913). (The footage, shot while under attack by the Colorado National Guard, was cranked out by a daring young cameraman, Victor Milner, who, twenty

Figure 8.9 Alexander Berkman, Pathé's Weekly No. 32, 1914.

Figure 8.10 Film Was Born Of An Explosive.

years later, would win the Academy Award for Cinematography for Cecil B. DeMille's *Cleopatra* in 1934).

In another Pathé reel, I found the anarchist Alexander Berkman, who had already served jail time for attempting to assassinate the industrialist Henry Clay Frick in 1892, heroically exhorting a crowd of Wobblies outside of John D. Rockefeller office in Union Square, New York, to rise up in solidarity with the striking coal miners (Pathé Weekly 32, 1914). But in another reel, five years later, Berkman and his partner Emma Goldman are shown being deported to Russia (International News, Vol. 1, Issue 52, 1919). While his face is recognizable, his name is not mentioned, and this story was not listed in the database describing the films.

Thinking with Film Images in Dawson City

Figure 8.11 *The Butler and the Maid* (Edison, 1912).

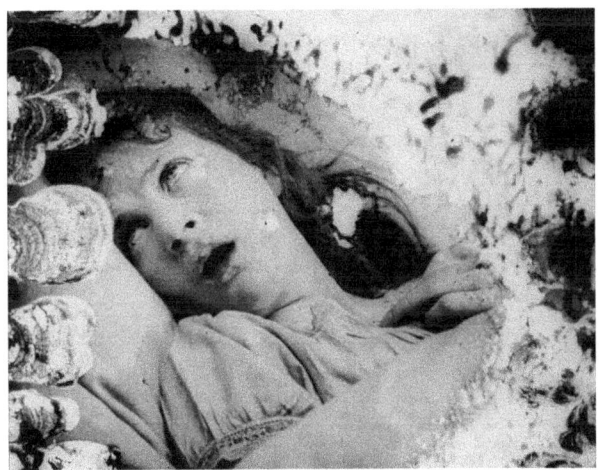

Figure 8.12 Mae Marsh in *Polly of the Circus* (Goldwyn, 1917) 01.

Cinema is Capitalism, which brings with it, on a razor's edge, both Dreams and Death. This is, in a nutshell, what the film is about. There is a line near the beginning of the film: "Film was born of an explosive." It speaks to the actual military origins of nitrate film. Military might is both the manifestation of Capitalism and the cogs that keep it running—a self-consuming death machine. Cinema is the entertainment division of that empire, colonizing capitalistic society the world over, which is central to this story in particular. Silver (nitrate) follows gold to the far corners of the earth, wherever it may be found. In Dawson, silver was literally buried in the same earth from which the gold was pulled—once the gold was gone, the silver died. I think it is why the story has resonance beyond simply being a story about lost films found. It is a story of the twentieth century

Practical Aesthetics

Figure 8.13 *Birth of Flowers* (Pathé, 1920) 02.

Figure 8.14 Florence Fleming Noyes dances in support of the suffragist movement (Pathé Freres, 1914).

and the forces that were at play in shaping the world we live in today, and that were starkly played out in black and white in Dawson City. It is Western expansionism and the rise and fall of Capitalism as seen through the movies.

The trash heap entombed by the Yukon permafrost turned out to be a singular long-term storage solution. The films buried there outlasted virtually every other copy stored elsewhere. And they were marked in a unique way, owing to their singular history. Either during the numerous Spring thaws they experienced or during the warm Summer of 1978 when they were suddenly exhumed from their cold storage vault, many of the reels suffered a distinct water damage. The undulating white waves we see washing the side of the frame is unique to the Dawson collection and is sometimes derisively referred to as "The Dawson Flutter" by film archivists.

In the finale of *Dawson City: Frozen Time*, I included several passages where the characters seem to interact with this patina, to regard the veil that encroaches into their frame with either horror or delight. The images that are marked in this way align with the notion of "practical aesthetics." The history of this collection and the many histories it contains—become the context for this encounter—and the images' apparent "reaction" to the formal condition of the frame creates our correspondence to those histories, in how they have reached us.

Ultimately, I feel the film speaks to the ephemeral nature of our cultural and personal memories. So much of our film history has been lost and will continue to be lost. That is the nature of film. By using these old, rare films, I am not just referencing what was photographed in the frame, but also the very reels themselves that were carried through time against all odds to reach us at the moment of projection. Thinking with these images, we are reminded of everything we may have forgotten, lost, or never have known to begin with.

Notes

1. "Up From The Permafrost: The Dawson City Collection," This Film is Dangerous: A Celebration of Nitrate Film, ed. R. Smither, Associate editor C. A. Surowiec, FIAF (Fédération Internationale des Archives du Film), London: United Kingdom, 2002.
2. Dawson Daily News, October 1, 1938.

CHAPTER 8
LAPSES, AFFECTS, SUPPLEMENT
HIRO MURAI'S AUDIOVISUAL ANACHRONISM
Tomáš Jirsa

Even though this chapter strives to think with moving images, sounds, and lyrics, at the very outset it is important to point out a constitutive paradox that underlies such an endeavor: Music videos dissolve their respective boundaries, obfuscating the point at which one medium ends and the other begins, thus merging its components into one hybrid audiovisual movement.[1] To think *with* music videos thus necessarily implies thinking *without* music *and* video, or, more precisely, in the absence of their alleged substantiality. This effectively means rejecting both moving images and sounds as already established, while moving away from their addition and, consequently, the imperatives of genre. Thinking with the music video calls for repetition—despite the risks of failures, lapses, and breakdowns this act involves—of its theoretical movement; in other words, instead of its main parts harmonically interconnecting, they *short-circuit*. And since the theoretical *praxis* of the music video operates in the short-circuiting way—for "[i]s not the shock of short-circuiting, therefore, one of the best metaphors for a critical reading?" (Žižek 2006: ix)—this chapter attempts to carry on the practical aesthetics by reading the music video precisely via and through its own short circuits. In order to follow the premise of this volume, which invites to think with art, images, and sounds, let us paradoxically begin by thinking at once with and without them. This involves considering music videos as forms just taking shape, hybrid configurations in motion and at work that is both aesthetically and epistemically generative. As a form of thinking driven by the interaction of sounds and moving images, the music video stands for their mutual and radical transformation.

But, first of all, how does a music video think? Not so much by what its images represent or its sounds express, but rather through its audiovisual gestures, performative mechanisms, and affective work of forms. Taking their theoretical force seriously, Steven Shaviro claims that music videos are "*machines for generating affect*" (2010: 3; emphasis in the original). This kind of affect, however, is not to be confused with an abstract placeholder for emotional or bodily intensity, since *affects*, as Eugenie Brinkema (2014) argues, are always plural, have distinct forms, and do far more than simply move with a subjective interiority. The music video *Day Ones* directed by Hiro Murai (2016), whose theoretical inflections this chapter attends to, is at once obsolete in its historical theme and contemporary in the affects of anger and violence to which it gives shape and makes them operational.[2] While probing the ways a music video thinks with—and therefore performs its own unsettling account of—history, the practical strategy of the present pursuit is to

Practical Aesthetics

think *with* the music video's thinking, in an attempt to imitate the conceptual operations which its aesthetic forms open up and develop. By showing that to think with something actually means to deconstruct it, to displace its hidden assumptions, and to read it in a short-circuiting way, Murai's video commits a double betrayal of history and structure. In so doing, it uncovers three overlapping paradoxes that critical language may articulate as questions: those of temporality, representation, and structure. These questions, however, are not propositional—they are not uttered or represented but performed and unfolded through the work of forms and affects. To keep up with their pace and to draw some consequences for the music video thinking, such is the aim of the following lines.

Rococo in the Hood: Anachronism

The American Revolutionary War did not finish on the battlefields in 1783; it's happening right now, somewhere on the nocturnal periphery of a deserted suburban parking lot. Thus goes the basic plot of the music video *Day Ones* directed by Hiro Murai, a filmmaker and video director who recently shot to fame for his subversive, gun violence-commenting video *This is America* (2018), starring the rapper Childish Gambino in a murderous Jim Crow–like dance. While Murai's previous productions typically generate a melancholic atmosphere with performers roaming through shady suburbs, especially his videos for the rapper Earl Sweatshirt and trip-hop group Massive Attack, in the case of his video *Day Ones*—a song from the album *Aa* (2016) by the trap and bass music producer Baauer—his preferred aesthetics of protagonists on the gloomy peripheries is played out to the backdrop of an anachronistic historical fresco. Accompanied by the dark escalating beats and aggressive rhymes of rapper Leikeli47 and grime MC Novelist, which are larded with allusions to street gang fights, drugs, and the harsh reality of life in the hood, a night battle between armed soldiers in tricorns and historical uniforms rages in a forsaken supermarket parking lot. But what may initially seem like a hallucinatory bad trip is quickly transformed into a refined historical deconstruction.

The intro to the video reveals a barely lit nocturnal parking lot set against the distant barking of a dog. Amid the soundscape created by a rugged electrified bass emerge marching shadows, which are soon revealed to belong to soldiers of the Redcoat infantry. And while the uniforms of their two serried legions marching past Novelist (sitting on the hood of a car and nimbly rapping) unequivocally refer to the Revolutionary War, their apathetic facial expressions hint at the anonymous passage of dark history (Figure 9.1). The British and American troops line up to do battle, drumming and shooting each other with muskets. But as soon as the first bodies fall to the ground, Leikeli47 appears on the scene masked in a black balaclava, delivering lyrics in a staccato rhythm through gilded teeth.

The unfolding narrative and music is then abruptly interrupted by a surreal intermezzo. Amid the sonic backdrop of atmospheric sounds, distorted reverberations, and amplified shouts, two kids dressed in the remains of the dead soldiers' uniforms enter on a bike, gazing upward at a levitating crystal chandelier. The sudden jarring appearance of this

Lapses, Affects, Supplement

Figure 9.1 *Day Ones ft Novelist & Leikeli47*, Directed by Hiro Murai © Doomsday Entertainment 2016. Vimeo. Screenshot by the author.
See https://vimeo.com/155932635, 01:04 (accessed November 15, 2018).

antiquated object brings into focus Murai's anachronistic gaze, blending retrospective and anticipated views into a single transhistorical moment, a strategy further disclosed in the ensuing shootout between past and present (Figure 9.2). The restored uniforms constitute a proleptic figure, framing the historical narrative of the War of Independence in the context of struggles to come. In a further arrangement of the scene, Leikeli47 is reintroduced in front of a spacious Rococo sofa under the same crystal chandeliers; yet this time the battle continues right behind her back while she spits the angry verses in incessant progression. The overall effect is to present a single allegorical setting, which *anachronistically* interconnects and blends the hip-hop suburban reality of the twenty-first century with an eighteenth-century war between Great Britain and its rebellious colonies.

The first question *Day Ones* asks both spectacularly and confusingly has therefore to do with temporality: How to dismantle the temporal succession without being ahistorical or, worse, naïvely anti-historical? The question points to an unsettling relationship between the obscure past, the insistent present, and the dark future, between the chronological order and the nonlinear historical leaps. Murai's transhistorical—one might even say "preposterous" (Bal 2001)—audiovisual gestures belong to the same conceptual repertoire that Georges Didi-Huberman has dubbed *anachronistic thinking*, which refuses the logic of causality, chronology, and representation as prerequisites for understanding both general history and the history of images. In his *plaidoyer* for anachronism, he explains this modality as a "temporal way of expressing the exuberance, complexity, and overdetermination of images" (Didi-Huberman 2003a: 37). Drawing on Aby Warburg's notion of *Nachleben*—a complex term denoting the *survival*: continual metamorphosis or afterlife of images and motifs throughout history (2003b: 273)—Didi-Huberman suggests, and so does *Day Ones*, that images resist the chronological order due to an atemporal resonance and intensity enacted by the symptomatic interplay of

Figure 9.2 *Day Ones ft Novelist & Leikeli47*, Directed by Hiro Murai © Doomsday Entertainment 2016. Vimeo. Screenshot by the author.
See https://vimeo.com/155932635, 02:14 (accessed November 15, 2018).

continuities and discontinuities through which past and present become entangled in one another (2002: 55). In this light, any image stands for a peculiar constellation of temporal crossings: "an object of complex, impure temporality: an *extraordinary montage of heterogeneous times forming anachronisms*" (Didi-Huberman 2003a: 38; emphasis in the original).

Since the problem of anachronism is at the crux of the "folding between time and history," the following question it poses reaches far beyond its original art-historical context: "Is it not, then, to the historical discipline itself that one must ask what it wants to do with this folding: to conceal the anachronism which emerges from it, and thereby mutely crush the time under the history—or open the fold and let the paradox germinate?" (Didi-Huberman 2002: 25; my translation). Through, against, and with this germinating and carefully arranged paradox, Murai's video opens up an avenue for the *anachronistic audiovisual thinking*, one that recasts the past through contemporary images and music while reshaping the present through the images of the past. Anachronism here becomes a generative deconstruction of all strict temporal partitions, keeping historical demarcations apart only to expose their permanent entanglement as they overlap and collapse.

With the concrete ground of the parking lot providing an incongruous setting for the enactment of the clichéd textbook bravery of the Patriots, who clumsily goose-step into battle before meeting their fates, any conceivable pathos one might attach to the historical legacy of the "Founding Fathers" is immediately deflated. However, this ironic recontextualization, which turns the glorious battle for the national self-determination into an awkward scuffle, is not ethically designed to highlight the evil, bestiality, or absurdity of war, but rather to stage—and thus enact the *survival* of—a universal cultural pattern of discord between different national, cultural, and ethnic groups, a pattern that pertains as much to the street gang wars as it does to an age-old conflict between colonialists and freedom fighters. And this is where the lyrics confirm the cannily anachronistic strategy: with verses abounding in allusions to the north-London criminal gang Tottenham Mandem and to the specific slang code of the Crips from south Los Angeles, the allegorical mise-en-scène contextualizes current conflicts, while at the same time actualizing the remote past. Instead of the classical mimetic gunfight between feuding gangs or the typical hip-hop depiction of murdered performers, the contemporary conflict is rendered obsolete through a procession of smoking muskets.

One of these musket gunshots in fact initiates the key moment of the video: Fired *within* but also *from* a war scene stylized in eighteenth-century props, a bullet smashes the rear window of a parked car, followed by a further rally of shots that successively crack the nearby storefront windows. Not only do the shots fired produce a temporal *lapse*—in both its meanings of a failure and a passage of time—suddenly blurring the gradually dissipating yet tenable distinctions between the realms of contemporary violence and historical conflict, they also trigger a powerful audiovisual moment, pitting the curated clamor of war against the contemporary voice of hip-hop subculture to encapsulate the anachronistic "montage of heterogeneous times." Having been effectively fired from one historical period into another, the gunshot is framed by a chilling short scene of blood—of the present or the past?—spilling down a traffic sign. As the video draws to a close, we find the living and the dead have disappeared; and yet through the abandoned parking lot shrouded in fading smoke, a lone Redcoat hobbles among the scattered hats of the fallen—as if to reassert that the events just witnessed, far from being a ludicrous hallucination, have in fact taken place "for real." Yet how is this reality shaped and through which forms is it conceived? That is the second cluster of questions *Day Ones* asks.

The Unreality Effect: Rhythms, Lapses, Anger

From beginning to end, supported by wobbling sounds, a thundering bass, and electronic beats, Murai's video highlights its artificiality, replacing the worn-out postmodern cliché "anything goes" with the postdigital "everything blows." As Steven Shaviro recently noted, contemporary music videos tend to collapse the distinction between diegetic and nondiegetic elements (2017: 32), so it comes as no surprise that *Day Ones* proudly draws attention to its own production, whether through the props of war, the pseudo-Rococo furniture, or the deliberately staged technical equipment such as the self-disclosing reflector that illuminates the parking lot. Instead of simply resorting to the Barthesian "reality effect"—produced by realist, seemingly redundant or narratively useless details whose aim is not to denote specific real contents but to connote "the category of the real" and thereby create a "referential illusion" (Barthes 1989: 148)—the video consistently reshapes this effect while undermining the very notion of representation. The formal affordances of Murai's video switch from the aesthetic model of the reality effect, whose main function is to evoke a realistic impression that "this really happened," to what I propose to call the *unreality effect*, or, to be more faithful to the original phrase—*l'effet de réel*—the "effect of the unreal." Far from merely negating the depiction of a historical event, the force of this effect is grounded in an operation that shifts from decontextualizing to *restaging*.

Enabled by the principle of anachronism, the unreality effect is stretched in two directions: recasting the present through its collision with the past, it makes this past both obsolete and contemporary; yet it does so in a tricky way. While the reality effect draws on details that connote reality in order to invoke a given historical moment or a particular "period" atmosphere, the unreality effect, which builds on a historical likeness at once highlighted and downplayed by the video mise-en-scène, fully fledges its own artificial illusiveness to produce a kind of referential anti-illusion. Take, for instance, the ironically twisted credibility of the museum-like uniforms: the spotless white pants, long blue jackets, black boots, and leggings—as historians remind us, such stereotyped representation is in no way an accurate depiction of the real state of affairs during the Revolutionary War and more "a far-fetched fantasy" (Lanning 2000: 173). In fact, the unreality effect uses such evocations only to exhaust and empty their historical core in favor of actualizing and unfolding their contemporary affective potential. In other words, the stiff eighteenth-century uniforms disappear yet the blood and anger remain on the parking lot.

In order to understand this logic, whose performative mechanisms are perhaps less "affectively oriented," as Erin Manning and Brian Massumi argue (2014: 106), but rather affectively *driven*, one should take a closer look at their formal activity. If the music video theorizes and critically engages with historical temporality, it needs to be noted that this speculative drive would quickly run dry without the work of what Brinkema calls the *formal affect*, which operates at the level of form, structure, and composition. This kind of affect is not about an emotional interiority of the classical subject, nor is it a matter of expression or of the spectator's bodily sensation, but rather affect as a "self-folding exteriority that manifests in, as, and with textual form" (2014: 25) is the force that operates within aesthetic matter, gives agency to forms, and shapes their thought.

From the outset, the video covers the whole scenery in a nocturnal murk. The dark images, which obscure visibility in favor of enhancing visuality and aurality, amplify the sinister beats as if to insinuate that despite refusing to see the bleak narrative of history, nothing can prevent its scream being heard. Structured by sudden cuts—here and there mischievously alluding to the genre of war reportage, with its emphasis on witnessing in real time—the darkness *gives rhythm* to the battle, creating a stifling soundscape and audiovisual atmosphere.[3] At the same time, this darkness is, from the intro onward, disrupted by the bright flashes and flickerings of the street lights and spotlights that frequently dazzle our view. The broken, blinking street lamp, which foreshadows the flashes of the reflectors at the end, is in fact anything but an innocent lighting effect: by making the flickering a framing device, the video imposes a spatiotemporal *short circuit* on its reading.

These dazzling effects are further elaborated through the camera movement and deviated angles that give rise to a perspective of anger, expanding on its etymological root, the Latin *angere*, meaning to strangle, to choke, to oppress. The quick close-ups of the blood-splashed sign and the cracked back window are never shot frontally—the same holds true for the frequent views of soldiers from behind and from the side—indicating that history usually comes unexpectedly and violently "from the reserves," as if demanding to be looked at askew. More importantly, the perspective of anger escalates with the merging of two scenes into a single shot—Leikeli47 rapping over the gun barrels and the inverse view of the soldiers behind her standing figure—the effect of which is to create a sort of dissolve without the usual temporal transit. But by no means does the shot blend the different temporalities harmoniously; rather, it creates a mutual "obstruction"—so that instead of sticking, it hinders, while still able, as Nick Salvato speculates (2016), to sustain generative thinking. The perspective of anger is fully fledged in particular *lapses* within the mise-en-scène, which appear not as unwanted errors, but as operations that place subjects and objects into "unreal" and anachronistic constellations. In the last third of the video, dirt and paving stones appear flung around the sofa (Figure 9.3). Referring, in a double irony, at once to the revolutionary slogan of the Paris protests of May 1968—"Under the cobblestones, the beach"—and to their obsoleteness as props, the objects almost seem to be relics of some archaeological excavation; in the next shot of the sofa, quite surprisingly, the paving stones have disappeared. How better, then, to imitate lapses in a historical scenario than by committing them in one's own script?

It would be reductive to understand the grounding of a lapse within an audiovisual composition uniquely in relation to moving images. Its essential counterpart lies in the irregular rhythms that peak and collapse, the creaking, ferocious voices often deviating from the tempo, and the contrast between the bursting chorus—"Still riding with your day ones? Let me hear you scream / You wish a nigga would, huh? Let me hear you scream"—and the monotonously sluggish, melodic bass line. As confirmed by Baauer in an interview, the lapse does not simply occur as a mere omission or serendipity; it is an elaborate strategy that integrates failure into the very structure of the music: "But more so than anything I discovered, what makes a sound special to me is its imperfections, its peculiarities. I spent the last couple years trying to get all of those imperfections into one record, and I think finally it makes sense" (Hughes 2017). Not only does Baauer's tactic make sense, it also forms the perfect complement to Murai's anachronistic "historicizing with a hammer."

This *strategy of failure*, made possible by the work of formal affects, does not articulate the music video solely as an aesthetic object, let alone a mere promotional product of the music industry but rather as a "theoretical object," which, according to Hubert Damisch, generates thinking in that it "obliges you to do theory but also furnishes you with the means of doing it" (1998: 8). This kind of theoretical production reaches its peak with a series of jerky close-ups and zoom-in shots of the soldier's white faces, driven by the verses: "To everybody locked up, I love y'all niggas / I'm the black elephant in the room / Don't swat flies, I go tick boom, boom / I, zoom zoom." Leveled by its explicit racial

Figure 9.3 *Day Ones ft Novelist & Leikeli47*, Directed by Hiro Murai © Doomsday Entertainment 2016. Vimeo. Screenshot by the author.
See https://vimeo.com/155932635, 02:49 (accessed November 15, 2018).

attribute, the literality of the idiom is extended further by the zooming motion of the camera, materializing the lyrics. In so doing, the video *performs* and *does*—rather than illustrates—not only what it shows and "plays" but also what it says.[4] Exceeding the music video's traditional fast editing, this aggressive zooming imitates the affective perspective of anger to enhance the strangling atmosphere of the sounds and images. The violent camera movements and scenes of blood splashing from the soldiers' heads combine to create a peculiarly claustrophobic mise-en-scène, with the mise en abyme gunshots perforating both the visual and aural spaces. As a result, the distinction between the scattered rhythms of the music and the disrupted dark images is dissolved to the point that the boundaries of the visual and the musical ultimately blur.

Toward the Audiovisual Supplement

The third question posed by the work of formal affects relates to the structure and, consequently, to the genre: Can music video think about its "preexisting" musicality and "added" visuality in a less arithmetic relation?[5] To flesh out the question further, let us take on the same movement Murai's video plays out, the constant back-and-forth switching between anachronism and irony. In *Day Ones*, history is reenacted in a twenty-first-century suburban parking lot and undermined by lapses and pseudo-historical details before arriving at a point where it makes sense only through temporal paradoxes. In its ironic and self-subverting references to the past conflict, the video thinks with history in terms of failure, offering its own take on a recent theoretical inquiry, which emphasizes, albeit in a different context, the fertility of disconnection and disassembly, and subscribes to the theorem that "failure is key" (Graham and Thrift 2007: 7). The anachronistic strategy of *Day Ones* posits that the audiovisual thinking music videos engage in is paradoxically most fruitful when it works with and operates through a *short circuit*.

If one of the most effective critical procedures, as Slavoj Žižek notes, is "to cross the wires that do not usually touch," and if reading in a short-circuiting way concerns the "inherent decentering of the interpreted text, which brings to light its 'unthought,' its disavowed presuppositions and consequences" (Žižek 2006: ix), then Murai's video makes this theoretical premise tangible. Not only does *Day Ones* uncover the contemporary affective force within the canonical past while reinterpreting contemporary violence in an anachronistic way, it also makes their mutual short-circuiting operate within their audiovisual forms. Undermining the representation of historical events through the contemporary affects, the way the music video thinks with history is grounded in a creative betrayal of the past—a *betrayal* that is always already incorporated into its audiovisual structure. In relation to the preexisting musical piece, this structure gains the role of both the additional complement *and* substitute: it accompanies the music while, at the same time, it replaces it.

This connection between moving images and sound in the music video thus invokes a relation that Jacques Derrida dubbed the *logic of supplementarity*. The supplement comprises two mutually opposed yet complementary meanings: as an addition it "adds itself, it is a surplus, a plenitude enriching another plenitude," yet it also functions as a substitute of something which is missing and fills a void: "It adds only to replace . . . it is not simply added to the positivity of a presence, it produces no relief, its place is assigned in the structure by the mark of an emptiness" (Derrida 1997: 144–5). To propose that the music video is an *audiovisual supplement* is not to claim that it ex post complements a musical object or replaces it through a sheer visual spectacle. In contrast to the recent "music video turn" and its usual understanding of the genre as a visual accompaniment to a preexisting musical piece—and somewhat more closely to Korsgaard's notions of remediation and interaction whereby music videos operate by "recasting a preexisting song visually" while "structuring the image according to musical logic" (2013: 509)—I argue that through its double bind of addition and substitution, the music video enacts the visual potential of music and lyrics, and, in turn, *transforms* them.[6] What enables the anachronistic strategy of Murai's video, which is to splash the Revolutionary blood onto a suburban parking lot, is this supplementary structure.

While music videos "express and reflect on experiences that cannot even be envisioned through traditional modes of representation" (Shaviro 2017: 18), *Day Ones* advocates thinking with the anachronism of the living present. To take one step further the impulse offered by Shaviro, which can be rephrased as "thinking the music video's thinking," it seems useful to take this hardly representable and yet thinkable experience seriously. It is precisely this experience—of anachronism, transhistorical lapses, and hybrid temporality—that Murai's video triggers, while at the same time opening the historical event up to the contemporary affects. There is a possibility, then, that by performatively thinking with history, the music video ultimately rewrites it. To pursue that avenue, one might just consider thinking with the music video by thinking without it.

Practical Aesthetics

Notes

1 Work on this chapter was part of the research project "Between Affects and Technology: The Portrait in the Visual Arts, Literature and Music Video" (JG_2019_007), funded by Palacký University Olomouc.
2 For a different analysis of this video from the perspective of "affective reenactment," see Jirsa 2019.
3 For an insightful discussion of the the term *soundscape*, coined by R. Murray Schafer in 1977, see Breitsameter 2017: 51–6.
4 My argument here is inspired by Ernst van Alphen's reading of the performative aesthetics of Francis Bacon's paintings which "*do* what they are about" (2019: 169; emphasis in the original).
5 The most elaborate and up-to-date discussion of the music video genre is provided by Korsgaard 2017: 16–40.
6 Although indebted to much of the recent music video scholarship—mainly the one by Shaviro and Korsgaard—for the sake of brevity I can only mention here the works I find particularly illuminating: Arnold et al. 2017; Vernallis 2013; Jullier and Péquignot 2013; Beebe and Middleton 2007.

References

Alphen, E. v. (2019), "Reading for Affects: Francis Bacon and the Work of Sensation," in E. van Alphen and T. Jirsa (eds.), *How to Do Things with Affects: Affective Triggers in Aesthetic Forms and Cultural Practices*, 163–76, Leiden: Brill.
Arnold, G., D. Cookney, K. Fairclough, and M. Goddard (eds.) (2017), "Introduction: The Persistence of the Music Video Form from MTV to Twenty-First-Century Social Media," in *Music/Video: Histories, Aesthetics, Media*, 1–19, London and New York: Bloomsbury.
Bal, M. (2001), *Quoting Caravaggio: Contemporary Art, Preposterous History*, Chicago: Chicago University Press.
Barthes, R. ([1968] 1989), "The Reality Effect," in R. Barthes, *The Rustle of Language*, trans. R. Howard, 141–8, Berkeley and Los Angeles: University of California Press.
Beebe, R., and J. Middleton (2007), *Medium Cool: Music Videos from Soundies to Cellphones*, Durham: Duke University Press.
Bois, Y.-A., D. Hollier, R. Krauss, and H. Damisch (1998), "A Conversation with Hubert Damisch," *October* 85: 3–17.
Breitsameter, S. (2017), "Soundscape as a System and an Auditory Gestalt," in B. Herzogenrath (ed.), *Sonic Thinking: A Media Philosophical Approach*, 51–63, London and New York: Bloomsbury.
Brinkema, E. (2014), *The Forms of the Affects*, Durham: Duke University Press.
Derrida, J. ([1967] 1997), *Of Grammatology*, trans. G. Ch. Spivak, Baltimore and London: John Hopkins University Press.
Didi-Huberman, G. (2002), *L'image survivante: Histoire de l'art et temps des fantômes selon Aby Warburg*, Paris: Les Éditions de Minuit.
Didi-Huberman, G. (2003a), "Before the Image, Before Time: The Sovereignty of Anachronism," trans. P. Mason, in C. Farrago and R. Zwijneberg (eds.), *Compelling Visuality: The Work of Art In and Out of History*, 31–44, Minneapolis: University of Minnesota Press.

Didi-Huberman, G. (2003b), "Artistic Survival: Panofsky vs. Warburg and the Exorcism of Impure Time," trans. V. Rehberg and B. Belay, *Common Knowledge*, 9 (2): 273–85.

Graham, S., and N. Thrift (2007), "Out of Order: Understanding Repair and Maintenance," *Theory, Culture & Society*, 24 (3): 1–25.

Hughes, J. (2016), "Baauer Taps Pusha T, Future, M.I.A. for Debut Album," *Exclaim!*, January 28, 2016. Available online: http://exclaim.ca/music/article/baauer_taps_pusha_t_future_m_i_a_for_debut_album (accessed June 26, 2017).

Jirsa, Tomáš (2019). "For the Affective Aesthetics of Contemporary Music Video," special issue "The Music Video in Transformation," ed. T. Jirsa and M. B. Korsgaard, *Image, Sound, and the Moving Image*, 13 (2): 187–208.

Jullier, L. and J. Péquignot (2013), *Le Clip: Histoire et esthétique*, Paris: Armand Colin.

Korsgaard, M. B. (2013), "Music Video Transformed," in C. Gorbman, J. Richardson, and C. Vernallis (eds.), *The Oxford Handbook of New Audiovisual Aesthetics*, 501–21, New York: Oxford University Press.

Korsgaard, M. B. (2017), *Music Video after MTV: Audiovisual Studies, New Media, and Popular Music*, London: Routledge.

Lanning, M. L. (2000), *Defenders of Liberty: African Americans in the Revolutionary War*, New York: Kensington.

Manning, E., and B. Massumi (2014), *Thought in the Act: Passages in the Ecology of Experience*, Minneapolis: University of Minnesota Press.

Salvato, N. (2016), *Obstruction*, Durham: Duke University Press.

Shaviro, S. (2017), *Digital Music Videos*, New Brunswick: Rutgers University Press.

Shaviro, S. (2010), *Post-Cinematic Affect*, New York: Zero Books.

Vernallis, C. (2013), *Unruly Media: YouTube, Music Video, and the New Digital Cinema*, New York: Oxford University Press.

Žižek, S. (2006), *The Parallax View*, Cambridge, MA: The MIT Press.

CHAPTER 9
SOME NOTES ON SOUND THINKING
Bernd Herzogenrath

I would like to start with a set of resonances. First of all, a resonance on the word "resonance": on the one hand, it means something like "echo" or "reverberation"; on the other hand, the word "reason" is somehow hidden in "resonance." The French verb *résonner* makes this resonance even stronger—one might even be tempted to invent the word *re(a)sonance* here.

Thus, a kind of knowledge is involved here. A kind of thinking—maybe not what we would call rational thinking, but a kind of thinking nonetheless. As the Polish philosopher and mathematician Józef Hoëné-Wronski has it, as quoted by Edgar Varèse: "Music is the corporealization of the intelligence that is in sound" (Varèse 1966: 17). Music as the becoming-body of the knowledge of sound—sound thinking.

Again, also this knowledge that sound is, has a highly interesting resonance in its "wordhood" in French: *connaître*, knowledge as a process of "being-born-with"; this could mean that this knowledge, this thinking, this re(a)sonance, which is that sound is not a knowledge *about* the world, coming to you only in retrospective reflection, but a thinking *of* and *in* the world, a part of the world we live in, intervening in the world directly.

Friedrich Nietzsche, in his unpublished early notebooks, dating from the period of his *Unfashionable Observations* (1872–3), relates the true philosopher to the scientist and the artist as listener "The concept of the philosopher ... : he tries to let all the sounds of the world reverberate in him and to place this comprehensive sound outside himself into concepts" (2009: 115), whereas the artist lets the tones of the world resonate within him and projects them by means of percepts and affects. So, here, sound-art practice becomes research and philosophy, and vice versa.

Rainer Maria Rilke, in his 1919 essay, "Primal Sound" (*Urgeräusch* in the German original), described an experience he had as a young boy, when introduced to a phonograph for the first time, seeing how the needle produced sounds out of grooves in a wax-cylinder, grooves that the recording of actual sounds had put there in the first place. Years later, while attending anatomical lectures in Paris, Rilke connected the lines of coronal suture of the human skull to his childhood observations—"I knew at once what it reminded me of: one of those unforgotten grooves, which had been scratched in a little wax cylinder by the point of a bristle!" (2001: 22). From this incident, Rilke derives the following "experimental set-up": "The coronal suture of the skull (this would first have to be investigated) has—let us assume—a certain similarity to the closely wavy line which the needle of a phonograph engraves on the receiving, rotating cylinder of the apparatus. What if one changed the needle and directed it on its return journey along a tracing which was not derived from the graphic translation of a sound, but existed of itself naturally—well: to put it plainly, along the coronal suture, for example. What would happen?" (23). Rilke's obvious answer is, of course, noise, music—sound! Probing further, Rilke asks himself, "What variety of lines then, occurring anywhere, could one not put under the needle and try out? Is there any contour that one could not, in a sense, complete in this way and then experience it, as it makes itself felt, thus transformed, in another field of sense?" (23).

In a letter, Rilke specifies this idea. Writing to Dieter Bassermann, Rilke speculates on "set[ting] to sound the countless signatures of Creation which in the skeleton, in minerals . . . in a thousand places persist in their remarkable versions and variations. The grain in wood, the gait of an insect: our eye is practiced in following and ascertaining them. What a gift to our hearing were we to succeed in transmuting this zigzag . . . into auditory events!" (2007: 391–2).

The project "sound thinking" aims to serve two interconnected purposes: on the one hand, it wants to develop an alternative philosophy of music that takes music serious as a "form of thinking" (and that might revise our notion of what "thinking" means). On the other hand, it aims to bring this approach into a fertile symbiosis with the concepts and practices of "artistic research": art, philosophy, and science as heterogeneous yet coequal forms of thinking and researching (and let me point out that we are using the concept of "artistic research" not in the meaning of art being a handmaiden subordinate to [and evaluated by] parameters of the sciences [a highly debatable practice], but more as a mediaphilosophical praxeology—artists [in this case: sound artists] thinking with and through their medium [in this case: sound]).

The debate about the sphere of sound is presently fought with high intensity. The emerging field of research "Sound Studies" is primarily discussed in the humanities and social sciences—the "Acoustic Turn" is tackled with the means of cultural sciences and semiotics. These disciplines are however based on foundations that could not be more alien to music (or sound, noise—the "sonic field"). Deeply rooted in one of the major strands of Western philosophy, the concepts of cultural studies and especially semiotics are based on what Gilles Deleuze calls "image of thought," dependent on the metaphysics of being, representation, and identity. Accordingly, a (passive) nature, matter, and so on is "informed" extrinsically, a substance affects existence, the subject organizes (the objects of) experience, progress determines the course of history, and so on.

On the other hand, how Hans Jonas, among others, has demonstrated in his groundbreaking essay "The Nobility of Sight" (1954), these foundations of Western existential philosophy are in turn rooted in the ubiquity of a "visual regime": a hierarchy of senses was established, in which the eye almost inevitably was declared the origin and foundation of all philosophy—central categories like "(in)finity," "distance," "abstraction," and "objectivity" are indebted to the intrinsic sensory qualities of visual perception. Since the dusk of the nineteenth century, the consequences of this hierarchization of the senses (and the "supremacy" of the eye) are discussed with increasing intensity. In his treatise about the origin of tragedy, Friedrich Nietzsche tried to regain the "aural culture" of the old, pre-platonic Greeks, and in a later note he hinted at the revolutionary implications for our culture, which a reorientation away from the eye toward the ear would trigger: "Images in the human eye! This governs the entire nature of the human being: from the *eye*! Subject! The *ear* hears sound! An entirely different, marvelous conception of the same world!" (2009: 25). Here Nietzsche is congruent with the bigger part of twentieth-century theoretical reflection that deems the prioritization of the visual sense as the original sin of Western thinking.

As Jonas further explains, the concept of "simultaneity"—and eventually of "identity"—is an effect of the visual regime: visual perception constitutes a "co-temporaneous manifold... at rest" (1954: 507), the sense of hearing however "construct[s its] perceptual unities out of a temporal sequence of sensations" (ibid.). Thus, the eye suggests the notion of a permanent existence we would not have, if we could merely resort to "time-senses" (like hearing and feeling).

Music and sound, however, can also be considered the "other" of this ontology of being and the visual regime—ephemeral, a time-art, nonvisual. So what could be the nature of a "sound thinking"? Initially, one would have to oppose (or accompany) the predominant discourses in sound studies to a philosophy that is process-orientated: an ontology of becoming, not of being, which recognizes entities as events and contingent actualizations of virtual potentiality, as a flow consisting of "variously formed matters, and very different dates and speeds . . . phenomena of relative slowness and viscosity, or . . . of acceleration and rupture" (Deleuze and Guattari 1987: 3–4), an "alternative" philosophical lineage, which relies on thinkers like Spinoza, Schopenhauer, Nietzsche, Bergson, Whitehead, and Deleuze. This perspective transforms "givens" with a preset and stable taxonomy of particular functions and agencies into "a construction site of exploration and connection" (Cox 2003: 3).

From this vantage point, the rigorous division between aesthetics and research (and the likewise rigorous division between the various related [academic] disciplines, for example "art" and "science") can no longer be seriously upheld.

Deleuze is also interested in "the relations between the arts, science, and philosophy. There is no order of priority among those disciplines" (1995: 123) for Deleuze. Whereas science involves the creation of functions, of a propositional mapping of the world, and art involves the creation of blocs of sensation (or affects and percepts), philosophy involves the invention of concepts. According to Deleuze and Guattari, philosophy, art, and science are defined by their relation to chaos. Whereas science "relinquishes the infinite in order to gain reference" (1994: 197), by creating definitions, functions, and propositions, art, on the other hand, "wants to create the finite that restores the infinite" (197). In contrast, "philosophy wants to save the infinite by giving it consistency" (197).

Yet, since "sciences, arts, and philosophies are equally creative" (5), it might be fruitful, as Deleuze proposes, "to pose the question of echoes and resonances between them" (1995: 123)—that is, to pose the question of their ecology.

As Deleuze specified in one of his seminars, "Between a philosophical concept, a painted line, and a musical sonorous bloc, resonances emerge, very, very strange correspondences that one shouldn't even theorize, I think, and which I would prefer to call 'affective' . . . these are privileged moments" (Deleuze 1983).[1] These moments privilege an affect where thought and sensation merge into a very specific way of "doing thinking" *beyond* representation and categorization.

The hiatus of art and research is the result of the idea of a linear process ranging from invention/concept (mental) to design (material realization). This however does not do justice to the complexity of the matter: mental and corporeal processes and interactions as well as "implicit/tacit/practical knowledge" become relevant on all levels, for all decisions. As Martin Tröndle has pointed out, conceptual cognitive and manual affective activities go hand in hand, and the sensual examination of the material and emotional reactivity is also of highest importance. As Deleuze and Guattari put it in their idea of the "artisan" (rather than the "artist"): "It is a question of surrendering to the wood, then following where it leads by connecting operations to a materiality, instead of imposing a form on matter: what one addresses is less a matter submitted to laws than a materiality possessing a *nomos*" (1987: 408).

The mind is tightly embedded into the interplay between body, environment, and matter. This is the quintessence of Embodied Mind Philosophy. Alva Noë, one of its originators, even takes it a significant step further: for him the mind evolves from the movements of the body in its environment—the mind is not a substance that could be simply located within the confines of our skull. Consciousness is not "something that happens in us, like digestion"—it is rather "something we do . . . a kind of living activity . . . the ways in which each of us . . . carries on the process of living with and in response to the world around us" (2009: 7).

Embodied Mind Philosophy, I argue, can stimulate a fertile resonance with the concept of *artistic research:* the artistic practice is here not (only) understood in terms of the finalized work of art (work-aesthetic), but rather in regard to the practices and strategies of artistic production (production-aesthetic). The process of the emergence of a work becomes the center of attention. Artists comprehend this process as the phase of examination or evolution of a work. With this shift from the work to artistic research comes also an altered handling of the work itself. It has become a medium of insight, at the latest since twentieth century's modernity (cf. e.g., Clement Greenberg). The work materializes knowledge—beyond the aesthetic experience it facilitates comprehension of the world. Making art then means, initially programmatically in general, to explore something with the specific means of art, to discover something about the world. This entails that art does not solely comprehend itself as a medium of representation and that artistic production does not solely revolve around questions of depiction. This alleged reduction of the artistic to a mere tool serving questions of content, turns out to be an actual extension far beyond self-occupation and the function of representation. The artistic position does not ignore the dimension of aesthetic experience; it rather collaborates with it and perceives it as a mode of negotiable understanding.

Not to be mistaken: it is not that art *morphs* into science. Art and science are rather poised in a force field of "mutual becoming." As Julian Klein has noted, "[a]rtistic experience is an active, constructive and aesthetic process, in which mode and substance are fused inseparably. This differs from other implicit knowledge, which generally can be considered and described separately from its acquisition" (2010: 4)—(cf. e.g.,

John Dewey, Michael Polanyi, Gilles Deleuze, etc.). The reflection of artistic research occurs on the plane of artistic experience itself. This neither excludes an interpretation on a descriptive plane, nor a theoretical analysis on a meta-level. It is however a false conclusion to assume that reflection is only possible from the exterior: artistic experience *is* a form of reflection. And affect-driven artistic production can arrive at more singular thought-positions than purely rationally organized philosophical systems of thought.

In the (American) musical avant-garde of the twentieth century, these perspectives of music as a contraction of forces, currents, and speeds coalesce with the notion of music as thinking, music as research—again, the "corporealization of the intelligence that is in sound" (Varèse 1966: 17). Varèse did not describe himself as a composer, or musician, but rather as "a worker in rhythms, frequencies, and intensities" (18). Without any interest whatsoever in traditional categories like melody, pitch, or form, Varèse turned to sound itself, the exploration of tone, timbre, and volume.

> When new instruments will allow me to write music as I conceive it, the movement of sound-masses, of shifting planes, will be clearly perceived in my work, taking the place of the linear counterpoint. When these sound-masses collide, the phenomena of penetration and repulsion will seem to occur. Certain transmutations taking place on certain planes will seem to be projected onto other planes, moving at different speeds and at different angles. There will no longer be the old conception of melody or interplay of melodies. The entire work will be a melodic totality. The entire work will flow as a river flows. . . . In these moving masses you would be conscious of their transmutations when they pass over different layers, when they penetrate certain opacities, or are dilated in certain rarefactions. (11–12)

To regard "form as a point of departure, a pattern to be followed, a mold to be filled" (16)—as being, as object—would be a mistake. Referring to Busoni, Varèse postulates, "Form is a result—the result of a process" (ibid.), a process of an impersonal becoming that is rather comparable to the formation of crystals than to any kind of "subjective intuition." Also John Cage, Morton Feldman, the Minimalists, and so on committed themselves to the musical exploration of the virtual and processual field of music, to the liberation from human subjectivity toward a realm of the experience of sound itself (cp. also Cox 2003).

As mediated by John Cage, a better part of the American musical avant-garde refers to the philosopher Henry David Thoreau, who conducted sound experiments at Walden Pond in the mid-nineteenth century.

In 1851, Thoreau notes an acoustic experience in his journals that reveals his particular sensibility to his sonic environment—"Yesterday and to-day the stronger winds of autumn have begun to blow, and the telegraph harp has sounded loudly . . . the tone varying with the tension of different parts of the wire. The sound proceeds from near the posts, where the vibration is apparently more rapid" (1962, III: 11). Far from being an isolated case, Thoreau focuses on the "sound of nature"—and in particular the "sound of the weather"—in various other entries in his journals: "Nature makes no noise. The howling storm, the rustling leaf, the pattering rain are no disturbance, there is an essential and unexplored harmony in them" (1962, I: 12). Thoreau is exploring the audible world like a sound-archaeologist, carefully distinguishing "sound" from "music:"[2] To fellow-transcendentalist Emerson, mind, not matter, is of prime importance—matter is only a manifestation of the mind. Thoreau, in contrast, stresses the material and sensual aspects of nature—"We need pray for no higher heaven than the pure senses can furnish, a *purely* sensuous life . . . Is not Nature . . . that of which she is commonly taken to be a symbol merely?" (1998: 307). Thoreau does not *read* nature like, and does not interpret nature according to, a spiritual principle external to it—such a principle, because of nature's manifoldness, is *immanent* to it. For Thoreau, nature's "music" is "the sound of circulation in nature's veins" (1962, I: 251). It is in this stress on nature as sensuous experience and materiality that Thoreau "deviates" from Emerson. Thoreau focuses on (the music of) nature as a material, physical process, not as an Emersonian emblem of reason—"The very globe *continually transcends* and translates itself. . . . The whole tree itself is but one leaf, and rivers are still vaster leaves whose pulp is intervening earth" (1973: 306–7). "Transcendentalism" is understood by Thoreau as completely "physical"—the natural, dynamic process of metamorphosis, of continuous change, transcendence becomes immanence.

In his journals, Thoreau writes: "Now I see the beauty and full meaning of that word 'sound.' Nature always possesses a certain sonorousness, as in the hum of insects, the booming of ice . . . which indicates her sound state." The pun on "sound" as acoustic sound and "sound" as a state of health even calls for a reference to Thoreau's dictum "in wildness is the preservation of the world" (from his essay "Walking"). Here "Wildness" refers to the untamed but also to anything that resists representation and any static thinking of identity: the continuous self-differentiation of the world, its growing, its dynamics, its processuality—here lies its "soundness" and also the "essence" of sound. Thus, "sound thinking" does not only imply "the thinking of sound," but also "healthy thinking," or, as Deleuze puts it: a thinking that rightfully earns its name, a thinking that does not derive its parameters/concepts from an exterior "verified knowledge" (Deleuze calls this "recognition") in order to adapt the object of investigation to these parameters, but rather a thinking that develops its very concepts from the examination of the object of investigation (Deleuze calls this "encounter"): here—a thinking *with* and *by means of* sound, not a thinking *about* sound, which eventually does not deal with the question what music *is*, but rather what music *can become*. And from this vantage point, research and art, theory and practice, are coextensive.

Notes

1. My translation: "Alors je dirais que le concept philosophique n'est pas seulement source d'opinion quelconque, il est source de transmission très particulière, ou entre un concept philosophique, une ligne picturale, un bloc sonore musical, s'établissent des correspondances, des correspondances très très curieuses, que à mon avis il ne faut même pas théoriser, que je préférerais appeler l'affectif en général . . . . Là c'est des moments privilégiés."

2. See also Thoreau's essay "Walking" and his/its concept of "wildness"—"sound" can be read as "wildness" with regard to "music" (as sound organized by a traditional composer), the unformed, unintended, untamed in comparison to John Sullivan Dwight's canonization in Thoreau's time of European Classical Music (and in particular the compositions of Beethoven) as *the* paradigm for a future American Music.

References

Cox, C. (2003), "How Do You Make Music a Body without Organs? Gilles Deleuze and Experimental Electronica." Available online: http://faculty.hampshire.edu/ccox/Cox-Soundcultures.pdf (accessed September 15, 2015).

Deleuze, G. (1983), "Vérité et Temps, le faussaire," *Cours Vincennes – St Denis: le plan* (November 2, 1983). Available online: https://www.webdeleuze.com/textes/69 (accessed June 11, 2019).

Deleuze, G. (1995), *Negotiations*, trans. M. Joughin, New York: Columbia University Press.

Deleuze, G., and F. Guattari (1987), *A Thousand Plateaus: Capitalism and Schizophrenia*, trans. B. Massumi, Minneapolis: University of Minnesota Press.

Deleuze, G., and F. Guattari (1994), *What Is Philosophy?*, trans. H. Tomlinson and G. Burchell, New York: Columbia University Press.

Jonas, H. (1954), "The Nobility of Sight," *Philosophy and Phenomenological Research*, 14 (4): 507–19.

Klein, J. (2010), "What Is Artistic Research?" Available online: http://www.researchcatalogue.net/view/15292/15293 (accessed September 15, 2015).

Nietzsche, F. (2009), *Writings from the Early Notebooks*, ed. R. Geuss and A. Nehamas, trans. L. Löb, Cambridge: Cambridge University Press.

Noë, A. (2009), *Out of Our Heads. Why You Are Not Your Brain, and Other Lessons from the Biology of Consciousness*, New York: Hill and Wang.

Rilke, R. M. (2001), "Primal Sound," in D. Rothenberg and M. Ulvaeus (eds.), *The Book of Music and Nature. An Anthology of Sounds, Words, Thoughts*, 21–4, Middletown, CT: Wesleyan University Press.

Rilke, R. M. (2007), *Letters of Rainer Maria Rilke. Vol. II: 1912–26.* trans. G. J. Bannard, Leiserson Press.

Thoreau, H. D. (1962), *The Journal of Henry David Thoreau*, ed. B. Torrey and F. H. Allen, in Fourteen Volumes (bound as two), New York: Dover Publications.

Thoreau, H. D. (1973), *The Illustrated Walden*, ed. J. L. Shanley, Princeton: Princeton University Press.

Thoreau, H. D. (1998), *A Week on the Concord and Merrimack Rivers*, Harmondsworth: Penguin.

Varèse, E. and C. Wen-chung (1966), "The Liberation of Sound," *Perspectives of New Music*, 5 (1): 11–19.

CHAPTER 10
THINKING WITH SOUND
PRELIMINARY THOUGHTS
François J. Bonnet

What is a sound? Here is a question that has been discussed and debated a thousand times. Nevertheless, to approach sound no longer as the object of a reflection but rather as a medium or *milieu* into which a reflection, a practice, enters inevitably implies to reexamine its status and to survey its extent.

What is a sound, then? Without seeking to repeat reflections presented elsewhere (Bonnet 2016), it is necessary to reaffirm the idea of a "schizological" approach to sound, that is, a thought that does not confine sound to its physical and event-driven reality, nor does it consider it as a mere phenomenal quality. Sound cannot be reduced to the vibratory event that generates it nor to the auditory phenomenon that one perceives. It is both one and the other or more precisely, it is neither quite one nor the other. Moreover, it binds and unites these two aspects around a common future. A sound *is* sound as soon as it *makes* sound, that is to say, it realizes and conjugates both an "event" and a "listening." The term "listening," here, must be understood in its broadest sense, that is, in a sense almost independent of its auricular modality. Isn't it said in kōdō, the Japanese art of smelling, that you listen to a perfume? Listening, in this sense, would be the counterpart, the mirror or the complement of an address, that is, a disposition to receive, an attention paid to, an opening to the sensitive world, and so on.

On the other hand, sound, as meeting point and interface, manifests itself by disappearing. Sound appears and disappears in an instant, not "without leaving a trace," but precisely by almost always leaving a trace. In fact, it entrusts the trace with the task of revealing it. If its transience is its condition, its survival lies only in its traces. Also, it's never really there. It has been and will be, but its present is entrusted to its resonances. Also, "sounding" is always already "resounding." The extension into a body or through a resonant space, the echo produced, the impression felt, are all moments when sound is printed in everything, in everyone, like a ray of ephemeral light on a photosensitive paper. The "phonosensitivity" of space and beings, this hybrid ability to extend sound over time, this resonance that is listening: this is the condition for the appearance of sounds and their possible persistence. Sound never really survives except through its avatar, through this trace which is already a link established with a listening. No sound lasts, but no sound that was not audible never completely disappears. Audibility, this linking of a sound and a listening, is in fact the only possible way for a sound to appear. This distinction between the unheard sound and the audible one is what reveals the discriminating modality of any sensorium.

Practical Aesthetics

It is therefore from such a conception of sound as relational and "schizological" that a sound can no longer be approached as a simple object of thought, but as a participating matrix: no longer think of sound, but think with it, follow its authority, through its currents, following its lines of force. But how can such a thought be practiced? How can the *implementation* of a thought that blossoms *within* sound be manifested? A track is emerging, and a possible horizon of its manifestation emerges. Thinking with sound, could it simply be *making music*? It is a difficult hypothesis that opens up here, a thousand traps are set, a thousand pitfalls are scattered. It nevertheless presents the fertility of complex territories and marshy areas but immediately raises a new and formidable question: What is music?

This question can be addressed, probably too briefly, by examining it from two perspectives: aesthetics and language. The aesthetic plane interrogates music as a form of sound, and considers its expressive domain. Any attempt at musical ontology has been confronted with this plan, because it seeks to define what the musical phenomenon is in essence. It is a classic posture, debated at length in the twentieth century and it is a question that has been constantly spurred on by the avant-garde, seeking to break or extend the traditional paradigms that governed the constitution of a musical nature. But seeking the nature of music has always been a misunderstanding, since the perimeter of music is not a constituted space, in which audible forms and proposals would be included or excluded, but rather a constituent space that defines itself in a dynamic way.

In the same way as for art in general, what is considered as "music" is what is constituted as such by a given group, or by an authority recognized by this same group, which ultimately amounts to the same. This is the constituent tautology of music: music is everything that is considered as such. If we embrace all the possibilities, through the ages, across continents, through aesthetics, that the notion of music can cover, we must admit that the question of a musical essence cannot be addressed through its sensitive manifestation, so much it takes different, sometimes contradictory forms, forms that evolve and expand unceasingly. It is the specificity of art, and therefore also of music, to be made up of moving territories, vortexes that already potentially integrate all future forms. And, in the case of music, it is listening that draws and redraws the boundaries. Music is, in this respect, what is listened to musically. Also, according to John Cage, "everything is music" from the moment you listen to sounds as you listen to music. In the end, listening to something *as music* is always already listening to music.

The second analysis plan can be deployed from the thorny problem of the relationship between music and language. Again, this is not a question to be approached with the hope of providing a clear and unambiguous answer. There is no solution to discover here for the same reason that there is not a single music, unique in its form, that can lead to a definition of its nature. In music, multiple realities coexist, sometimes irreconcilable. It is certain that music can have a linguistic character when it unfolds through a set of rules and conventions, and as such it can sometimes be anticipated, understood, and in a certain way read. But it is also certain that in music something outside language arises, something that exceeds language, as in any sensitive manifestation.

One musical genre in particular has revealed this constitutive tension between music and language: *musique concrète*. By professing to start from the preexisting "concrete" sound, that is, from all the possible "given" sounds, Pierre Schaeffer extends the universe of musical sounds to all possible sounds. However, any noise, any sound, has such a formal and energetic complexity that it is impossible to reduce it to a simple notation, and therefore, *in fine*, to a standardized language. The composition itself, in *musique concrète*, emancipates itself from the score. There is no symbol to write *musique concrète*, no sign to anticipate, plan, or reproduce it. It is discovered, revealed, as sculpture emerges from rock or earth through the sculptor's gesture, who models and evaluates his work and perceives the evolution of his work at the same time as silent creation. Nothing in this process is stated. The programmatic, communicable, transmissible aspects, inscribed on a score in the case of instrumental music, that what it shares with human language, are absent from the concrete world.

And it is indeed, to a certain extent, to compensate for this lack of marking—which some, moreover, have hastened to associate directly with an "unthinkable" of this emerging music—that Pierre Schaeffer felt the need to invent a musical theory. And this music theory, moreover, was less thought of as a set of rules to be strictly followed than as a corpus of markings and concepts to say this music that can be composed without resorting to the symbol.

What *musique concrète* reveals particularly clearly in its relationship to language is what it deploys *outside* language, that is, its *figurative* modality, which we have also called the sonorous. In Jean-François Lyotard's work, the figural refers precisely to the sensitive modality that cannot be reduced to a text. For Lyotard, the given has a thickness, "or rather a difference, which is not to be read, but rather seen; and this difference, and the immobile mobility that reveals it, are what continually fall into oblivion in the process of signification" (Lyotard 2011: 3). Lyotard also reminds us that if the world were reducible to a text and if the whole of such a world were readable, then it would imply a writer:

> That the world remains to be read basically means that an Other, on the other side, transcribes the given objects, and that with the appropriate point of view I could theoretically decipher it. (Lyotard 2011: 4)

It is to deny the thickness of the world, and reduce it to an inscription surface.

Music, as a hybrid device between a construction and a given, and especially as a sensitive phenomenon, has a thickness that exceeds a simple code, a simple text. Also, through it, a world is expressed outside the field of discourse, outside the structures of language.

This is why the question of the place of language in music is particularly fertile when it is linked to the problem that occupies this short text, namely that thinking with sound could, perhaps, be reduced to making music. And it is a whole new meaning of music that emerges here, and which stands, with mistrust, against that which assimilates music to another form of language. The question of language thus always remains central. Because thinking with sound, and not thinking of sound as an object, that is, sonic thinking, can thus, and in the first place, be approached as an alternative to thinking based on pure logos. But what can a thought of sound bring that could not be delivered by a thought that only turns toward language and is mobilized by it? What can be a sensitive thought excluded from the world of words? And how can it manifest itself? Can such sensitive thinking then be reinvested in language? But perhaps it can only do so through a practice of mediation. That's how the music hypothesis is understood here: a sensitive thought can only really be thought through a practice, which is in a way a thought in action.

Giorgio Agamben writes:

When we walk through the woods at night, with every step we hear the rustle of invisible animals among the bushes flanking our path. Perhaps they are lizards or hedgehogs, thrushes or snakes. So it is when we think: the path of words that we follow is of no importance. What matters is the indistinct patter that we sometimes hear moving to the side, the sound of an animal in flight or something that is suddenly aroused by the sound of our steps. The animal in flight that we seem to hear rustling away in our words is—we are told—our own voice. . . . But the voice, the human voice, does not exist. We have no voice . . . We can only think if language is not our voice, only if we reach our own aphonia at its very bottom (but in reality there is no bottom). What we call world is this abyss. (Agamben 1991: 107–8)

This constitutive impossibility for language to really tell the world is an ancient subject in philosophy and literature. Language is always a coding, and therefore, intrinsically, a betrayal. Writing about Maurice Blanchot's work, Michel Foucault extends this impossibility to the speaker himself: "Mallarme taught us that the word is the manifest non-existence of what it designates; we now know that the being of language is the visible effacement of the one who speaks" (Foucault 1987: 54).

There is thus a mistrust of language in its own right, from an affirmation of incompleteness illustrated, for example, in the concept of figural developed by Lyotard and mentioned earlier, to the impossibility even for language to say the world, but which is the very price and condition of the possibility of language. "Words are not of this world," wrote Hofmannsthal, but only they can tell it. Language persists, thus, in its failures and even in its absences. It is always tempting to evoke the unspeakable with words, even if they are powerless. If words, through appropriate discourse, are often solicited and invoked to get as close as possible to this unspeakable world, it is always at the risk of avoiding other possible modalities of access, alternatives, and in particular sensitive access.

Music, in this sense, is a fascinating "field," because it has too often sought to reinvest the world of words, to reintegrate itself into logos, forgetting, sometimes, that its sensitive "carrier," that is, sound itself, opened up to other axes of expressive deployment. However, this double destination of music, one aiming at its inclusion in the logos, the other, on the contrary, establishing it as a possible alternative, can no longer be maintained when precisely the possibility of a different thought, flourishing outside of discourse, is observed. It is then necessary to take a stand and affirm that a whole section of music has gone astray by singling out reason and denying its profoundly excessive dimension.

Thinking with sound, therefore, may be first of all to establish and affirm a choice about how one makes music and understands it. It is, perhaps, even better: it could amount to redefining music through this use. If thinking with sound does indeed mean making music, it opens the doors of such a proposal to infinite or at least unexplored horizons. Thus, making music, as such, could very well mean simply listening to the sound of the sea, feeling and experiencing it, and incorporating it. It can also mean the virtuoso musician's acute and precise listening to the inflection of a touch, nuance, or timbre, as well as the rough gesture of an apprentice sound artist who for the first time mixes two sounds recorded with a mobile phone. But, on the other hand, such an understanding of the musical fact, as thinking of sound in action, ultimately excludes from its scope any practice aimed at using sounds and notes to illustrate an idea, tell a story or even make the use of sound a confirmation of a formula, a formal logic or a structure. Any use of music for the purpose of inserting it into a discursive field, aesthetic or not, de facto destroys the possibility of music as a sound thought. Thinking with sound, making music, already prevents any attempt to reduce sound to a *pretext*.

Such music, which moves away from language by revealing its flaws, and which evokes the sensitive by the sensitive, deepens the figurative furrow of expressiveness, disdaining to withdraw into the pseudo-known world of words and things, refusing to be put into objects, its reification. It is a thought in the making, which straddles the sound avatars, the spectra, celebrating at every moment the life and death of all things, invokes the Universe, never constant, never static, never predictable, far away, far from a harmony of the spheres. It is also a thought that occurs from the extreme locality of the sensitive, concrete appearance.

"The eye," says André Breton, "exists in its savage state" (Breton 2002: 1). The ear too. To put it in thought is not to put it in word, which would be like domesticating it. To put sound into thought is to act with it, to make thought into sound, to reinvent music by silencing it. Music no longer says anything, it just is, in silence. According to Lyotard, "[w]hat cannot be tamed is art as silence. The position of art is a refutation of the position of discourse" (Lyotard 2011: 7).

As such, thinking with sound, *making music*, is already taking sides. It is opening up to the silent but sonorous world that speeches cannot reach. It is to be on the lookout for the future of the world, that is, to embrace the field of metamorphoses, and of worlds in the making. To think with sound is to refuse to base any reflection on the imperial logic of words and speeches. It means exploring what is hidden outside words, outside the logic of power, outside the control zones. It is about turning around ideas, like turning around a sound, which never repeats itself, always almost the same but never itself. It does not build, but collects, accepts. It is to trace from traces, to walk in the dust. It is thus learning to deal with the unspeakable, without seeking to pacify or tame it. It is living in the company of shadows and resonating with them.

Translated from the French by Louisa Collenberg.

References

Agamben, G. (1991), *Language and Death: The Place of Negativity*, trans. K. E. Pinkus and M. Hardt, Minneapolis: University of Minnesota Press.

Bonnet, F. J. (2016), *The Order of Sounds: A Sonorous Archipelago*, trans. R. Mackay, Falmouth: Urbanomic.

Breton, A. (2002), *Surrealism and Painting*, trans. S. Watson Taylor, reprinted edition, Boston: MFA Publications.

Foucault, M. (1987), "Maurice Blanchot, the Thought from Outside," trans. B. Massumi and J. Mehlman, in *Foucault/Blanchot*, 7–60, New York: Zone Books.

Lyotard, J.-F. (2011), *Discourse, Figure*, trans. A. Hudek and M. Lydon, Minneapolis: University of Minnesota Press.

CHAPTER 11
IN SEARCH OF SACRED SPACE
John Luther Adams

A young composer and I were sitting on a bench in Central Park, talking about music. He asked me about form.

"I want my music to be intensely sensuous," I said. "But I also want it to be rigorously formal."

"Why?" he asked.

"Form gives the music a deeper coherence. It also protects the music against the bad taste of the composer!"

He laughed.

I added: "But recently I've begun to relax a little in my obsession with form..."

"Then what will take the place of form?" Without hesitating I replied: "Space."

It was a prescient question, and my answer surprised me a bit. I wasn't entirely sure what I meant, but it had the ring of truth. And it got me thinking.

When I was twenty-one, I became captivated by the songs of birds. In the woods and fields of rural Georgia, I began trying to write down what I heard. Before long I had a collection of miniature portraits, a bit like pages in a musical field guide to the birds. But that wasn't enough. I wanted to evoke something of the magic that I felt listening to the birds in the places where they sang. So to my first settings of birdsongs, scored for piccolos, I added parts for percussion—rattles, sizzle cymbals, woodblocks, bells, and the like—that I imagined as the wind, the rain, the light, and the weather. This was the beginning of a lifelong exploration of place and space in music.

The following year, in Alaska, I experienced landscape on a scale I'd never known. Enthralled, I began to sketch out broad harmonic fields that I hoped would echo those sprawling expanses of mountains and glaciers, forest, and tundra. Eventually, those sketches became an orchestral work titled *A Northern Suite*. From the subtitle—"Tone Paintings of Alaska"—it was clear that I was thinking of this music in a pictorial way. And for more than a decade, in works such as *Night Peace* and *The Far Country of Sleep*, I continued this kind of landscape painting in music.

There was a profoundly romantic dimension to this early passion for place, fueled by my reading of Thoreau and Muir, and by contemporary writers like Annie Dillard and Barry Lopez. I found special inspiration in the poetry of John Haines. And when I was not yet thirty, I had the extraordinarily good fortune to begin a long, close friendship with John, working with him on *Forest Without Leaves* (1984)—a choral work grounded in his cycle of poems about humanity's inextricable roots in the earth.

Practical Aesthetics

Several years later, I ventured to combine the poetic and the pictorial in *Earth and the Great Weather* (1991). This "sonic geography of the Arctic" mixes instrumental music for strings and percussion with sounds recorded in the landscapes of the North. But the real conceptual ground of this work was a series of "Arctic Litanies"—found poems composed from indigenous names for places, plants, birds, and the seasons. Spoken and sung in the Gwich'in and Iñupiat languages, these words seemed to me to come directly out of the earth itself and to constitute an authentic poetry of place.

Yet music is not poetry or painting. And even while I was painting musical landscapes, I was committed first and foremost to music as *sound*. I wanted my landscapes to have depth. I wanted the listener to be able to enter into, to *inhabit* those musical spaces.

Early on I'd encountered Henry Cowell's visionary book *New Musical Resources*. In the chapter on rhythm, Cowell proposes nothing less than a unified field theory of music—compositions that encompass not only tonal harmonies but also rhythmic harmonies derived from the whole number relationships of the natural harmonic series.

Most Western music is constrained by regular meter and a single audible pulse. But ever since my days as a rock 'n' roller this has struck me as curiously two-dimensional. In the works of Conlon Nancarrow and Johannes Ockeghem, I found inspiring models from the twentieth and the fifteenth centuries of multitemporal music. And for decades now most of my own music has encompassed three, four, or more different tempos simultaneously. Somewhere along the way it occurred to me that these tempo layers could allow me to create a larger sense of musical space.

Beginning with *Clouds of Forgetting, Clouds of Unknowing* (1996), and continuing with *In the White Silence* (1998), and *For Lou Harrison* (2004), I employed large-scale, multidimensional orchestral textures in an effort to move beyond landscape painting. In this music, I wanted to create inherently *musical* landscapes that immerse and envelope the listener. Yet even as the music became less pictorial, I was still enamored of color.

We often speak of sound in visual terms. Timbre—the unique sonic profile that allows us to distinguish one instrument from another—we call "tone color." I love working with the broad palette of acoustic instruments, mixing their colors in different ways. I also enjoy creating new colors with electronic media.

But beyond timbre, I also think of *harmony* as color, and over the decades my music has traversed a wide territory of harmonic colors. When I'm working in standard twelve-tone equal temperament, I usually mix my colors from the interval of a Perfect Fifth (or its inversion, the Perfect Fourth)—superimposing that single interval on itself in varied ways to create chords, clouds, and fields of distinctive harmonic hues.

I also work frequently in non-tempered tunings derived from the harmonic series and its theoretical inversion, the subharmonic series. Digital media make it relatively easy to explore unfamiliar harmonic territory, and in electronic works such as *Veils and Vesper* (2006), *The Place Where You Go to Listen* (2007), and *The Wind Garden* (2017), I've worked with a wide range of new harmonic colors. Over time, some of those new harmonies have found their way back into works for human performers and acoustic instruments.

In Search of Sacred Space

As I became less interested in painting musical landscapes, I began to study the nonrepresentational art of Mark Rothko, Jackson Pollock, Helen Frankenthaler, and Barnett Newman, as well as the history of color theory. This led me to a compose a series of "color field" pieces, beginning with *The Light That Fills the World*, and continuing with *Dark Wind*, *The Farthest Place*, and *The Immeasurable Space of Tones* (all completed in 2001). This music is composed from long clouds of harmony and timbre, moving slowly in multiple tempos—rising and falling, merging and dissolving, drifting together and drifting apart. At the time, this sounded radically new. I wasn't even sure it was music. Yet ironically, over the years these pieces that I originally conceived as floating fields of color have come to sound melodic, almost songlike, to me.

While I was working on my "color field" series, I also composed *Red Arc/Blue Veil* for piano, mallet percussion instruments and electronic sounds. Inspired by the forms and colors of the aurora borealis, *Red Arc* was the first piece in which I created an "aura" of electronic sounds derived directly from the acoustic instruments. This "aura" allowed me to create an almost orchestral field of sound, while the "live" musicians animated the surface with touch.

Following *Red Arc*, I've employed auras in a number of other pieces, including *The Light Within*, *Four Thousand Holes* and *Ilimaq* (Spirit Journey). This technique has also influenced the sound of my music even when a composition doesn't include an electronic aura. In *Dark Waves*, I embedded an electronic aura within the sound of a full symphony orchestra. But in *Become Ocean*, I decided to dispense with the electronic sounds and compose the aura directly into the orchestra.

As John Cage observed, most of what we hear around us most of the time is noise. When we try to ignore it, it disturbs us. But when we listen to noise with our full attention, we find it fascinating. So what happens when we invite noise into our music? Suddenly the whole world becomes music.

In this spirit, I began work on *Strange and Sacred Noise*—a concert-length cycle of pieces for percussion quartet, celebrating elemental violence in nature. In my travels throughout Alaska, I'd experienced howling storms, raging wildfires, and glaciers crashing into the sea. I'd also been reading books about chaos theory, which inspired me to imagine a kind of "sonic geometry"—sounding fractal forms with noise.

Strange and Sacred Noise roars, howls, and thunders. But it evokes the unbounded spaces of the natural world within the enclosed space of a concert hall or theater. In fact, this music relies on four walls, a ceiling, and floor to saturate the acoustic space with sound and overload our psychoacoustic perceptions, provoking us to hear things that aren't really there.

One section of *Noise* is scored for four tam-tams. When I first heard this piece, amid the dense waves of broadband noise, I clearly heard voices—like a choir of spirits singing long, wordless tones. I promptly dubbed these "angel voices." And I wanted to hear them alone.

In Papua New Guinea, when a Kaluli songmaker searches for a new song, he will sometimes camp by a waterfall or a running stream. It's said that all the songs in the world are contained in the noise of the water. And the songmaker listens carefully, sometimes

Practical Aesthetics

for days, until he hears the voice of his new song. All broadband noise contains within its pure tone. And the complex sonorities of percussion instruments conceal choirs of inner voices.

In *The Mathematics of Resonant Bodies* (2002), my search would be to find and reveal those voices. Working with a recording of those tam-tams from *Strange and Sacred Noise*, I filtered out most of the noise until all that was left was that choir of angel voices. This became the point of departure for an exploration of the inner resonances, the sonic spaces hidden within noise.

I continued by composing a complete cycle of new pieces for percussion quartet. Then I assembled recordings of those pieces and then began filtering—selectively erasing them, as I'd done previously with the tam-tams. The result was a series of "auras" derived from the inner resonance of the instruments themselves. As the final step, I composed a series of solo parts to be performed within these sonic fields.

For years I had been working with the *idea* of space and place, imagining each new composition as its own metaphorical space and place. But the time came when this was no longer enough.

In a sense, my music was becoming less painterly and more sculptural.

My continuing interest in visual art led me to the so-called "Light and Space" artists who came of age in southern California in the 1960s and 1970s. I found the light art of James Turrell and the perceptual art of Robert Irwin especially compelling. And I began dreaming of musical equivalents to their immersive visual environments. If their basic materials were light and space, mine were sound and space. And just as they were creating the physical spaces in which their work is experienced, I wanted not only to compose the music but also to design the space in which it was performed and heard—whether indoors or outdoors.

The Place Where You Go to Listen is a small room at the Museum of the North in Fairbanks—an interior space that echoes the music of the larger world around it. Inside this room the rhythms of night and day, the phases of the moon, the seismic movements of the earth, and the dance of the aurora borealis are all transformed into sound and light.

Loudspeakers all around the room—in the walls, in the ceiling and near the floor—allowed me to place the sounds relative to one another in a way that echoes the geographic locations of those vibrations from the outside world. After working inside this immersive space for more than two years, I became more aware than ever of the flatness of hearing music played on a proscenium stage in a conventional concert hall. And I began to think about utilizing those spaces in a fuller, more dynamic way.

In *Become Ocean* (2014), a full symphony orchestra is deployed in three different ensembles separated as widely as possible. Each of these groups has its own distinctive instrumental and harmonic coloration, and each moves at its own tempo.

Become River (2014) is scored for a smaller orchestra, turned upside down. Rather than their usual position near the edge of the stage, the violins are seated far upstage and elevated, and the entire ensemble is raked. Over the course of twenty minutes, three different musical streams moving at different speeds flow downstream, from high sounds to low—taking the listener on a musical journey from the headwaters to the edge of the sea.

Become Desert (2017) is a forty-minute symphonic work that completes a trilogy that I didn't set out to write. In all three of these works, space is a fundamental compositional element. I'm not speaking only of poetic or metaphorical space, but also of the physical, acoustic, and volumetric space of the musical ensemble and the place in which the music is heard.

For decades now, one of the most fundamental questions I ask myself when I begin a new composition is: "What are the instruments?" With *Become Desert*, this became two questions: "What are the instruments? And where are they located?"

For a long time, I pondered the floor plan, the physical deployment of the instrumental and vocal choirs within and around the performance space. Ultimately, I decided to disperse the strings all over the stage, with four harps and four percussionists interspersed among them.

The other four choirs are elevated on high risers, in balconies, lofts, or boxes around the performance space. Upstage, a choir of sixteen woodwinds and a percussionist playing crotales (antique cymbals) is elevated as high as possible above the strings. A choir of eight horns and a percussionist playing chimes is elevated on one side of the space. A choir of four trumpets and four trombones and a percussionist playing chimes is elevated on the other side of the space. And a choir of singers and handbells is elevated at the rear of the space.

Only when I arrived at this layout, only when I could begin to hear this sonic space in my mind was I ready to begin writing the score.

For decades, my music had been inspired by the outdoors, but it was almost always performed indoors. Then I heard *Strange and Sacred Noise* performed outdoors, and everything changed.

It was in the Anza-Borrego desert of southern California. I settled in to listen to what I thought of as my big, powerful piece performed in a stunningly beautiful natural setting. But in all that sprawling space, a lot of it just blew away in the wind, and I realized that it was time for me to make music conceived from the outset to be heard out of doors.

The result was *Inuksuit* (2008) for nine to ninety-nine percussionists, which was inspired by the stone sentinels constructed over the centuries by the Inuit in the windswept expanses of the Arctic.

Inuksuit is a concert-length work in which the performers are widely dispersed and move throughout a large outdoor area. The listeners, too, may move around freely and discover their own individual listening points. Every performance of *Inuksuit* is unique, in response to the topology, vegetation, and acoustics of the performance site. This is music as a kind of echolocation or GPS, a vehicle for reminding us where we are and how we fit in with the never-ending music of the world around us—in the hope of transforming seemingly empty space into more deeply experienced *place*.

Composing *Inuksuit* in my cabin studio in Alaska with the image of those solitary stone figures standing on the tundra, I imagined each performing musician and each individual listener as a solitary figure in a vast enveloping landscape. I thought this was a piece about solitude. It was only when I heard the first performances of *Inuksuit* that I realized that this is a piece about community. Although the experience of each solitary listener is unique, out of the experience of shared solitude an extraordinary sense of community emerges.

In a relatively brief time, *Inuksuit* has taken on a robust life of its own, independent of the composer. From the Canadian Rockies to New York City, from Europe to Australia, from Hong Kong to Valparaiso, people around the world have utilized *Inuksuit* to celebrate their own communities and their unique places on the planet. One of the most extraordinary performances was given by musicians on both sides of border between Tijuana, Mexico, and San Diego in the United States.

For an hour or so, as the music sounded, the looming wall that divides the two countries seemed to disappear. Before the performance began, the percussionist and conductor Steven Schick looked through the wire mesh of the wall and said to his fellow musicians on the other side: "Con la música nunca se puede dividirnos." ("With music we can never be divided.")

Following *Inuksuit*, I've gone on to compose the choral/orchestral work.

Sila: The Breath of the World (2013) and *Across the Distance* (2015)—an outdoor work for a large ensemble of horns. I've also returned to my original point of departure with *Ten Thousand Birds* (2014) for performance outdoors in locations where the same species of birds included in the score are present on the performance site.

The Wind Garden (2017) is my first work employing electronic sounds to sound outdoor space. This is a musical composition in the form of a landscape. Composed with and within a eucalyptus grove on the campus of the University of California San Diego. Creating *The Wind Garden* involved not only composing the sounds, but also designing the landscape.

Hidden in the trees are thirty-two small loudspeakers. Attached to the highest branches are thirty-two accelerometers that measure the movements of the trees in the wind. As the velocity of the wind increases, the amplitude of the sounds grows louder. And as the velocity of the wind diminishes, their amplitude grows softer. Occasionally, when there is no wind in a particular tree, the sounds from that tree fall silent.

At midday, the sounds in the grove are high and bright. At night, they are lower and darker. On overcast days, all the sounds are more subdued. And the sounds of summer are generally brighter than the sounds of winter. Throughout the day and throughout the year, at every moment the sounds in the grove seem to rise and fall with the wind.

The artist Robert Smithson is perhaps best known for his earthwork *Spiral Jetty*, which curls gently out into the Great Salt Lake. In his brief, explosively creative life, Smithson made works both on the land and in art galleries. The outdoor works he called "sites" and the indoor works he called "non-sites."

In Smithson's lexicon, non-sites are fragments of land, removed from the places from which they came. In a non-site, we feel the absence of the original place and our own remove from it. Sites, by contrast, are authentic places. In a site, we feel ourselves present in a place in which (to paraphrase Pascal) the center is everywhere and the circumference is nowhere.

Today, in this time when we humans have become a dominant geological force, we are creating for ourselves a world in which there are fewer and fewer sites and more and more non-sites. We seek refuge in the comfort of partitions—in the rectilinear geometry of our houses and buildings and by carving up the landscape into ever-diminishing rectangles and squares.

We know this cannot continue. There are simply too many of us to live so heavily on the earth. But what can we do? How do we get from where we are to where we need to be?

This is a perilous moment in the history of our species. If we don't know where we are, we don't know who we are or where we are going. Lost and wandering on the edge of our own extinction, perhaps we need new maps to help us find our way—to rediscover and reconsecrate our sites, to reclaim and reinhabit our non-sites.

As present-day geographers have observed, maps are not objective representations. They are propositions. Historically, maps evolved in conjunction with the rise of nation states. Maps are tools that we use to diminish and control the land and its inhabitants, both human and other-than-human. Throughout history, people have used maps to prosecute wars against one another and against the earth.

But maps can also help us understand more deeply the places we inhabit. And if we better understand where we are, we may better understand who we are, and how best to live.

In the Name of the Earth (2018), a large-scale work for massed human voices, is my musical map of North America—a refutation and a counterproposal to the official maps of state highway departments and the corporate worldview of Google, a celebration of this beautiful continent where the only real borders are watersheds and coastlines.

As in *Earth and the Great Weather* many years ago, my texts for *In the Name* are litanies of names—the names of mountain peaks and ranges, rivers and glaciers, forests and plains and deserts—in English and Spanish and the older indigenous names that reverberate like words spoken by the earth itself.

By singing these names, I hope to draw music not only from my own imagination, but also from the older, deeper music of this continent:

Katadhin, Agiocochook, Yuhaihaskun, Absaroka, Uncompaghre, Culebra.

Citlatépetl, Tajumuleo, Usumacinta, Popocatépetl, Nevado, Sonora. Tahoma, Klickitat, Wy'east, Shasta, Mojave, Toomanguya.

Iliamna, Tsalxhaan, ShaaTlein, Ahtna, Dinadhi, Igikpak, Kuukpak . . .

The resonance of these names invokes the presence and the memory of the people who have inhabited this continent since long before the arrival of Europeans. In the poetry of these names, I listen for spirits that are still present on the land and echoes of how it was before the rise of nation states. But there is no turning back. And my real work is to give voice to a vision of how our world might be after their fall.

As I write now (in early 2019), I'm immersed in composing *Crossing Open Ground*—a new outdoor work for woodwinds, brass, and percussion. I've borrowed the title from a book by my friend Barry Lopez. As Lopez observes: "*Each place on Earth goes deep. Some vestige of the old, now seemingly eclipsed place is always there to be had.*"

Practical Aesthetics

In this spirit, *Crossing Open Ground* invites us to experience the older, deeper resonances of place—wherever we may be—and to practice walking as a form of resistance and hope. From the freedom marchers of the civil rights movement to the refugees from Central America currently seeking asylum in the United States, walking is an expression of devotion and an assertion of freedom—a transgression of the borders we construct to separate ourselves from one another, and from our true nature as thinking animals and citizens of the earth.

In this time when we humans have become a geologic force, most of us live in increasingly homogenous environments, and in the amorphous non-places of "cyberspace." Searching for real experiences in real places, we travel to far-flung destinations, where we make photographs of ourselves to prove that we were there. But it's increasingly rare that we are fully present *anywhere* and the knowledge that we truly belong to a place eludes many of us. Growing from my own deep desire to feel at home in the world, *Crossing Open Ground* is a ceremony of rediscovery, reconsecration, and reinhabitation of place—wherever we may be.

While *Inuksuit* and my previous outdoor works all utilize timelines, *Crossing Open Ground* does not. The notation for this music is arrayed in a series of 27 "stations," showing not *when* but rather *where* the notes are played. The exact moments at which the sounds occur are determined by the breath of each musician and by the topography of the site.

Composing this music requires me to think more deeply about the orchestration of space. Each musician follows her or his own individual path from station to station—playing, walking, playing again, and walking on. And a performance will last as long as it takes all the musicians to move from one side of the space to the other.

For more than four decades now, I've explored these and other manifestations of musical space and place. My journey continues, and I hope to continue composing music specifically for outdoor performance for years to come. But what is this obsession all about?

As an artist, I see myself as a worker for a culture I will never live to inhabit, in a society that may never come to be. And I know that I'm not alone. All over the world there are artists and scientists, teachers and activists, people in every field of labor who, each in their own way, are working in the belief that the only possible future for our human species is to discover a new way of being on this earth. Together and alone, we are doing our best to imagine and to create new cultures and new societies to come after the inevitable collapse of the global monoculture that is driving us toward oblivion. We are working as if our survival depended on it because, very likely, it does.

Music is my way of understanding the world, of knowing where I am and how I fit in. This isn't just an emotional, a psychological need. It's a spiritual hunger—a search for the sacred. Yet in these troubled times, in a secular society in decline, what does that mean? Just what, if anything, is sacred anymore?

Composers from Johann Sebastian Bach to Arvo Part have found courage and musical inspiration in their faith. So do I. Although I don't follow any established religious tradition, the practice of my art is the practice of my faith. However, my faith is not in the church. It is in the earth.

For me, the earth itself is sacred. The natural world is an inexhaustible source of inspiration and music. Whether in the Arctic or the desert, most of my works have begun with some small epiphany, some moment of grace that I've experienced outdoors, in what I call "the real world."

Music for me is a form of prayer. It is a call to attention, an invitation to enter into sacred space, to be more deeply aware, to feel the presence of mysteries larger and older and deeper than I can fathom. In my work, I aspire to discover new musical spaces that invite us to lose ourselves, to step out of time as we usually experience it.

In *Parsifal*, Gurnemanz sings: ". . . here time becomes space." Or as Samuel Beckett puts it: "Time has turned into Space and there will be no more Time."

The Book of Revelations is filled with apocalyptic visions of the end of time. But even as human society seems to be rushing headlong toward oblivion, I hold no dreams of escaping via messiahs or spaceships. My deepest longing is to be fully present in the fullness of the present moment in *this* world, here on this beautiful stone spinning in space that is the only home I will ever know.

I find something like a credo in the words of the poet Pedro Salinas:

Earth. Nothing more. Earth. Nothing less.
And let that be enough for you.

CHAPTER 12
THINKING IN SOUND
Craig Shepard

Every human being has the capacity to hear sounds in the mind. The musician dedicates time, attention, and energy to develop five capacities:

(1) to listen with discrimination,
(2) to hold sounds in the mind,
(3) to hear sounds in the mind that they've never heard before,
(4) to make sounds in the world, and
(5) to know what resonates.

In this chapter, I will talk about my understanding of how listening works, share some of my own experiences bringing sound into the world, and give some practical suggestions for others looking to deepen their music practice.

Let's begin with a listening exercise:

Listening Exercise

Take a moment to relax and listen. What do you hear? Can you direct your attention to your breathing? Can you hear your breath coming in and going out? What does it sound like? Can you hear your heartbeat? Nervous system? Can you hear a car on a distant highway? The sound of heating in the room in which you are sitting? Take a moment and rest with these sounds.

Sounds are happening within and around us all the time—it's we who are not always here. Sometimes we only notice when there is an alarm or a siren, or someone calls our name. We come back to where we are and listen.

The musician develops the capacity to listen and to direct attention to fine details of tone, rhythm, pitch, volume, and timbre. The more the musician listens, the more he or she hears, and the more details he or she can distinguish.

The musician also holds sounds in the mind. Most of us can do this when we remember sounds.

Practical Aesthetics

Memory Exercise

> *Now direct your attention to your memory. Can you hear the sound of your mother or father calling your name? What does it sound like? What qualities does it possess? What does it feel like when you hear it in your mind? Can you hear them angry? Scolding? Can you hear in your memory a group of friends calling your name? At a birthday party?*
>
> Sounds leave a memory—an echo—in the mind.
> The more we hear a sound, the stronger is the echo.
> The more often we hear the sound, the stronger is the echo.
> The more we pay attention, the stronger is the echo.

Most of us know the sound of our own name, and can call to mind this sound very clearly. We know the sound of our family and close friends calling to us when they are happy to see us, when they are angry, and when they are sad. We know the particular tone they take, the tenor of their voice, the way they pronounce consonants, and the emphasis they place on certain words. We know what these sounds feel like in our body.

In the same way each of us can call to mind the sound of our name in many different situations, a musician can call to mind the sound of his or her instrument.

The English word "rehearse" comes from the Anglo Norman "rehercier," literally "to rake over again" (Kelly 2018). When we listen to a sound over and over, we can hold that sound in our mind. This is an essential part of the work of a musician.

The musician often begins learning a song he or she loves, memorizing the words and melody. The jazz musician memorizes solos from their favorite recordings. A young musician often takes private lessons, listening to his or her teacher.

While practicing, the musician rehears the sound of his or her instrument over and over again, until he or she can call it to mind quickly and clearly. As the musician repeats a scale, the scale becomes clearer. As the musician sings a chord, he or she develops awareness of the sound of that chord. Repeating this over and over, the awareness becomes finer. The musician learns to hear a pitch, then learns to hear the tiny vibrations and beating patterns when two pitches resonate at slightly different frequencies.

As the musician practices this capacity, he or she can hear his or her instrument in many different situations: solo, duo, high range, low range, chords, scales, melodies, songs, and styles. The musician also goes beyond his or her primary instrument and can hold other instruments in the mind. Over time, the musician fills a reservoir of sounds in the mind, and is able to call them up individually, and in different combinations.

Reading sheet music is the practice of associating the sounds in the mind with a symbolic representation of sound. This too can be developed, refined, and clarified to the point where seeing a symbol on a piece of paper recalls a sound immediately. After developing the capacity to read music, when a musician sight-reads, he or she is hearing a sound in the mind that he or she hasn't heard before.

I believe we all have the capacity to hear sounds in the mind we've never heard before.

New Sounds

In your mind, can you place yourself in an arena at a sporting event? Can you hear the sound of the announcer over the loudspeaker? Can you hear the announcer say the starting line-up? Now, can you hear your name coming over the loudspeaker?

For most people, hearing their name over the loudspeaker in the arena has never happened before. So far, everyone who has joined me in this exercise has reported that yes, they could hear their name coming over the loudspeaker at an arena. Many of us also have the experience of hearing a melody very clearly in our minds: we can't get the tune out of our head. When this is a melody that we have never heard before, the mind is composing.

It's one thing to hear a sound in the mind, it's another to bring this sound into the world.

Making New Sounds

Take a moment to hear the sound of your name in your mind. Call to mind a memory of someone you love calling your name. What does it feel like? What does it sound like? How would you like it to sound? Take a moment to hold it very clearly in the mind. Now, speak that name.

Many of us do have awareness of sounds in the mind, but have not developed the facility to make them. We know the joke, but can't deliver the punch line. The spouse wants to comfort his partner—but the words come out harsh and end up pushing the partner further away. The musician can hear the melody clearly in the mind, but the fingers just won't follow.

As the performing musician practices, he or she develops the facility to bring sound into the world. This is physical technique on the instrument. The brass player builds small muscles in the cheeks and jaw. The guitarist develops strength and flexibility in the hand and fingers. The singer develops control over the diaphragm and the vocal chords. The electronic musician learns what sequence of electric impulses through which circuits create which sounds.

The composing musician also develops the facility to bring sound in the mind into the world. One direct route is to perform one's own compositions. Another route is writing symbols on paper for others to perform.

In a scene in the movie *Amadeus*, Wolfgang Mozart bends over the billiard table, writing notes on a sheet of paper. The soundtrack of the film plays one of his symphonies, and we see him writing while absent-mindedly rolling a billiard ball. The scene suggests Mozart was taking dictation directly from the sounds in his mind.

This is one model; many composing musicians also go through a testing process, trying different sounds to see which one rings true.

Practical Aesthetics

Resonance

Take another moment to hear the sound of your name in your mind. Hold the sound for a moment. Now speak the sound and record yourself. Listen to the recording. Does it match what you were hearing in your mind? What's different? How is it different? Try this with a group of people speaking each others' names. Do your colleagues say your name as you would like to hear it? What's different?

This exercise begins to develop the capacity to pay attention to how sounds resonate with the listener. Does the sound in the world match the sound in the mind? Is it in tune? Is it in harmony with the sound in the mind? Developing the capacity to know what sounds we resonate with is part of developing intuition.

"The rewards of listening to our inner voice without the masking effects of language are immediate. We all have a kind of knowing that comes to us from our inner voice. We may think of it as intuition, or call it a hunch or a feeling in the bones" (Tomatis 2005: 46).

The musician develops the capacity to know what resonates. One situation where this occurs is hearing when two tones are out of tune. Two tones sounding together make a distinct vibration. Over time, the musician learns to recognize this quality. Upon further repetition, the musician can hear this resonance in their mind. When these two tones vibrate just slightly apart, they make a pulsing or beating pattern which is often called "out of tune." Over time, the musician learns to recognize this quality. He or she makes a sound and knows when it's in tune.

The composing musician learns to recognize when a certain organization of sounds resonates with the sounds in her or his mind. For many composing musicians—often early on in their development—there is a testing process. First, the composer has a slight intuition—like a half-heard echo from another room. He or she might try to play that sound on the piano, and it's not quite right. So the composer tries another sound, and so on. At some point, the sound on the piano resonates. It's a "yes," or an "ah-hah"; something "clicks" inside—it *feels* right. The process can involve compositional techniques including chance procedures, electronic circuits, twelve-tone rows, algorithms, counterpoint, and harmonic systems; listening and knowing what resonates is essential.

I suggest that many more composers work by intuition than is at first apparent. Christian Wolff writes: "[John Cage] described the difficulties of making the orchestra piece *Apartment House 1776*—the chance procedures hadn't worked out quite right, the sound was too thick, he had to start over again" (1998: 384). This suggests that Cage had a sound in his mind and the music which resulted from his chance procedures did not match that sound. He then adjusted the chance procedures. Despite all of John Cage's writings about chance, it seems he also worked intuitively.

Although I write about resonance last, I believe it's actually the first impulse in becoming a musician. Most of us can remember the first song we really fell in love with. It still resonates with us; it excites and moves us, giving us energy and direction. It moves the musician to keep going, to practice, and to develop.

Thinking in Sound

This is my understanding so far of how listening works and how we make music. I came to this understanding by examining my own experiences, and I'd like to share both those experiences and the lessons I learned about situations which support creating new music.

Practical Experience

Looking back on some of my own projects, I can see that each had elements that supported the process of listening, holding sounds in the mind, listening to new sounds, bringing them into the world, and paying attention to resonance.

Walking Projects

In 2005, I organized a small tour with a brass sextet. Once the tour fell apart, I decided I wanted to simplify how I was working. I asked myself: What are the essential elements of a concert tour? I came to: music, multiple dates, multiple venues, transportation, and a place to sleep. Then it came to me that I could do a minimal tour where I played my own music, performed outdoors, slept in a tent, and walked from place to place.

This became *On Foot*, in which I walked 250 miles in thirty-one days across Switzerland. Every day, I composed a new piece, wrote it down, and performed it outdoors in a public space. Each day I walked between two and nine hours. Usually, after walking for three hours, my thoughts settled, and I began to hear music in my mind.

Some pieces, such as "Vallorbe, le 23 juillet," used a pattern for the pitches. I wrote out the pattern, and then played it on the trumpet. Once I heard it, I asked myself: "does this piece work or not?" When it did, I wrote out the piece. When it didn't, I changed the pattern until the piece "hit the spot." Many composers work this way with a system or procedure, trying things out until it rings true in the mind.

For other pieces, such as "Grottes de l'Orbe, le 22 juillet," I wrote down the melody that was in my head. As I walked, I heard a fragment of the melody, stopped, and wrote it down. Continuing my walk, I heard another fragment, and then wrote that down. When I heard another part, I'd stop and write that down, and so on, until the piece felt good enough to perform that evening.

I saw that the structure of *On Foot* supported composing. I had a simple activity (walking), a clear deadline to share the music with the world, and time to listen to resonance.

I wasn't entirely sure that these structures worked until I did another walking project in 2012. I lived in New York and worked forty-five to fifty hours a week at an office. I found it difficult to find enough time to write music. I had seen pictures from the 2003 three-day blackout in New York City, during which people walked from their homes in Brooklyn to work in Manhattan. One day, I tried walking the three hours

Practical Aesthetics

round-trip to the office, and found that—as during *On Foot*—I began to hear music in my mind.

This was the beginning of the project *On Foot: Brooklyn*, in which I walked everywhere I went for ninety-one days—at least three hours each day—composed a new piece of music every week, and performed it outdoors on Sunday in the middle of a silent walk. Again, ample time, a simple activity, and clear deadlines for public performances supported me in completing new works.

I knew that these structures supported me while working alone. The next step was exploring which structures supported creating in groups.

Creating Music Together

Beginning in 2018, Tony Geballe, Dev Ray, Erin Rogers, and I have organized workshops and retreats in which a group of people practice listening exercises, write music, and perform each others' compositions. On the seven-day retreats, the group lives together and participants take turns cooking and caring for the house. Days usually begin with a group sitting, and sessions feature listening exercises like the ones mentioned earlier. There is silence every day from 10:00 p.m. through 8:00 a.m. and on two days from 10:00 p.m. through 1:00 p.m. During a performance cycle, we break up into small groups of three to five, within which everyone writes and everyone rehearses and performs each others' music.

As with the walking projects, we had dedicated time to work, deadlines for performances, and a simple physical activity in cooking. Further, in the rehearsal stage, we could test what we were hearing. On each workshop and retreat, many more compositions came to me than I had time to write down. Other participants have reported the same.

Suggestions

This is my understanding of listening and creating music. Each of us can listen closely, pay attention to how sounds and music resonate with us, take time to listen to sounds in the mind, and share them in the world.

In my walking projects, I needed time, a simple repetitive activity, performing in front of others, and paying attention to what resonated with me. These practices also support musicians working in groups.

To those looking to establish or deepen a musical practice, I hope you will take the time to really listen, to give yourself the support you need, and to share what you hear with others.

We can all hear more than we think we can. We all have more to share than we know.

References

Amadeus (1984), [Film] Dir. Milos Forman, USA: AMLF.
Kelly, J. (2018), "What in the Word?! Raking over the Roots of Rehearse." Available online: https://blog.oxforddictionaries.com/2018/03/07/what-in-the-word-raking-over-the-roots-of-rehearse/ (accessed February 25, 2019).
Tomatis, A. (2005), *The Ear and the Voice*, trans. R. Prada and P. Sollier, adapt. R. Prada and F. Keeping, Toronto and Oxford: Scarecrow Press.
Wolff, C. (1998), "Benign Ghosts. On John Cage," in C. Wolff (ed.), *Cues: Writings & Conversations*, Cologne: MusikTexte.

CHAPTER 13
MUSIC AS SONIC PRAXIS
ON THE WORK OF CATHERINE CHRISTER HENNIX
Marcus Boon

1

One afternoon in Berlin in 2016, when I was talking with composer/mathematician Catherine Christer Hennix at her house, I saw a copy of Alain Daniélou's *Tableaux Comparatif des Intervalles Musicaux*—the 1958 booklet in which Daniélou, the French musicologist, lists every pitch that has been used by human beings within the octave. The booklet was important to minimalists such as La Monte Young, who worked with Just Intonation, since the book is effectively a catalog or recipe book of tuning systems. When I asked Hennix about the book, she said, "It is, you may say, the continuum of the octave."[1]

What did she mean by this? The continuum or continuity refers philosophically the notion of a partless or undifferentiated whole—for example, the space-time continuum in physics, or nonduality in certain religious traditions such as Advaita Vedanta or Dzogchen in Tibetan Buddhism. Continuity can also be thought of more locally, as the continuum of mind, body, and world. In mathematics, the continuum refers to the set of real numbers on a number line, that is, all of the points on this line. This set, like the set of natural numbers on the number line, is infinite. But while the set of natural numbers on the number line is countably infinite, that is, you can keep counting ever greater natural numbers, the set of real numbers is uncountably infinite, due to the infinitesmal differences marked as real numbers that can be demonstrated between any points on the line. Cantor determined in the late nineteenth century that the magnitude of the infinity of these real numbers was demonstrably greater than the infinity of the natural numbers. This magnitude he referred to as cardinality, and he hypothesized that there was no cardinality between that of the real numbers and that of the natural numbers. This claim, which is foundational for modern mathematics, is known as the continuum hypothesis, which Hilbert listed as the first of his famous twenty-three problems in modern mathematics in 1900, and there remains no consensus as to whether the hypothesis holds.[2] The relation between the mathematical and philosophical meanings of the word "continuum" is complex—most mathematicians would probably prefer to restrict their use of the word to the frameworks set out earlier. But since the problems raised by the continuum as to the foundations of mathematics are unresolved—and since these problems find an analogy in philosophy and elsewhere—an openness as to where, disciplinarily, the problem (and explanation) of the continuum is located is I believe permissible.

In these terms, to speak of "the continuum of the octave" is to speak of an uncountably infinite number of pitches that exist within the octave, and via a kind of set theory to speak of tuning systems as subsets that are somehow sutured to this continuum. For musical systems such as South Asian raga or Arabic maqam, which use a variety of tuning systems, this is self-evident—and may offer a first perspective on the question of music and pluralism. There is a plurality of tuning systems and a plurality of ways of moving within specific tuning systems. Going beyond the specific just intonation-based systems that are used in traditional musics around the world, contemporary Just Intonation musics from Harry Partch onward propose a much larger possible number of pitches within the octave that accord with the mathematics of harmony, being based on ratios of prime numbers. This raises a broader issue of the relation of music to ideas of the continuum. On the one hand, "the continuum of the octave" suggests the possibility of musics of infinitesmal subtlety, in which the differentiation of musics has its roots or core in tiny but decisive decisions and events as to the ordering by which tones and tone clusters occur. On the other hand, all music would appear to emerge from the indifferentiation of the continuum itself—in other words, a kind of super-sameness that underlies difference and which iterates the problem of the one and the many, monism and pluralism, and so on. Here, I offer some thoughts on the ways in which the problem of the continuum has been presented philosophically as the basis for thinking about a pluralist and pragmatic ontology of music.[3]

From the point of view of "practical aesthetics," we might ask: What is it that makes the practical practical? When we speak of practical aesthetics, we are talking about that which can be or rather is realized or revealed or actualized. That which can be realized cannot be restricted to or framed as "thinking with sound"—an approach that still imagines sound as a preexisting material that then is deployed like pieces in a chess game, or the execution of a code. Practical aesthetics must mean thinking the immanence of aesthetic unfolding of the real. That sounds like a Deleuzian proposition. But that is not intention here—as I understand it, what I am arguing for is closer to what Badiou argues in *Being and Event 2: Logics of Worlds*. That the realm of the practical, and the emergence of aesthetic propositions, objects and events out of the immanence of an infinite potentiality—is guided by logics which structure this experimentation. And those logics are grounded as much in the qualities of the materiel of sound (as vibration) as they are by thought. It is in this way that what we call music emerges from what we call sound—an "aesthetic" differentiation, a differentiation that comes to define what we call "aesthetic," a differentiation discovered "in practice."

2

An initial hypothesis: considered globally, the practice of music in toto addresses and articulates the continuum.

Mental exercise: imagine the totality of all musical activity on the planet at this particular moment. Include the 400 million times Kanye West's *The Life of Pablo* was streamed on Tidal in the first month of its release. Include the anonymous bossa nova singer and guitarist who was playing Milton Nascimento's "Tudo Se Voce" on a makeshift stage on the roof of a beach bar in Trindade, Brazil, last March while a group of us played or floated in the waves. Include animal sounds. Include all organic life. Include all of the sounds of inorganic life. Now extend this in time. Now extend this across the cosmos. Now imagine all of that happening within the framework of the octave(s). From there you begin to approximate the continuum. A very large number of cuts, marks, traces, local mappings of the continuum, happening in space-time. This is what music is: a binding to/of the continuum. A supermultitudinous vibration, both metaphor for and articulation of the continuum itself.

In speaking this way, I am drawing on the work of Colombian philosopher of mathematics Fernando Zalamea, who, in his book *Peirce's Logic of Continuity: A Conceptual and Mathematical Approach* (2012a), sets out a striking rethinking of what is meant by the continuum through the work of American philosopher and a founding voice of both pragmatism and pluralism, Charles Sanders Peirce. Peirce's work on the continuum is complex and evolved over the course of his career. Zalamea's presentation emphasizes that Peirce's idea of the continuum was of a continuity beyond that of Cantor's mathematics yet still able to support mathematical ideas of the continuum. In other words, points on a number line are insufficient for representing the continuum in its full reality. He describes it as a supermultitudinousness, a multiplicity so dense that in the end all possible singularities fuse into continuity and vice versa (Peirce 2010: 198). The point is that this is not a confabulation of science fiction or fantasy, but the basis of our own reality. Zalamea describes Peirce's theorization of the continuum and how particularity emerges from it as involving a modal logic. The continuity of the "true" continuum, which is ultimately unrepresentable, supports the discontinuity of particular points and relationships of points. In other words, it supports modes and modalities.

> Peirce's continuum is general, plastic, homogeneous, regular, in order to allow, in a natural way, the "transit" of modalities, the "fusion" of individualities, the "overlapping" of neighborhoods. The generic idea of a continuous flow is present behind those transits, fusions and overlappings, ubiquitous osmotic processes that Peirce notices in the plasticity of protoplasm and human mind, and that, in a bold abduction, he lifts to a universal hypothesis. (Zalamea 2012a: 17)

From thinking about the continuum in this way, Peirce derives a pragmatic and pluralist logic: pragmatic because all existent forms and events are local arrangements of and improvisations on/in the continuum, pluralist because the local constructions that constitute cuts or workings in/of the continuum are variable types of discontinuous pragmatic constructions. In other words, there is not just a single relation of continuity to discontinuity. If we apply this way of thinking to music, we might interpret "modality" in the strict or literal sense of modes as scales. In a 1976 interview, Hennix described her own musical work as "intuitionistic modal music," meaning that the construction of modes proceeds from the existential engagement of the mathematician with the "two-ity" through which continuity breaks into the temporal sequence of before and after, and the full Parmenidean immanence of the NOW is rendered/reduced to a phenomenological object—the two-ity which is the basis of Brouwer's intuitionism and his theory of the foundation of mathematics (Hennix 1976a). Hennix transposes this to music and sound, emphasizing that "we aim at evolving frames of musical structures, rather than trying to obtain completeness." However, we might speak of improvisation in general as a local articulation of a structure, or more generally of a musical event per se as being "modal" in some broader sense of the word. Musical genres such as the blues, musical practices such as "possession" in the sense that Gilbert Rouget (1992) uses the word, events such as the Jamaican sound system clash could all be thought of in this expanded sense of "modal."

The entire data of ethnomusicology could be seen as evidence of this. To take but one example, Jose Maceda's wonderful book *Gongs and Bamboo* (1998) in which he describes the varieties of gonged and bamboo instruments and the ways they are played in different parts of the Philippines, today, but also historically. Every regional variation in the music played constitutes a kind of act of musical pragmatism, that is, the form that music takes in that time and place, but also the form that musical access to the continuum takes in that time and place. In other words, there is no music without the continuum. As soon as an act of sound shaping occurs, the continuum appears as the space produced by sound shaping. To make musical sounds is to sound shape—not any particular shape, but a shape in the sense of a geometric invocation (a few points/tones, some kind of harmonic and/or melodic organization, rhythm, timbre) nonetheless. And of course there are more or less arbitrary shapes and more or less significant ones. Music is the pragmatic local elaboration of that. Even at the level of the construction of musical instruments, Maceda notes that in order to understand the forms of bamboo instruments played in the Philippines, you need to know the botany of Bamboo varietals, just as the history of trade routes is revealed by the ways in which the resonant forms of the gong are used in different geographical regions of the Philippines. Music emerges out of a certain material set of histories and practices and potentials for the making of sounds. The important thing to understand here is that if pragmatism is merely considered the local arrangement of things, what we would have is a fairly unremarkable sociology of music or even ethnomusicology. But there are constraints on pragmatic local elaboration which remove music from being arbitrary, though not from being diverse or pluralistic. And these constraints have to do with the relationship between music and the continuum.

3

In giving a more precise meaning to the expanded sense of "modal music" that I introduced earlier, we should further track Zalamea's thought, in his work on Peirce and in his later book, *Synthetic Philosophy of Contemporary Mathematics* (2012b)—precisely because Zalamea attempts to show the ways in which contemporary mathematics explores plural ontologies. Key in this undertaking is category theory and its offshoot/relative topos theory as developed by mid-century mathematicians such as William Lawvere and Alexander Grothendieck. For Zalamea, topos and category theory point to the need for a "synthetic philosophy" in which the pragmatic elaboration of connections or "transits" between different modalities is emphasized over a concern with a singular fundamental ontology or "foundation of mathematics." Here, "topos" will be used to explore an expanded sense of the ways in which modality works in music.

To present this in highly oversimplified but still hopefully useful terms, the ontological implications of category theory are pluralist; in other words, each category presents an ontology according to its own logic and method, and the possibility also exists of making mappings between categories—for example, geometry and algebra. Category, for the purposes of this chapter, would be a kind of mode. Topos theory then explores making a taxonomy of mapping methods and practices between categories. The word "topos" means site or space in a very general sense of that word—a site being a formal space which intersecting or overlapping ontologies, logics, categories might simultaneously or prospectively or speculatively occupy. In Olivia Caramello's gloss (2017), topos theory concerns the building of bridges between mathematical theories or models. How might one think of music in relation to topos theory? I would like to present two possibilities: one the work of Guerino Mazzola, whose book *The Topos of Music* (2002) sets out in 1,500 pages a detailed elaboration that among other things has received the approval of Grothendieck. The other is Hennix, for whom the figure of the topos, and crucially, toposes, has been important since the mid-1970s both in her writings about music and sound and in her compositions.

Mazzola uses the notion of topos to present as thorough and deep a set of parameters as possible by which to model or "categorize" music via a "musical semiotics." The importance of this work cannot be overstated since Mazzola makes a compelling and rigorous argument that despite all the random, improvisatory, spontaneous, and singular aspects of a musical performance that would seem to place it "beyond" science or mathematical description, contemporary mathematical tools are capable of rigorously describing—at least in principle—even the most chaotic or arbitrary sounding free jazz performance. Which is simply to say that music does always involve structure. Here it should be understood that words like "noise," when applied to music, are often merely ethnocentric or ideological weapons for dismissing musics that do not conform to the patterns established by a particular hegemonic musical system. Beyond that, the so-called noise music is subject notions of pattern and dispersal as much as any other. Unfortunately, Mazzola then tries to measure the success of his theory by the ability of computer software to analyze a musical performance in sufficient detail as to describe it accurately and to offer the possibility of significant improvisations or musical events that are novel. The difficulties involved in this endeavor become evident when one compares them with the recent work of Julian Henriques, who in his book *Sonic Bodies* (2011) attempts to give a full account of the "sounding" "wavebands" that go into a single session of the Jamaican sound system Stone Love Movement at one of their weekly dances. Henriques identifies the descriptive musicological qualities of the sound as just one element of a threefold structure that includes material (the physics of sound and electricity), corporeal (the way particular bodies shape both the production and reception of a specific musical event), and sociocultural (the "ways of knowing" that give particular kinds of social meaning to a musical event) (2011: 20–4). While the sum total of these qualities may indeed still constitute a "topos of music" or maybe even THE topos of music, it is hard to see how they could be quantified by computer software in any meaningful way. Or even why that would be an interesting thing to do. In this sense, we can raise a question of the magnitude of pluralisms that Mazzola's model of music is able to contain or account for—and in this sense we might speak of degrees of pluralism internal to a single model of what music is.

To consider music a topos then, as Mazzola does, is to say that the totality of music has one logic within which there are a variety of permutations which constitute specific musical forms and events. Mazzola dismisses the question of "What music is?" saying that it is meaningless after Kant's bracketing of the "thing in itself" and the resulting displacement of the problem of "ontology" to one of locating the concept within the categories of knowledge. Although I do not wish to imply that I think that the ontology of music involves recourse to the "thing in itself," the question of "what music is?" in fact remains unanswered by Mazzola. Or rather, Mazzola gives a reductionist answer to the question, even as he proposes what he considers to be a nonreductionist solution, that is, a topos theoretical model, to the problem. In the end, Mazzola is concerned with generating computational models to provide an adequate representational or descriptive rendering of music. What is absent in Mazzola's work is precisely the notion of the continuum and the topos of music's essential relationship to it.

Hennix's interest in topos theory is different because it is not focused on issues of representation, but on a formal language that allows one access to something unrepresentable, which nonetheless can be made to appear, via sound and music. It is not clear, by the way, that this "something unrepresentable" is "the thing itself" since the continuum, if that is what is at stake here, is not reducible to thinghood. As such, what is important is the suture of the topos to being-as-void or—the continuum. (Hennix, as we noted in an earlier chapter, returns continually to the problem of the Parmenidean "One.") Recourse to the idea of the topos relates to the possibility of a variety of fields of formalization of this relationship to the continuum and the construction of fields grafted onto fields which head in the direction of this voidness. Perhaps the major difference in approach is once again Hennix's interest in intuitionism and the necessarily improvised construction of topoi and connections between topoi—which in turn radically changes what is at stake in exploring topoi in music: not representation, but construction, creation, and these latter acts as necessarily oriented in relation to ecstatic nonknowledge.

What is gained by calling this music work a topos? To this obvious question, the best answer I can give is that Hennix's work actually inverts what Zalamea (and likely Mazzola) believes to be at stake in topos theory. Rather than suggesting that questions of fundamental ontology are misguided or irrelevant because densifying the weave of interconnected and verifiable mathematical models via toposes produces a pragmatically deepened kind of description that is actually more ontological than "ontology," Hennix focuses on topos as the site of ontology, and topos theory as offering the intuitionistic construction of mathematical models and practices for revealing that site "in itself." Furthermore, and via her readings of Lacan, Hennix recognizes that what is at stake here is perhaps beyond language, though not perhaps beyond mathematics or music. As such, musical practice or performance carries the weight of the actual and "practical" revealing of being to be found in a topos/site. At an ontological level, suggested by the idea of a topos as a generalized notion of space, place, or location, Hennix's work often succeeds, at least in my experience, in producing an uncanny wavering of the phenomenality of the room one is in. Sometimes when listening to her work, it feels like the floor is melting. Hennix is concerned with the possibility of designing, or bringing into being toposes that are mathematical entities, musical compositions but also new kinds of ontological frameworks. In a recent text, she says:

> In the passage to this topos of maqam during Sam'a (Sufi congregation for prayer), the ultimate goal is to experience fan'a, a state of annihilation carrying the subject fading into infinity, a state that comes in distinct degrees and modalities all of which are accompanied by specific inner sounds that arise in the course of arriving at the crossings of remembrance and oblivion. (2017: 16)

In her notes to *The Electric Harpsichord*, her 1976 drone-based composition, she elaborates a series of abstract musical ideas which she names toposes, most of which involve the production of drones, or sustained tones, which work at various levels to produce a "continuous musical event" along with various other kinds of continua (continua of memory, of perception, of time) (2010).

Hennix's work introduces a new kind of pluralism to our thinking about music. In other words, musical pluralism is not just the set of iterations occurring in a single but variable field which we might call following Mazzola "the topos of music" whether defined in a strictly musicological sense, or in a broader sociocultural sense. Musical pluralism, in Hennix's version, may be understood as the possibility of variable ontologies of sound and vibration—a possibility, which, in *Intensions, Illuminations and Toposes* (1981), she relates to a kind of synaesthesia. To complicate matters—in a recent poem entitled "Topos 1," Hennix explores the notion of Islam as a "master topos" (a paradox or even a contradiction, as she is well aware) (2017: 5). As far back as 1976, she proposed "monistic universes" (in the plural) and recently coined the term "mono-monism" to describe her thinking).[4] How to resolve this paradox? Elsewhere, Hennix writes of music as "the shortest path to monism" (2016). Ontologies are pathways, "logics." Thus, they are plural in relation to an ultimate referent which is the continuum or the One, but a "One" and a "monism" that need to be understood differently precisely because of the introduction of modes as mediators of "the one and the many."

Hennix's proposal may at first appear a fantastic or unreasonable one since it may be argued that few musical works are literally concerned with revealing an ontology of music. I myself am not sure I accept it (although I have no difficulty in accepting topos and category theory as pluralist mathematical practices, or in thinking about Badiou's turn to "logics of worlds" or for that matter Zalamea's reformulated pragmatism). But it does forcefully make the argument that the ontology of music matters and that the question of "what music is?" cannot be answered without considering it.

4

There has been a modal turn in a number of quite different recent philosophical texts, including Bruno Latour's *An Inquiry into Modes of Existence* (2012), his response to those who argue that his work lacks an ontology; Alain Badiou's *Logics of Worlds* (2006), the second volume of *Being and Event*, and his modification, via Grothendieck's work on toposes, of the first volume of that book's claim that set theory provides a fundamental ontology; Giorgio Agamben's *The Use of Bodies* (2014) in which the problem of "bare life's" elaboration as social and political form is worked through via the idea of modes as "forms of life." While each of these texts uses sound as an analogy at certain points (Latour reflects on "tonality" [375]; Agamben on "originary echos" [149]; Badiou on serial music [79–89]), none of them considers sound and music in any depth in their elaboration of modal ontologies. In each case, what is missed is that sound and music are not just arbitrary examples or peripheral to ontological inquiry—they are "the shortest path to monism" and offer the clearest embodiment of a modal ontology.

What is at stake in Zalamea and Hennix's work is a pragmatic or practical sense of what it means to elaborate a mode—as creative mathematical endeavor for Zalamea, and as musical, aesthetic, ontological wager for Hennix. Still, at least in Hennix's case one might wonder whether we are really talking about "practical aesthetics" any more. Hennix has repeatedly observed that music's place in Medieval Europe was as a component of the quadrivium (arithmetic, geometry, astronomy, and music)—which were "arts" of course in a different sense to that of post-eighteenth-century European aesthetics. Yet the opening up of the problem of practice within the arts, whether associated with Duchamp, or Cage, or Coltrane, always leads to a collapse of the coherency of that modern notion of aesthetics, such that art must be abandoned either for some version of life itself, or Being or to a generalization of aesthetics, such that aesthetics becomes the practical principle of the organization, design, or form of life and living. In Hennix's case, what is most important is the status of the subject (also a topos, or site, one might say), and the possibility of a "practice of the unconscious" (a phrase Hennix adopted from certain Italian Marxist-feminists of the 1970s [Melchiori 2015]) that exposes or opens up that site to divine influence, psychotropic transformation, and ekstasis. The practice of making music is directed toward this goal.

Notes

1. Interview with author, May 2016.

2. Many of the great mathematicians of the twentieth century, including Brouwer, Weyl, Gödel, and Cohen, responded to the problem of the continuum. There is no single book that surveys this history. See however Buckley 2012.
3. Christoph Cox has emphasized the importance of the idea of the continuum in his work on the ontology of sound. In Cox's work, the continuum consists of an infinite sonic multiplicity or flux, one that is virtual in relation to music and speech, which consist of local "contractions" of this continuum. Cox draws on Leibniz and Deleuze in his work—I believe that the model Hennix proposes (and which I draw on) has some affinities with this work, not least because of Deleuze's interest in Peirce (though Hennix does not refer to Peirce), but also certain differences which could (and should) be drawn out. See Cox 2009 and 2018.
4. "The world de-signifies itself by being re-centered around a single signifier which is immediately recognized and that reveals a parallel world with an alternative semantics which abolishes all distinctions, and, therefore, necessarily, but not, perhaps, without a sense of paradox, also the distinction between the lover and the Beloved. This is the ultimate form of monism of Unity of Being—ana'haq" (Hennix 2017: 11).

References

Agamben, G. (2014), *The Use of Bodies*, Stanford: Stanford University Press.
Badiou, A. (2006), *Being and Event II: Logics of Worlds*, London: Continuum.
Buckley, B. L. (2012), *The Continuity Debate: Dedekind, Cantor, du Bois-Reymond and Peirce on Continuity and Infinitesmals*, Boston: Docent.
Caramello, O. (2017), *Theories, Sites, Toposes: Relating and Studying Mathematical Theories Through Topos-theoretic "bridges,"* Oxford: Oxford University Press.
Cox, C. (2009), "Sound Art and the Sonic Unconscious," *Organized Sound*, 14 (1): 19–26.
Cox, C. (2018), *Sonic Flux: Sound, Art, and Metaphysics*, Chicago: University of Chicago Press.
Daniélou, A. (1958), *Tableau Comparatif des Intervalles Musicaux*, Pondicherry: Institut Français d'Indologie.
Hennic, C. C. (2016), "OM: When a Divine Name Confers a Radiance of Infinite Blessings', Self-published poem.
Hennix, C. C. (1976), "Aspects of Intuitionistic Modal Music," *Brouwer's Lattice, Moderna Museet 20 March 76-30 March 76*, exhibition catalogue, Stockholm: Moderna Museet.
Hennix, C .C. (2010). Sleevenotes to *The Electric Harpsichord* (CD plus booklet). Milan: Die Schachtel.
Hennix, C. C. (2017), *Sonoilluminescences* [booklet], self-published. Available online: http://www.annesenstad.com/SonoilluminescencesCCHtextVeniceBiennale2017.pdf (accessed June 6, 2019).
Hennix, C. C. With H. Flynt (1981), "Intensions, Illuminations and Toposes," draft 3, manuscript.
Henriques, J. (2011), *Sonic Bodies: Reggae Sound Systems, Performance Techniques, and Ways of Knowing*, New York: Continuum.
Latour, B. (2012), *An Inquiry into Modes of Existence: An Anthropology of the Moderns*, Cambridge: Harvard University Press.
Maceda, J. (1998), *Gongs & Bamboo: a Panorama of Philippine Music Instruments*, Quezon City: University of the Philippines Press.
Mazzola, G. (2002), *The Topos of Music: Geometric Logic of Concepts, Theory, and Performance*, Basel: Birkhäuser Verlag.
Melchiori, P. (2015), "Psychoanalysis in Early Italian Feminism: The Contributions of the Practice of the Unconscious," in A. Calcagno (ed.), *Contemporary Italian Political Philosophy*, 75–97, Albany, NY: SUNY Press.

Practical Aesthetics

Peirce, C. S. (2010), "On Multitudes," in M. E. Moore (ed.), *Philosophy of Mathematics: Selected Writings*, Bloomington: Indiana University Press.
Rouget, G. (1992), *Music and Trance: A Theory of the Relations Between Music and Possession*, trans. B. Biebuyck, Chicago: University of Chicago Press.
The Electric Harpsichord (2010), [CD with booklet] Hennic, C. C., Milan: Die Schachtel.
Zalamea, F. (2012a), *Pierce's Logic of Continuity: A Conceptual and Mathematical Approach*, Boston: Docent Press.
Zalamea, F. (2012b), *Synthetic Philosophy of Contemporary Mathematics*, Falmouth, UK: Urbanomic & Sequence.

CHAPTER 14
THE AUDIO PAPER AS AFFECTIVE ATTUNEMENTS
THINKING, PRODUCING, AND LISTENING
Sanne Krogh Groth and Kristine Samson

Introduction

The audio paper is a publication format shaped, produced, and perceived in sound. The core of the audio paper is an academic argument, as it is positioned in ongoing research; it brings in new perspectives to a defined research topic; and it argues with adequate and sensible means. The means involved in this argumentation are all presented in sound. A written abstract and bibliography is added to the interface where the audio paper is accessed, but the argument itself is presented in sound.

The core issue of the audio paper is often introduced by a narrating voice, being the voice of the author, a participant, or an actor. The argument is further explored, discussed, or problematized through other sounding sources. These sources can be music, field-recordings, "acted" sounds, real sounds, interviews, just to mention a few. And just as the voice does it, so do these composed sounds bring semantic and aesthetic dimensions to the argument. The audio paper is a fixed production and runs in real time. What is of importance is not the clock time, but the experienced time and the timing throughout the paper.

Besides being an academic genre, the audio paper draws upon other time-based formats, such as the musical composition, theatrical drama and dramaturgy, and radio montage. It is a new and an experimental format, but also one that builds on various existing disciplines and methodologies. One way of categorizing and institutionalizing the audio paper is to place it as a hybrid between anthropological field research, its orality and the documentation (e.g., Ingold 2016; Feld 2015), practice- and arts-based and artistic research (Borgdorff 2012; Leavy 2015 Springgay and Rotas 2015; Schön 1983).

As a media and methodological hybrid, the audio paper can also be seen as a redisposition of Deleuze's definitions of thought in science, philosophy, and art. In *What Is Philosophy?* Deleuze states, "What defines thought in its three great forms—art, science, and philosophy—is always confronting chaos, laying out a plane, throwing a plane over chaos" (Deleuze 1994: 197). Whereas Deleuze does not privilege one form of thought over the other, he distinguishes between how they each create a plane of consistency. As the audio paper draw on science, art, and philosophy as hybrids in its production and composition, we are interested in how these "three great forms" are entangled and attune to one another. Such exchanges might even "privilege an affect where thought and sensation merge into a very specific way of 'doing thinking' beyond representation and categorization" (Herzogenrath 2017: 5; see also Introduction, this volume).

Introducing the notion of differential attunement, we look into how the audio paper is a *reflection-in-action* (Schön 1983) or *thought in the act* (Manning and Massumi 2014). Both when it comes to production and reception, the audio paper is a composition in which the academic argument and the semantics are entangled with a plethora of practices. As a format, the audio paper itself is in flux as it often leads to new questions and challenges the dissemination of research. It is a format that presents research, while it also explores and opens for aesthetic sensation and affects, for the open-ended potentiality of knowing and feeling.

To outline the practical knowledge situation of the audio paper, we introduce the term "attunement" as understood within poststructuralist theory, and as it more recently has appeared within the field of sound studies. With this term, we structure our reflection in three modes inspired by Molino's semiotic three-part model (Molino and Underwood 1990): First, we reflect the researcher's work when articulating the argument and producing the audio paper reflected as *field attunement*; second, the published production is reflected as a composition with *multifocal attunement*; third, the position of the listeners' is discussed as a *relational attunement* opening toward broader ecologies.

This approach is not unlike tendencies in recent sound studies where, for example, Marie Thompson positions affect as an extension of twentieth-century critical theory:

> An affective approach, by contrast, deals first with an a-signifying register—the modulations of intensity, sensation and feeling that occur at the level of matter and constitute an encounter, happening or event. However, despite certain polemical overstatements so its "newness," affect theory is not a straightforward disavowal of these previous modes of understanding—a radical overthrowing of these "wrong" approaches in favour of a new, "correct" model. Rather it extends beyond, while also drawing from and working alongside, these modes of analysis. (Thompson 2017: 9)

In a similar way, we see the audio paper carrying and engaging both affects and semiotics. This approach can lead to a multilayered and sensational knowledge on the topic explored and welcomes an ecology of practices and forms to shape the academic argument.

Practical Aesthetics: Affect and Attunement

Recently, new materialism and the so-called affective turn (Clough and Halley 2007; Thrift 2007) has put an emphasis on embodied experience and how the world matters into cultural production and humanities. As pointed to by Springgay and Truman, new materialism expands beyond reflective modes of production:

> In shifting the prioritizing of mind over matter, human over thing, culture over nature, materialism with its attention to affect, movement, and agential matter develops theoretical possibilities where art is no longer understood as a reflection of reality, but as intensities and dynamic flows. (Springgay and Rotas 2015: 553)

Also Massumi notes that there seems to be a growing feeling in media, literary, and art theory that "affect is central to an understanding of our information—and image-based late capitalist culture, in which so-called master narratives are perceived to have foundered" (Massumi 2002: 27). The audio paper as an academic format deals with a variety of matters and affects, and can in this regard be seen as a format welcoming the material and affective turn in art and humanities. Together with the developments in the technology and media, the audio paper is a fruitful encounter between a material, affective turn and an increasingly hypermediated world.

No longer focusing solely on semantic meanings, but attuning into a variety of sense-making expressions, knowledge ecologies and material matters, the audio paper opens for such explorative and embodied engagement in its production, in its dissemination, and in its reception. Hence, we see the audio paper as a processual media informed by an affective and material mode of knowledge production. As stated in our audio paper manifesto, "The aesthetic, material aspects of the audio paper produce affects and sensations" (Groth and Samson 2016). We see the audio paper as an aesthetic academic practice working with auditive and affective production of knowledge and sense-making. Similar to artistic research, it is the process of emergence that is in the center of attention (Herzogenrath 2017). As an academic media format, we argue that the audio paper contributes to an aesthetic-affective encounter enabling the researcher and the listener alike to attune into a field of research.

As a practical aesthetic assembling diverse means of expression, the audio paper is an interface for acting otherwise—a thinking in action that diverts from the linearity of the academic argument and introduces heterogeneity and simultaneity as a timely knowledge form. As a practical mode of production, the production enables blocs of sensations to be brought forth in the environment. For instance, when the audio paper researcher records and organizes sounds in the research process, she actualizes the sensations and affective materiality of places, people, and environments. The simultaneity of expressions in blocs of sensation implies that heterogeneous voices and meanings are assembled in the audio paper, and spatially redistributed in its reception. Hence, the processes and attunements that relate production and composition of the paper can be seen as when "science passes from chaotic virtuality to the states of affairs and bodies that actualize it" (Deleuze 1994: 155–6).

Massumi notes that whereas perception is structural or interactive, sensation is eventful or processual (Massumi 2002: 295). This in particular applies to the audio paper as a bloc of sensation and as a composition of conceptual argumentation. Unlike emotions, affects are unqualified and nonsubjective and question already-fixed meaning. Affects are in this regard meaning coming into being, and can be understood as a process of attunement both in the situation of producing the audio paper, in its aesthetics, and in the listening situation.

The Differential Attunements of the Audio Paper

Attunement is closely related to affect, and we unfold affect in the Deleuze-Spinozist framework as the capacity of a body to affect and to be affected and can further be related to attunement as to what happens in the immediacy of an event. Massumi expands:

> That's what I mean by differential attunement: a collective in-bracing in the immediacy of an affective event, but different in each case. Attunement refers to the direct capture of attention and energies by the event, "differential" refers to the fact that we each are taken into the event from a different angle, and move out of it following our own singular trajectories, riding the waves in our own inimitable way.
>
> *(Massumi 2015: 115)*

Attuning to the immediacy of the event includes also the various affections of the body by which the body's power of acting is increased or diminished, aided, or restrained. Hence, we see affective means of knowledge production such as the audio paper, as a power that enables knowledge to be bodily felt by the listener. In this sense, a potential for multiple "knowledges" to come into being at the same time. Furthermore, the capacity to act and to be acted upon that is not limited to the human body alone but to any body, material, spatial sensory, or even a body of thought. In the ladder, we regard the capacity to affect in how the audio paper can contribute with new or traditionally hidden information into a body of thought. For instance, by bringing site-specific, regional, or gendered aspects of knowledge into the knowledge situation. Importantly, the capacity to affect and to be affected governs a transition and can be understood as an increase or a decrease in the power to act. Hence, we argue that nonlinear transitions from one state to another appear in the audio paper. One thing is related to how knowledge and material agencies can be perceptually felt or as a resonance with the expressive potentials of a given materiality or field. Here, affective attunements are "a directly relational immersion in a field of immi(a)nence from which determined actions and determinate thoughts have to emerge" (Massumi 2015: 116). This also goes for the composing of the audio paper which can be understood as a transition from a field of immanence into more determinate thoughts and actions—for example, the transformation from material agencies into aesthetic composition.

In the following discussion, we will work with two sides of affect, longitude and latitude, and explore how affect emerges in the audio paper as attunements. With reference to Deleuze and Spinoza, Thompson writes: "The longitude of a body can be understood as *the structural composition* of dynamic relations. As Spinoza states, 'Bodies are distinguished from one another in respect to motion and rest, quickness and slowness, and not by reason of substance'" (Thompson 2017: 47). Hence, the longitude of the body is, for instance, what we refer to as compositional means, whereas the latitude of the body can be understood as its intensity or its capacity *to affect and to be affected*. In relation to the audio paper, we find dramaturgy and aesthetics in its longitude and its latitude as compositions of dynamic relations affecting one another. We also see the composition as a capacity to affect the listener of the audio paper, and at the same time also attuning to a certain field of investigation allowing for the complexity of the field to emerge. Thompson sums it up: "In other words, the individual body—its structure and its power to act and to be acted upon—is constituted by its engagement with a wider milieu" (Thompson 2017: 47). The relationality of such affective attunement will be expanded in the following three sections.

Field Attunements

Our first aspect of the audio paper concerns the production of the audio paper in which attunement is related to the researcher's *reflection-in-action* or *thought in the act*. During a research process, thinking through materials, environments, bodies of texts, and disciplines or people's statements is a central part of the exploration. In the production of the audio paper, this process becomes even more fleshed out, as the researchers, while recording, editing, and mixing sounds, are in an ongoing immersion in the world's manifold rhythms. In other words, we see not only the mind operating as conceptual thinking, but an embodied mind entangled with its environment. Hence, the affective attunement in the production of the audio paper can be seen in how the researcher relates to her (empirical or theoretical) field, how she makes her subject matter come into being through, for instance, the sound recordings. Any field can be said to have capacities to affect as long as it encourages engagement. Any field resonates with what Ikoniadou has called "rhythmicity" (Ikoniadou 2014: 3), attuning into the rhythms and intensities of a field we understand as a modulation of its affective potentiality. Reorganizing the rhythmicity in the editing phase of the audio paper can be said to be an attunement to what is bodily felt, or what resonates in the body and mind of the researcher. Sound recordings and production are here not understood as a method, but rather as a way of thinking in action allowing thinking to "arrive in the middle and be immanent to the event itself" (Springgay and Truman 2018: 3). In other words, it is a method beyond a linear "proceduralism," as argued by Springgay and Truman. Hence, producing the audio paper is a thinking-in-action that works from the middle of a field folding the rhythmic materiality of a given field into an argument, a dramaturgy, and the aesthetics of the paper. Here, affective field attunements allow for augmenting and strengthening materiel agencies in the field.

Practical Aesthetics

Fields that resonate can be any field with the capacity to affect. In the first production series of the audio paper (see Groth and Samson 2016), the field of study was the urban-rural landscapes of the island Amager in Denmark. Attunement to the field involved attuning to the landscape and its soundscapes, to the discursive practices and actions taking place on Amager (Holt and Nielsen 2016) and attunements to specific sites and cultural institutions at Amager (see Kreutzfeldt and Pedersen 2016).

The production of the audio paper as a certain attunement to a field is related to audio ethnographies, anthropology of sound and the notion of "acoustemology," a conjunction of "acoustics" and "epistemology" "to investigate sounding and listening as a knowing-in-action: a knowing-with and knowing-through the audible . . . [engaging] the relationality of knowledge production" (Feld, 2015: 12). The audio production opens to a specific and direct field engagement that enables sensory modes of affective attunement that do not think human rationality first. Here, attunements to the field open up the researcher's preset definitions and understandings. As argued by Springgay and Rotas, "We must disrupt the idea that the human/self exists prior to the act of research and rather envision research in the milieu" (Springgay and Rotas 2015: 557). In this sense, the audio paper is a way of doing field research attuning to the emergence of a field, rather than representing already-established "knowledges" of a field. Listening while recording is an attunement that enacts a field's capacity to affect and to be affected: A kind of radical empiricism that explores the affective milieu of the field. For instance, in an audio paper on the non-place of the radio studio designed to be inaudible, the lack of a specific soundscape emerged as an affective environment affecting the researcher to define it as a non-place. At the same time, the audio production affects back on the broadcasting studio as sound qualities are attributed to the non-place, it is "like sitting inside a phone" (Kreutzfeldt and Pedersen 2016). In the second series of audio paper productions (Groth, Vandsø, Schmidt and Søndergaard 2017), sound art was the field of investigation. In the audio papers, the materiality of sound as medium was explored in relation to "the implications of sonic production, exchange and experience in a hyper-mediatized culture saturated with sound" (ibid.). Here, attuning into the field is to a larger extent attuning into the hyper-mediatized culture, in which sound art potentially matters. Hence, we understand producing (recording, editing, and mixing) the audio paper as an entangled practice that involves a wide range of human and nonhuman actors—technologies, sounding materialities, environmental qualities, voices, and discourses and even paradigms.

Multifocal Attunement

As argued by Deleuze (1994), art involves the creation of blocs of sensation (affects and percepts), whereas philosophy proposes the invention of concepts. The audio paper is a "bloc of sensation"; meanwhile, it also is a construction of concepts, as seen in philosophy. Hence, we can understand the audio paper as an experimental and hybrid encounter, in which "blocs of sensations" as in the work of art *and* the concepts found in philosophy appear simultaneously and are entangled in the composition. Here composition and argument are composed on the same plane of consistency. Drawing on affect as a body's capacity to affect and to be affected, the audio paper can be seen as an interface assembling and relating diverse voices and sound material. An interface in which blocs of sensations affect the construction of arguments and vice versa. All components carry a capacity to affect and to be affected as they form relations in the sound composition. The components are, for instance, the dramaturgy, voice, environmental sounds, pitch, and rhythm and how they relate affectively to one another.

As a practical aesthetic bringing diverse expressions together, the audio paper diverts from the linearity of the conventional academic argument by offering an interface for a thinking-in-action that introduces heterogeneity and simultaneity as a durational knowledge form. Thus, the audio paper enables affective attunement and implies that heterogeneous voices and meanings can coexist. The audio paper allows several voices to come to the fore, and allows for front and back staging of voices and sounds throughout both production and reception of the paper. As previously stated in the audio paper manifesto, "The audio paper is multifocal; it assembles diverse and often heterogeneous voices" (Groth and Samson 2016).

What in a written paper is left to the inner voice of the reader's own imagination becomes expressive utterances in the audio paper with all that comes with it. In the audio paper, not only language's semantics and syntax are of importance, so is the presenters' tone, rhythm, pitch, and timing, as well as age, nationality, and gender. The voice in the audio paper is by the technological circumstances an objectified and acousmatic voice detached from the human being who once brought it to life. From a Lacanian perspective, Mladen Dolar has stated about the voice as such: "The voice stems from the body, but is not its part, and it upholds language without belonging to it, yet, in this paradoxical topology, this is the only point they share" (Dolar 2006: 73). Such reflection of the voice can be explicated in the audio paper through the conscious use of aesthetic means. For instance, voices played simultaneously as composed cacophonics, as well as electronically manipulated voices pitched, speeded up, or slowed down, stress the materiality of the voice, pointing toward neither the body nor the language (e.g., Robinson 2016). Hence, we might say that the voice in the audio paper becomes further detached from the body and the human-centered voice narration. Instead, it opens up for aesthetic modulations of affect and the voice's capacity to affect and to be affected through technological montage aesthetics.

However, the voice is not only to be understood as an autonomous abstraction. It can also, as argued by Brandon LaBelle, be defined as a situated and partial phenomenon attached to the body through the mouth: "The voice does not move away from my body, but rather it carries it forward—the voice *stretches* me; it drags me along, as my body bound to its politics and poetics, its accents and dialectics, its grammars as well as it handicaps" (LaBelle 2014: 5).

Following the latter, the voice never leaves the idea of the body behind. This situated thinking of the voice is also at stake in the audio paper bringing in political aspects touching upon race, gender, regionality, nationality, and the environment, among others. Hence, the acousmatic voice not only is listened to as an abstraction, but also appears

Practical Aesthetics

as an embodied voice expressing historical and social matters directed by certain sets of listening.

In *The Sonic Color Line* on the relationship between "sound, race, and American life" (2016: 7), Jennifer Lynn Stoever introduces the notion of the *listening ear*. The *listening ear* leaves listening to a cultural understanding, described as "the hierarchical division sounded between 'whiteness' and 'blackness.'" Stoever argues that listening practices change over time and that "the dominant culture exerts pressure on individual listening practices to conform to the sonic color line's norms. Through the listening ear's surveillance, discipline, and interpretation, certain associations between race and sound come to seem normal, natural, and 'right'" (Stoever 2016: 7–8). The presented voices are in this interpretation not universal, but are depended on the listener's cultural and social habitat.

This leaves us with three theoretical framings of the voice: the acousmatic, the embodied, and the one defined by the listening and cultural ear. These three aspects are necessarily not only reserved for the voice but can broadly be understood as how affective attunements take place between listener and audio production; attunements that are mutual and transitional—capacities to affect and to be affected, that, in Stoevers perspective, are culturally embodied.

Relational Attunement

Following Massumi and Manning's use of Sterne's notion of "relational attunement," we see listening as an emergent quality based on relationality (Manning and Massumi 2014: 217). An attunement in Sterne's sense "does not subsume the singularity of the contributing actions that come into relation, even as it brings them together to joint affect" (Manning and Massumi 2014: 118). In listening to the audio paper, we can understand attunement as a listening practice that opens up toward nonlinear reception, or knowledge as a singular event. Relational attunements allow, for instance, for heterogeneous sensations and meanings to coexist in listening. Hence, we might say that rather than establishing a linear communication situation from research into a listening audience, the audio paper folds together researcher, producer, and listener together in a temporal emergence of sound.

In the reception and listening to the audio paper, several relational attunements can be registered, attunements in the sense that attuning to here becomes a question of how to engage not only cognitive reason but a continuum of sensory regimes. Here the audio paper potentially establishes other learning situations in which experiencing and learning is to a broad extent qualified by the listening body's capacity to affect and to be affected. Being affected does, for instance, cover how the audio paper enables the felt sensations of a given academic argument. It does not only communicate, rather it realizes knowledge in the body of the listener.

In the aesthetic components of the audio paper, the organizations of sound material (e.g., voice, dramaturgy, and rhythm) work as blocs of sensation that are immediately felt. Sensation, according to Massumi, "is the mode in which potential is present in the perceiving body.... In that sensation, a heterogeneity of levels contract into the body from which they reissue in an action—in a unity of movement through which their multiplicity is singularly expressed" (Massumi 2002: 75). Hence, sensation is potentially open to what is not yet finally captured. This applies to the listening situation of the audio paper. In the reception, there might still be a hierarchy between producer and listener, but not necessarily a linearity. As pointed to by Herzogenrath, linearity "does not do justice to the complexity of the matter: mental and corporeal processes and interactions as well as 'implicit/tacit/practical knowledge' become relevant on all levels, for all decisions" (Herzogenrath 2017: 5).

We might say that listening to the audio paper makes space and place polyvocality into communication between producer and listener as many voices are assembled in the audio paper. Here, the listening situation opens up for sensations understood as what is not yet finally captured: for instance, the researcher can participate in the listening of her own audio production; she can engage with it from the outside as a depersonalized expression of what no longer belongs to her and maybe never has. The researcher has a fragile and indeterminate position. In a similar way, compared, for instance, to a reading of a paper, the reception of the audio paper opens up for listening in a variety of situations and environments, listening situations that can both be practiced individually and collectively. We can imagine listening-learning situations in which actions such as drawing, walking, dancing, and writing take place simultaneously while listening. Hence, affective attunement in the listening situation can imply "an opening up of the body to shared and collective registers of the experiential" (Thompson 2017: 11).

Concluding Remarks

As such, we argue that the audio paper works with knowledge *production* in all cases rather than knowledge as objectified and stable data. We might say that the creative process of producing and listening to the paper forms the pathway through which experience, knowledge, and understanding come into being. Here the knowledge situation of the audio paper resembles artistic research understood "not only as the result of the research, but also its methodological vehicle, when the research unfolds *in and through* the acts of creating and performing" (Borgdorff 2012: 46).

Both in terms of its production and its reception, the audio paper relies on differential attunement and relationality, in which sense-making engages wider ecologies of differential attunements. Whereas qualitative studies often extracts meaning from the environment as data to be captured by the researcher and brought into academia (see Springgay and Truman 2018), we have argued that attunement on various planes characterizes the audio paper insofar as it allows for a thinking-in-action that takes place from the middle. Likewise, reflexivity and critique is not something that takes place only after presenting the paper. In the production/composition of the audio paper, reflexivity is already there, and happens in the making as the artist-researcher thinks and reflects in recording and listening.

To sum up, the audio paper is a bloc of sensation that through relationality attunes the researcher into potentials in empirical fields and attunes the listener into the sensorium of knowledge. We see the audio paper as a relational and nonlinear knowledge production that makes meaning felt and thus rather understood in an affective register of existence. Here, the concepts of affect and attunement are helpful as to soften the distinction between the human and the nonhuman, the voice as a carrier of meaning and semantics and sound as a background noise. As Thompson notes "Affect involves, but is not limited to, the affectations of the body-as-subject: it pertains to a web of relations that traverses the divisions that hold apart the human and non-human, being and things" (Thompson 2017: 46). In the composition of the audio paper, we have seen this in particular in how the (human) voice is folded together with the various sounds of the environment, or how it is dispersed and rendered sensible through the tonality and materiality of the voice. In this sense, we see the audio paper as an encounter between listeners, researchers, and nonhuman agencies alike. As a technological medium and interface, it moves away from a human-centered ideology and the linearity of communicating knowledge as data extracted from the field. Instead, it allows for a variety of cultural, technological, and material agents to speak. It carries the traces of media technologies and environments, sound materials, and the cultural, ethnic tonalities between the voice and the listener.

References

Borgdorff, H. (2012), *The Conflict of the Faculties. Perspectives on Artistic Research and Academia*, Leiden: PB- Leiden University Press.
Clough, P., and J. Halley (2007), *The Affective Turn. Theorizing the Social*, Durham and London: Duke University Press.
Deleuze, G. (1994), *What Is Philosophy?*, New York: Columbia University Press.
Dolar, M. (2006), *A Voice and Nothing More*, Cambridge: MIT Press.
Feld, S. (2015), "Acoustemology," in D. Novak and M. Sakakeeny (eds.), *Keywords in Sound*, 12–21, Durham and London: Duke University Press.
Groth, S. K., and K. Samson (2016). "Audio Papers - A Manifesto," in *Seismograf*, #16. Available online: http://seismograf.org/fokus/fluid-sounds/audio_paper_manifesto (accessed February 28, 2019).
Groth, S. K., A. Vandsø, U. Schmidt, and M. Søndergaard (eds.) (2017), "Sound Art Matters," in *Seismograf*, #19. Available online: http://seismograf.org/fokus/sound-art-matters (accessed February 28, 2019).
Herzogenrath, B. (2017), *Sonic Thinking, a Media Philosophical Approach*, New York: Bloomsbury Academic.
Holt, M., and K. P. Nielsen (2016), "A Sound Factory on Amager' (audio paper), in *Seismograf*, #16, Available online: http://seismograf.org/fokus/fluid-sounds/a-sound-factory-on-amager (accessed February 28, 2019).
Ikoniadou, E. (2014), *The Rhythmic Event, Art, Media, and the Sonic*, Cambridge, Massachusetts London, England: MIT press.
Ingold, T. (2016), "From Science to Art and Back Again: The Pendulum of an Anthropologist," *ANUAC*, 5 (1): 5–23.

Kreutzfeldt, J. and S. Pedersen (2016), "Like Sitting Inside a Phone" (audio paper) in *Seismograf*, #16. Available online: http://seismograf.org/fokus/fluid-sounds/like-sitting-inside-a-phone (accessed February 28, 2019).

LaBelle, B. (2014), *Lexicon of the Mouth: Poetics and Politics of Voice and the Oral Imaginary*, New York: Bloomsbury Academic and Professional.

Leavy, P. (2015), *Method Meets Art: Arts-Based Research Practice*, New York: Guilford Publications.

Manning, E., and B. Massumi (2014), *Thought in the Act. Passages in the Ecology of Experience*, Minneapolis, London: University of Minnesota Press.

Massumi, B. (2002), *Parables for the Virtual: Movement, Affect, Sensation*, Durham, N.C. and London: Duke University Press.

Massumi, B. (2015), *Politics of Affect*. Cambridge: Polity Press.

Molino, J., and J. Underwood (1990), "Musical Fact and the Semiology of Music 'with an Introduction by Craig Ayrey'," *Music Analysis*, 9 (2): 105–56.

Schön, D. A. (1983), *The Reflective Practitioner: How Professionals Think in Action*, New York: Basic Books.

Springgay, S. and N. Rotas (2015), "How Do You Make a Classroom Operate Like a Work of Art? Deleuzeguattarian Methodologies of Research-creation," *International Journal of Qualitative Studies in Education*, 28 (5): 552–72, DOI: 10.1080/09518398.2014.933913.

Springgay, S. and S. Truman (2018), "On the Need for Methods Beyond Proceduralism: Speculative Middles, (In)Tensions, and Response-Ability in Research," *Qualitative Inquiry*, 24(3): 1–12.

Thompson, M. (2017), *Beyond Unwanted Sound: Noise, Affect and Aesthetic Moralism*, London and New York: Bloomsbury Academic.

Thrift, N. (2007), *Non-Representational Theory: Space, Politics, Affect*, Florence: Routledge.

Robinson, A. (2016) "Through the Air with the Greatest of Ease: Phonogenie" (2016) (audio paper) A. Robinson, in *Seismograf*, #16, Available online: http://seismograf.org/fokus/fluid_sounds/through-the-air-with-the-greatest-of-ease-phonogenie (accessed February 28, 2019).

Stoever, J. L. (2016), *The Sonic Color Line, Race and the Cultural Politics of Listening. Postmillennial Pop*. New York: New York University Press.

CHAPTER 15
GENEALOGIES OF IMMERSIVE MEDIA AND VIRTUAL REALITY (VR) AS PRACTICAL AESTHETIC MACHINES

Michael N. Goddard

Toward a Media Archaeological Approach to Virtual Reality

Advertising and promotional hype for commercially available Oculus Rift VR headsets and related content give the impression that VR is a new, emergent twenty-first-century phenomenon, facilitating never-before-experienced potentials for "immersion," "presence," and perceptual realism:

> Rift's advanced display technology combined with its precise, low-latency constellation tracking system enables the sensation of presence—the feeling as though you're actually there. The magic of presence changes everything. (Oculus Rift 2017: n.p.)

Such claims to novelty should give anyone attuned to cultural histories of technology pause, especially if we want to adopt a media archaeological perspective attuned to both what is old in the new, as well as what is new in the old (see Parikka 2012: 10–14). VR, and the dreams of total presence it sustains, is especially prone to periodic bouts of historical amnesia, so much so that reading contemporary "practical" accounts of VR it is as if it had no history. However, if one retains any memory, or does any research into the cybercultural discourse of the 1990s, one can find here both the same, if not more, prominence accorded to VR, and an even greater level of hype, in some instances, as well as paranoia in others. As with other audiovisual media technologies like 3D and stereoscopy, technological development is cyclical rather than progressive, with different technical assemblages returning when conditions, whether technical, economic, cultural, or all of the above are right. As Parikka puts it:

> Thinking cyclically has been one media-archaeological strategy for critiquing the hegemony of the new. . . . Zielinski's development of media archaeology as research into the deep time of the media—modes of hearing, seeing and sensing in general—is another way of developing an alternative temporality that moves away from a hegemonic linearity [that works] towards improvement and something better. (Parikka 2012: 11–12)

Practical Aesthetics

Without following Zielinski into thousands of years of deep time (see Zielinski 2006), it is clear that VR devices and the more general field of immersive media have followed distinct cycles across the last century or more with high points in the 1960s and 1990s, as well as in the present. Another key insight is that more than technologies, there are specific ways of organizing the senses, hence aesthetic machines. As such, they are part of the nonlinear history of audiovision, a specific assemblage related to previous ones such as cinema and television, except that they have different affordances in terms of tactility, agency, and the generation of a 360-degree environment that renders VR a distinct type of aesthetic machine. Furthermore, VR is not a distinct, isolated phenomenon but part of a continuum of technical devices and assemblages including such dominant ones as cinema and television, as well as more specific arenas such as cinematic special effects, histories of simulation, and conjunctions between moving images and computing that go back at least to the 1960s.

VR and Genealogies of Audiovision

VR, as argued earlier, can usefully be situated as part of a broader history of audiovision in several interlocking ways. Siegfried Zielinski proposed the term "audiovision" in his book *Audiovisions* (1999) as an alternative way of understanding both cinema and television as "entr'actes in history," meaning as contingent and far-from-stable assemblages, enabled by practices of invention that have also led to other audiovisual arrangements that are "no longer film, no longer television" (see Zielinski 1999: 219–72). While he acknowledges theories of the cinematic apparatus in his introduction to this work, it fundamentally goes against static ideas of any "basic apparatus" as theorists like Baudry proposed (see Baudry 1985), and is much more in line with Casetti's appropriation of the concept of the assemblage (2015: 67–98), to account for the "cinematic" as dispersed across a heterogeneous post-cinematic field. What all of this has to do with VR is that while going further than other post-cinematic assemblages in terms of levels of immersion and interactivity, even apparently dispensing with the need for a screen or interface, it nevertheless remains post-cinematic because it is still concerned with moving image and sound environments, even if augmented by increased tactile potentials via sensors. As such, it is part of what Zielinski characterized in the following terms, bearing in mind that this was originally formulated in the late 1980s before even first-generation VR:

> Advanced audiovision, as a complex construction kit of machines, storage devices, and programmes for the reproduction, simulation and blending of what can be seen and heard, where the trend is their capability of being connected together in a network but which . . . display a similar heterogeneity to that which was characteristic of a large part of the nineteenth century. (Zielinski 1999: 19)

This cyclical return to the nineteenth-century exhibition of diverse attractions in the form of multiple devices for generating the illusion of movement in space and time has not been lost on other authors, for example in the volume *The Cinema of Attractions Reloaded* (Strauven ed. 2007) in which a range of authors demonstrate the ways in which the fascination with technological machineries of illusion, rather than immersion in narrative, characterize the contemporary era of fantasy blockbusters, CGI, Imax presentations, and the return of 3D cinemas.

The latter collection of post-cinematic phenomena, also brings up the importance of sound in VR and experiences of media immersion more generally; while initially considered to be primarily a visually defined experience, increasingly sound, as Frances Dyson argues (Dyson 2009), has proved essential in actually generating the sought-after senses of immersion and presence. This has also proven to be the case in cinematic special effects development in which the development of sonic special effects was arguably more sophisticated and in advance of visual effects.

But there is another more specific reason to relate VR to genealogies of audiovision, namely that it emerges directly out of the intersection of computing and specifically computer interfaces and moving image technologies, a process that began in the 1960s but really accelerated in the 1990s. Initially, these technologies had little in common, as cinematic moving images were generated by industrial, mechanical technologies for simulating illusions of real movement and thereby facilitating new forms of narrative, whereas computers were largely concerned with calculation, and its software was either algorithmic or related to technologies of writing. Hence, the first technological coupling of the computer was with the typewriter, not with anything audiovisual. However, as computers started to become a more graphical medium in terms of both interfaces and at the level of now-object-oriented software, its artistic applications became increasingly apparent leading to computer art, which soon took the form of moving images. This becoming visual of computing has been discussed in more detail by Casey Alt, who argues that it was only with object-oriented software that computers became a medium (see Alt 2011: 278–301). Similarly, innovative filmmakers wanted to go beyond the possibilities not only of the photographic images but even of analogue varieties of animation, and turned to computer animation as a way to achieve this. This intersection of cinema and computing played a key role in what would be named by Gene Youngblood as "Expanded Cinema" (1970), which is really where VR begins.

What Is Virtual and What Is Real in VR?

Many of the contrasting responses to VR in the 1990s came down to different positions on how virtuality could be understood. In terms of a dictionary definition, the virtual is usually understood as not quite real, or having an "as if" quality, in other words as a form of simulation or illusion. For relatively paranoid theorists like Baudrillard, Virilio, and their followers such as Kroker (1993), VR could be seen as the culmination of tendencies toward simulation and annulling of reality already enacted via earlier technologies like photography and cinema. In this sense, without the direct reference to VR itself, the virtual is seen as an annihilation of the "real world," if not proof that such a thing no longer exists, whether via simulation or substitution, the "precession of simulacra" (Baudrillard 1994) or the "aesthetics of disappearance" (Virilio 2009). On the other hand, other writers such as Howard Rheingold (1991) or Pierre Levy (1996) embraced the actual development of virtual technologies including VR with undisguised enthusiasm. However, especially in the case of the latter, this was a very different concept of the virtual, more derived from Bergson and Deleuze than these more pessimistic accounts. For Deleuze, following Bergson, the virtual is not opposed to the real but is in fact what is really intensively real about reality, as the reservoir of past potential, actualizable in any given situation. Another term Deleuze uses is the "Powers of the False" (see Deleuze 1989: 126–55), which suggests a more affirmative take on simulation, which dates back to his earlier aim of reversing Platonism by affirming simulacra (see Deleuze 1990: 253–65). If in the 1990s few writers were able to avoid the polarization of either radically affirming or rejecting VR, at least they had the virtue of adopting a speculative, philosophical approach, nowhere more apparent than in the work of Michael Heim, whose books *The Metaphysics of Virtual Reality* (1993) and *Virtual Realism* (1998), tended to situate VR as opening up new possibilities for metaphysical experience, continued in a recently initiated ten-volume series *VR Metaphysics* (Heim 2017–). These distinctions and assumptions about virtuality, whether a text is explicitly philosophical or not, are fundamental to how VR, and indeed cyberculture more generally, is understood. As Heim puts it:

> The ultimate VR is a philosophical experience, probably an experience of the sublime or awesome. The sublime, as Kant defined it, the spine-tingling chill that comes from the realization of how small our finite perceptions are in the face of the infinity of possible, virtual worlds we may settle into and inhabit. The final point of a virtual world is to dissolve the constraints of the anchored world so that we can lift anchor. (Heim 1993: 137)

If this still sounds like a transcendent understanding of virtuality, Heim's philosophical reference points are multiple, encompassing in addition to Kant, Heidegger, Leibniz, and going back as far as Duns Scotus, which are also key reference points for Deleuze's immanent concept of the virtual. A virtual world is neither equivalent to "reality" or more precisely "real reality" but nor is it imaginary. Instead, Heim claims it is relatively unanchored: "A virtual world can only be virtual if we can contrast it with the real (anchored) world. Virtual worlds can then maintain . . . a multiplicity that is playful rather than maddening" (Heim 1993: 133). Even if Heim is still using the language of the imaginary that Deleuze explicitly rejects to some extent, it resonates with ideas of crystalline perception from Deleuze's cinema books and even more with the concept of the plain of immanence from Deleuze and Guattari: VR in this sense would not be a substitute for reality nor its transcendence but a step into the immanent diagram of a world of experience; not an escape from reality or being but a form of ontogenesis in which one becomes other to oneself, has other sensory experiences, while experiencing a form of blended embodiment combining a here and an elsewhere, self and other, being and becoming. In order to flesh out this theoretical approach to virtuality and to VR as an aesthetic machinery, it is necessary to take a step back to the precursors of VR in so many varieties of what was once called expanded cinema.

Primal Scenes of VR: *Vertigo* (1959) and the Stargate Corridor in *2001: A Space Odyssey* (1968)

Alfred Hitchcock certainly was one of the filmmakers open to innovations in visual arts, up to and including early computer animation. In the film *Spellbound* (1945), he invited Salvador Dali to create the sets for scenes that were less a dream sequence than the psychoanalytic recall of a dream; but while these Daliesque images were striking in their deliberate artifice, they were also somewhat corny and stagy, reminiscent of the artificial sets of German expressionist films of the 1920s. For some of his later films, Saul Bass had already been creating abstract animated sequences but for *Vertigo* he wanted a series of rotating abstract geometric figures that should be mathematically precise. They turned to the artist John Whitney, who had already been experimenting with these kinds of moving images, by adapting the Second World War military technologies for rotating antiaircraft guns:

> Whitney realized that the gun director could rotate endlessly, and in perfect synchronization with the swinging of a pendulum. He placed his animation cels on the platform that held the gun director, and above it suspended a pendulum from the ceiling which held a pen that was connected to a 24-foot high pressurized paint reservoir. The movement of the pendulum in relation to the rotation of the gun director generated the spiral drawings used in *Vertigo*'s opening sequence. (Guo 2018: 54)

The results, which can be seen both in the opening credits to *Vertigo* and in Whitney's own film *Catalog* (1961) [see Figure 16.1], literally a catalog of the visual effects generated by this machine, already point to the generation of abstract virtual spaces with immersive and hypnotic qualities, as the realization of the conjunction of computing and audiovisual media.

Jordan Belson, working at the same time, also followed a similar trajectory and also explored the possibilities of expanded cinema involving computer animation and often with a cosmic, mandala-related theme, as can be seen, for example, in his film *Allures* from 1961. While technologically less sophisticated than Whitney's contemporaneous work, it is aesthetically and philosophically more complex, described by Youngblood as "a 'mathematically precise' film on the theme of *Cosmogenesis*, Teilhard de Chardin's term to indicate that the universe is not a static phenomenon but a process of becoming,

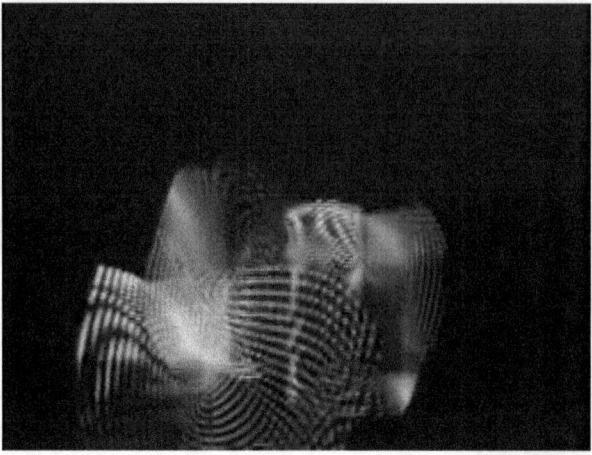

Figure 16.1 "Catalog," Directed by John Whitney Sr., ©John Whitney Sr., 1961 (Held at Academy Film Archive).

of attaining new levels of existence and organization." (Youngblood 1970: 160, emphasis in original)

The ultimate realization of such aesthetic practices cinematically was in the famous "Stargate Corridor" sequence of *2001* in which the special effects supervisor Doug Trumbull turned to such preceding experiments in order to create a new technique for producing special effects, the "Slit Scan technique." This was developed by Whitney in order to generate continuous variation of abstract shapes, but then modified for the film by making it more three dimensional (see Youngblood 1970: 151–6). While this was all a purely analogue process, the effect of the final sequence was absolutely formative in terms of the look of future computer animation. It also had a huge impact on the imagination of cyberspace both in science fiction such as in the equally formative *Neuromancer* (Gibson 1984) and in the development of cyberspace itself as a multidimensional graphically generated space, functioning as an interactive virtual world.

All of these examples were central to Gene Youngblood's concept of Expanded Cinema which, while having its roots in experimental animation, was already having a marked influence on Hollywood. In a sense, these experimental practices already crossed commercial and creative worlds in new ways; developing out of a fine art context, they nevertheless found application for use in title sequences, logos, and advertising, a tension that would continue to mark technologies of virtuality up to contemporary VR. While John Whitney's children would continue his work by becoming computer programmers, it was really George Lucas who fully brought digital computing technologies into the world of Hollywood filmmaking, and not just for title or dream sequences; these technologies would become essential for the *Star Wars* franchise, but also the development of digital effects through his Industrial Light and Magic Studio and its computer animation offshoot Pixar, which would lead ultimately, in the twenty-first century, to the production of VR films.

Genealogies of Immersive Media and Virtual Reality (VR)

Back to the Future, According to the 1990s

There are several accounts such as by Hillis (1999) and Heim (1998) of the direct history of VR including such things as Viewmasters and 3D stereoscopy, flight simulators as developed in the 1960s, and Ivan Sutherland's "Sketchpad" "an interactive program that enabled a user holding a light pen to make designs on a screen that could be stored, retrieved and superimposed" (Hillis 1999: 11). Later, Sutherland developed the concept of the "ultimate display" in which the computer would control the existence of matter, resonating with and extending earlier theories of "total cinema." Finally, there is the development of head-mounted displays, compared by Howard Rheingold to "exceptionally bulky sunglasses," and data gloves which more fully enable the experience of virtual environments by in principle eliminating both the screen as interface and the bracketing out the perception of surrounding reality.

It is this suspension of one's lived spatial reality and its substitution with another that led many writers and developers to see in VR dreams of transcendence of the body and hence to imagine it as the facilitator of a form of disembodiment. But there were always voices cautioning against this kind of approach. N. Katherine Hayles, for example, argued in 1996, "As anyone who designs VR simulations knows, the specificities of our embodiments matter in all kinds of ways, from determining the precise configuration of a VR interface, to influencing the speed with which we can read a ... screen" (Hayles 1996: 1). If there is nevertheless "so much noise about the perception of cyberspace as a disembodied medium" (1996: 1), it is due to making a cut between the embodied experience of the user and the alternate virtual world, the attribution of more reality to the latter, due to the desire to leave the former behind, by disavowing the technical and perceptual process by which it is generated in the first place. This is a precise articulation of the differences between posthuman immanence and transhuman transcendence. The gendered nature of such fantasies of disembodiment hardly needs to be spelled out or repeated, and by now have been fully critiqued. Yet such desires and fantasies still attach themselves to VR, and are as hard to shake as the implications of its military origins, as artists like Harun Farocki have explored in works like *Serious Games 3: Immersion* (2009). As more perceptive commentators like Hayles have noted, VR might have less to do with *Neuromancer*'s fantasy of leaving behind the "meat" of the organic body and more to do with pattern recognition: "People have something to lose if they are regarded solely as informational patterns, namely the resistant materiality that has marked the experience of living as embodied creatures" (Hayles 1993: 73).

Such a polarization between transhuman and posthuman accounts of VR seems today to be exaggerated but is understandable in the context of 1990s speculations about VR and its future as a synecdoche for cyberspace itself. The idea that we were on the verge of a world in which we would all be engaging in virtual environments for most of our activities (in an era when even email was relatively novel). In actual fact, the dreams and anxieties surrounding VR barely survived the late 1990s dotcom crash, and until recently it seemed consigned to being just another technological novelty, suitable for amusement parks and the peripheries of gaming. One problem was the hype itself,

Practical Aesthetics

which was basically impossible to live up to, and another was the level of technological development; certainly there were some admirable experiments in VR art, but their realization was not the overwhelming technological experience it was supposed to be; in other words, the fantasies of immediacy, of surpassing the need for an interface, returned in the form of effects of hypermediacy in anything from the delay time of loading necessary information, to the so-called Alternate World Syndrome, which could leave some users in a state of nausea and disorientation. Taking as an example the 1990s VR artwork "Dancing with the Virtual Dervish" (Figure 16.2), far from being an experience of disembodiment, it was, in fact, all about kinesthetic and proprioceptive embodiment. Michael Heim describes the aftereffects of his two-and-a-half-hour experience with this work in the following terms:

> Even the next day, my optical nerves held the imprint of the brightly coloured transhuman structures. I could summon them with the slightest effort—or see them sometimes in unexpected flashes of cyberspace. (Heim 1998: 51–2)

Of course, much of this kind of embodied reaction or abreaction to VR had to do with levels of technological development; too low a frame rate apparently produced such effects, a problem that has since been overcome in twenty-first-century VR apparatuses with much higher processing rates and hence the ability to generate relatively seamless virtual environments. But the problems with 1990s VR were not just a question of technical obstacles, high costs, and lack of a clear idea of its potential uses; there was also a fundamental misperception of what its affordances and limits were, namely that what it enabled was not an experience of immediacy, of being transported into another body

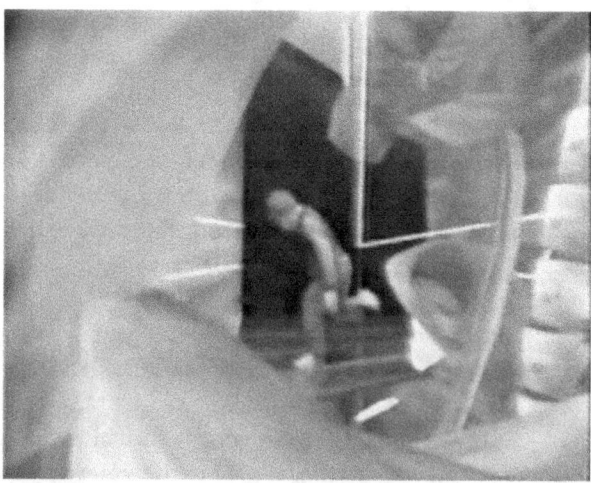

Figure 16.2 "Dancing with the Virtual Dervish: Virtual Bodies," Created by Diane Gromala and Yacov Sharir, CC, Attribution-Non Commercial-NoDerivs 3.0 United States, 1994 (Virtual Reality event) first "performed" at Banff centre for the Arts, 1994.

in another space, but just another modality of remediation to use Bolter and Grusin's term (see Bolter and Grusin 1999: 2–19). As with all forms of remediation there is no pure immediacy attainable via technologies of perception, only an oscillation between immediacy and hypermediacy which are always mixed. This perhaps accounts for VR being eclipsed in favor of other technologies, principally the mobile smart phone and augmented reality developments that dominated the first decade of the 2000s, and which foreground rather than hide their processes of hypermediation. Nevertheless, in a nice irony, mounting a VR-enabled phone within a headset has become a new way of generating VR experiences, rendering them cheaper and more accessible. Conversely, the supposed next step forward in augmented reality in such devices as Google Glass has met with unanticipated unpopularity, in its adding of new layers of surveillance or at least interveillance to a world already saturated with such practices: don't objectify me into my data body, at least not so obviously.

This underlines the point that VR does not do away with the screen or interface, so much as render it imperceptible, displacing it to the nonperceived display or even the retina. But how new is this process? Are cinemagoers ever aware that they are watching a screen when immersed in a spectacular cinematic presentation, especially when immersion is aided by HD or IMAX technologies, complex sound environments, or 3D effects? Is VR just the latest in a line of immersive audiovisual technologies, a kind of post-cinematic supplement or actually a medium or artform in its own right?

It may still be too early to give definitive answers to these questions, but other than medical and military uses of VR, it is now being developed largely as a way of producing supplementary content, extending the repertoire of games, cinema, especially animated cinema, music video, and slightly more sophisticated versions of virtual environments already well known from MMORPG's like *World of Warcraft* or even *Second Life*. Certainly, VR has progressed from being limited to use by either military-industrial or artistic elite projects, to becoming more available and accessible, as well as becoming commercialized as a desirable consumer product, but whether it will develop some of the artistic, let alone the ontogenetic potential imagined for it in the 1990s, still remains to be seen. Certainly, if the works produced by the now-defunct Oculus Rift Studio are anything to go by, things have not yet progressed all that far beyond Pixar animations.

Also, as Hito Steyerl has suggested, there are other limits to VR as a kind of "bubble vision" in congruity with a range of twenty-first-century spherical technologies and architectures of seeing (Steyerl 2017). Steyerl references the philosopher Peter Sloterdijk's concept of spheres as inherent to Western metaphysics (see Sloterdijk 2011) and suggests that we should be wary of this mode of experience of spherical alternate worlds, which she labels as an aesthetics of isolation. This raises the specter of the VR user in full headgear clumsily banging into gallery walls and other people, since the payoff for a rich spherical, immersive VR experience is a bad relationship to exterior surroundings. However, the strongest resonance of VR with Western metaphysics is really the monadology of Leibniz, which was presented in terms of so many incompossible subject-centered points of view on a "possible world" each closed off from the other, with only God seeing all of these worlds clearly. This Leibnizian resonance was not lost on early theorists of

Practical Aesthetics

VR like Michael Heim, who saw Leibniz as laying the foundations for the emergence of cyberspace through his "electric language" of symbology (Heim, 1993: 92–6). The question then for VR might be of how to "overtake monadology with a 'nomadology,'" as Deleuze suggested in *The Fold* (1993: 137), by constructing and imagining ethical openings between individuated VR spheres and other horizons of aesthetic potentiality, so that the monadic VR experience becomes "astraddle over several worlds [and] kept open as if by a pair of pliers" (1993: 137).

Perhaps some richer inspiration for designing really ontogenetic VR experiences might rather be gained by reengaging with the lesser-known histories of abstract cinema, audiovisual experimentation, and computer art presented here, which might form the basis of aesthetically rich, immersive, ontogenetic, and open experiences. Something like a VR equivalent of *Twin Peaks: The Return* (2017), episode 8, which can be seen as a kind of negative Stargate Corridor, could be a more aesthetically challenging starting point for such experimentation than the insipid work of Oculus Studios. At any rate, it seems important to find a point somewhere between the banality of discourses surrounding contemporary VR and the speculative spasms of the 1990s, in order to grasp what is really, potentially new in VR as an aesthetic, ontogenetic machine, while remaining fully aware of both its limits and affordances.

References

2001: A Space Odyssey (1968), Dir. Stanley Kubrick, USA, UK: Stanley Kubrick Productions, Metro-Goldwyn-Mayer (MGM).
Allures (1961), [Film] Dir. Jordan Belson, USA.
Alt, C. (2011), "Objects of Our Affection: How Object Orientation Made Computers a Medium," in E. Huhtamo and J. Parikka (eds.), *Media Archaeology: Approaches, Applications, and Implications*, 278–301, Los Angeles: University of California Press.
Baudrillard, J. (1994), *Simulacra and Simulation*, trans. S. F. Glaser, Ann Arbor: University of Michigan Press.
Baudry, J.-L. (1985), "Ideological Effects of the Basic Cinematic Apparatus," in B. Nichols (ed.), *Movies and Methods: Volume 2*, 531–42, Berkeley and Los Angeles: University of California Press.
Bolter, J., and R. Grusin (1999), *Remediation: Understanding New Media*, Cambridge, MA and London: MIT Press.
Casetti, F. (2015), *The Lumière Galaxy: Seven Key Words for the Cinema to Come*, New York: Columbia University Press.
Catalog (1961) [Film], Dir. J. Whitney Sr., USA.
Dancing with the Virtual Dervish (1994), [VR Artwork], Artists D. Gromala and Y. Sharir, Canada: Banff Centre for Arts and Creativity.
Deleuze, G. (1989), *Cinema 2: The Time-Image*, trans. H. Tomlinson and R. Galeta, London; New York: Continuum.
Deleuze, G. (1990), *The Logic of Sense*, trans. M. Lester with C. Stivale, ed. C. Boundas, New York: Columbia University Press.
Deleuze, G. (1993), *The Fold: Leibniz and the Baroque*, trans. T. Conley, Minneapolis and London: University of Minnesota Press.

Dyson, F. (2009), *Sounding New Media: Immersion and Embodiment in the Arts and Culture*, Berkeley and Los Angeles: University of California Press.
Gibson, W. (1984), *Neuromancer*, New York: Penguin.
Guo, C. (2018), "The Successful Chorus of the 'Second Wave': An Examination of Feminism's 'Manifesto'of Digital Art," in F. Bruckner, N. Gilić, H. Lang, D. Šuljic, and H. Turkovic (eds.), *Global Animation Theory: International Perspectives at Animafest Zagreb*, 51–60, London, New York: Bloomsbury.
Hayles, N. K. (1993), *How we Became Posthuman: Virtual Bodies in Cybernetics, Literature and informatics*, Chicago: University of Chicago Press.
Hayles, N. K. (1996), "Embodied Virtuality: Or How to Put Bodies Back in the Picture," in D. MacLeod and M. Moser (eds.), *Immersed in Technology: Art and Virtual Environments*, Cambridge Mass. and London: MIT Press.
Heim, M. (1993), *The Metaphysics of Virtual Reality*, Oxford and New York: Oxford University Press.
Heim, M. (1998), *Virtual Realism*, Oxford and New York: Oxford University Press.
Heim, M. (2017), *VR Third Wave: Book One of Virtual Reality Metaphysics*, Seattle: Amazon Digital Services.
Hillis, K. (1999), *Digital Sensations: Space, Identity and Embodiment in Virtual Reality*, Minneapolis, London: University of Minnesota Press.
Kroker, A. (1993), *Spasm: Virtual Reality, Android Music and Electric Flesh*, New York: St. Martin's Press.
Lévy, P. (1996), *Qu'est-ce que le virtuel?* Paris: La Découverte.
Oculus Rift (2017), [Webpage], Available online: https://www.oculus.com/rift (accessed November 1, 2017).
Parikka, J. (2012), *What Is Media Archaeology*, Cambridge: Polity Press.
Rheingold, H. (1991), *Virtual Reality*, New York: Touchstone.
Serious Games 3: Immersion [Video Installation], Dir. Harun Farocki, Harun Farocki Filmproduktion, Germany.
Sloterdijk, P. (2011), *Bubbles: Spheres 1*, trans. W Hoban, Los Angeles: Semiotext(e).
Spellbound (1945), [Film] Dir. Alfred Hitchcock, USA: Selznick International Pictures, Vanguard Films, United Artists.
Steyerl, H. (2017), *Bubble Vision* [Lecture Performance], London: Serpentine Gallery. Available online: https://www.youtube.com/watch?v=boMbdtu2rLE (accessed March 1, 2019).
Strauven, W. (ed.) (2007), *The Cinema of Attractions Reloaded*, Film Culture in Transition, Amsterdam: Amsterdam University Press.
Twin Peaks: The Return (2017), [Television Series], Dir. David Lynch, USA: Showtime.
Vertigo (1958), [Film] Dir. Alfred Hitchcock, USA: Alfred J. Hitchcock Productions, Paramount Pictures.
Virilio, P. (2009), *The Aesthetics of Disappearance*, trans. Sylvère Lotringer, Los Angeles: Semiotext(e).
Youngblood, G. (1970), *Expanded Cinema*, New York: E. P. Dutton.
Zielinski, S. (1999), *Audiovisions: Cinema and Television as Entr'actes in History*, trans. G. Custance, Film Culture in Transition, Amsterdam: Amsterdam University Press.
Zielinski, S. (2006), *Deep Time of the Media: Towards and Archaeology of Hearing and Seeing by Technical Means*, trans. G. Custance, Electronic Culture: History, Theory and Practice, Cambridge, MA and London: MIT Press.

CHAPTER 16

AS *DUO*

THINKING WITH DANCE

Elizabeth Waterhouse

Program Note—William Forsythe's Choreography *Duo*
In the small space just in front of the curtain, just at the edge of the stage, Duo is a clock composed of two women. The women register time in a spiraling way . . . they pull time into an intricate, naked pattern in front of the curtain, close to the eyes of the audience. . . . Their bodies brilliant in a shimmer of black, the women fly with reckless accuracy, their breath sings of the spaces in time. Distant music appears and vanishes as the women follow each other through the whirling, etched quiet. A clock which regards the limitless by returning to where it began.

—Dana Caspersen[1]

Part I: Introduction

To think *with* dance and to speculate upon a form of practical aesthetics is a new invitation—dance having not played a prominent role in the development of aesthetic theory (Cvejić 2015b). This is shifting. Recently, many texts have engaged dance *and* or *with* philosophy—referencing performances that also process philosophical discourse.[2] The scope of these artworks is manifold and heterogenous, but in their expansive view of choreography they have come to a consensus of sorts: that choreography can be broader than the register of experiencing humans dramatically in movement (Cvejić 2015a: 17–22). As dancer Dana Caspersen indicates in the abovementioned quote, dance performance has a specific potentiality for crafting time and space between bodies—according to artist-scholar Erin Manning, of making felt "the dissonance, the dephasing, and complementarity of the between" (Manning 2016: 51). This is an initial answer to Baumgarten's question of art's "specific potential for expressing sensible cognition" (Herzogenrath, in Introduction, this volume). My task here is to develop this answer further.

Based upon a life as a dancer and extensive research of the duet practice of dancers performing William Forsythe's choreography *Duo* from 1996 to 2018, this chapter thinks *with* dance, *with* movement, and *with* choreography, and examines the particular manner of this thinking *with*.[3] I ask: What aesthetic theory emerges from the example of *Duo*? What ways do practical aesthetics of dance contribute to the broader contemporary field of aesthetic theory? When, or can, such theoretical contributions be relevant to both scholars and dancers? And how, using what methods, would thinking *with* dance become inscribed?

Without sealing any of these questions with final answers, here I present a case study as a raw proposition for how this might go forward: poetically evoking the choreography of *Duo* for the reader. This translation of *Duo* is, as revealed in the footnotes, based on extensive learning from the artists' practice enacting the choreography. Methodologically, it proceeds from a dance studies analysis, including the ethnographic method of writing "thick description" about experiences in the field: attending performances, interviewing the artists, reviewing archival material, and even dancing with the dancers (Geertz 1973).[4] As a former Forsythe dancer, the perspective I bring to this research bridges many voices and multiple times across the history of *Duo*, creating an analysis composed of many parts. One term that could be given to identify this way of understanding performance might be borrowed from philosopher Alfred North Whitehead, *concrescence*, which "presupposes the notions 'creativity,' 'many,' 'one,' 'identity' and 'diversity'" (1985: 21). Concrescence embodies "production of novel togetherness" through "creating a novel entity other than the entities given in disjunction" (ibid). Concrescence as a sort of thinking *with*, bringing dance and aesthetic theory together—to consider the artwork as a complex unity, in process and creative advance.[5]

William Forsythe is a well-known choreographer prominent in the field of contemporary European dance.[6] The short duet *Duo* was created in 1996 for the Ballett Frankfurt and is still being performed at the present time of writing, in 2019.[7] Danced by either two men or women, the dancers move in and out of synchrony, breathing-movement audibly. The choreography of *Duo* echoes a history of ballet steps and involves a practiced art of interpretation. Negotiating the sequence of steps, creating a push and pull of time, the aesthetics of *Duo* are more than structural abstractions. *Duo* is a journey through ethical time-space. It is a process of a common-ing and creating time between dancers and the audience.

It is this main idea, modeled in *Duo* and in my research of *Duo*, that I put forth for thinking *with* dance. More generally, performances like *Duo* encourage scholars to move beyond thinking of art as an object-bound representation that is a singular, finished, and pure expression of the author, to thinking more fluidly and from multiple perspectives. Choreography is not only ephemeral but in fact an "enduring" process, historical, and situated in a sociocultural field.[8] From my perspective as a practitioner, I describe aesthetic dynamics as discoveries made through a human's way of moving with, making experience, and reflecting about time-durational activities—in short, grounded in my real contact with the dance field. Such a view rifts with earlier modernist aesthetics, enforcing the timeless and autonomous nature of art, and grounds any speculation about the infinite and mystical aspects of art in the real. Drawing from process philosophy, I propose the working hypothesis of art as *pluralistic creative process*—admittedly an argument has already been raised before under various guises.[9] But this refrain is a principal shift that dance asks of traditional aesthetics: to open to the dynamics of art. My claim is intended to designate the medium of dance not only as time-based (which it is) but as a complex, multimodal interweave, based on and superseding material registers.

A processual view foregrounds experiencing, attuning, apprehending art—streams of consciousness, as opposed to consciousness-of. This widens the aesthetic view from direct focus upon the object (i.e., on a performance) to experiencing artistic activity. Borrowing from William James' poetic language, Alfred North Whitehead describes: "We find ourselves in a buzzing world, amid a democracy of fellow creatures" (Whitehead 1985: 50). Whitehead and James are both pluralists. The sense of creative pluralism that I develop here is what one could call an ontology of the many parts, and an epistemology, in which a whole cannot be known through any singular view. Again, Whitehead's term *concrescence* expresses this. He writes:

> The word Concrescence is a derivative from the familiar latin [sic] verb, meaning "growing together." It also has the advantage that the participle "concrete" is familiarly used for the notion of complete physical reality. Thus Concrescence is useful to convey the notion of many things acquiring complete complex unity. But it fails to suggest the creative novelty involved. For example, it omits the notion of the individual character arising in the concrescence of the aboriginal data. (1967: 236)

True to *Duo*, here I consider not only the intersubjective, as in between the two dancers or the dancers and audience, but along all pluralistic relations of budding subject-objects—materials, energies, feelings, forces. In my analysis, I condense these, weaving the rhythm and structure of the choreography into my writing, hoping to evoke *Duo* (a new *Duo*) for the reader. Thinking aesthetic process with history, I juxtapose observations across the piece's history from 1996 to 2018. Close to the practitioners, I bridge from my awareness to what I have learned from the artists involved—telling *Duo* in a way that I hope contributes to both theory and practice.[10]

Part II: *Duo*

The choreography of *Duo* activates a field. The audience is essential to what transpires, as is the vast space of the theater: each stage providing a large, flat horizon that holds *Duo* together. The gap between the performers and the audience is a blank space, in German a *Leerstelle*, a space proposing to be filled.[11] It is an architectural holding, creating betweenness.

Theater performances convene a group of people according to a learned ritual of collectively framed attention. Audience members for *Duo* (whether in Tokyo, Paris, Melbourne, or New York) follow the norm not to speak. They pause, defer, or minimize social interactions with their neighbors. Each presentation of *Duo* is accompanied by a hush. The air of listening is palpable with attention. The *Leerstelle* of the room provides a type of resonance, creating intensity. Dancers can feel, in a vague way that culminates through years of performing experience, the changes in the audience's attention: how quiet or focused they are between coughs, murmurs, or shifts in position. No audience member or audience is alike, though en masse they resemble one another: all quiet, listening, attuning.

In this hush, warmth is given to the stage. The warmth is brought by stage lights, which heat the air and materials they illuminate. The theatrical beaming of light in *Duo* performances varies over the years, sometimes using harsh fluorescent lights, which give the dancers a top-down illumination, other times warmer and more glowing, allowing for better discernment of the dancers' facial features. Light provides orientation to the dancers who can see-feel: up and down, front and back, more or less heat. In this temperature gradient, the dancers can navigate. Their pupils dilate: background is black, the audience this way, backstage that way right and left. For the audience, the lighting makes *Duo* dancers stand out in strong relief, as shifting forms taking priority in this space. The light focalizes the audience's attention away from the mass of them (in the dark) to the dancers (in the light). The two dancers share this illuminated field, this *Leerstelle*, together: on the same stage, in the same hush, with a common past and future in mind. The situation is a flux of solidarity.

Each performance of *Duo* is slightly different, due to interpretation but also due to changes made by the choreographer. The dance alters but does not progress: adapting to context, need, and desire. From 1996 to 2016, there are two main versions of *Duo*: the structure (movement, light, sound, costumes, dancers) performed by Ballett Frankfurt from 1996 to 2004, and the version renamed *DUO2015* performed exclusively by dancers Riley Watts and Brigel Gjoka since 2015.

DUO2015 begins this way: the dancers, side by side have started making small movements, nearly silently. In this duet, they will never touch one another—though their closeness feels like touch (Gjoka and Watts 2017). To begin, they play and riff upon subtle variations of a theme—improvising similar positions. They use easy effort and jest with one another, prolonging arrival into unison. Suddenly they reference the same theme. The ensuing synchronization crystalizes something that had been etched and sketched with nuance just before. Time has stretched and then fractured: sync.

In a different beginning, performed in *Duo* between 1996 and 2004, two female dancers have run backward and swiftly laid themselves down on the floor. A few, long seconds pass, before they gently fold their bodies into unusual poses, lumping into delicate piles of limbs (see Figure 17.1).

These appear novel, not like balletic glyphs—though they are constructed by the dancers transposing poses from elsewhere in the sequence, to a horizontal axis. The dancers take turns, one moves and then the other, slowly enough so that time suspends. The sound of distant piano notes mixes with the intermittent sand-like swoosh of their limbs shifting position. Experiential time is relative. The floor-laying version of *Duo* presets a horizontal pallet and long smooth-durations—very different to *DUO2015* with its prologue of upright, fast-ticking gestures. Both versions eventually sync into a unison "phrase" that is the heart of *Duo* (see Figure 17.2).[12]

The costumes are minimal. The female dancers wear black leotards, sheer at the top and slightly different for each dancer. As women, they are aware that their bodies and breasts are exposed to the eyes of others—the skin of their hands, necks, and thighs reflecting the

Figure 17.1 Regina van Berkel and Jill Johnson Performing William Forsythe's *Duo*. Photo © Dominik Mentzos.

Figure 17.2 Riley Watts and Brigel Gjoka Performing William Forsythe's *DUO2015*. Photo © Bill Cooper.

light. Since 2015, the male dancers have foregone, with Forsythe's permission, wearing designed costumes and, instead, are clad in ordinary training clothes: sweatpants and tank tops, of nonmemorable colors and cuts. Like the women, they too have exposed chests; air circles underneath their armpits and around their nipples as they move their arms, sweat dripping down their backs. The pants create a millisecond echo of their movement as the fabric folds around their calves. Their socks mediate stops and steps, allowing for moving quietly, like a cat. The dancers enjoy the repetition of wearing their costume-clothes, becoming part of the regular presence—part of knowing that they are doing *Duo*.

The men and women have never danced *Duo* on stage together. This piece is always performed by a same-sex couple, never coed. Pairs work consistently together, rather than by swapping partners. Between them is another *Leerstelle*, or gap: two distinct people, two fully different bodies, unique but entwined. In dancing, they cleave. The dancers assure me that gender is not important in dancing *Duo*—even if it shades the audience's interpretation. What is important to them is the quality of *Duo*'s movement, the specific chemistry of each *Duo*, and the art of sharing time. The duet transforms when new dancers enter, with Forsythe's directions and edits, and when new contexts are found for promoting the work (such as a gallery space, even a church).[13]

In 2015 Forsythe made significant changes to *Duo*'s choreographic sequence (insertions, expansions, additional solos, and improvisations). These adjustments were welcomed by the new performers, who had not embodied *Duo*'s history in the Ballett Frankfurt and were excited by change. Forsythe revised the title of the piece to show its discontinuity: *DUO2015*. The dancers and Forsythe recognize these versions as "one"— as well as that the two titled versions only outline the piece's many variations. *Duo* as a genetic project of creative evolution, not progressing but changing: a work-in-process. Performance iterates, both ephemeral and enduring. Performers inhabit a history going further.

Performances also rekindle the past. The movement of *Duo* echoes ballet symmetries, although they are not comprised of ballet steps: the movements are in Forsythe's characteristic style (twisted, polycentric, polyrhythmic, vibratory) and unique to this dance only. *Duo* steps are recalled by the dancers through abstract images, forms of the body, or sensations: for example, "to be light in our feet like crystal," the knee lifting the hand, the fingertips drawing an arc (Watts 2013; Gjoka 2017; Forsythe 1996). The whole body is involved through the panoply of torsions, breath, and movements, strung together rhythmically through symmetries and repetitions. A reality is made in movement: in a workshop one *Duo* dancer coaches, "Really touch the back of your head. Really grab it. Really fall. Never kind of dance, really dance" (Watts 2017b). A requisite to thinking with embodied and performative artworks is following how movement and the body create change—always awash in a new reality.

The choreographic sequence of *Duo* is comprised of many internal loops and repetitions of movement. Each step is thus not singular, but a portal into different dimensions of its structure. Dancer Regina van Berkel remembers the dance fitting together like a "puzzle." She recalls: "We create a whole. But it is all about—made together from little puzzle parts. And we also puzzle up, I call it, the phrase sometimes" (2017). As two dancers move through this puzzle together, simultaneously, on stage they follow and recapitulate this historic plan: co-navigating. I am reminded of a labyrinth, where any turn can conjure a semblance of a previous location; one's sense of time is linked to an exploration of place. Not alone, but in solidarity, the two dancers move within the conceptual labyrinth. From the audience I see this too. Sometimes the dancers progress in perfect unison, for example, making the same walk with "Baroque arms" or leaning together in three consecutive falls (Watts 2017a). Other times, the choreography prescribes that one dancer performs a sequence on his or her own, while the other does a different movement series, or waits. They check in constantly with eyes and ears: At what point are you? Are we on time? Which way next? Are we together?

Co-navigating, feeling the push and pull of timing in the sequence puzzle-labyrinth, *Duo* dancers move through ethical time-space, sharing and creating time. The choreography is only atomistically comprised of steps. From these Forsythe constructs a larger compositional plane of goings and comings, waiting and arriving, certainties and uncertainties: Are we there yet? To navigate this, even after much practice, the dancers must meet eyes and pass subtle vocal signals—negotiating the sequence in a way that is virtuosic and virtuous. The choreography is distributed: across memories and dancers, in spaces and times, always being deciphered.

On the plane of rhythm, Forsythe calls the dancers' time-aligning "entrainment."[14] Rich in tone and communicative like language, *Duo* dancers breathe as they gesture, exfoliating sound that performers (in other traditions, like Ballet) learn to keep silent. One repeated unison movement is a key point of breath connection: while turning their right finger tips around a spiral. Typically, the dancers inhale audibly through their noses, sniffing (never snorting), and then exhale through open lips. The sound has two distinct phases—in and out—parsing time through the soft palate equivalent of tick-tock. While dancing, the dancers sometimes open their vocal tracts wider to vocalize an "ah" or "e"— at most, a tennis like grunt. Rules imply that such sounds should not be exaggerated— never ornamental or indulgent, only functional for attunement (Watts 2017b; van Berkel 2017; Johnson 2018). *Duo* communication through breathing-movement functions holistically not propositionally, like the pleasure of talk.

The "breath song" gives continuities between actions, providing a sonic rhythm or envelope around the movement, congealing entrainment (Watts 2017a). Like whistling while you work, breathing is the dancers' implicit way of thinking with the sequence and each other. Each pair finds their own negotiation style: fast or slow, quiet or loud. Forsythe and dancers Brigel Gjoka and Riley Watts tell me that the breath is the choreography: a formed practice that is deeper than the movement, and an indicator of how together the dancers really are (Gjoka 2016; Watts 2017a). Breathing-movement fuses dance, music, and speech, making an in-between form of composition.

Each iteration of *Duo* fulfills breathing-movement differently. Over *Duo*'s history Forsythe has explored many relations of movement and sound. Between 1996 and 2004, a score for live piano and acoustics by Thom Willems resonates the space, alternating between sound and silence; ideally, this music should not overpower or give the dancers timing mandates, but support them (Willems 2018). The sound shapes mood and atmosphere. At its climax, three-quarters into the piece, the music swells as if ascending to speakers placed at the top of the theater. In a later version of *Duo*, Forsythe chose to leave Willem's score out entirely: the dancers' "breath song" is the only thing audible

Practical Aesthetics

(Watts 2013).[15] In another version, Forsythe selected a recording of aleatoric birdcalls, whose unpredictability of call comes in and out of correspondence with the dancers.[16] With these different ways of pairing sound and movement, various modes of attention are created. Each iteration of the piece composes a palpable push and pull of time, seen-felt-heard.

Microphones have been placed upon the stage to capture the *Duo* dancers' sounds. They operate in real time—a technician takes care to slowly move the fader, bringing the volume of the dancers' sound more audibly into the spectators' chamber. Forsythe describes this amplification as an "audio zoom" (Forsythe 2019). Not too loud and gradual is important, so that it is imperceptible to the audience. Thereby Forsythe composes attention to an emerging visual-acoustic counterpoint. As spectator, one becomes caught in the grasp of the dance's evolving closeness: looming and zooming in. The "effect" is being more "affected." Forsythe augments the sound, to make the dance feel near.

The dancers meet up in the same pose, with their right elbows lifted and one leg stretched in a balletic *tendu*. It is a beautiful resolution: previously fast movements suddenly resolve into stillness. The dancers appear to be perfectly identical, but they are not. One dancer delicately makes two movements and then they resolve into perfect symmetry. Forsythe constructs choreography according to his expectations of how humans learn and anticipate based upon patterns in time and space: artfully making and breaking expectations. This reflects Forsythe's concern for choreography as an open art of composing attention.

Again, the dancers meet up in the same pose, with their right elbows lifted and one foot pointed in *tendu*. Again they are not together and one dancer switches legs: coming into perfect symmetry.

By choreographing attention and teaching the dancers to feel and modulate their own and the audience's attunement, Forsythe hopes to hold the audience close, to bring them *into* and *with* the unfolding of performance. *Duo* experience is intense. Not just intense, but a timeline of variation and contrast: proportions and scales, shifts, and dilations, first and second times, synchronization and dephasing. The dynamics of *Duo* have changed considerably over its history. Recent versions are more dynamically variable than earlier ones, providing more frequent and greater contrast (energy, effort, tempi). Variable, not forceful. The dancers' exertion is always accompanied by listening—never force against one's partner but an impulse that tightens the negotiation, to catch up or surprise. This force is linked to play, rather than violence.

Synchronously, the dancers collapse upon the floor with barely a sound, in the time of a candle being blown out. Building tension continuously, they rise up to standing while listing from their right ear (the choreography prescribes this experience, and the dancers enjoy its distinctness) (Watts 2017b; Gjoka 2017). They continue into the rhythm of a repeated twisting fall: one, two, three times. Contrast ensues: the dancers exit into the shadow upstage before returning.[17] They pause, with their hands on their thighs, like winded basketball players, to breath audibly after a particularly hard phase of exertion.[18] Dancing *with*: phases of intensity, pulses and playful pushes, patterns of (a)symmetries, repeated efforts and dynamics.

As *Duo*

Duo is about relations, sensations, and affects, as composed around moving bodies exfoliating breathing-movement—a thinking *through/in/with* dance. But when Forsythe and the dancers make and rehearse choreography, they need to talk. It would be impossible to create without sharing information about their intentions and offering names to common features. The dancers are also highly reflective and intelligent about what they do. But on stage, *Duo* dancers exchange words only occasionally. I find out in my fieldwork that these utterances are traces of the language used in the choreographic process—often inherited names for things, passed down from pair to pair: "New Beginning" names a repeat of the first move. "Snake" names a point in the sequence where the body slithers right. "Almost there" is an encouragement at the end (Johnson 2018). In watching archival videos of performance, I catalog the utterances, watching them come and go, across history—each performance, the dancers tell me, provides its own logic of what needs to be said, or left unsaid. The speaking is a reverence for the dance's history: one more "New Beginning," another "Almost There." According to Whitehead, novelty always lends potential to experience the refrain anew: not the "newest new" of capitalism, but the eventfulness of experience in the specific now unfolding (Manning 2016: 58).

Duo concresces composition across registers: coeval movement, the sounds of the room, the quality of the light, the gaps between partners and audience, the shifts in

Figure 17.3 Image by *DUO2015* Dancer Riley Watts, Superimposing His Body with His Partner Brigel Gjoka's.
Photo © Riley Watts.

Practical Aesthetics

recognition and attention, occasional words. Intensity dilates. History unfolds, thinking past, toward this iteration's new. Intensities and relays of attention: negotiating memory and experience.

Epilogue

And *Duo* continues. One example is Figure 17.3, by *DUO2015* dancer Riley Watts.

During the downtime between tours, Watts continues to "process" his thoughts about performing *Duo* through making digital art—using digital tools to recompose an archival video recording of *DUO2015*, making images and short videos (Watts 2019). In Figure 17.3, Watts has superimposed his body with his partner's, becoming one: concrescence. Like my aforementioned written concrescence of *Duo*, Watt's photo illustrates the open channels of creativity that the dancers and Forsythe delight in, asking how else they can view the dance or their bodies differently. Artwork is both a product and a means of passing through. The refrain again anew: pluralistic creative process.[19]

Notes

1. Program note from the Ballett Frankfurt tour to the John F. Kennedy Center for the Performing Arts, USA June 17–19, 2004.
2. See Cull for a detailed introduction.
3. I was a guest dancer (2004) in the Ballett Frankfurt, a dancer (2005–12) and guest dancer (2012–15) in The Forsythe Company. See endnote 6 for a short biography of William Forsythe.
4. Geertz develops the term "thick description" from Gilbert Ryle, writing "The aim is to draw large conclusions from small, but very densely textured facts" (1973: 28). In my case I differ from a cultural view that might read dance movement as a form of symbolic action, seeking to systematically decode the conceptual structures of Forsythe dancers or *Duo* spectators.
5. Another valuable reference is Cvejić's writing on performance process, see 2015a: 195–224.
6. William Forsythe is an American choreographer who has been active in the field for over forty-five years, producing a wide range of projects—including performances, installations, films, and knowledge creation. He danced in the Stuttgart Ballet before directing Ballett Frankfurt (1984–2004) and The Forsythe Company (2005–15). His work has reoriented ballet to a dynamic twenty-first-century art form.
7. Since 2018 a revised version of the work, titled *Dialogue (DUO2015)*, has toured internationally on Forsythe's program *A Quiet Evening of Dance*.
8. On endurance in Whitehead, see, for example, Whitehead 1985: 136–7. Discussing formal vs. sociocultural aspects of dance, see Siegmund 2013: 81–2.
9. Erin Manning defining "art-as-practice," proposes "we engage first and foremost with the manner of practice and not with the end-result." (2016: 45). Umberto Eco describes "an open product on account of its susceptibility to countless different interpretations" including structures that may be "unplanned or physically incomplete" requiring interpretation (1989: 4, 12). Roland Barthes differentiates the material object of the book from the Text, which is "*experienced only in an activity of production.*" (1977: 157). Nicolas Bourriaud writes, "it is

10. The "dissonance, the dephasing, and complementarity of between" is made palpable during an exercise at a workshop for dance scholars with *Duo* dancer Allison Brown (Manning 2016: 61). I have invited Brown to teach us something from her practice of *Duo*, something without virtuosic movement so that my fellow scholars can join in. Brown asks us to find a partner. She gives us the task: "You go, I go, we go" (Brown 2018). Without music, she asks us to improvise movement together accordingly. She lets us negotiate the transitions, some speaking, others sensing. The instructions render aspects of dancing William Forsythe's duet *Duo*, of which Brown is an expert, palpable to those outside it and inexperienced in moving-with others. True to Brown's assignment, *Duo* is a duet in which dancing together happens quite barely upon the stage, without touch and plot, putting relations in motion as forms in and of time. But it is not only the movement or the dancers that are important: dance is working across many registers.

11. On the difficulty of translating this term into English see Thomas: "A *Leerstelle* is not merely an emptiness; it is a form of emptiness that determines to an extent how it can be filled." (1982: 56).

12. A phrase is a general term for a movement sequence.

13. In 2016 *DUO2015* was performed in the Philadelphia Museum of Art and the church of Saint Eustache in Paris.

14. Entrainment as the ability to synchronize and interlock rhythms, necessary for communication as well as in music and dance (Spier 1998: 142–3).

15. Gala performance of *Duo* performed by Riley Watts and Brigel Gjoka on June 1, 2013, at Staatstheater Darmstadt.

16. Performances of *Dialogue (DUO2015)* October 4–6, 2018, at the Sadler's Wells Theatre of London. This performance is currently touring internationally under the title *A Quiet Evening of Dance*.

17. Performances of *DUO2015* September 17–18, 2015, at the Théâtre des Champs-Elysées in Paris.

18. Gala performance of *Duo* performed by Riley Watts and Brigel Gjoka on September 12, 2013, in Weimar.

19. I am exceptionally grateful to the dancers, whose diverse experiences with *Duo* I can only touch upon in this short paper: thank you Cyril Baldy, Regina van Berkel, Allison Brown, Brigel Gjoka, Jill Johnson, Roberta Mosca and Riley Watts. Great thanks as well to Christina Thurner and Tilman O'Donnell for their helpful feedback on a draft of this paper.

References

Barthes, R. (1977), *Image, Music, Text*, trans. S. Heath, London: Fontana Press.

Bourriaud, N. (2002), *Relational Aesthetics*, trans. S. Pleasance and F. Woods, with Mathieu Copland, Dijon: les presses du réel.

Brown, A. (October 25, 2018), Dancing Together Workshop, University of Bern.

Cull, L. (2014), "Performance Philosophy—Staging a New Field," in L. Cull and A. Lagay (eds.), *Encounters In Performance Philosophy*, 15–38, Basingstoke: Palgrave Macmillan.

Cvejić, B. (2015a), *Choreographing Problems: Expressive Concepts in Contemporary Dance and Performance*, Basingstoke: Palgrave Macmillan.

Cvejić, B. (2015b), "From Odd Encounters to a Prospective Confluence: Dance-Philosophy," *Performance Philosophy*, 1: 7–23.
Eco, U. (1989), *The Open Work*, trans. A. Cancogni, London: Hutchinson.
Forsythe, W. (January 2, 1996), archival video of *Duo* rehearsal, Ballett Frankfurt.
Forsythe, W. (January 30, 2019), interview with the author.
Geertz, C. (1973), *The Interpretation of Cultures*, New York: Basic Books.
Gjoka, B. (March 6, 2016), interview with the author.
Gjoka, B. (October 23–27, 2017), *DUO2015* Workshop, Art Factory International.
Gjoka, B., and R. Watts, (October 25, 2017), interview with the author.
Johnson, J. (June 28, 2018), interview with the author.
Manning, E. (2016), *The Minor Gesture*, Durham: Duke University Press.
Siegmund, G. (2013), "Aesthetic Experience," in G. Brandstetter and G. Klein (eds.), *Dance [and] Theory*, 81–8, Bielefeld: transcript Verlag.
Spier, S. (1998), "Engendering and Composing Movement: William Forsythe and the Ballett Frankfurt," *The Journal of Architecture*, 3 (2): 135–46.
Thomas, B. (1982), "Reading Wolfgang Iser on Responding to a Theory of Response," *Comparative Literary Studies*, 19 (1): 54–66.
Van Berkel, R. (April 22, 2017), interview with the author.
Watts, R. (February 27, 2019), interview with the author.
Watts, R. (January 10–15, 2017a), interview with the author.
Watts, R. (March 3, 2013), email to the author.
Watts, R. (October 23–27, 2017b), *DUO2015* Workshop, Art Factory International.
Whitehead, A. N. (1967), *Adventures of Ideas*, New York: The Free Press.
Whitehead, A. N. (1985), *Process and Reality*, corr. edition D. R. Griffin and D. W. Sherburne, New York: The Free Press.
Willems, T. (November 21, 2018), interview with the author.

CHAPTER 17
THE HEART AND OTHER ORGANS OF DARKNESS IN THE YEAR 2019
Allen C. Shelton

In February 2018, I had just started my sabbatical, ostensibly to finish a project I had already begun, a collection of letters from the Civil War sent home by my ancestor Eli Pinson Landers. I first conceptualized this project in the early 1980s after becoming aware of my ancestor's trove of letters. I even bore a striking family resemblance to Eli according to my mother. I wanted the writing to look and feel like his letters and reproduce the texture, the sadness, and the stray pieces of cloth that kept coming up in his prose: shirts, coats, socks, pants; and the dark in his sunny South. I imagined I would pull a comb through Eli as the nurse might have as she combed his hair and washed his face as he lay dying in the field hospital. I had pages and pages of this in piles on my desk—notes, lists, and paragraphs already written in longhand on at least one hundred sheets of large French paper on tiny grids. I'm sure it was cold outside. The sidewalks and streets were slushy. The sky was overcast. That is a persistent feature of winter in Buffalo. One of Eli's brothers was a prisoner of war in Elmira, so he too knew this gray cold world. I lived a mile away from the college, though it might as well of been across the country I had so little contact with anyone there. My work there felt like a disaster in the distance, a Pompeii from afar or Vesuvius waiting for me to return to it in the fall before erupting.

Then my plans changed. My editor at the University of Chicago Press told me they were no longer interested in another book after the disappointing sales of the first. I had been clinging to this. After my partner had left two years earlier, this commitment from Chicago was a relationship that comforted me. Now it was gone. The world around me was gray. I couldn't think straight.

What memories I have of that time are like weather fronts passing through with ghostly outlines rather than discrete shapes. Nothing was safe. Important dates or events which I had used as markers in my life were shadows. I had an uneventful Christmas that now a year later I have no memories of other than being alone, as if that was a tangible shape next to me. On Valentine's Day, another important marker, I was alone that night in bed scanning my iPhone for a text message from my ex-partner, but I was in the sunny South in Boone, North Carolina, staying with a couple who I cared about, the anthropologists Jon Carter and Christina Sorinito-Carter, giving two talks to their department. This would turn out to be one of my few memorable and happy times that year. Ironically, on the day before Valentines I was on the same flight as my ex. We sat next to each other. Our shoulders touched. We may have even held hands. For this talk

Practical Aesthetics

I needed an abstract and a title. I couldn't come up with either. Looming up behind me was the same request from another quarter, which felt in my state like a demand for this very chapter. In a panic I recalled an essay I had written years before that had gotten little attention, "The Heart and Other Organs of Darkness." It was impossible to find the original abstract if there ever was one. The essay itself seemed to have been erased. I couldn't find it online or in my library at school. Why this essay came to me as a solution to my immediate needs for a talk in Boone and this essay wasn't clear to me yet. It would come to be clear piece by piece in time. One morning, the sudden appearance of the sun cast shadows on my apartment floor. They made me think of x-rays that had spilled out of a file, another intangible shape, like my aloneness next to me (see Map 5).

Dorian Gray

The essay contains a portrait of me at a critical point in my biography that initiated my long stay in Buffalo, which is nearing the weight of my home in Alabama. Looking at this portrait gives me a feeling what Dorian Gray must've felt if he'd had a photographic record of his portraits over time. It's vertigo. There is a scene in Alfred Hitchcock's *Vertigo* that I only more or less remember after seeing it many times; my own vertigo keeps distorting the scenes so that I'm not sure what's in the movie and what's my own version. The detective Scotty, played by Jimmy Stewart, is in a redwood forest outside San Francisco. He's there with a woman named Madeleine, who he's been hired to follow. He's in love with her. They're looking at a redwood stump on which important historical dates have been marked going back hundreds of years. Madeleine, the wife of a rich businessman, has increasingly become obsessed with a dead woman Carlotta Valdes, who bears a remarkable resemblance to her. At this moment, she is possessed by her and she places her finger on, first, her birthdate and then her death. It makes Scotty's head spin. It makes my head spin. But this is only the first level of the vertigo. Scotty is a former cop whose vertigo causes the death of his partner and pushes him into retirement. The possessed wife is not the businessman's wife but a salesgirl who has been hired to impersonate the wife to facilitate her murder. Scotty will meet her again as the salesgirl and fall in love with her and the ghost of the now dead wife. His vertigo will claim at least one more life. Inside this memory I recall the actress Kim Novak's hair wound into a bun, her figure wrapped in elegant fabric, her inappropriate heels stood out in the woods like a prehistoric prosthesis, Stewart's suit (was it gray), hat, slick leather-soled shoes on the forest floor, and the dappled light. I see these pieces alien as creatures in a woodland.

Like Stewart in another version of my reimagined scene, I am placing my finger on a tree ring where my vertigo either originated or became clear enough to see. I arrived here in Buffalo twenty years ago at the end of August. I'm trying to remember where I was in that past on this date. I can't. It's likely I was still in Alabama visiting what was left of my family and my life there. I would've been staying at my brother's house. I would start back teaching on January 3. I barely have any memories. It's the same blank landscape I see around me now as if something was devouring my memories. How could

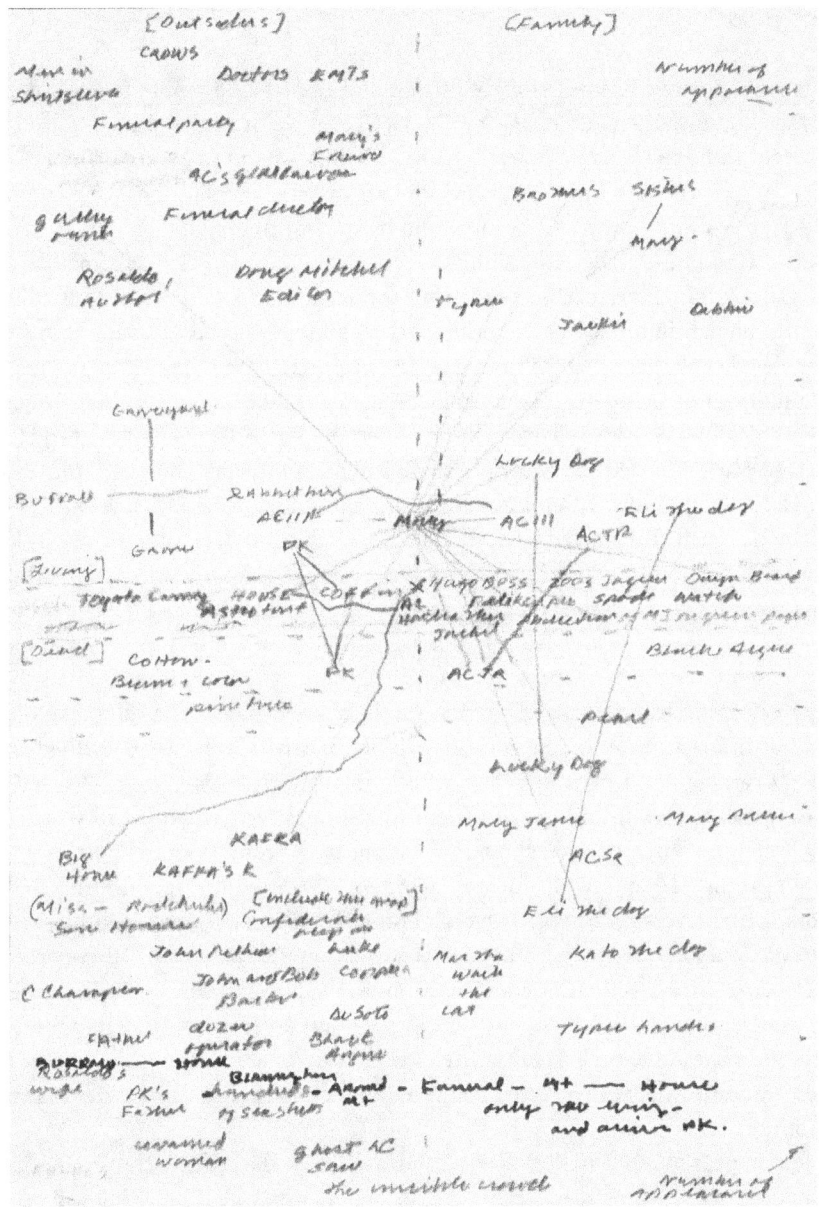

Map Draft 5 Courtesy Allen C. Shelton.

this feeling that I'm soaked with now reach back and find another helical thread in the screw set in me or what Sebald would describe as another ring in the rings of Saturn? If I go back another two decades, it's 1978. I'm married. I live on my farm with two dogs, three horses and a cat. The last stop is 1958. I'm three years old. It's Rome, Georgia. There's a pond near the house where I see a king snake wearing a yellow crown. If I look to the future, I will be eighty-three years old. I can't see where I'll be.

Practical Aesthetics

Marco Polo

In this 1998 portrait I'm in my early forties, and I have a desperate but still hopeful look that this essay would change my inevitable trajectory toward insignificance. It turned out to be the longest essay I would ever publish and has proportionately the largest bibliography of all my works including my books. Perhaps most importantly, it marked a transition in my writing. It would be the last time that locations other than Alabama would be equally represented. Over the arc of my work, Alabama has acted like a growing sinkhole reaching even into my accounts around me in Buffalo much as Walter Benjamin looked back on his Berlin childhood as an entrance to his work on his new home, Paris, which contains no accounts of him. The essay is likely the most unknown of any of my published work, a point made tellingly by an anonymous reviewer in 2004 as she looked over a book project of mine. All my work was forgettable, she wrote. She described the book as a small insignificant work. What she means here by small is synonymous with minor and is like and unlike what Deleuze and Guattari mean by the term. They mean to describe a high degree of deterritorialization. In my minor work she points out my bitterness toward established professors and institutions while remaining a small person and in the wrong. In a recent work I described myself as a minor Southern sociologist only to have another anonymous reviewer single out that one sentence out with particular scorn. I couldn't tell what he meant by "self-proclaimed minor Southern sociologist." He never elaborated what he meant by the phrase in the review unless he meant it to be related to what he described as my deliberate ambiguity. I can't help but think of Kafka's circuitous prose, his desire to become small to escape and out of which his critiques are written. I had written this essay over the course of several years reaching back from 1998 in Buffalo to 1991 on my farm in Alabama with my son laying on the desk playing with his trucks as I wrote the first version of what I would come to call my meeting with the garbage madonna for a job talk at Oberlin which is at the center of the essay. Other parts were conceived or written in South Bend, Des Moines, Walla Walla, Las Vegas, Tacoma, and Geneseo. The essay indirectly records my zigzagging career as an itinerant scholar. It's indirect because at the time it was written I was afraid or at least reluctant to reveal my movements and what that revealed about me though looking at it now it's clear that I hid nothing.

I don't appear to move in the essay, but I drove across the country three times in that span of time. The opening scene takes place in an unnamed café in an unknown location. The final scene occurs in an unknown office. In between are two episodes in Alabama, one occurring at my son's school and the last in the hills ringing what was my farm. Calvino's *Invisible Cities* recounts a conversation between Kublai Khan and Marco Polo in the palace garden. Marco describes city after city in the Empire that he's visited—none are real in that they can't be found on a map except those in the future, some seem to be his home in Venice. Each is told without accounts of how they were conquered or how Marco traveled there. The Khan never moves, Marco has ceased moving. Except for short trips to Boone and Bloomington, I barely moved during my 2018 sabbatical other than the three-quarter mile to the café to write. I'm lying in bed, my arms folded across my chest like I am an Egyptian prince flying into myself. First there is dark as if I'm in a theater and then flashes of memory repeated many times before I fall asleep.

Bathysphere

The anguish of my heart is everywhere in the essay, but it doesn't begin to acknowledge the other organs of darkness that were in my world then. It seems Conrad's heart of darkness was a means of containing and insulating myself from the disasters in my life as if it were a bathysphere and I were descending into my own depths. Of all the books mentioned in the essay, it's the only one that has a specificity and weight like a body and from which my own title is taken. I mention a reader in my essay close to me, a blonde poet. She shows up again named in my acknowledgments. There's even a specific bookmark, a postcard with an African fertility symbol on it, sent to me by a former professor, an Englishman married to a Polish woman. Conrad was Polish who wrote in English. I even name the edition I own, a Penguin paperback. The small novel pops up more often than any other book in the essay. But it doesn't appear in the bibliography. It's part of a network of omitted books that hold up the pages of the essay, a visible but unofficial bibliography that doesn't show up in the official record. I can't say why this occurred. I can't type so adding in these other citations would've been stressful, if not impossible. The essay was published as it was. No one said where's Conrad? One clue as to why is on the first page when the chair of my department asks out of boredom, "Did you read it in graduate school?" She sipped her mocha through a mound of whipped cream. "We didn't read books like that where I went to school." My response tells why it was gone; "No, I read it on my own." What was listed on my final pages were the most acceptable texts.

The power of Conrad's book lay outside the pages in my past. The first time I ever articulated the phrase the heart of darkness wasn't in school but at a party sitting in a circle in a living room as a joint was being passed from person to person as if it were a secret. Next to me was a young woman I vaguely knew who went to the same charismatic churches I did. I'd only spoken to her once before when she came up to me, hugged me, and thanked me for sharing Jesus with her alcoholic brother. She was older, the daughter of a plumber I knew. What work she did after high school I didn't know. We were talking about sin and I described it as a heart of darkness, like a continent floating inside the person. Where this image came from wasn't Conrad, I hadn't read him yet but from Victorian portraits of Africa in old books and missionary talks in the churches around my town. With that I had one half of Conrad's discourse on this horror and I was just beginning to suspect that the other half was in my own life in Alabama. Now, like the romantic breakup, the disasters that surrounded me seem trite in retrospective. Some of them I've written about in my other works. I produced some for my therapist. At best, these other organs peek through the surface prose of the essay, hiding behind the official bibliography.

Practical Aesthetics

Nadja

Out of this I wrote seventy-two love letters to her from late August to early January. Even as I was writing the scriptural recordings of my broken heart, I sensed they were somehow related to Eli's letters though part of a much smaller configuration than the war he was trapped in. He never saw the ocean or anything the size of the man-made lakes that are part of the South today. He makes no comment on any of the large rivers he saw other than to say the name of the river, and like the river or its shores he can barely see how large the war is surrounding him. Eli wrote almost a hundred letters from the Eastern front to his mother and sister. How this related to me seemed at the tip of my tongue except for where the object of my letters lived was for me a hell made up of strip malls and casinos. It in no way resembled my home in the sunny South. Did that mean my very person in Buffalo was the new front in a war? I would walk five miles to sit in my office or the library work room to peck out letters to send as emails and somehow this essay. If there were editorial comments, none have survived. While this essay was written about losing K, it's now about losing M. I've moved up the alphabet. It's easy to substitute the loss now for the old one, particularly since the original woman only appears once by name in the essay. The only obstacle is the dedication borrowed from Benjamin's *One-Way Street* to his short-term but intense love, Asja. My copy reads "In memory of Asja, who first touched my imagination and memory from very far away." Benjamin's is more forceful; "This Street is named after Asja Lacis Street after her who as an engineer cut it through the author." The rest of Benjamin's collage text is seldom read as evidence of a hole, a single one-way street running out of his heart. Here at least, in this line, Benjamin's heart appears; if it appears elsewhere, it's so disguised that it's unrecognizable. Even sex in this portrayal is dada. It's in his *Moscow Diaries*, which was never meant to be seen by others that Benjamin cries. In a sled headed to the depot, he turns back to look at Asja as she walks away. He cries.

M is not Asja, except like K she blasted a hole through my heart. The book that M and I share is Andre Breton's *Nadja*, though neither of us can be found in the pages. The new dedication should be something about convulsive beauty and haunting, but it was her cat named Nadja that I came to love who's is a direct descendent of that book.

Three Axes

What I meant to do once I had the title eluded me. The original essay was in many ways dated by its baroque bibliography and pop cultural references. There was a section devoted to the David Lynch film *Blue Velvet*, which was and is for me a deeply moving work. I had recently found out that the movie was set in Lumberton, North Carolina, and not in some mythical town in the Northwest. What I originally meant by that title was wrapped up for me in my thoughts about this film; a young man back from college after his father has a heart attack watering the lawn, finds an ear covered in ants, like it was made of sugar in the grass cutting across an empty lot, and from there Jeffrey, which is the same name as my grandfather, the nickname of my aunt Jeffy, and my brother, descends into a dark town beneath the surface of the pastel-colored one he has known. My own life in a small southern town was marked by these same entrance points, a place of dreams, the dead, and memories. The anthropologist Michael Taussig referred to zones like this as a "space of death." For him, this space was mythic cauldron of haunted art, literature, and theologies of the afterlife as well as a concrete place in the Amazonian rain forests along the Putumayo River, which framed the violence around the rubber boom there in the early twentieth century and then, later, the dream space of shamans. How the forest thought and moved as a space of death isn't articulated at this point in his work. Perhaps it can't be. Tree species, animals, insects, and the temperature are absent in his portrayal. Instead, he relies upon stories from travelers and other eyewitnesses from the late nineteenth and early twentieth century which form another kind of haunted rain forest. No steel ax or machete touches his hands in this forest. In the corner of my apartment are three Swedish axes of different sizes. Tellingly, the death space doesn't infiltrate him in the text, filling him with dread. My own exploratory representations soak up the taste of a death space in my own fat.

Minotaur

I'm half asleep. It's before seven in the morning. I've already gotten up and taken a pill for my cholesterol. I left the light on in the adjoining room looking into my bedroom to act as the sun coming out. It was dark and snowing outside. I was trying to solve a dream. I was back in the house I lived in when I was ten years old. It was a two-story house on what was a dairy farm on the outside of Lebanon, Ohio. My mother and father, now dead, were there. Around the house was a ten-foot wire fence which was in my memory a regular three-foot wire net fence found in the suburbs or around houses in the cities. This dream fence was military. My mother and I spoke about it. I was concerned about who did the maintenance, and it was then I realized that in the dream I was a visitor. I was no longer part of the same time zone as my mother, father, and this house but an outsider coming back, unable to alter what I saw. My mother took me through the house. There were so many rooms. The hallways were narrow. I wanted to see the room where I as a child had recuperated in bed for weeks after surgery and a month in the hospital. When we walked into the room, I immediately recognized it. It seemed to be ready for me. The bed was made. There was a toilet and sink next to the bed because I couldn't walk. The curtains were drawn. And yet I'd never seen this room before. But in my dream this room at the center of a labyrinth was made for me and me alone. It was then that I looked at my phone and saw two emails from B asking about the status of the essay I had promised him. It was due in a month and whatever I had wasn't an essay but fragments, snatches of things like tendrils from a psychic encounter, pieces of cloth from a hundred ghosts. I keep returning to this old essay to find traces of my future to solve this problem of producing an essay now.

Practical Aesthetics

I carry on me a reminder of that past time. On my back the surgery left the imprinted scar in the shape of a bull's head with its horns reaching to either side of my waist. There is no doubt I was meant for this space. I had the Minotaur hovering above my ass. I'm dreaming this just over an hour away for where I lay in the original essay.

M

Instead of working on my talk, I retreated to a project my ex-partner and I had started at least two years earlier. The reasons for that seem easy enough to understand now. I wanted to be in a space where we were together. Even before it was clear that my last book was a commercial failure, she had hit on the idea to dissemble the book into a collection of pages which we would alter. She cut the spine and the book was rendered into a long accordion of pages that if they had been written only on one side would've resembled what Walter Benjamin's *Arcades Project* must've looked like; he had no binding holding the work together. Instead, the handwritten pages in different-colored ink were stored in some sort of box of which I know of no mention of. At that point, the project with my partner sputtered, as did our relationship. "What should we do next?" I had written in my own illegible handwriting a passage on the first typed page. But that's as far as we got. Together we never came up with a solution. Apart, preparing for the talk, an answer came to me.

I had a practical question: Where is my heart in the book? Which is I suppose like asking where the heart in Conrad's novel is. Ordinarily that answer points to where Kurtz resided in the far reaches of the Congo and then back to Belgium where his fiancée mourns at the center of the origin of the violence. But what of Marlowe? He is unattached. If he is Conrad's double as the novel's narrator, the answer lies outside the text in Conrad's biography. There was what seemed to be the obvious answer in my case since it was a book devoted to the memory of a friend who committed suicide. But in the public readings of the book I never teared up around him; it was the death of the small cat named Nadia that caused me to cry. Behind me, pushing was this old essay and in front of me yanking on me was a new one with the same title. Each was sharpened by failed love and academic pressures. What seemed doable was to translate my introduction into a Dogan map of a kind. At the center of the map was my father's house. I then moved out in increments, drawing a series of nestled rectangles moving from my father's house and family further and further out to zones completely dominated by outsiders. At the far extreme was my home in Buffalo. I used the zones to place the actors, animal, human, and objects as they appeared. M appeared in every zone. Then I drew a line to each entry she was connected to. It was virtually all of them. On the edge of the map I rewrote the only entry we'd done together. I placed the image of my father and I, my suicidal friend, and my mother onto the map. Each time I found M in the text, my heart beat faster; but however much she was there, she wasn't. She was somewhere else. A simple word search pulled up her name, but if it was untangled from the thicket of other relationships and movements, there would be holes left on the page like a series of drain plugs that had been pulled. Likely all my memories would drain away.

At the beginning I thought I was what held the story together. I'm certainly there. I tell the story. What would happen if I were removed? Just after the book was published, I found a blog entry from a man named John Shaplin. It was titled "Dark Waters" by Allen Shelton, a title I thought was mine and an image deeply embedded in my book. It appeared he had typed out his nine favorite paragraphs from my work. The entry was about four pages long. It was I thought a good summary of my work. Then it was just there. I would see it online searching for reviews. Preparing for the talk in Boone brought me back to it. I needed a summary of my book. He had produced a good one. It was then I found that none of the paragraphs were exactly as I had written them. I had written every sentence, but he had picked through my book like it was a Lego set to produce new paragraphs by breaking up my paragraphs into sentences and then reassembling them into his own. The title wasn't even mine. It was clear then that his version of my book was perhaps better, certainly shorter, and didn't contain me. He had deleted Allen Shelton and his narrator from the book. I lingered behind his title but for how long? His version of *Where the North Sea Touched Alabama* contains no Allen Shelton. It or I wasn't needed. One heart beat for another in this internet space.

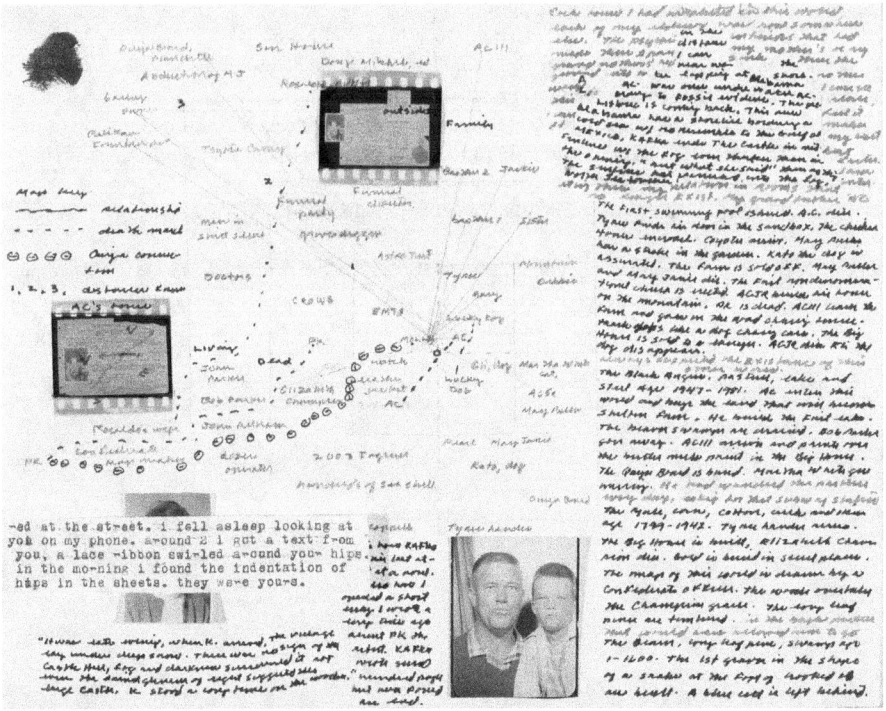

Map Draft 11 Courtesy Allen C. Shelton.

Practical Aesthetics

References

Barthes, R. (1977), *Roland Barthes by Roland Barthes*, trans. R. Howard, New York: Hill and Wang Publishers.
Before and After Science (1978), [LP] Brian Eno, Island.
Benjamin, W. (1986), *Moscow Diaries*, trans. R. Sieburth, Cambridge, MA: Belknap Press of Harvard University Press.
Benjamin, W. (1999), *The Arcades Project*, ed. and trans. H. Eiland and K. McLaughlin, Cambridge, MA: Belknap Press of Harvard University Press.
Benjamin, W. (2006), *Berlin Childhood around 1900*, trans. H. Eiland, Cambridge, MA: Harvard University Press.
Benjamin, W. (2016), *One-Way Street*, trans. E. Jephcott, Cambridge, MA: Belknap Press of Harvard University Press.
Borges, J. L. (1984), "Partial Enchantments of the Quixote," trans. R. Simms, in *Other Inquisitions: 1937–1952*, 43–6, Austin: University of Texas Press.
Blue Velvet ([1986] 2002), [Film] Dir. David Lynch, Los Angeles: MGM.
Breton, A. (1960), *Nadja*, trans. R. Howard, New York: Grove Press.
Conrad, J. (1986), *Heart of Darkness*, New York: Penguin Books.
Darwin, C. (1985), *On the Origin of Species*, New York: Penguin Classics.
Deleuze, G., and F. Guattari (1986), *Kafka: Toward a Minor Literature*, trans. D. Polan, Minneapolis: University of Minnesota Press.
Deleuze, G., and F. Guattari (1987), *A Thousand Plateaus: Capitalism and Schizophrenia*, trans. B. Massumi, Minneapolis: University of Minnesota Press.
Discreet Music (1975), [LP] Brian Eno, Obscure.
Kafka, F. (1998), *The Castle*, trans. M. Harman, New York: Schocken.
Leiris, M. (1984), *Manhood: A Journey from Childhood Into the Fierce Order of Virility*, trans. R. Howard, San Francisco: North Point Press.
Sebald, W. G. (1999), *The Rings of Saturn*, trans. M. Huss, New York: New Directions.
Shelton, A. C. (1999), "The Heart and Other Organs of Darkness," *Cultural Studies: Research Annual*, 4 (Winter): 71–97.
Shelton, A. C. (2013), *Where the North Sea Touches Alabama*, Chicago: University of Chicago Press.
Taussig, M. (1987), *Shamanism, Colonialism, and the Wild Man: A Study in Terror and Healing*, Chicago: University of Chicago Press.

CHAPTER 18
ESSAYISTIC IMAGINATION AS THINKING *WITH*
PRACTICAL AESTHETICS AND MAX BENSE'S ESSAY ON THE ESSAY
Christoph Ernst

I. Practical Aesthetics and Media Aesthetics[1]

The idea behind this book is to propose that practical aesthetics explicates our ways of "thinking with" media and its forms (images, sounds, etc.) (see Introduction in this volume, by Herzogenrath). The roots of practical aesthetics can be traced back to the eighteenth century. Its appearance in the twentieth century is associated with the growing awareness of the importance of media technologies for aesthetics. Practical aesthetics can even be considered as a particular form of media aesthetics. But if this is true, one has to take into account that media aesthetics is a transgression of aesthetics itself.

The development of media aesthetics is closely linked to the tradition of essayistic writing about media in the German-speaking world. Authors such as Walter Benjamin, Siegfried Kracauer, and others provided impulses for media theory and media aesthetics (Ernst 2005). From the 1920s onward, the essayistic was (re)discovered as a cipher for a specific form of thinking. Essays about the essay reflect a way of thinking that—in essayistic fashion—focused on the emerging "media culture" and its aesthetics. In this tradition art was used as an example to illustrate fundamental changes between human perception and media technologies. Inaugurating the discourse on media aesthetics, Walter Benjamin famously spoke of the historical interrelations between media and what he called "human sense perception" (*Sinneswahrnehmung*) (Benjamin 1936).

Times and technologies are changing. At the beginning of the twenty-first century, a shift in the mediation of "human sense perception" is on the horizon. Computer-based media technologies developing toward ubiquitous computing, the internet of things, and artificial intelligence (machine learning) lead to questions about the role of aesthetics in the era of distributed human-machine cognition. From this perspective, older notions of media aesthetics are suffering from a humanistic bias. To talk about media aesthetics today means not only to "deconstruct" subject-centered notions of aesthetics but to talk about the cognitive abilities of machines as well. This new "posthuman" program of media aesthetics is, for example, linked with new speculative realisms (Askin et al. 2014). Influenced by critics of theories of subject-centered perception such as Gilles Deleuze and Félix Guattari, these challenges of traditional notions of aesthetics indicate a crucial tension within current media aesthetics for which the discussion of practical aesthetics can be fruitful.

Practical aesthetics is the elaboration of a theory of epistemic practices which are not covered by notions of "representation" or "concept" in conventional theories of thinking (see Introduction in this volume, by Herzogenrath). To explicate the idea of "thinking with" as a form of perceptual involvement implies an experiential dimension of human thought processes. What makes the notion of practical aesthetics interesting is its emphasis on the relation between perception and thinking. This is especially true if "practice" is the basic category of the proposed form of aesthetics. Semiotics, pragmatism, phenomenology, and the philosophy of cognition have shown that perception and thinking must be considered as embodied and situated practices. Viewed from this angle, practical aesthetics concerns the problem of a translation between two groups of practices—perception and thinking. A "practical" perspective on aesthetics comes into play when aesthetics is considered to be a theory about connections between perception and thinking in which thinking cannot be separated from the specific qualities of an actual perceptual involvement.

In this text, I propose that an elaboration of this practical dimension is of particular importance for media aesthetics. Discourses on practical aesthetics contain knowledge of practical ways of thinking. However, one has to be careful here. Neither are understandings of thinking which rely on the notion of "concepts" opposed to practical aesthetics nor are representational theories of thinking false. I would like to propose a "moderate" reading of practical aesthetics. Practical aesthetics develops a heterodox vocabulary for certain types of epistemic practices which are often overlooked. As I will try to show in a case study of Max Bense's theory of essayistic writing, the epistemological program of practical aesthetics can be discussed under the heading of a theory "proto-theoretical thinking." In order to do that, I will read Bense from a "media philosophical" standpoint. As Lorenz Engell showed in his works, media philosophy can be understood as an endeavor to decipher the theoretical knowledge of media about themselves (Engell 2014). Following this approach, I am not primarily interested in the historical contexts of Bense's essay on the essay rather than in its media theoretical implications and connotations.

II. Essayistic Writing as *Thinking With*: The Case of Max Bense

Max Bense is well known as a semiotician and a pioneer of computer theory. Yet, Bense has disappeared from consciousness as a cultural theorist (Fröschle 2016). While he is renowned for his works on information aesthetics, Bense can be placed in a tradition of essayistic forms of reflection on media aesthetics as well. In this regard, Bense's theory of essayistic writing is important.[2] His essay *On the Essay and its Prose* is one of the most interesting essays about the essay.[3] For many years, there was a tendency to overlook Bense. When it came to essays on the essay in German-speaking countries, usually Theodor W. Adorno's essay *The Essay as Form* was cited (Adorno [1958] 2017). Adorno, however, was referring to Bense. This is illustrated by two key quotes Adorno takes from Bense's text (Zima 2012: 164–5). The first quote is:

> This, then, is how the essay is distinguished from a treatise. The person who writes essayistically is the one who composes as he experiments, who turns his object around, questions it, feels it, tests it, reflects on it, who attacks it from different sides and assembles what he sees in his mind's eye and puts into words what the object allows one to see under the conditions created in the course of writing. (Adorno [1958] 2017: 74)

The second quote is:

> The essay is the form of the critical category of the mind. For the person who criticizes must necessarily experiment, he must create conditions under which an object becomes visible anew, and do so still differently than an author does; above all, the object's frailties must be tried and tested, and this is the meaning of the slight variation the object experiences at the hands of its critic. (Adorno [1958] 2017: 74)[4]

Both quotations describe an epistemic situation and are inspired by metaphors which consider the essay as a form between "experience" and "experiment" (Müller-Funk 1995). Essayistic thinking is for Bense "experimental thinking" ("experimentelles Denken," Bense 1952: 28).[5] If we follow this metaphor and take a look at Bense's text from the perspective of media theory, then Bense does not only speak of an unprejudiced examination of an object. He also states that this examination is a varying, perspectival work under the conditions defined by the medium, in his case, writing. Thinking *with* writing is, at least metaphorically, understood as a physical-haptic process of working with the medium ("turns his object around," "feels"). Thus, Bense can be read in such a way that writing is for him more than just "written language."[6] Writing has to be regarded as a materially realized, semiotic medium that has properties that go beyond language, for example it has a visual form (Krämer 2003).

According to Bense, the essay is characterized by a tension between poetry and prose, aesthetics and ethics, creation and tendency (Bense [1947] 2017: 49–51). Like other authors, he sees the essay as a discursive borderline between literature (or art) and philosophy (or science)[7]:

> Therefore, I arrive at the conclusion that there is a strange border area [confinium] that develops between poetry and prose, between the aesthetic stage of creation and the ethical stage of persuasion. It always remains somewhat enigmatic, but it captures a well-known literary position. This is because the "essay" is the unmediated literary expression of this strange border area between poetry and prose, between creation and persuasion, between an aesthetic and an ethical stage. (Bense [1947] 2017: 52)

Practical Aesthetics

Bense has a clear idea of what the essay should be used for, namely as a counter-model to the "treatise." The treatise discusses an object based on a theoretical way of thinking. But the essay does not fall into the registers of art and literature. It is something independent, something third, located in a "confinium," a strange borderland. In order to grasp this, Bense assigns the essay with the methodic quality of a "proto-theoretical" procedure. The function of the essay is not simply to implement a theory, but first and foremost to develop a theoretical perspective on an object:

> "Essay" means "attempt" or "experiment" [*Versuch*] in German. This raises the question whether this expression means that a literary-leaning person "attempts" to write about something, or whether the writing about an explicit or a partly explicit topic has the character of an attempt, an experiment with that topic. (Bense [1947] 2017: 52)

The essay is "experimental" because it arranges and configures an object so that it becomes accessible for systematic investigation. In the later version from 1952, Bense describes this proto-theoretical method of experimental practice with the words:

> The essay is an expression of an experimental method of thinking and writing as a justified or animated action of the mind, but also an expression of literary activity to lend contours to certain objects, to give to reality existence. Neither the objects nor the thoughts about them appear in the state of eternity or existence, they appear as relative objects and the thoughts are slowly brought into an arrangement that they can become the subject of a theory. (Bense 1952: 27, my translation)

And:

> An experimental thought process is the more or less experimental preparation of an idea, a thought, a subsuming image from a certain amount of experiences, considerations and ideas. One senses a certain truth but does not yet have it; one circles it in repeatedly starting chains of inferences, descriptive turns and perhaps excessive reflections, in order to discover gaps, contours, cores, circumstances. The prose that emerges is not transparent like a theory. One encounters here, at best, the genesis of a theory, attends a birth, and accordingly does not get rid of the feeling that the actual process of creation obscures or even conceals a complete overview. The highest mastery of the essay would thus be based on leading the experimental thought process in the act of linguistic expression towards the arrangement of theory, up to a certain boundary, because beyond that the other kind of prose, theory, already begins. (Bense 1952: 28, my translation).

In the "act of linguistic expression," an "arrangement" is created. This arrangement leads to a "theory" but is not yet theory. The essayistic experiment constitutes the "genesis of a theory" to the extent that this experiment is a step into an unknown. In accordance with the tradition of essayistic writing, Bense connects this with a dialogical metaphor of question and answer.[8] While in a treatise one already knows the answer to a research question, the question in the essay is an open question. The questioner does, as in every good experiment, not know *that* and *how* she will ask the question (Ernst 2005: 159–85, Fröschle 2016: 402–3). Yet, Bense describes the proto-theoretical epistemology of the essay with strong "aisthetic" overtones. The essayistic experiment offers space for the appearance of a phenomenon or object through the way it is arranged.

III. Essayistic Thinking as Imaginative Practice

An essay serves as a medium to differentiate question and object in the process of writing. And it does so without the subject as the carrier of thought:

> Hence, "attempting" something within the essay does not signify true writing subjectivity. Instead, it produces conditions under which a topic is moved closer into the context of a literary configuration. There is no attempt to write or to recognize. There is an attempt to see how a topic behaves in a literary manner. Hence, a question is posed, an experiment conducted on a topic. This allows us to see that the character of the essay is not defined by the literary form in which it is composed, but rather the content, the topic that is treated, appears "essayistic" because it appears under conditions. (Bense [1947] 2017: 53)

Most important here is Bense's notion of a literary configuration as a "condition" for the essayistic experiment. Read as a material condition, the formation of an implicit assumption happens within the formation of writing. Thus, the assumption is realized through the performative act of observing the difference between material form and meaning. In consequence, the process of configuring the question has to be understood as a spatialized and temporalized form. Subsequently, the formation of a hypothesis is necessarily subject to transformation. This transformation reflects on the cognitive value of a written configuration that is also conditioned by the literary form. Bense speaks of "a type of philosophical perspectivism in the sense that . . . a specific viewpoint in thinking and perception" (Bense [1947] 2017: 53) is applied. Following his assessment of the proto-theoretical status of the essay, he understands the essayistic experiment as "crypto-rational": "This curious calculative prose naturally contains the specter of strongly expressed precision; it is crypto-rational. It hides its reason. Why? Because this prose is not pure persuasion, but coinciding persuasion. It is still poetry. It performs for the sake of creation, not for persuasion" (Bense [1947] 2017: 51). The essayistic experiment cannot be viewed isolated from its medial realization. It is based on a "poetic" interaction between perception and materiality of the medium. Only the process of perceiving and arranging the "form of writing" produces genuine ideas (Luhmann 1993). Thinking is not made explicit from the depth of any "inner dialogue" of the subject but arises from the exterior material arrangement of writing, where it is objectified and subjected to the possibility of a theoretical examination. Thus, the essayistic experiment becomes a genuine act of "creation." The method of this kind of thinking is based on an interaction of cognitive activity and an autonomous medial "operating space"—recognized by Bense as a relevant epistemic dimension for the genesis of knowledge in its own right (Krämer 2005). If we follow Bense's metaphors, the notion of experimenting means varying the materialized and spatialized "literary configuration":

> The essayist is a combiner, a tireless creator of configurations around a specific object. Everything that is even somewhat in the vicinity of this object, defining the subject of the essay, giving it the possibility of existence, enters into the combination and causes a new configuration. The transformation of a configuration, in which the object is located, is the point of the experiment, and the goal of the essay is less the revelation of the object's definition than is the sum of factors, the sum of configurations, in which it becomes possible. That is also of scientific value, because the circumstance, the atmosphere, in which something flourishes wants to be recognized and, after all, reveals something. Therefore, configuration is an epistemological category that cannot be achieved through axiomatic deduction, but rather through a literary "ars combinatoria" in which imagination has replaced pure knowledge. Because new objects are not created in the imagination, but configurations for objects are, and the configurations do not appear with deduced but with experimental necessity. All great essayists have been combiners and possessed extraordinary imagination. (Bense [1947] 2017: 57)

If the hypothesis is materialized in writing and thus realized in a medium, the work of finding a perspective begins with an "ars combinatoria," as Bense calls it. Different aspects of the object are tested in essayistic experiments from different points of view. In the process, the configuration also changes which implies an "experimental necessity." This "literary 'ars combinatoria'" of the essayistic experiment is clearly distinguished from the "axiomatic-deductive" thinking of the scientific treatise.[9]

Again, Bense emphasizes the pre-theoretical and passive character of the essayistic experiment. The experiment aims neither at substance nor at a definition. Its goal is to try out possible configurations that allow a thought to emerge in the "arrangement" of writing.[10] The guiding principle of knowledge seems to be the visually connotated way in which the arguments are arranged in writing. Bense extends this distinction through a specification of the cognitive faculties mobilized in the essayistic experiment. Especially, the power of imagination forms an "essayistic necessity." Imagination experiments with "configurations for objects." It does so, as Bense emphasizes, not deductively, but "essayistically"; imagination *creates* the possibility for deduction. A deductive theory as the basis for the "theoretical" analysis of the object has not yet been found.

These ideas are reminiscent of Charles S. Peirce's notion of "abduction." Not only is abduction famous for being an inventive, speculative, and risky type of inference. As Peirce pointed out, it is closely related to the interplay of perception and imagination as well (e.g., Peirce 1998: 209–241).[11] This complex entanglement of thinking with perceptual processes can be illustrated with a very brief look at underlying philosophical ideas. In his book *Kant and the Platypus*, Umberto Eco discusses reworking of Immanuel Kant's Schematism by Charles S. Peirce. In this context, Eco refers to a distinction made by Wilfrid Sellars. According to Sellars, there is a difference between "imagining" and "imaging" (Sellars 1978). Eco refers to this distinction with the words:

> There is a difference between "to imagine$_1$," in the sense of calling up an image (we are now in the realm of fancy, the delineation of possible worlds, as when my desire portrays a stone I would find to crack a nut with—and this process does not call for the experience of the senses) and "to imagine$_2$," in the sense that, on seeing a stone as such, precisely on account of and in concomitance with the sensible impressions that have stimulated my visual organs I *know* (but I do not *see*) that it is hard. (Eco 2000: 80)

While imagining ("imagine$_1$") is closer related to the use of concepts in thinking, imaging ("imagine$_2$") is characterized by Sellars as a "sensing-cum-imaging." In both cases, there is a process of conceptualization involved, in the first case a "unified image structure" and in the second case a "sense-image structure" (Sellars 1978). In the case of "imaging," our bodily senses and their experience of an object are involved as a necessary condition of any inferential process. Umberto Eco remarks: "I propose to translate *imaging* with 'to figure' (both in the sense of constructing a figure, of delineating a structural framework, and in the sense in which we say, on seeing a stone, 'I figure' it is hard inside)" (Eco 2000: 81). Obviously, imagining is closer to reflexive modes of thinking, while imaging can be considered closer to the modes of a practical "thinking with." To back this assessment, one can point at the fact that both, Sellars and Eco, associate "imaging" with sensing as the empirical underside of perception. Of particular importance in the given context is what connects "imaging" and the notion of "thinking with."

Eco and Sellars don't make an argument about aesthetics. They talk about "aesthetic" aspects in human practices of applying concepts in mundane situations. In Bense's case, the situation is different. He talks about a way of "doing thinking" in a philosophical and artistic context.[12] Nevertheless, from this angle, we can see the connecting lines between pragmatist notions of perception and a notion of the essay as practical aesthetics. What Bense calls an *"essayistic* form of imagination" can be understood—if taken as a form of "creative" (abductive) imagination—as being closer to the practice of *imaging* than of *imagining*. Read in analogy to Bense's terms, imagining would be related to practices of "theory" and the "treatise" and not to the proto-theoretical practices of the essay. For Bense, it is clear that in order to shape an understanding of a theoretical perspective on an object, sensual acts of "imaging" within the material confinements of a medium have to be conducted in the first place. In consequence, it is no surprise, as Ulrich Fröschle writes, that for Bense the essay is always both, a "thinking process" ("Denkvorgang") *and* a "mode of concrete affixation" ("Modus konkreter Affizierung," Fröschle 2016: 398).

IV. Conclusion

Transferred into the context of media aesthetics, we can find in Bense's ideas a reflection on a perceptual involvement with a medium which becomes a proto-theoretical condition for more abstract thoughts (and complex "theories"). The essay is a "borderland" (confinium) because—within the confinements of the materiality of a medium—a specific type of "thinking *with*" is realized as a blend of imaging and thinking.

Bense's Text approaches practical aesthetics via the discussion of a literary form. The reflections provide insight into an independent epistemic mode related to practical aesthetics. For media aesthetics, one consequence is that Bense conceptualizes the essayistic experiment as a theory involving a creative processual logic of the material "form" of a medium. Essayistic thinking appears as a practice of configurative arrangement, in which the momentum of thinking itself is created. Thus, Max Bense is an example of how a reflection on media was developed in the essayist tradition in the twentieth century. In this regard, Bense's reflections can even be read as a pretext for more modern theories of "epistemic writing" in which the epistemic potentials of writing are understood in the context of its spatialized visuality (Krämer 2005: 42–43).

What Bense describes is certainly no "deconstruction" of traditional philosophical theories of thinking. Given the theoretical frameworks of poststructuralism, actor-network-theory and especially media philosophy,[13] far more radical notions of "thinking with" are possible. Still, Bense's notion of a proto-theoretical method associated with the essay delineates an involvement of the imaginative side of perception into a materialized medium. And it does this in order to describe (in more or less "pragmatist" terms) a process in which thinking evolves from an autonomous state of "thinking *with* (a form in medium x)."

Notes

1. The passages on Max Bense are a substantially modified and translated version of my text "Der Essay als Form der Medientheorie. Max Benses essayistische Medienreflexionen" (Ernst 2018). I am grateful to the publisher J. B. Metzler for the rights for an English version. All translations in this text were assisted by the free online service *deepl* (www.DeepL.com/Translator.com).

2. For an excellent discussion of Bense's text in the context of the 1940s and 1950s, see Fröschle 2016: 386–98; for a broader look on Bense's works, see Uhl and Zittel 2018. My first discussion of the Bense's text was in Ernst 2005: 135–44.

3. The text was published in 1947 in the journal *Merkur* and again as a modified version in 1952 in *Plakatwelt*. There is also an early version from 1942 (Bense 1942; Bense 1947; Bense 1952). For the reference to the version from 1942, I thank Elke Uhl. An English translation of the version from 1947 is Bense [1947] 2017. I use this translation wherever possible. Quotes from the version of 1952 are my own translations.

4. Cf. Bense [1947] 2017: 52, 55 for slightly different translations of both quotes.

5. See for German research on the essay Ansel, Egyptien and Friedrich 2016; Braungart and Kauffmann 2006; Ernst 2005; Müller-Funk 1995; Schärf 1999; Zima 2012.

6. Cf. Krämer 1996. Krämer provides a critical discussion of the idea to consider writing as written language in the age of digitization. Bense later became associated with the Stuttgart School of Concrete Poetry.
7. Cf. Zima (2012: 1–34) for an overview.
8. Cf. Zima (2012: 23–9) for dialogical potentials of the essay.
9. Zima (2012: 166–7) compares this with the notions of "configuration" and "constellation" in the works of Benjamin and Adorno.
10. Fröschle (2016: 400) comments on a remark from Harry Walter on the montage-like character of Bense's writing practice. It would be interesting to do more research on this.
11. Read as an argument in the context of the genealogy of Bense's writing, this could be interpreted as an anticipation of Bense's interest in Peirce.
12. Fröschle (2016: 401) argues that imagination can be seen as precondition for Bense's notion of rationality within his idea of essayistic thinking.
13. A discussion of Bense in the context of theories of the essay film has been made possible thanks to the important collection of texts on the film essay in Alter and Corrigan 2017. It would be interesting to see how such a discussion plays out in the context of a media-philosophical discussion of the essay in literature and film.

References

Adorno, T. W. (2017), "The Essay as Form," in N. M. Alter and T. Corrigan (eds.), *Essays on the Essay Film*, 60–82, New York: Columbia.
Alter, N. M., and T. Corrigan (eds.) (2017), *Essays on the Essay Film*, New York: Columbia University Press.
Ansel, M., J. Egyptien, and H.-E. Friedrich, eds (2016), *Der Essay als Universalgattung des Zeitalters. Diskurse, Themen und Positionen zwischen Jahrhundertwende und Nachkriegszeit*, Leiden: Rodopi.
Askin, R., P. J. Ennis, A. Hägler, and P. Schweighauser (eds.) (2014), *Speculations V. Aesthetics in the 21st Century*, New York: Punctum.
Benjamin, W. (1936), "The Work of Art in the Age of Mechanical Reproduction." Available online: https://www.marxists.org/reference/subject/philosophy/works/ge/benjamin.htm (accessed February 22, 2019).
Bense, M. (April 19, 1942), "Über den Essay," *Kölnische Zeitung* 197–8: 5–6.
Bense, M. (1947), "Über den Essay und seine Prosa," *Merkur* 1 (3): 414–24.
Bense, M. (1952), "Der Essay und seine Prosa," in *Plakatwelt. Vier Essays*, 23–37, Stuttgart: DVA.
Bense, M. ([1947] 2017), "On the Essay and Its Prose," in N. M. Alter and T. Corrigan (eds.), *Essays on the Essay Film*, 49–59, New York: Columbia.
Braungart, W. and Kauffmann, K. (eds.) (2006), *Essayismus um 1900*, Heidelberg: Winter.
Eco, U. (2000), *Kant and the Platypus. Essays on Language and Cognition*, San Diego: Harcourt.
Ernst, C. (2005), *Essayistische Medienreflexion. Die Idee des Essayismus und die Frage nach den Medien*, Bielefeld: transcript.
Ernst, C. (2018), "Der Essay als Form der Medientheorie. Max Benses essayistische Medienreflexionen," in E. Uhr and C. Zittel (eds.), *Max Bense. Weltprogrammierung*, 121–31. Stuttgart: Metzler.
Engell, L. (2014), "Medientheorien der Medien selbst," in J. Schröter (ed.), *Handbuch Medienwissenschaft*, 207–13. Stuttgart: Metzler.

Fröschle, U. (2016), "Max Bense zum Beispiel. Zur Essaykultur und Essaytheorie in der frühen Bundesrepublik," in M. Ansel, J. Egyptien and H.-E. Friedrich (eds.), *Der Essay als Universalgattung des Zeitalters. Diskurse, Themen und Positionen zwischen Jahrhundertwende und Nachkriegszeit*, 386–405, Leiden: Rodopi.

Krämer, S. (1996), "Sprache und Schrift oder: Ist Schrift verschriftlichte Sprache?," *Zeitschrift für Sprachwissenschaft*, 15 (1): 92–112.

Krämer, S. (2003), " 'Schriftbildlichkeit' oder Über eine (fast) vergessene Dimension der Schrift," in S. Krämer and H. Bredekamp (eds.), *Bild, Schrift, Zahl*, 157–76, Munich: Fink.

Krämer, S. (2005), "Operationsraum Schrift: Über einen Perspektivenwechsel in der Betrachtung der Schrift," in G. Grube, W. Kogge, and S. Krämer (eds.), *Schrift. Kulturtechnik zwischen Auge, Hand und Maschine*, 23–57, Munich: Fink.

Luhmann, N. (1993), "Die Form der Schrift," in H.-U. Gumbrecht and L. Pfeiffer (eds.), *Schrift*, 349–66, Munich: Fink

Müller-Funk, W. (1995), *Erfahrung und Experiment. Studien zur Theorie und Geschichte des Essayismus*, Berlin: Akademie.

Peirce, C. S. (1998), *The Essential Peirce. Selected Philosophical Writings, Vol 2: 1893–1913*, ed. N. Houser and C. Kloesel, Bloomington: Indiana University Press.

Schärf, C. (1999), *Geschichte des Essays. Von Montaigne bis Adorno*, Göttingen: Vandenhoeck & Ruprecht.

Sellars, W. (1978), "The Role of Imagination in Kant's Theory of Experience." Available online: http://www.ditext.com/sellars/ikte.html (accessed February 22, 2019).

Uhl, E. and C. Zittel (eds.) (2018), *Max Bense. Weltprogrammierung*, Stuttgart: Metzler.

Zima, P. V. (2012), *Essay und Essayismus. Zum theoretischen Potenzial des Essays: von Montaigne bis zur Postmoderne*, Würzburg: Königshausen & Neumann.

CHAPTER 19
RADIOACTIVITY AND THE TYPEWRITER'S BREATH
PRACTICAL AESTHETICS IN POUND AND OLSON
Julius Greve

This chapter starts with two quotes by the poets Ezra Pound and Charles Olson, whose versions of what may be termed "practical aesthetics" are both idiosyncratically pathbreaking with respect to the subsequent development of twentieth-century American poetry. Given the highly suggestive arsenal of metaphors Pound mounts in one of his most important early essays, "The Serious Artist," what could the word "radioactivity" in the following statement possibly mean in the context of modern American poetry, and what are the consequences of that term for the latter? This is Pound in 1913: "The thing that matters in art is a sort of energy, something more or less like electricity or radioactivity, a force transfusing, welding, and unifying" (Pound 1960: 49). Conversely: how is the process of breathing aligned with the intricacies of the typewriter, this recording instrument Charles Olson hails as revolutionary for the practice of poetic expression and innovation in the following quote from "Human Universe"? This is Olson in 1951: "What it comes to is ourselves, that we do not find ways to hew to experience as it is, in our definition and expression of it, in other words, find ways to stay in the human universe, and not be led to partition reality at any point, in any way. For this is just what we do do, this is the real issue of what has been, and the process, as it now asserts itself, can be exposed" (Olson 1967a: 56).

If the first of the abovementioned two quotations is relatively straightforward, the other is deliberately obscure. In what follows, I hope to clarify these two conundrums of *radioactivity* and what I call *the breath of the typewriter* in my chapter on what could be termed Pound's and Olson's respective forms of "practical aesthetics." I am interested in the connection between the practical aspect of poetry—that is, of poetry as an activity, a performance, or simply as something that one does rather than defines—and the notion of the aesthetic in poetry—that is, at least according to Alexander Gottlieb Baumgarten's multivolume *Aesthetica* (1750–8), the realm of sense, of perception, and of corporeally being in the world and knowing the world.

In the wake of Baumgarten and his contemporary heirs, I want to address a set of issues and, specifically, their examination in the work of the aforementioned modern American poets, Pound and Olson: How to determine the relation between doing (or *praxis*), making (or *poiesis*), and sensing (or *aisthesis*)? How is thinking (or *theoria*) to be reconceived along the lines of a firmly practical approach to the realm of literary activity, in general, and to that of poetry, in particular? In what sense can we describe poetry as *a material articulation of thought*—meaning both a consequence of its immediate and intermediary environment, and a technique for generating concepts of materiality as such? In other words, how to grasp poetry's capability for both enacting and conceptualizing the material conditions of its mediation and remediation, on the one hand, and its ostensible channeling of affective immediacy, on the other? Finally, how to think the reciprocation of social and aesthetic activity in early to mid-twentieth-century poetry?

With these more general questions used as a conceptual backdrop, I will trace the adamantly practice-oriented strands of thought in Pound's and Olson's work (meaning, their respective emphases on the poetic act as a form of doing that is imbricated in a social, political, and historical circumstance), thus delineating their practical aesthetics. I will do so, first, by briefly contextualizing the question concerning the return of or to aesthetics in contemporary theory—or, rather, the continuous emphasis on the aesthetic at least since what has been called "the affective turn" (see Clough and Halley 2007)— in order to address the cleavage between practice and technique that both Pound and Olson seem to circumvent in their respective projects. Second, I will discern the main assumptions of Pound's essay fragment "Pragmatic Aesthetics" (written around 1940–3[1]) and then compare these with two of Olson's most influential essays, "Projective Verse" (1950) and "Human Universe" (1951). Third, I seek to examine the pragmatic lineage of Pound and Olson by looking at how their poetry stakes out specific conceptions of materiality that include distinct visions of the social. This examination will entail looking at what each poet means by "pragmatic" or "practice." As will become apparent, they do not always mean the same thing when it comes to both material practices (or *praxis*) and a pragmatic understanding of discourse about the sensible (or *aisthesis*). In any case, neither for Pound nor for Olson do literature and the arts exist in a vacuum. On the contrary, poetry and poetics become diagnostic and quasi-gnostic tools with which to intervene in the social fabric. In this sense a practical aesthetics is one that links literary and media-technological technique with its social and political complement. Emphasizing the thematic intersections of history, philosophy, and scientific method in the idiosyncratic styles of both poets, I will delineate the conditions of possibility for thinking their poetics as individual attempts at *a pragmatic "science of the human" by poetic means*.

I

A contemporary understanding of aesthetic discourse in reference to Baumgarten may be seen in a variety of contexts. One of these, unsurprisingly, is critical and cultural theory—or what has also been called "Continental philosophy." In the past few decades, Jacques Rancière has spoken of the "distribution of the sensible" (*le partage du sensible*), a notion of the aesthetic determination of everyday experience, in terms of participation and nonparticipation, inclusion and exclusion in regard of the dynamics of the social.

It is important here to note the etymology of the original French, insofar as this term, which "is a principle of aggregation that configures the forms of participation in a political community . . . , a *partage* is at once a sharing and a division" (Panagia 2014: 96). This term, which is central to Rancière's project as a whole, is highly productive in our present discussion of Pound's "radioactive" poetics, as will become clear. For the moment, however, it is important to mention that Rancière's notion—which evokes direct interventions in the political arena he calls the "aesthetic regime of art" (Rancière 2009: 22–3)—indexes modes of sensing, making, and doing that intersect in reciprocal kinds of human activity by which social life comes into being and perpetuates itself. Importantly, this broad definition of the aesthetic realm and its political nature is strictly opposed to what Rancière calls "the political (*le politique*)" or, in a more provocative inflection, "the police order" (ibid., 29–30, 2–3). Before Rancière, Gilles Deleuze and Félix Guattari have conceived of the realm of art as one of three specific modes of thought, working in terms of affects and percepts, rather than concepts or propositions—as would be the case in the adjacent realms of philosophical or scientific practice, according to them (see Deleuze and Guattari 1994).

Both of these comparatively recent approaches to the problem of aesthetics are directly linked to the long trajectory of "aesthetics" as a discipline, as Christoph Menke's important book *Force: A Fundamental Concept of Aesthetic Anthropology* (originally published in 2008) has shown by implication (see Menke 2013, 2017). While others have linked Deleuze and Guattari's philosophy of art to Baumgarten's notion of aesthetics as the *analogon rationis* (see, for instance, Leyla Haferkamp 2010: 62)—thus, as a different kind of thought that is practical rather than theoretical or rational, yet which is nonetheless analogical to the latter—I am specifically interested in the way in which Deleuze and Guattari's work, but also Rancière's approach corresponds to the problem pointed out by Menke with respect to Johann Gottfried Herder's critique of Baumgarten's discourse, because it neatly prefigures my argument concerning Pound and Olson. Herder's critique, in a nutshell, points to the crucial Baumgartenian definition of artistic practice as a mode of thought, rather than a mode of feeling. For Herder, as Menke demonstrates, aesthetics does not need reason to serve as a legitimizing force, thus realizing the "force" inherent to artistic practice and its discourse. Even if aesthetic cognition is defined vis-à-vis the domain of the sensible, Baumgarten's concept of the *analogon* eschews art's emphasis on human feeling. Instead, from Herder's point of view, aesthetics harbors a "dark" or "obscure" component that is determined thus because of its indefinably nonpractical, nonsocial, and, consequently, unreasonable character (Menke 2013: 32–3).

This is the point, also with respect to Deleuze, Guattari, and Rancière, at which I want to distinguish between "practice"—the social realm of human activity, of habit, and of disposition—and "technique"—the realm of activity that may or may not entail a social or political element, and which refers to the concrete manufacture or construction involved in the poetic act. In other words, while practice imbricates aesthetics and politics, technique may or may not combine notions of the sensible as feeling or affect with its political consequence. The difficulty of differentiating between specific practices and their techniques and vice versa points to the way in which practice and technique, conceptually speaking, reciprocally presuppose each other in the context of modern American poetry I am concerned with here.[2] This is also how Rancière's conception of distribution (*partage*) comes to bear on the terminology employed in my discussion, first, to point to the difficulty of distinguishing between practice and technique and thus to acknowledge their both shared and divided space of thinking social and artistic forms of articulation, and, second, to note the etymological vicinity of *partage* in a political context to *partage* in the context of the history of broadcasting.[3]

Menke's commentary on the conceptual developments from Baumgarten all the way to the late nineteenth century also distinguishes between aesthetics in the light of "force" and practice in terms of "faculty" or capability. This distinction ultimately arrives at an idea of aesthetic articulations and artistic expressions as the realm in which what is at stake is "human freedom"—the freedom of choosing between useful and useless activity within the social realm and the reciprocity between force and faculty that is the precondition of that choice (Menke 2013: 98). In this sense, aesthetics deals with an ethico-political panorama of practices and medial and material relations (which also entails intermedial and intermaterial relations) within which a quasi-anthropology—or "science of the human"—becomes possible with respect to sensible and social experience.[4]

II

It seems that the issue of defining social practice in contradistinction to (or in tension with) aesthetic technique in the context of modern American poetry would apply to the majority of twentieth-century authors, not just to Ezra Pound or Charles Olson. The cleavage between practice and technique—between act and form—and the struggle between aesthetic autonomy and engaged literature are the hallmarks of modern verse, that is, versified literature responding to or assimilated in the reality of the modern. Yet, in this case, Pound and Olson, figuring as what could be called the hubs of influence when it comes to modern American poetry, explicitly react to that cleavage, namely by dissolving it in unique identifications of the one with the other.

Pound's essay fragment "Pragmatic Aesthetics," which he jotted down into a notebook in the early 1940s and which was published as part of Maria L. Ardizzone's edition of Pound's work on aesthetics in 1996, called *Machine Art & Other Writings* (thus comprising work from several decades), is a highly unsystematic, albeit instructive text. It suggests, in retrospect, the clear direction Pound assumed with regard to aesthetic discourse from his early prose onward. Some of the doctrines to be found in his Imagist phase, and in particular in his 1913 piece "The Serious Artist," via Vorticism and his engagement with Ernest Fenollosa's notebooks on *The Chinese Written Character as a Medium for Poetry* (1919) can be rediscovered in the form of fragmentary notes and queries, as well as a few unmistakably declarative sentences. Recalling Imagism's earlier dictate "Go in fear of abstractions," Pound's tone has changed slightly in congruence with the time- and site-specific "structure of feeling" in the late 1930s and early 1940s—both in Europe and the United States. The writer no longer "goes in fear of" but vouches for an "Attack against abstraction" (Pound 1996b: 157). Not just harkening back to "A Few Don'ts" but especially to "The Serious Artist," Pound is deeply involved in what, back then, he had called "an art of diagnosis" that was correlated to "the cult of ugliness," and the revelation thereof, at a specific historical moment in time (Pound 1960: 45). And yet, curiously, this type of diagnosis seems to be nonnegotiable in any intersubjective mode whatsoever: "The point is not to agree or disagree but to show . . . true thinking is ideogrammic in the sense that the general is composed of *definite particulars known directly* by the thinker. Art is the particular declaration that *implies* the general; and being particular. . . . may not divert, distract, melt and muddle like an abstract declaration which becomes a party cry; or cloak or mask for a hundred different ideas" (Pound 1996b: 158).

Pound is alluding to multiple aspects here, one of which is the amplification of precision and the concrete in the art of poetry. From Imagism's "direct treatment of the thing" that would be referred to in the making of a specific poem, such as "In a Station of the Metro" (published 1913, the same year as "The Serious Artist"), what we have in Pound's "Pragmatic Aesthetics" is a well-nigh denunciation of other forms of thought, and one in particular: "Philosophy, philosophical expression," he describes as "nothing but vague fluid approximation; art achieves a MORE PRECISE manifestation" (Pound 1996b: 159). Which type of thinking, however, does he align with poetic practice and which kind of practical consequence of that type may be found in society at large? In other words, what about the materialization of that specific mode of thought? The answer to the first question is given in the diagram Pound employs to clarify the new handmaiden of poetry:

mathematics, the writing
arithmetic
algebraic
geometric
analytic.

(Pound 1996b: 157–8)

This alignment of poetry with mathematics, in accord with his earlier reference to "the fourth dimension" of non-Euclidean geometry vis-à-vis a certain literary pastoralism in Canto 49 of his epic poem's 1937 section *The Fifth Decad of Cantos*, is not a new gesture at all in the trajectory of Pound as a writer (Pound 1996a: 245). It is the distinctly social and political usage of mathematical science in the form of technology that is of interest to Pound. Human technology—and specifically its ancient Greek etymology of *technê* as "skill in art, in making things" (Pound 1970: 327)—from the mid-1930s onward becomes increasingly important for the poet who begins to regard his practice and form of writing as *functionally* significant in political terms. As he states in his 1938 book of criticism, *Guide to Kulchur*: "The history of a culture is the history of ideas going into action" (Pound 1970: 44).

If Pound's image of "the serious artist" was already characterized by a "scientific" disposition (Pound 1960: 46), during the Second World War poetry ought to become

Practical Aesthetics

imbricated in politics in order to stay relevant: practice and technique, act and form, become one. And for Pound, it is in the context of a specific technological apparatus—the radio—that political action (or *praxis*), literary making (or *poiesis*), and lived experience (or *aesthesis*) converge (see also Bacigalupo 1980: 230). It is important to remember at this point that Pound was at first skeptical with regard to this new communicational medium. On March 31, 1940, in a letter he wrote to George Santayana from his home in Rapallo, Italy, he mentioned that a few of his "blasted friends left a goddam radio here yester. Gift. God dam destructive and dispersive devil of an invention. But got to be faced. Drammer has got to face it, not only face cinema. . . . Anyhow what drammer or teeyater *wuz*, radio is. Possibly the loathing of it may stop diffuse writing" (Pound 1950: 342). Moreover, he complained about "the *personae* now poked into every bleedin' 'ome and smearing the mind of the peapull" (Pound 1950: 343). Ironically, it is this "poking" and "smearing" that he set out to do in the form of anti-Semitic speech-acts "broadcast over Rome Radio between 1941 and 1943" (Flory 1999: 284), showing his endorsement of Fascist Italy—speeches that eventually led to his arrest as a traitor to the United States and a collaborator with Benito Mussolini's regime.

One of the poet's particularly anti-Semitic Cantos—that is, Canto 46—broadcast on Rome Radio in early 1942, refers to the essential concept "usury" or "usura"—in this case, "hyper-usura"—which he identified as the sin of making money from nothing, or, as he himself writes elsewhere, "the use of purchasing power, levied without regard to production" (Pound 1973: 355). What is interesting in this context is his Jeremiad-like emphasis on the downfall of the American empire after Thomas Jefferson and John Adams. Even though this Canto, as part of *The Fifth Decad* was published only a year before Pound's *Guide to Kulchur*, I would argue that it is particularly in the epic's next section, on Chinese history and Adam's biography, that Pound's radio-inspired poetics come to full fruition. This kind of poetics recalls the first of the two quotes with which I began: "The thing that matters in art is a sort of energy, something more or less like electricity or radioactivity, a force transfusing, welding, and unifying" (Pound 1960: 49). Daniel Tiffany comments on this sentence thus: "In the 'unifying' power of 'radioactive' images we discover the origins of *paideuma*—the fascist 'world-picture'—in which the disparate features of history are fused into mythological coherence. More remotely, we also discover in Pound's theory of radioactive art the origins of a conception of radio as a medium that is capable of unifying the 'subconscious energies' of an entire population" (Tiffany 1995: 224–5). Pound's organicist worldview, which is apparent throughout the majority of his writings on the level of content, and which I will revisit in the direct comparison with Olson's work—this worldview is curiously amplified (in both senses) at the moment the poet's writing style of documentary technique and archival accumulation goes full throttle. At this point of his career, poetic practice, on the level of "ideas going into action" via "skill in art, in making things," means the underlining of *poiesis as archeology*.

Yet, while others have commented on Pound's "poetic archaeology" in the past (see, for instance, Mottram 1992: 109), it is important to underline what this means in the context of "radioactivity, a force transfusing, welding, and unifying." While Pound had cited from literary, historical, economical, mythical, and philosophical sources long before this critical phase of his epic poem, there is a certain media-technological particularity to this "radioactive" context that sheds light on Pound's oeuvre as a whole. In other words, what is the connection between the wirelessness of radio broadcasting and the organicism proclaimed politically and philosophically in the poet's Cantos and his other writings?

I have already mentioned Pound's ambivalent—or, rather, contradictory—relation to radio, or what he called a "destructive and dispersive devil of an invention." Along these lines, Tiffany notes how Pound saw how "the insidious power of technology reaches deep into our hereditary past, the realm of the dead, as well as into the future, the realm of the unborn. What's more, Pound's fears about technology coincide with this condemnation of usury" (Tiffany 1995: 246), once again the chief factor that, according to Pound, had led to the downfall of US culture in the course of modernization. It is precisely the combination of the technological and the organic, of the modern and the archaic, and of the contemporary with the historico-mythological that defines the poet's practical aesthetics. Tiffany helpfully suggests: "Given the historical speculations about radio's relation to spiritualism, we might usefully ask whether Pound's conception of radio doesn't resemble a kind of ventriloquism originating with the dead.... The exteriorization and projection of the voice that occurs on the radio has obvious parallels with the act of ventriloquism, as well as with the experience of haunting" (Tiffany 1995: 250). It is as a consequence of this tension between embodiment and disembodiment, and between appropriation and depersonalization, in his radio speeches and Cantos, of various controversial historical and contemporary voices including Jefferson and Adams, Mencius and Confucius, Mussolini and Hitler that Pound would turn to a full-fledged fascist and racist poetics that was more tacit at earlier moments of his career. What needs to be remembered is not merely that he was eventually indicted as traitor to the United States because of his radio speeches, but that the latter are demonstrations, among other things, of his approach to poetic practice itself. The radio apparatus and the form of broadcasting it allowed for is key for any understanding of Pound's fascist politics of medial distribution grounded in a univocal, rather than equivocal, notion of communication.

III

After being "interned at the US Army 'Disciplinary Training Center' north of Pisa" (Flory 1999: 284) in 1945, he was eventually found as unable to stand trial and thus transferred to St. Elizabeths Hospital in Washington, DC. One of the many authors and artists that visited Pound in this psychiatric hospital was Charles Olson, whose fascination with Pound's *Cantos* is visibly present in many of his own writings, in particular his epic, *The Maximus Poems*, a work that he started writing in the early 1950s. Much has been said about Olson's debt both to the *Cantos* and to the comparable works, such as William Carlos Williams's *Paterson*, yet it is the relationship between Pound's "Pragmatic

Practical Aesthetics

Aesthetics" and Olson's critical work that I am interested in here (see, for instance, Beach 1992). Especially the text "Projective Verse," in many ways a manifesto for the postwar generation of American poetry, provides insight into Olson's dissolution of the chasm between social practice and literary technique, between the faculties of political life and the force of art. However, it is important to remember that, politically speaking, Olson was on the other side of the spectrum—different from Pound, his politics were guided by a left-leaning liberalism. This poet, who had worked as a political activist for the Democratic National Committee during the closing years of the Second World War under Franklin D. Roosevelt, had picked up on Pound's formalisms, while inverting the political orientation of his poetics.

"Projective Verse," borrowing its name from the mathematical branch of projective geometry, also praised the poetic act itself (which, especially in Pound and Olson, includes both the composition and the recitation of poetry): if for Pound, "the history of a culture" was regarded as "the history of ideas going into action," for Olson it was the history and geography of a region—of the locale—that was synonymous with specific "ideas going into action." This locality was connected to the lived experience of the poet himself; in *The Maximus Poems*, Olson depicted his home and its environment in Gloucester, Massachusetts, adding to it the history and geography of it, from this emplaced point of view. As Olson writes in his 1950 manifesto, "the projective act, which is the artist's act in the larger field of objects," points to a distinctly ecological ethics that presents "man [as] himself an object, whatever he may take to be his advantages" (Olson 1967b: 25, 24), the projective stance leading to a kind of humility with respect to the poet's environment, a stance that would regard humankind as "participant in the larger force" that is "nature" (25). Olson would use the notions of poetic "speech-force" and "THE LAW OF THE LINE" rather than more traditional forms of meter and rhyme. Different from many versions of high modernist free verse, however, his take on what he also called "composition by field" focused on the poet's site- and time-specific process of breathing while making the poem. This somatic "breath poetics" would then be reflected in the lines typed onto the page, the typewriter being christened as the technological apparatus that, "being the personal and instantaneous recorder of the poet's work," somehow correlated with "the *kinetics*" and "the *process* of the thing" (23, 16) of the poem in the making.

Like Pound, in his comments on "radioactivity," Olson, too, relies on a semantics of force: the force of speech, of poetic construction in a kind of immediacy that seemingly denies what is so central even—or especially—in the kind of poetry Olson would go on to write. Note, in this regard, that according to an idiosyncratic poetological inference of Olson's, the word "myth" in "mythology" is derived from "mouth," rather than "story," as other ancient Greek etymologies would have it (see Pattison 2015: 61–2 on this issue). And it is this form of understanding the use of myth—that is, not merely the use of mythological references as in high modernism, but literally, the use of one's mouth—that the alignment of a poetics of breathing in Olson with the technological particulars and practical intricacies of the typewriter lead to a poetics of ventriloquism in Olson, if by ventriloquism we may also denote the disassociation of a voice from its usual origin (see Connor 2000: 22–4). It is only by means of the typewriter that the poet may breathe and thus produce the poetry that is most pressing in the time of what Olson calls "the dispersion," the time after a new lapse of the human in the form of all that was endured as the collective experience of the Second World War, the Holocaust, and, more generally, the processes of modernization that led to that lapse. Olson's (or any projective writer's) breath *is* the typewriter's breath, because otherwise, paradoxically, it would be impossible to escape the metric grid of the modern.

To return to the issue of a "pragmatic aesthetics" as conceptualized by both poets, I would like to argue that it is not just in Pound's case that "pragmatic" means "functional" as "opposed to something merely theoretical," as Ardizzone has stated (1996: 14). Olson, too, will condemn the theoretical overdetermination of sensible or lived experience by any universalist standpoints whatsoever; he will also equate such a nonlived overdetermination with the process of modernization itself (see Mark Byers 2018: 133–4). Pound had referenced pastoral scenes taken from Chinese literature and historiography (filtered predominantly through the Orientalist lens of the Jesuit missionary Joseph-Anne-Marie de Moyriac de Mailla's *Historie générale de la Chine*), and he was thus concerned with the rhythms of the working day in the aforementioned Canto 49 and even more so the Chinese Cantos. This idealization of the days' rhythms of labor, with all its political implications can be witnessed in another sense, in a 1939 recording of Canto 56, in which Pound's voice is accompanied by a beating drum. This time, however, the beating drum is that of the war between insurgents and imperial soldiers from the rule of the Chinese emperor Yao onward.[5]

Olson, in a similar manner to that of the pastoral theme in Canto 49, praised Gloucester's famous culture of fishing. The reader of both *The Cantos* and *The Maximus Poems* should take seriously the respective expressions of scorn in regard to the destructive processes of modernization, and should indeed take note of the respective versions of the aforementioned "cultural organicism" these expressions entail—in Olson's case, "the wondership" of supposedly "older" forms of living being "stolen by, / ownership" (Olson 1983: 13) of bigger companies, invading his beloved sea town on Cape Ann, Massachusetts; in Pound's case, the notorious rants against "usury" from *The Fifth Decad* onward, and the penetrating commendations of Confucian ethics of feudal order and virtue, as well as Mencian paternalist affection or "benevolence" represented by the aforementioned historical figures Adams, Jefferson, and/or Mussolini.[6]

The identification of practice (*praxis*) and technique (*technê*), again, leads both to a skeptical take on modernity's advantages in view of ordinary lives *and* to a technologically informed—that is, *materially inflected*—approach to literary activity vis-à-vis the question concerning the "use" of oneself in the social realm. In this sense, for both Pound and Olson, the medial cross-fertilization of modern *technê*—of "skill in art, in making things"—between poetry, radio broadcasting, and typewriting also gives rise to adamantly practice-oriented strands of thought that tend either toward the imaginary of what Rancière terms the totalitarian "police order" or toward the reverence of humankind as one object among many within local geographies. As Olson writes in "Human Universe," a text that can readily be called his critical statement on ethics,

Practical Aesthetics

especially because it recalls the aforementioned problematic of *partage*: "What it comes to is ourselves, that we do not find ways to hew to experience as it is, in our definition and expression of it, in other words, find ways to stay in the human universe, and not be led to partition reality at any point, in any way. For this is just what we *do do*, this is the real issue of what has been, and the process, as it now asserts itself, can be exposed" (Olson 1967: 56; emphasis added).

Regardless of Pound's and Olson's idiosyncratically staged identifications of practice and technique, the identification itself relies on a unilateral determination that goes from the performance of the poetic act to that of the social objective, thus inquiring by means of versification into the ways in which "men do use / their lives" (Olson 1983: 63). In other words, if there is a quasi-anthropological, or, rather, nonstandard anthropological impulse in *The Cantos* and in *The Maximus Poems*—that is, a "science of the human"— it is by way of the "forwarding" (6) poetic force, of poetry as a project, and of verse as projection that material practice, pragmatic aesthetics, and thus practical aesthetics become possible.

Notes

1. I take this assumption from Maria Luisa Ardizzone (1996: 164–5).
2. This account is similar to, yet not entirely isomorphic with, contemporary theories of practice (see Reckwitz 2002).
3. Compare with Selena Savicic, who connects Rancière's notion to the history of technologies of wirelessness (2012: 49).
4. The notion of "intermaterial relations" is derived from Kleinschmidt (2012), while I take the idea of a quasi-anthropology or science of the human from François Laruelle's conception of non-philosophy as a "science of the human" (Laruelle 2012).
5. I am referring to the recording from Pound's 1939 visit to Harvard, before the publication of the Chinese Cantos and the John Adams section; that is, 52/71. See the PennSound webpage: http://writing.upenn.edu/pennsound/x/Pound.php. On Pound's poeticization of Chinese history, see Park (2008: 41).
6. In terms of this organicist parallelism between Pound and Olson, see Stimpson (1995: 152).

References

Ardizzone, M. L. (1996), "Note on the Texts," in E. Pound, *Machine Art and Other Writings: The Lost Thought of the Italian Years*, ed. M. L. Ardizzone, Durham: Duke University Press.
Bacigalupo, M. (1980), *The Formèd Trace: The Later Poetry of Ezra Pound*, New York: Columbia University Press.
Beach, C. (1992), *ABC of Influence: Ezra Pound and the Remaking of American Poetic Tradition*, Berkeley: University of California Press.
Byers, M. (2018), *Charles Olson and American Modernism*, Oxford: Oxford University Press.
Clough, P. T., and J. Halley (eds.) (2007), *The Affective Turn: Theorizing the Social*, Durham: Duke University Press.

Connor, S. (2000), *Dumbstruck: A Cultural History of Ventriloquism*, Oxford: Oxford University Press.
Deleuze, G., and F. Guattari (1994), *What is Philosophy?*, trans. H. Tomlinson and G. Burchell, New York: Columbia University Press.
Flory, W. S. (1999), "Pound and Antisemitism," in I. B. Nadel (ed.), *Cambridge Companion to Ezra Pound*, 284–300, Cambridge: Cambridge University Press.
Haferkamp, L. (2010), "*Analogon Rationis*: Baumgarten, Deleuze and the 'Becoming Girl' of Philosophy," *Deleuze Studies*, 4 (1): 62–9.
Kleinschmidt, C. (2012), *Intermaterialität: Zum Verhältnis von Schrift, Bild, Film und Bühne im Expressionismus*, Bielefeld: Transcript.
Laruelle, F. (2012), "A Rigorous Science of Man," in R. Mackay (ed.), *From Decision to Heresy: Experiments in Non-Standard Thought*, 33–74, Falmouth: Urbanomic.
Menke, C. (2013), *Force: A Fundamental Concept of Aesthetic Anthropology*, trans. G. Jackson, New York: Fordham University Press.
Menke, C. (2017), *Kraft: Ein Grundbegriff ästhetischer Anthropologie*, 2nd edn, Frankfurt a. M.: Suhrkamp, 2017.
Mottram, E. (1992), "Ezra Pound in His Time," in J. Kaye (ed.), *Ezra Pound and America*, 93–113, London: Macmillan.
Olson, C. (1967a), "Human Universe," in R. Creeley (ed.), *Selected Writings*, New York: New Directions.
Olson, C. (1967b), "Projective Verse," in R. Creeley (ed.), *Selected Writings*, New York: New Directions.
Olson, C. (1983), *The Maximus Poems*, ed. G. F. Butterick, Berkeley: University of California Press.
Panagia, D. (2014), "'*Partage du sensible*': The Distribution of the Sensible," in J.-P. Deranty (ed.), *Jacques Rancière: Key Concepts*, 95–103, New York: Routledge.
Park, J. N.-H. (2008), *Apparitions of Asia: Modernist Form and Asian American Poetics*, Oxford and New York: Oxford University Press.
Pattison, R. (2015), "'Empty Air': Charles Olson's Cosmology," in D. Herd (ed.), *Contemporary Olson*, 52–63, Manchester: Manchester University Press.
Pound, E. (1950), *The Selected Letters of Ezra Pound, 1907–1941*, ed. D.D. Paige, New York: New Directions.
Pound, E. (1960), "The Serious Artist," in T. S. Eliot (ed.), *Literary Essays of Ezra Pound*, 41–57, London: Faber and Faber Ltd.
Pound, E. (1970), *Guide to Kulchur*, New York: New Directions.
Pound, E. (1973), *Selected Prose, 1909–1965*, ed. William Cookson. New York: New Directions.
Pound, E. (1996a), *The Cantos of Ezra Pound*, New York: New Directions.
Pound, E. (1996b), "Pragmatic Aesthetics," in M. L. Ardizzone (ed.), *Machine Art and Other Writings: The Lost Thought of the Italian Years*, Durham: Duke University Press.
Rancière, J. (2009), *The Politics of Aesthetics: The Distribution of the Sensible*, trans. G. Rockhill, London: Continuum.
Reckwitz, A. (2002), "Toward a Theory of Social Practices: A Development in Culturalist Theorizing," *European Journal of Social Theory*, 5 (2): 243–63.
Savicic, S. (2012), "Immaterial Public Space: The Emperor's New Architecture," *Digimag Journal*, 73: 45–55.
Stimpson, C. R. (1995), "Charles Olson: Preliminary Images," in P. Bové (ed.), *Early Postmodernism: Foundational Essays*, 140–62, Durham: Duke University Press.
Tiffany, D. (1995), *Radio Corpse: Imagism and the Cryptaesthetic of Ezra Pound*, Cambridge, MA: Harvard University Press.

CHAPTER 20
CAN PRACTICAL AESTHETICS CHANGE LIVES?
Jill Bennett

Practical aesthetics, I proposed in my book of that name, is the study of aesthetic or sensori-affective perception (aesthesis) in a social field. Engaging an embodied process, carried forward by art as much as by theory, practical aesthetics confounds theory-practice distinctions. It is not simply a branch of philosophy, analogous to practical ethics; nor is it the exclusive domain of art, an area of practice that provides rich resources and techniques to aesthetic inquiry:

> To engage in practical aesthetics is not to contest directly the philosophical ground of Aesthetics or its historical determinations; nor is it simply to "apply" aesthetic theory. It is to conceive of an aesthetics informed by and derived from practical, real world encounters, an aesthetics that is in turn capable of being used or put into effect in a real situation. (Bennett 2012: 2)

As an inquiry into the process of aesthesis, practical aesthetics is also an examination of lived experience—and a valuable method for working in the field of mental health. In this chapter, I consider practical aesthetics in terms of the creation of a transformative space at the intersection of disciplines and practices, drawing in particular on my own practice-based mental health work on *The Big Anxiety – festival of people + arts + science*. Within this sphere of inquiry, a central question for the theory of practical aesthetics is, as I argued in my book, "what can art—or the study of aesthesis more generally—actually do in this field of social relations that is not already accomplished by social science? And in what sense can we talk about the practical value of aesthetics without merely placing art in the service of a social agenda or promoting its 'application' to other fields?" (Bennett 2012: 5).

Compared to art, the traditional practice of aesthetics has a limited history of engagement with social inquiry. The association with judgments of taste and beauty has prevailed over theorizations linking aesthetics to the continuum of everyday sensori-affective interactions that shape psychosocial life. And what aesthetics has to say about art tends toward generalizing or high-level theory rather than the particularities of engagement.

However, if aesthesis is embodied experience, it is also situated; if it is subjective, it is also intersubjective. If aesthetics engages "inner" experience, this internal realm is not a given but may be envisaged as imbricated within environmental settings (Bennett et al.

2019). Rancière's work on the distribution of the sensible (Rancière 2004) has grounded an approach to aesthetics that opens up exploration of the politics of experience at macro levels—the sensible, understood as inscribed within social and institutional systems. Psychoanalytically informed theory focuses on the inverse—on how the social impacts at the micro level of interpersonal sensibility. Most notably, Bollas has mobilized the notion of an "aesthetic intelligence" at play in interactions between people and with the material world (Bollas 1987, 1992; Bennett and Froggett 2020; Bennett et al. 2019). This usage of the term "aesthetic" is distinctive as it pertains both to unconscious process (originating in the way in which the environment of the mother holds and attends to a baby) and to reflective professional practice. Hence, Bollas writes of therapeutic practice that "the analysand whose self has been lost is working with a sensory system in the other who senses his self"; in this process, the analyst's technical decisions (relating to comments, diction texture, use of feelings, choosing to pause or speak and so forth are similarly "aesthetic choices" in tune with the analysand's "aesthetic presence and its articulation" (Bollas 1995: 171).

Here I am not concerned with psychotherapeutic process per se but with the implications of identifying such skillful transactions as aesthetic. Notwithstanding one's commitment or otherwise to a psychoanalytic paradigm, this offers a radical framework for understanding the procedures of art and design as practical and generative, countering the tendency to discuss art as object or the deposit of expression. For me what is at stake in practical aesthetics is not just the expressive process but the intersubjective and transactive process of engagement in both the production and "use" of art. How does a practitioner of practical aesthetics feel into and attune to a situation by aesthetic means and what happens when they do? How, in other words, are people transformed by art or through an aesthetic transaction?

To take an example: *Parragirls Past, Present* is a twenty-three-minute-long, experimental 3D immersive film, commissioned by *The Big Anxiety*, 2017 (Figure 21.1). It was developed by a team of artists working collaboratively with "Parragirls"—women who as teenagers in the 1970s were deemed by the courts to be "neglected, uncontrollable or in moral danger" and placed in the Parramatta Girls Home in Western Sydney, Australia. While in the Home, women were routinely subjected to physical, emotional, and sexual abuse, as many of them had been on the outside. In this respect, the work may be considered to be primarily reparative. In the terms of psychoanalytic trauma studies, we might deem its function to be a "working through" of complex trauma. It also serves personal and political agendas, defined by the Parragirls. These included the women's desire to control their own narrative at a point where there was significant media interest in institutional abuse cases—and also to register the history of the site as it faced the prospect of redevelopment. It was important for them to communicate their experience to children and grandchildren—and more broadly to the community so that no children would suffer in future. These distinct objectives are, however, inseparable from the considerable psychological and social challenge of bearing witness to trauma that has been denied and effaced in the public record.

Can Practical Aesthetics Change Lives?

Figure 21.1 (a) *Parragirls Past, Present* (viewer in immersive 3D film), 2017. Photo: Saeed Khan/ AFP. (b) Parragirls Past, Present. 2017. Immersive 3D Film (Still). Bonney Djuric, Jenny McNally, Lily Hibberd, Volker Kuchelmeister, Alex Davies. Lynne Edmondson Paskovski, Gypsie Hayes, Denise Nicholas. Commissioned by: *The Big Anxiety: festival of art+science+people*, Sydney 2017.

As such, this is a definitive work of practical aesthetics—not simply because the film is used to advance these agendas, but in the way that these goals are integrated into a reflective creative process. *Parragirls Past, Present* is not only a registration of individual or shared "past" trauma but is concerned with its continual unfolding as present experience. The immersive film constitutes a ground or container for this experience through its realization of the entire Girl's Home site in a 3D topographic image. Visitors move through the environment, which is rendered with photorealist fidelity but tempered by a "point-cloud" aesthetic in which objects and surface textures appear to break into luminescent colored pixels (Kuchelmeister et al. 2018). This evokes the fragmentary nature of memory but also the erosion of institutional boundaries as space opens up to the Parragirls' narrative. They do not appear on screen but are heard talking to one another, not only of the abuse during their time in the Home but of the ways in which institutional power is reinforced in contemporary interactions at the site (e.g., in the way that visiting government officials casually disregard their presence; Bennett et al. 2019).

In a video interview at the time of the work's exhibition, Jenny McNally, one of the former residents collaborating on the work, described its impact on her: "the most amazing thing [is] that I was believed. To . . . have my first-born son, who was taken from me . . . say, 'Mum, this is stunning and now I understand your story, I understand who you are.' It gave me back my reality" (McNally 2017).

Such an outcome was unforeseeable, unpredictable, yet in other ways unsurprising. The nature of massive trauma and institutionalized abuse is such that "the inherently incomprehensible and deceptive psychological structure of the event precludes its own witnessing" (Laub 1995: 65; Bennett et al. 2019). Reparative work thus focuses on the complex process of enabling the telling of survivors' stories in a context where these have been systemically denied both within the institutional complex and outside it. This process entails creating the conditions within which such stories may be elaborated and believed, the latter requiring significant critical examination of structures of exclusion and suppression. In this case, the Parragirls are not only telling their stories but establishing the ground on which they can be shared. Colleagues and I have elsewhere discussed this in terms of creating a holding space (Bennett at al. 2019), the emphasis being not solely on designing an outcome, or even registering traumatic experience but on supporting a different form of transaction. There is more to say on the techniques used in the arts to create such a holding space but here I want to highlight a shift away from a linear model of art production (in which expression leads to an output, which in turn engages audience) to a paradigm that envisages aesthetic experience at each point as a transactive process. Most writing on art and trauma focuses on expression of experience, and on the imperative to register trauma, rather than on reparative impact—particularly when it emerges from literary or art studies prioritizing the text/object rather than interactive process.

The notion of "being transformed" is not routinely ascribed to the process of art engagement in the Western tradition. It sounds excessive in relation to the modest measurables, routinely captured in surveys of cultural experience. The way in which art objects are positioned and accessed as autonomous entities within a public exhibition context makes personal transformation a somewhat unrealistic expectation. It is more redolent of the religious ecstasy associated with premodern devotional art, which was, conversely, conceived with the objective of transformation in mind. This is not only a function of the secularization of Western art but of the concomitant acculturation of a less-embodied viewing experience. And yet, it is not uncommon for the use of art (particularly art forms accessed privately) to be envisaged in such terms by artists; David Foster Wallace, for example, spoke of "fiction, poetry, music" as a means by which the loneliness of mental illness may be "stared down, transfigured, treated" (Bennett 2017a).

The idea that art "treats" or mitigates a depressive condition—by something other than distraction—has been given attention in the tradition of Kleinian aesthetics developed first by Hannah Segal and then by C. Fred Alford. Segal sees art as an expression of the depressive position and the task of the artist as the creation of another reality. This new reality is the recreation of a ruined inner world (Alford 1989: 111). Thus, the appeal of the artwork lies not only in sharing the joy of the creator at restoring this world but also in simultaneously allowing the viewer to experience the artist's depression at the loss that is addressed in this process. Alford takes up this proposition in an important move that argues for art as an expression not merely of eros but of caritas or the reparative impulse. Moreover, he is alive to the tendency for reparation to remain abstract: "reconciliation with one's internal objects in phantasy sometimes seems more important than . . . reconciliation with external objects: people" (Alford 1989: 107). Yet in spite of his critique of "the errors of transcendence," Alford insists, "my goal is not to make aesthetic theory more practical or more relevant to the real world" (Alford 1989: 108).

But why is the practical such a stumbling block? Alford (like Segal) inclines toward the Frankfurt school argument that the autonomy and sheer impracticality of art is what makes it critical and resistant to appropriation by the establishment: the social function of artworks is their "functionlessness" according to Adorno (Adorno 1997: 227). In the case of *Parragirls Past, Present*, it is within an aesthetic framework that the site of institutional abuse can be reclaimed. But the reparative nature of the work cannot be confined to the exhibiting space—which may be understood as one among many intersections. The film, itself only one facet of the process, was premiered in an immersive theater, and simultaneously shown via virtual reality headsets in public sites; it was accompanied by the opening of the Girls' Home site itself, and by programs designed to engage community and also the state welfare authorities implicated in historic abuse. It might be argued that all of this is cultural activity; but as a practical aesthetics endeavor, its autonomy—and the hard-won autonomy of trauma survivors—cannot rest on the separation of the artworld from other institutional space, even if the latter enables the constitution of a holding space that was lacking elsewhere. Thus, we need to consider—and invent—the institutional arrangements necessary to its function and critical discussion, and to its longer-term value for the community. Such projects necessarily emerge from extended community work; they neither begin nor conclude with their public display. In this sense, they are as much about ongoing reparative work as they are about an artwork—and as such they are too rarely envisaged and supported within conventional exhibitionary (or health) frameworks.

In the United Kingdom, the chair of a recent parliamentary committee on arts and health observes in his report that there is a "chronic and sterile altercation" between two camps: the proponents of art for art's sake versus those who promote the practical, community benefits of art (Howarth 2017: 5). This schism is enshrined in the discourse of the contemporary artworld, which embraces a radical social agenda but forecloses on the project of practical aesthetics. An explicit example: during the 2016 Sydney Biennale, the artistic director Stephanie Rosenthal insisted in an interview with *The Guardian* that art can do no more than "talk about" political matters: "you're cheating yourself if you think you're going to change the world" (Bennett 2017b). An activist working through art, she suggests, does not compare to "to someone who has given his whole life to work for human rights." As a philosophical proposition, this is questionable; as an institutional or curatorial prescription, its force is carried forward in practice. Unless we are actively open to work that pursues practical goals beyond exhibiting, the role of art is effectively curtailed. Institutional settings promote only weak engagement, with the expectation that art reflects or represents its outside, rather than entering into another sphere with the aim of transforming it.

This raises the question of how we can open up spaces for more expansive transdisciplinary practice—not only the kind of theoretical transdisciplinarity that remains within academic parameters but a practice that can operate across often inhospitable or skeptical domains in ways that challenge the limits of existing institutional practice. Where might an artist go to do "human rights" or reparative work if the artworld is inadequate to practical, life-changing endeavors? Is there a way to leverage the arts without turning inward so that the effects of radical practice are not limited to existing art audiences?

Change occurs at the edges of disciplines and practices, not only because it is here that those ill-served by the center congregate but because license granted in one field is withheld in another. Hence, the edge is not only a refuge but a place where fields can be reformed and opened to outside influence. Artists work freely in mental health in ways that the protocols of health fields restrict; their outputs, which may generate a qualitative experiential knowledge base of value to health objectives, will not conform to the demands of evidence-based research in health and medical fields. Thus, there is benefit in activating from an arts base and constituting a "third space"—a genuine intersection where, for example, health objectives can be addressed directly through collaborations of arts, science, and community that are not instrumental or hierarchical but that move outside disciplinary structures in order to refocus (Muller et al. 2018).

Fields do not readily accommodate each other's paradigms and methods without extensive theoretical and practical effort. Given this, we should not settle for the easy collaborations alone. There is increasing enthusiasm, for example, for Arts on Prescription, whereby health professionals or GPs write prescriptions for patients to participate in the arts. In 2018, the Montreal Museum of Fine Arts announced that it would allow physicians to write prescriptions for free museum visits on the basis that the "neutral, beautiful, inspiring space" of a museum can boost mood, improve well-being (BBC 2018). As those involved acknowledge, this move usefully affirms the value of cultural experiences, like physical activity, for their health benefits. It does not entail the critical inquiry that would constitute practical aesthetics, nor question the model of art consumption at its core.

In different ways, both museum visits on prescription and Alford's "non practical" reparative encounter with art disregard the practicalities and politics of setting. Both take for granted the (neutrality of the) scene in which a spectator encounters an artwork, read implicitly as the deposit of an artist's process. Equal access to art, its discourse, and its buildings is presumed. But a more ambitious and "practical aesthetic" approach to mental health must ask the question, who is in the building and how is access granted? This is not only a question of social demographics but one that goes to the core of the mental health challenge; who feels that they belong? Accordingly, in developing *The Big Anxiety* as a strategic arts-led mental health project, we started from this position, acknowledging the value of leveraging the arts and arts institutions but at the same time asking who is missing?

The question can be posed two ways: Who is missing in mental health and who is missing in arts? In the mental health field, there is increasing interest in "lived experience" but mental health research is dominated by the medical model. "Knowledge translation" is conceived on a pipeline model with the goal of getting the message out from those with the medical answers to those who need help. There are few tools and techniques for bottom-up research, or for cultivating languages of experience. Yet in Australia, where the festival operates, at least 65 percent of those with lived experience of mental health concerns don't seek help (far higher in certain populations). This points to the need for richer engagement methods within mental health, as well as to the value of extending the sphere of operations to new ground.

There is of course a tension in bringing transdisciplinary aesthetics to mental health: this negatively defined cohort of "non help seekers" is arguably not a clinical group at all. The reasons for nonengagement are various but include stigma and skepticism, raising the question of whether medical labels are effective. Rather than simply doing communications work for mental health, then, art practice may work from experience, or from the ground up. In so doing, it may move into new spaces, constructing projects which may have one or several exhibited outcomes but which are conceived as more expansive engagements. In this regard, *The Big Anxiety* does not follow an agenda defined by either health or arts but it does pursue what may be broadly defined as a mental health objective—the challenge of broadening and deepening engagement and of understanding lived experience. But it does this by means of practical aesthetics, resisting the instrumentalization of art. What this means is that while a high-level goal may be shared, methods must be derived from the exigencies of collaboration in a genuine "third space," and through a reflective practice where all structures and institutional precepts are subject to scrutiny.

Alford proffers a general theory of art, which (like Arts on Prescription) is content agnostic and therefore not directly concerned with the politics of exclusion—something that may be implicit and alienating within certain spaces and works, and addressed productively and practically in others. To take a straightforward example, a gallery installation by Italian artist Monica Bonvicini comprises a sign in giant illuminated letters, created from rows of light bulbs. The paradoxically welcoming sign reads NOTFORYOU (*Not for You* 2006; Bennett, 2017a). Whether read as a reference to the illusory offerings of consumerism or to the trappings of wealth, it addresses (amuses, connects with, touches) those who know implicitly that that affordances are always already in play in any display of art, that we are not always welcome. Art thereby "speaks to us" by acknowledging felt experience as good and bad. It may do this fleetingly or unexpectedly, as may be the case on encountering the spectacle of Bonvicini's sign; or it may do this more programmatically (as in the Parragirls project), aiming to promote transformative experience: "transformation does not mean gratification . . . likewise aesthetic moments are not always beautiful or wonderful . . . many are ugly and terrifying but nonetheless profoundly moving because of the existential memory tapped" (Bollas 2011:12).

Transformation through art need not be an unplanned, exceptional occurrence—though for it to become a planned occurrence requires a shift in paradigm—specifically a shift toward an experiential understanding of art/aesthetics, away from one that privileges the object in isolation. Bollas's account of aesthetic relations locates the development of aesthetic sensibility in "the mother's idiom of care and the infant's experience of this handling," which he argues "will predispose all future aesthetic experiences that place the person in subjective rapport with an object" (Bollas 1987: 32–3). In such a context, transformation is not exceptional but axiomatic: "the nature of the self is formed and transformed by the environment." It is in this sense that I would argue that the potential for transformation is a function of design and access; it is enabled, or conversely restricted, by art and institutional contexts.

But following Alford and Bollas, we might also argue that the ability of art to engender transformation is dependent on its capacity to provide a space in which loss, fear, and the "depressive" condition can be held and processed. In this respect, art doesn't design experience in some prescriptive Disneyesque fashion, but it does create and activate potential space and its relational possibilities. This, as my colleagues and I have argued elsewhere, entails attending to affordances (Gibson 1979)—the possibilities for action and experience that exist in the relationships between participants and the environment and which are felt, sensed, and implicitly understood (Bennett et al. 2019). Affordances may be designed within a project to support particular kinds of transactions, but also within the encasing structure of a gallery, venue, or curated festival. In *The Big Anxiety* festival, we have undertaken projects that design for/from neurodiversity, as well as projects that promote "awkward conversations"; we have also created an Empathy Clinic, opening up the potential for transforming experiences of people, places, and things.

The clinic as art can be neither a self-help tool nor ironically detached. Practical aesthetics entails critical attunement to the means by which experience is accommodated, appropriated, shaped, and managed. If, as Adorno claims, the ultimate value proposition of art lies in its functionlessness, this remains one of the touchstones for art that is simultaneously focused on promoting its usefulness. Such a resolution might be contradictory if we focus solely on the autonomy of the artwork as object. If, instead, we focus on experience—the lived experience of participants—and on how art can respond to and transform that experience, then the value of art lies in its capacity to attune to subjectivity and to the emotional valence that inflects our relationships to people, places, and things. If art is to transform experience, it must offer the means to escape prescriptions as much as to pursue a course of action. Currently, the field of "arts and health" is gaining momentum, its traction due in part to its measurable health benefits. These are tangible; cultural activity might productively be envisaged within a health framework, as the Arts on Prescription movement suggests. But the forms that a genuine practical aesthetics may take, its distinct modes of criticism, its transformative modes of engagement, its impact on health, human rights, institutional practice, and the way that exhibitions operate, are yet to be fully imagined.

References

Adorno, T. ([1970] 1997) *Aesthetic Theory*, trans. R. Hullot-Kentor, Minneapolis: University of Minnesota Press.

Alford, F. (1989), *Melanie Klein and Critical Social Theory: An Account of Politics, Art and Reason Based on Her Psychoanalytic Theory*, New Haven and London: Yale University Press.

BBC "Montreal Museum Partners with Doctors to 'prescribe' Art," *BBC News*, October 26, 2018. Available online: https://www.bbc.com/news/world-us-canada-45972348 (accessed May 28, 2019).

Bennett, J. (2012), *Practical Aesthetics. Events, Affect and Art after 9/11*, London: I.B. Tauris & Co.

Bennett, J. (2017a), "Are We All Anxious Now?" *Tate Etc.* (39) (Spring): 96–9. Available online: https://www.tate.org.uk/context-comment/articles/jill-bennett-are-we-all-anxious-now (accessed May 28, 2019).

Bennett, J. (2017b), 'Editorial: Anxiety', *Artlink* issue 37 (3): 10–11.

Bennett, J., and L. Froggett (2020), "Aesthetic Intelligence," in J. Bennett and M. Zournazi (eds.), *Thinking in the World Reader*, 223–37, London: Bloomsbury.

Bennett, J., L. Froggett, and L. Muller (2019), "Psychosocial Aesthetics and the Art of Lived Experience," *Journal of Psychosocial Research* 12 (1–2): 185–201.

Bollas, C. (1987), *The Shadow of the Object: Psychoanalysis of the Unthought Known*, London: Free Association Books.

Bollas, C. (1992), *Being a Character: Psychoanalysis of Self-Experience*, New York: Hill and Wang.

Bollas, C. (1995), *Cracking Up: The Work of Unconscious Experience*, London: Routledge.

Bollas, C. (2011), "Psychic Genera," in *The Christopher Bollas Reader*, London: Routledge, 57–78.

Gibson, J. (1979), *The Ecological Approach to Visual Perception*, Boston: Houghton Mifflin.

Howarth, A. (2017), "Foreword," All-Party Parliamentary Group on Arts, Health and Wellbeing Inquiry Report, "Creative Health: The Arts for Health and Wellbeing," Available online: http://www.artshealthandwellbeing.org.uk/appg-inquiry/Publications/Creative_Health_Inquiry_Report_2017_-_Second_Edition.pdf (accessed June 2, 2019).

Kuchelmeister, V., L. Hibberd, and A. Davies (2018), "Affect and Place Representation in Immersive Media: The Parragirls Past, Present Project," in J. Bowen, J. Weinel, G. Diprose, and N. Lambert (eds.), *EVA London 2018: Electronic Visualisation & the Arts. Proceedings of a conference held in London 11th–13th July*, 71–8.

Laub, D. (1995), "Truth and Testimony: The Process and the Struggle," in C. Caruth (ed.), *Trauma: Explorations in Memory*, 61–75, Baltimore: Johns Hopkins.

McNally, J. (2017), *Jenny McNally Interview, Parramatta 2017*. Available online: https://www.youtube.com/watch?v=4hFS8-Fq-c8 (accessed May 28, 2019).

Muller, L., L. Froggett, and J. Bennett (2018), "Emergent Knowledge in the Third Space of Art-science," *Leonardo* 53 (3) (June 2020): 1–11. Available online: https://doi.org/10.1162/leon_a_01690.

Rancière, J. (2004), *The Politics of Aesthetics: The Distribution of the Sensible*. London, UK: Continuum.

CHAPTER 21
CONTAMINATIONS
TOWARD AN EMPATHIC MUSEOLOGY
Mieke Bal

Do the words "practical" and "aesthetics" really go together to form a concept different from each one of them alone? How art can be practically useful in the world by participating in thinking is a question that has preoccupied me for a long time, along with many others. Often, my primary focus has been violence and its consequences. The current situation of the world, with migration, dictatorships (whether or not "democratically elected"), and poverty-driven violence, religious and nationalistic strife, and more, makes a deeper, more creative reflection on violence and its assault on human subjectivity (trauma), an urgent task for art, with its access to the imagination that can help think up hitherto unknown possibilities. That question includes that of the potential of art for contributing to making a social change. I have recently finished work on an interdisciplinary case study anchored in critical reflection and a special educational method. In this project, a group of artists, educators, and scholars seek to achieve a larger societal goal: to deploy art to affect spectators, and even slightly contaminate them by way of inoculation, with the sociocultural state of violence-induced "madness." The resulting trauma leads routinely to isolation and ostracization; but this can be counteracted by empathy.

How art can help achieve this, by using and strengthening the position of museums as motors for social change, is the central question of the project. Theoretically as well as practically, we concentrate this question on the way theatricality can be deployed for museological presentations. The practical goal is to solicit a form of "contamination" that makes visitors vulnerable to, and thereby understanding of, the traumatic states of others. The impact of this project is located at the crossroad of an innovative approach to museum display for learning and practicing empathy in a world of traumatizing violence, and the difficulty, well known in psychiatry and psychoanalysis, of treating traumatized people without disempowering means (medication, hospitalization).

My commitment to this issue has been nourished especially when I made, with British artist Michelle Williams Gamaker, and with the participation of psychoanalyst of trauma Françoise Davoine, the theoretical fiction film A LONG HISTORY OF MADNESS (2011). This film is "about" madness, but it also stages, performs, enacts, and critiques ideas about madness and their cultural history. Based on the 1998 book *Mère Folle* by Davoine (2014), the film stages the question and practice of the psychoanalytic treatment of people diagnosed as "psychotic" and who, for the sake of avoiding narrowing diagnostic discourse, we simply call "mad."[1]

Practical Aesthetics

One issue is the status of images different yet on a par with words. To explore how this works in practice, I have been making videos. There, I am interested in how images can help articulate and embody *thought*. Images can perform an equivalent of speech acts; they can respond ("speak back") to the look cast onto them, and that they can entice viewers to theorize, think, and feel all at once. They are *performative*. They *do* something; they act. I call such "speaking images," which resist (parts of) my interpretation and make me think, "theoretical objects." The task of the art writer and teacher is, then, to focus on thinking *with* such art.[2]

With my title I seek to draw attention to the fluidity between domains. In the recent project, we study and experiment with learning to listen to trauma, and respond to it with empathy. "Contaminations" occur when different people, things, states, and illnesses come in close proximity with one another. Thus, in the catalog text for a 2019 exhibition of my video work in Murcia, Spain, titled *Contaminations: Reading, Imagining, Imaging*, I argued for the permeable distinctions between cultural activities:

> The cultural activities of reading, imagining, and seeing or making images all hang together. The title "contaminations" indicates this overlap, the fluid demarcations we are used to bring to cultural domains, between words and images, still and moving images, material and mental images. The key word is "between." . . . The underlying thought is that cultural life consists of performative events.

A socially productive contamination can be forcefully explored around the topic of the social recognition and acceptance of traumatic life, because this is where a change in attitude is necessary, and can be solicited and assessed. The deployment of theatricality for museological innovation is a fitting means to that end.

Transformations

The transformation from "theater film"—a lengthy projection in a darkened theater with seats facing the screen—to "gallery film"—disposed in a semi-dark setting where visitors are free to determine their own pace—can be considered as "spatializing film." The primary distinction is the concrete and material space in which it is presented, in which both the images and the viewers move. Gallery films use cinematic techniques and aesthetics to partly dislodge the primary feature of cinema, its temporality, and turn it into a spatial feature. Conversely, the alleged primary spatiality of paintings and photographs can be thickened with temporality. Gallery films function differently both in space and in time. That they seem to turn time into a spatial feature is what Lev Manovich proposed: multiscreen works function as "spatial montage" (2001: 325).[3]

But film's temporality does not disappear, which complicates the implied opposition between time and space, and also the distinction between the different screens. In the gallery, space is the context, or environment—or in the terminology of my view of affect, the medium—within which the film develops its specific effects, such as immersion.

"Immersive" includes creating a fictional environment within which viewers can be steeped for the duration of the visit. They can walk around or sit down in a world of images and construct the content they prefer, under the noncoercive guidance by the art and its curating. But they are not alone. The immersive space is an ideal setting where thinking with the art, or as I have called it, "thinking in film" can be practiced.[4]

Space and time collaborate with and confuse each other. Moreover, an immersive presentation solicits moods, emotions, and affects before contents, and hence impacts on the way the latter is taken on and interpreted by the visitor. Whatever content viewers construct is inflected by those moods, emotions, and affects. For the curator, the task is to offer such artistic experiences that bring past insights back to life, to today. In the case of an exhibition that mixes media as well as older and contemporary art, the underlying novel, the videos, and the paintings and sculptures together can resonate without the one dominating the other. Spatial proximity and temporal synchronicity are tools to achieve this resonance, through which the art writer can think.[5]

The same holds for the relationships between videos. Like paintings and other artworks, each one of them functions on its own, while their sequence, suggested but not imposed, can function as a narrative framework, or an atmospheric, philosophical, or artistic one. The videos must achieve performativity: *do* something to their viewers—but without machine-driven manipulation. The immersion enhances the viewer's agency in choosing her duration of watching, a direction of looking, and a response to the images. They help visitors to think, with and in the video works, through the creation of an environment and a time-space that is conducive to thinking. Such transformations help rethink film, literature, and exhibition together.

In our project, the integration of such "contaminating" objects is geared toward a clearer practical goal: to raise empathy (an attitude) for the traumatized (a state), caused by violence (an event). The contamination is to occur between a theatrical video installation and its viewers, who will be encouraged to give their time to the integrated activities of looking and listening, reflecting and feeling, in the face of the *form* of a traumatic state created by artistic means. To this purpose we have transformed (parts of) an episodic, chaotic novel into an equally chaotic, hectic video installation: *El Ingenioso Hidalgo Don Quixote de la Mancha* by Spanish baroque author Miguel de Cervantés Saavedra (1547–1616).

Reactivating Cultural Heritage

Cervantes wrote one of the world's primary best sellers after experiencing five years of captivity as a slave in Algiers (1575–80). The novel—the first part published in 1605, the second in 1615—reads like a parody of medieval epics and romances, and as a precursor of later novels that also mock adventure stories, and also resonates with postmodern novels. Most importantly, the novel stands out in its intensity and creative expression of prolonged hopelessness. This, we speculated, led to what is termed trauma, a notion overused and in danger of losing its specific meaning. In this project, "trauma" is a state of stagnation and the impossibility of subjective remembrance that results from traumatogenic events; not the events themselves; the distortion of time and its forms that results, rather than the violence that causes the trauma.[6]

If such a literary work has achieved and retained worldwide status as a masterpiece, it is first of all because it has not lost any of its actuality. Not coincidentally, the novel is based on what the Cervantes specialist María Antonia Garcés has called "an early modern dialogue with Islam" (Garcés 2005). Formerly, in deep history, things happened that still happen, or happen again, today. Hence, "formerly is today." With a research group at the Linnaeus University in Växjö, Sweden, we could call it "concurrences."[7]

Every epoch knows of situations where the event of violence leads to the state of trauma, situations that push people out of humanity. The recurrence of violence and the subsequent traumatic states makes it useful to think, not only with and through art, but to keep the past in view in that endeavor. One of the missions of art is to keep the past alive, as a vital interlocutor for art in the present. Cervantes's novel carries not only the traces of the absurdity and madness that suggest the inevitably traumatic state in which its creator must have been locked, as transpires in the stories told. It also foregrounds this consequence of war and captivity in the madness of its literary form. Long as it is, the novel could continue endlessly, for the sense of time is what has been disrupted by the traumatic state. Explaining the main character's madness with reference to his eager reading is a superficial interpretation that is subservient to explicit mentions and blind to what underlies these. It is, in other words, ignoring what art as such can help us think.[8]

The sheer-endless stream of "adventures" makes all film adaptations more or less pointless. One can barely read, let alone watch all those senseless attempts to help others, the repercussions of which involve cruelty, mutilation, and pain. If we nevertheless have sought to make an audiovisual work based on this novel, it was because the aftermath of violence, of hopeless stagnation in situations of which the end is not in sight, needs exploration. Making an artwork can help thinking through what captivity really means and does. Thus, by being touched by the installation's form, viewers can learn from it for dealing with their own experiences of the violence contemporary society can generate, their own as well as those of others, in order to repair what Cervantes called the "broken thread" of memory, and, we add, of social connectivity.[9]

This work pertains to what is most frequently called "artistic research"—a search and analysis through artmaking (Borgdorff 2012). The specific genre of video production where making produces thinking, I call "theoretical fictions." This term indicates the deployment of fiction to understand difficult theoretical issues and to develop theory through what fiction enables us to imagine. This is how Leonardo da Vinci solved his problem of making his complex, abstract knowledge understandable through visualization in painting (Fiorani and Nova 2013).

"Theoretical fiction" is the genre here as well, with its implication that the art, the visualization and theatricalization, generates ideas, if only we heed them, listen to them. The challenge to make a video installation project based on *Don Quixote* appealed to two ambitions. First, to reflect deeper on trauma and its disruption of subjectivity. Due to its creative source and different rationality, art is more suitable than academic research only to do this. The insights Cervantes's novel harbors connect to other experiences of war, violence, and captivity. Second, a well-thought-through video project can explore and transgress the limits of what can be seen, shown, narrated, and witnessed specifically in relation to trauma, which is notoriously unrepresentable (Alphen 1999; Hirsch 2008). But that is not a reason to turn our backs to the traumatized.

As a mostly narrative medium, film seems the least apt to do justice to the turbulent incoherence, repetitiveness, and incongruous "adventures" told in the novel. Yet thanks to its capacity for audiovisualization, a video installation consisting of different, nonlinear episodes may instead be more effective in showing, not the moment trauma occurs but violence-generated traumatic *states*. The importance of showing is to enable *witnessing* as an engaged activity against the indifference of the world.

Traumatic Form: "Sprinkling Events in Which Formerly Is Today"

In order to do justice to the peculiar, cyclic, perhaps even "hysterical" form of the novel while pursuing these two goals, only an equally "incoherent," chaotic, episodic artwork can be effective. But a different medium works with different forms. Thus, we aimed to turn the hysteria of endless storytelling into a reflection on communication beyond the boundaries that madness draws around its captive subjects and, instead, open up their subjectivity.[10]

To achieve this, we expected that the creation and production of singular installation pieces would facilitate experimenting with the episodic nature of the literary masterpiece. These pieces, presenting "scenes," are presentations of situations. To give insight into the stagnation that characterizes the adventures, hinting at a traumatized state, these pieces are predominantly descriptive. Any attempt at narrative is "stuttering," recurring, without any sense of development. And often, the images do not match the dialogues. But most importantly, the installation itself enhances the chaotic and temporally disturbed nature of the traumatic state.

What French psychoanalyst and theorist of violence-induced madness Françoise Davoine calls, citing historian Fernand Braudel: "poussières d'événements" (dust of events) (2008: 43–4) is the motto of this work's form: sprinkling situations, moments, over the stage or throughout the gallery space, creating confusing on different levels. These moments are suspended between the past and the present, and thus they confuse chronology. Like specters, they cast their shadow over the present, the time frame that is ours when we see images. This conception of spectrality has been convincingly proposed by Esther Peeren (2014). Thus, the tenuous line of a single narrative yields to an installation that puts the visitors in the position of making their own narrative out of what is there, on the basis of their own baggage, while witnessing the events and being touched by it.

This is adequate to the state of trauma presented in the pieces and in the juxtapositions among them, and to the need to stretch out a hand to, instead of turning away from, people hurt so deeply. The trauma incurred by Cervantes, after being

Practical Aesthetics

held in captivity as a slave without any sense of an ending to his disempowered state and his suffering, has been beautifully traced, narrated, and explained by Colombian literary historian scholar María Antonia Garcés. This traumatic state looms over the entire project and determines its form. Therefore, we wanted to try something we never do: completely merging the author's biography, the main character's ostensive and much commented-upon madness, and the main character of the one narrative unit or inserted novella we selected for a narrative element, "The Captive's Story." This merging indicates that these are three incarnations of the desperate attempt to recover from the world's most horrid crime: to destroy the subjectivity of others by captivity.

The form of these pieces are experimental in many different ways, so that a contemporary aesthetic can reach out to, and touch, a situation of long ago that, as befits the stilled temporality of trauma, persists in the present. Where possible, long, enduring shots predominate, eight minutes per shot, or per scene. Soundwise, some are quiet, some loud. This allows the simultaneity, the proximity, and even the superposition of different scenes. Another experimental form concerns the dynamic relationship between visibility and invisibility, image and writing. The actor Mathieu Montanier, co-initiator of the video project, is visible, but so are, sometimes, the letters of inscriptions, in association with other texts, to foreground the nature of video*graphy* as a form of writing. We also experimented with different combinations of sequences, including mounting multiple images on a screen; this, also, for the practical purpose of facilitating the project to travel and to be combined with other artworks. Hence, through experimenting with possible forms of the art of video, we have sought to invent new forms for the formlessness of trauma.

In order to include, while questioning it, the narrativity that is, after all, the novel's primary mode, "The Captive's Tale" (DQ I, ch. 39–41) was developed in four scenes. It is the one "captivating" story of captivity, an embedded novella, with a plot of sorts, of a soldier taken in slavery, clearly based on autobiography, supplemented with dreams of wish fulfillment. The Captive is played by the same actor who plays Don Quixote, just slightly younger in appearance. This allows viewers to reflect on, and decide, how they consider narrative itself. These three scenes have also been edited as a single short narrative film (twenty-four minutes).

Collaboration, Interdisciplinarity, Intermediality

The starting hypothesis was that theatricality ("live") can be usefully transformed into forms of museal display that get closer to the visitors and thus turn "live" into "life." Since this is a project of artistic research, integrating creation and analysis, in addition to theoretical work on theatricality (Röttger 2017, 2018a, 2018b), educational experiments (Lutters 2015, 2017, 2019), and a thorough study of Cervantes's novel, we have collaborated closely with two experts, one on trauma and one on Cervantes: Françoise Davoine, psychoanalyst of trauma and madness (2008; 2014), and the biographer María

Antonia Garcés, who wrote her masterful, thoroughly documented book after having been held captive herself by Colombian terrorists. With the former, we already worked for the production of the film and installation project *A Long History of Madness*, 2008–11 (see note 1). She also collaborated and played in *Madame B*. Davoine has also published two books on *Don Quixote* as a source for insights into trauma and the possibility to "cure" it analytically (Davoine 2008; Davoine and Gaudillière 2013). Garcés as a literary scholar helped with the delicate task to stay "loyal"—rather than "faithful"—to Cervantes's work, not in spite of, but due to the modifications of form. Rather than an "adaptation," the work we have made is a response, a mode of turning a historical object into an interlocutor with suggestions for today's world.

Collaboration is one crucial aspect of this project, and I would venture to affirm that it is indispensable, of the logic of 1+1=3, and makes for a spontaneous interdisciplinarity. The work with actors, as I have been able to understand before, contributes insights that, in light of artistic research, are quite simply inherent in the actors' art. Between theater studies and pedagogy, there is already quite a history, especially in Brazil (Boal 1995). Literary analysis and video installation bring us to intermediality (Röttger 2018b). And the approach to cultural heritage to the anachronism for which I have made a plea in a study of our film *Madame B*. In this film and video installation, also made with Michelle Williams Gamaker, anachronism is of vital importance (Bal 2017b).

These "interships" resulting from the inherent collaborative aspect of this project are a primary outcome of the stimulating "hands-on" interaction with art and its making. This is perhaps the closest I can come to theorizing thinking with, through, or in art. If aesthetics, as based on Baumgarten's sensuous interaction between artwork and spectator, is to have practical sense, it, too, must collaborate with both makers and spectators. See Bennett (2012) The latter can then become, as per Boal, "spect-actors" and actively participate in addressing acute problems of the world. This is a way art can be practical.

Since I wrote this essay the project has been finished, thanks to the generous help of many. It has already been exhibited three times, in Sweden, Spain and the UK. Each time my intuition about its potential to perform "practical aesthetics" has been confirmed.

Notes

1. On our films, see http://www.miekebal.org/artworks/films/. Michelle Williams Gamaker's PhD dissertation (2011) develops the concept of art practice on which our film is based.
2. On Damisch's concept of the theoretical object, see Yve-Alain Bois et al. (1998). For the performativity of images, which is modeled on speech act theory, see Culler (2007) and Bal (2002).
3. With the term "gallery film" and the placement of video exhibitions in a museum, we also participate in the so-called high culture and the social divide that term entails. For a wide range of views, see Grisprud (2001; 2002). I borrow the term "gallery film" from Catherine Fowler (2004). For the deictic aspect of gallery films, see Butler (2010). I refer to gallery film as a genre, something close to *dispositif*. See Bellour (1999). For a comparative analysis of video installation and film, see Houwen (2017).

4. For *Thinking in film*, see my book on Eija-Liisa Ahtila's installation works (2013). More on affect and its political effectivity in my 2019a article, inspired by Alphen (2008).
5. I use the generic term "affect" in the sense of Deleuze ([1968] 1994). I have had the opportunity to experiment with such mixings in an exhibition in the Munch Museum, Oslo (Bal 2017a).
6. For a lucid explanation of trauma, see Alphen (1999).
7. "Concurrences" is a center of colonial and postcolonial studies. The name is an attempt to decenter the problematic term "postcolonial," which wrongly suggests that we have left colonialism behind. See Bryson et al., eds. (2017).
8. On the disruption of temporality in baroque art and today, see the article I wrote in collaboration with Norwegian artist Jeannette Christensen in *ASAP* (Bal 2019b).
9. Cervantes wrote this in the Prologue to the *Persiles* (1617); quoted in Garcés (2005: 252). Films based on *Don Quixote* are either unfinished (Orson Welles) or take refuge in a parodic postmodern aesthetics (Terry Gilliam) without acknowledging the traumatic state that sustains the novel.
10. On the need for witnessing, see Felman and Laub (1992).

References

Alphen, E. v. (1999), "Symptoms of Discursivity: Experience, Memory, Trauma," in M. Bal, J. Crewe, and L. Spitzer (eds.), *Acts of Memory: Cultural Recall in the Present*, 24–38, Hanover NH: University of New England Press.

Alphen, E. v. (2008), "Affective Operations of Art and Literature," *RES: Journal of Anthropology and Aesthetics*, 53/54: 20–30.

Bal, M. (2002), "Performance and Performativity," in *Travelling Concepts in the Humanities: A Rough Guide*, 174–212, Toronto: University of Toronto Press.

Bal, M. (2013), *Thinking in Film: The Politics of Video Installation According to Eija-Liisa Ahtila*, London: Bloomsbury.

Bal, M. (2017a), *Emma & Edvard Looking Sideways: Loneliness and the Cinematic*, Oslo: Munch Museum / Brussels: Mercatorfonds, Yale University Press.

Bal, M. (2017b), "Intership: Anachronism between Loyalty and the Case," in T. Leitch (ed.), *The Oxford Handbook of Adaptation Studies*, 179–96, New York and Oxford: Oxford University Press.

Bal, M. (2019a), "Affectively Effective: Affect as an Artistic-Political Strategy," in E.v. Alphen and T. Jirsa (eds.), *How to Do Things with Affects: Affective Triggers in Aesthetic Forms and Cultural Practices*, Leiden: Brill.

Bal, M., in collaboration with J. Christensen (2019b), "An Aesthetic of Interruption: Stagnation and Acceleration," *ASAP Journal*, 4(1): 85–112 (with Jeannette Christensen).

Bellour, R. (1999), *La querelle des dispositifs. Cinéma – installations, expositions*, Paris: P.O.L.

Bennett, J. (2012), *Practical Aesthetics: Event, Affect and Art after 9/11*, London: I.B. Tauris.

Boal, A. (1995), *The Rainbow of Desire. The Boal Method of Theatre and Therapy*, New York: Routledge.

Bois, Y.-A., D. Hollier, R. Krauss, and H. Damisch (1998), "A Conversation with Hubert Damisch," *October* 85 (Summer): 3–17.

Borgdorff, H. (2012), *The Conflict of the Faculties: Perspectives on Artistic Research and Academia*, Leiden: Leiden University Press.

Bryson, D., P. Forsgren, and G. Fur (eds.) (2017), *Concurrent Imaginaries, Postcolonial Worlds*, Leiden: Brill|Rodopi.
Butler, A. (2010), "A Deictic Turn: Space and Location in Contemporary Gallery Film and Video Installation," *Screen*, 51 (4): 305–23.
Culler, J. (2007), "The Performative," in *The Literary in Theory*, 137–65, Stanford, CA: Stanford University Press.
Davoine, F. (1998), *Mère folle: Récit*, Strasbourg: Arcanes.
Davoine, F. (2008), *Don Quichotte, pour combattre la mélancolie*. Paris, Stock.
Davoine, F. (2014), *Mother Folly: A Tale*, trans. J. G. Miller, Stanford: Stanford University Press.
Davoine, F., and J.-M. Gaudillière (2013), *A bon entendeur, salut! Face à la perversion, le retour de Don Quichotte*, Paris: Stock.
Deleuze, Gilles ([1968] 1994), *Difference and Repetition*, trans. P. Patton, New York: Columbia University Press.
Felman, S. and D. Laub (1992), *Testimony: Crises of Witnessing in Literature, Psychoanalysis, and History*, New York and London: Routledge.
Fiorani, F., and A. Nova (eds.) (2013), *Leonardo's Optics: Theory and Pictorial Practice*, Venice: Marsilio Editore.
Fowler, C. (2004), "Room for Experiment: Gallery Films and Vertical Time from Maya Deren to Eija-Liisa Ahtila," *Screen*, 45 (4): 324–43.
Garcés, M. A. (2005), *Cervantes in Algiers: A Captive's Tale*. Nashville, Tennessee: Vanderbilt University Press.
Garcés, M. A. (ed.) (2011), *An Early Modern Dialogue with Islam: Antonio de Sosa's Topography of Algiers (1612)*, trans. D. de Armas Wilson, Notre Dame, IN: University of Notre Dame Press.
Gripsrud, J. (ed.) (2001), *The Aesthetics of Popular Art*, Kristiansand: Norwegian Academic Press.
Gripsrud, J. (2002) *Understanding Media Culture*, London: Arnold.
Hirsch, M. (2008), "The Generation of Postmemory," *Poetics Today*, 29 (1): 103–28.
Houwen, J. (2017), *Film and Video Intermediality: The Question of Medium Specificity in Contemporary Moving Images*, London: Bloomsbury.
Lutters, J. (2015), *Teaching Objects: Studies in Art-based Learning*, Amsterdam: Idea Books (ArtEZ Press).
Lutters, J. (2017), *Ema (Nude on a Staircase): Studies in Art-based Learning*. Amsterdam: Idea Books (ArtEZ Press).
Lutters, J. (2019), *In the Shadow of the Art Work: Art-Based Learning in Practice*, Amsterdam: Valiz.
Manovich, L. (2001), *The Language of New Media*, Cambridge, MA: MIT Press.
Peeren, E. (2014), *The Spectral Metaphor: Living Ghosts and the Agency of Invisibility*, London: Palgrave.
Röttger, K. (2017), "Towards a Pedagogy of Cultural Translation: Challenges for an International Classroom," in S. Bala, M. Gluhovic, H. Korsberg, and K. Röttger (eds.), *International Performance Research Pedagogies: Towards an Unconditional Discipline?* 41–54, Cham: Palgrave Macmillan.
Röttger, K. (2018a), "The Eventization of Tragic Experience at the Threshold of the 19th century: The Raft of the Medusa," in J. Dünne, G. Hindemith, and J. Kasper (eds.), *Catastrophe & Spectacle: Variations of a Conceptual Relation from the 17th to the 21st Century*, 58–67, Berlin: Neofelis.
Röttger, K. (2018b), "The Mystery of the In-Between: A Methodological Approach to Intermedial Performance Analysis," *Forum Modernes Theater*, 28 (2): 105–16.
Williams Gamaker, M. (2011), *The Relocation of Art Experience: Social Interrelations and Therapeutic Negotiations in Art Practice*, Goldsmiths College, University of London.

CHAPTER 22
THINKING WITH ARCHIVAL ORDERING, OR THE POLITICS OF DESTRUCTION
Ernst van Alphen

In her book *Practical Aesthetics: Events, Affects and Art After 9/11*, Jill Bennett defines practical aesthetics as follows: "to conceive of an aesthetics informed by and derived from practical, real-world encounters, an aesthetics that is in turn capable of being used or put into effect in a real situation" (2). This assessment explains especially the qualifier "practical." At the same time, she emphasizes that "practical" does not imply an application of aesthetic theory; it modifies aesthetics. It concerns art and its study as a means of apprehending the world through sense-based and affective processes. This implies that such studies do not oppose thinking to sense-based and affective processes, but consider aesthetic perception *as a mode or form of thinking*. Bernd Herzogenrath conceives practical aesthetics as "thinking with art, in order to find new ways to create worlds and thus to make the world perceivable in different ways" (see Introduction in this volume, by Herzogenrath). This implies a distinction between rational knowledge and aesthetic knowledge. Whereas the former is thinking *about* art, the latter is a thinking *with* art, or with artistic material or forms. Although Herzogenrath's notion of practical aesthetics has much in common with Bennett's, I follow Bennett because of the special ramifications of her understanding of "practical." In what follows, I explain what these ramifications are.

To conceive aesthetic perception as a form of thinking has at first sight much in common with French philosopher and art historian Hubert Damisch's notion of art as developed in his *Theory of the /Cloud/* (1972), *The Origin of Perspective* (1987), and *The Judgment of Paris* (1992). Damisch argues that artworks perform an intellectual or philosophical project. He never deals with art as mere passive manifestations of a culture or a historical period, nor as the product of the artist's intention. Instead, he conceives art as a special mode of thinking. An artwork is for Damisch a reflection—not according to the passive definition of the word, as a mirror image, but to the active definition: as an act of thought.

Damisch's notion of art as a mode of thinking differs, however, from the way practical aesthetics thinks with art. With art as a mode of thinking, Damisch resists the disciplinary principles of art history to understand artworks historically. The full significance of artworks cannot be appreciated through history as an absolute concept. History is, but also has, a subject. The subject of art engenders general, transhistorical, and philosophical questions.

Practical Aesthetics

> Historical are the parameters within which a specific artist works, the idioms that have been passed on to her, and the specific articulation of her answers to a more general problematic or issue. It is at least also philosophical or theoretical and, hence, transhistorical. This general issue cannot be reduced to historical terms. It pertains to the world of thought that we are steeped in at all times. (van Alphen 2005)[1]

This notion of art as thinking has resulted in a concept Damisch created, namely "theoretical object." Damisch explains this concept in an interview with Yve-Alain Bois. A theoretical object

> obliges you to do theory but also furnishes you with the means of doing it. Thus, if you agree to accept it on theoretical terms, it will produce effects around itself . . . [and] forces us to ask ourselves what theory is. It is posed in theoretical terms; it produces theory; and it necessitates a reflection on theory. (Bois et al. 1998: 8)

Bal comments: "In the dynamic between the art works as objects, their viewers, and the time in which these come together, accompanied by the social buzz that surround both, a compelling collective thought process emerges" (Bal 2010: 7).

The thought process set into motion by a theoretical object is intellectual and rational, even though it is generated by artistic work. The mode of thinking activated by practical aesthetics is, in contrast, sense-based. Bennett explains: "The object in this sense is not merely the subject of layered interpretations but is, in essence, the infolding and unfolding of ideas and perceptions" (Bennett 2012: 9). These perceptions are not restricted to sensorial perceptions but also to the transmission of affects. As she argues, affect is the natural medium of aesthetics (13).

Bennett distinguishes philosophical from practical aesthetics, as concerned with points of theoretical difference versus concerned "to use ideas about aesthetics to illuminate the connections and processes that give life to visual culture" (26). That concern of practical aesthetics makes affective transmissions vitally important: "it is because affect is what gives us the feeling of life; it makes us feel alive . . . and in turn gives images life" (26). Affects move in the space between the visceral body and the consciousness, and manifest themselves bodily. The disciplinary boundaries of art history and visual culture studies have difficulty in taking the mobile quality of affect into consideration:

> Unlike meaning, iconography or a formal quality, affect is not easily anchored in an image. It may be expressed, activated or incited by an image; but at the same time, affect does not always come *from* a single image. . . . Moreover, strong affect seems sometimes to pursue the image; as Nietzsche argues, it seeks out effigies against which to vent. (21; emphasis in original text)

Because of the central role of affect and its mobile quality, practical aesthetics is transdisciplinary, for it relates a great number of disciplines to one another: from art history and visual culture studies, to philosophy, politics, psychology, sociology, and more.

In her fundamental assessment of practical aesthetics, Bennett emphasizes one more element: contemporaneity. Affect is not transmitted from the past to the present. When it concerns an image or a text, it is in the act of reading or viewing that affect is being transmitted or released. Because viewing and reading take place in the present of performing the practice of practical aesthetics, this transdisciplinary focus is necessarily anchored in contemporaneous affects, feelings, and emotions. And many of these contemporaneous affects are deeply political. The importance of the political is the final element I would like to foreground as a defining element of practical aesthetics. As Bennett explains, 9/11 reoriented many art practices to the real. Affects and emotions have become increasingly the focus of political analysis:

> The intractable pull—and insufficiency of the empirical facts of the event have, at the same time as making actuality and politics a necessary topic, engendered a focus on how the event is apprehended: on perception and feeling as constitutive of the event itself. (Bennett 2012: 20)

To put this view to the test of its yield for understanding specific artworks, I will now read a political artwork in practical-aesthetic terms. I will not focus on assertions, denunciations, or programmatic statements in this work; not only because they are absent in it, but, more importantly, doing so would violate the sense-based orientation of practical aesthetics. The aesthetics of this artwork is informed by and derived from a practical, real-world encounter, namely the conflict between Israel and Palestine about the ownership of their homeland. The specificity of its aesthetics "is in turn capable of being used or put into effect in a real situation" (Bennett 2012: 2) by actively transforming the trauma caused by this destructive conflict into a memory.

The Politics of the House

What does one destroy when one destroys a house? First of all, the building that the word "house" refers to. Although today more and more people live in tents or other temporary constructions, and a house can also be a houseboat, we think of an architectural construction, a building, in which people live and have made their home. But the word "house" also stands for "family." When we talk about the House of Orange, we do not refer to one of their royal palaces. The term covers the complete lineage and ancestry of the family, not only the family members that are still alive. In other words, the word "house" also refers to a family and its roots, to genealogical memory.

In languages such as English and Dutch, this use of the word "house" is metaphorical. Only in special contexts and cases does the word "house" have this meaning of "family" as intertwined with the architectural meaning. The best-known example is Edgar Allen Poe's story *The Fall of the House of Usher*. *The Fall* concerns primarily a family and not a building, although the collapse of the building materializes the downfall, indeed the extinction of the family. In Arab and Hebrew, however, one word denotes these two different meanings systematically. The Arab "bait" and the Hebrew "bet" are homonyms. They each concern a concept, or two words that are both spelled and pronounced identically, but have different meanings. In those languages the destruction of a house is ambiguous: it refers to the destruction of a building that serves as a home to people and to the destruction of the genealogical memory of a family; and the one through the other, because the physical construction is the equivalent of the roots of the family it harbors.

In the recent art projects by Marjan Teeuwen, the term "destroyed house" contains yet another ambiguity.[2] Most titles of these projects are specified by the location of the house: *Destroyed House Krasnoyarsk (2009), Destroyed House Piet Mondriaanstraat (2010–11), Destroyed House Leiden (2015), Destroyed House Gaza (2017), Destroyed House Arles (2019)* and, most recently, *Destroyed House Kyoto (2020)*. All these projects were interventions in discarded houses. Destruction was their fate. Teeuwen's interventions in these ruined houses look at first sight like a further destruction of houses that are already being destroyed. She breaks away floors or walls, which seems to perform the finishing stroke. The project of the artist is, then, not an act of creation, but an act of destruction; or better, creation is a form of destruction. But there is more to it.

Teeuwen reuses the remainders of the ruined houses. They are piled up; windows or other kinds of openings are closed off by leftover materials. She also creates sculptures out of debris of used materials. The reused materials are selected and categorized according to materials and colors. Her works demonstrate an obsessive practice of ordering and structuring. Whereas a house designated to be destroyed tends to look chaotic, Teeuwen's interventions create order and structure. Her ordered piles of whatever kind of materials adds harmony to the desolate spaces of the deserted building, no longer a house, for no longer the haven of a family. This creation of harmony out of chaos and destruction is, however, not an end in itself. The beauty of the practice of ordering is highly significant; it symbolizes, embodies the ordering activity of memory. The activity of memory is explicitly evoked by the titles of a series of works she made between 2007 and 2010 in the Archive—series: *Archive 1-4, Archive Sheddak SM's, Archive Johannesburg*, and a recent commission, *Archive Temporarily Hall of Justice Amsterdam 1-5*. Although not situated in discarded houses, and not dealing with architectural interventions like destroying walls, floors, and ceilings, these works share all characteristics with the *Destroyed Houses*. Archives are physical storages of memory; in archival processes, we can recognize the activity of memory. Archives and memory collect objects and events. But they do not do this arbitrarily. Archives and memory are selective in how they collect. If they did not select, they would end up as arbitrary storage. But the ordering activity of archives and memory implies that many objects and events are discarded, refused, repressed, and forgotten. What is selected to be kept and cherished is not just stored. Archives and memory categorize; they put together objects or events with similar qualities. They create links between objects and events that are different in some respects but share qualities in other respects.[3]

Thinking with Archival Ordering, or the Politics of Destruction

This view of the archive and/or as memory suggests that Teeuwen's interventions in discarded houses should be understood as archival practices embodying the work of memory. Her creation of order in chaos concerns both a rebuilding/the transformation of the house and a return of memory to the house. She visualizes and materializes the house-as-memory, the work of memory, and the rooting of the people who lived there, which are embodied by the house. Not the roots, but the rooting. From this perspective, it is important to notice that her interventions in the discarded houses do not only consist of pilings of selected leftover materials. She also opens up floors or removes walls, creating views in spaces that were so far closed off. Connections and associations established by the activity of memory are enabled by opening up and connecting all spaces in these houses. The house as embodiment of memory depends on the intensification and materialization of links, relations, and connections, performed through opening up the surfaces that so far blocked views.

The different projects of the *Destroyed House* series that Teeuwen realized have in common are that they create order out of chaos and beauty out of ugliness. Moreover, they deconstruct the notion of destruction itself, proposing creation not as the opposite of destruction, but as intimately entangled with it, as its precondition. By performing creation as an activity that establishes a new architectural sculpture with a new order, structure, links, and relations, she evokes the ordering, archival activity of memory. In fact, memory is already suggested by the location of her performances of creation: the house, not only referring to an architectural construction but also to the rooting of human beings and genealogical memory.

When she realized her *Destroyed Houses* in several locations in the Netherlands, and in Russia with *Destroyed House Krasnoyarsk*, this evocation of memory remained abstract. The embodiment of memory in these projects remained implicit because no specific memories were involved, no specific pasts imposed themselves. Most visitors of the *Destroyed House* series were impressed by the obsessiveness of the performance that resulted in this stirring, unconventional beauty, but they did not make the association with the "work of memory." In the case of *Destroyed House Gaza*, the recognition of the destroyed house as an embodiment of the work of memory is unavoidable. It is the context of Gaza that transforms the abstract idea of memory into a concrete one.

The conflict between Israel and Palestine originates in historical ruptures of their respective bonds between the land and the people.[4] The ancient Jewish people were exiled by the Romans from the land they felt connected to and identified with. It was only after 2,000 years, in 1948, that they were able to return to the land they originally came from by establishing the State of Israel. This led to a relay of exilic existence: Palestinians have experienced exile in more recent times, since the foundation of that state. This has resulted in the expulsion of hundreds of thousands of Palestinians from the land in which they have been rooted for thousands of years.

The Israeli/Palestinian conflict is not just an armed conflict fought by means of conventional weapons. Ultimately it is a war on memory, in which houses and trees are employed as powerful instruments of warfare. Both states claim to be rooted in the same land, and those claims are based on memory. Houses and trees have become important

Practical Aesthetics

cultural symbols that are central in their respective articulations of rootedness. As one scholar put it, these cultural symbols claiming rootedness and ownership over the land have become major stakes in this war of memory, "of which some of the most salient examples are Israel's massive uprooting of Palestinian olive trees, the punitive demolition of Palestinian homes, and the Israeli overplanting of bulldozed Palestinian orchards and villages with non-native pine forests," and the construction of settlements in East Jerusalem and at the West Bank (van Gelder 2016). Israeli legal scholar Irus Braverman suggests that the seeming unimportance of houses and trees to the Israeli-Palestinian conflict harbors a denial of their true significance. He argues that acts of planting/uprooting and building/unbuilding are in fact "acts of war," regulated by a range of legal strategies (Bravermann 2007, 2009).

In the context of this memory war in which houses and trees are powerful cultural symbols as well as instruments of warfare, *Destroyed House Gaza* does not evoke memory abstractly, but utterly concretely and politically, albeit implicitly—as it becomes art. In difference from political journalism and propaganda, political art achieves its convincing effect by an appeal to viewers to reconsider their routine convictions because they are touched on an affective as well as an intellectual level. This makes Teeuwen's interventions instances of practical aesthetics: in *Destroyed House Gaza*, they are at the same time interventions in the Israeli/Palestinian memory war, making visible that the Arab homonym "bait" and the Hebrew homonym "bet" refer to the destruction of a building that serves as a home to people as well as to the destruction of the genealogical memory of a family. For the rooting of human beings is embodied in the cultural symbol of the house; their uprooting in its destruction.

Transforming Trauma into Memory

The house in which Teeuwen performed her intervention in 2016–17 is located in the town of Khan Younis, near Rafah, in the South of Gaza near the Egyptian border. Since 1948, the town is a major part of a refugee camp. The center of the town has been demolished in order to create a buffer zone between Gaza and Egypt. The concrete wall, which Israel built to close Gaza off from Israel, also continues here between Gaza and Egypt. The house put at Teeuwen's disposal was owned by a member of Hamas and bombed by Israel in the 2014 Gaza War. The bomb created a big hole in the roof and in the floor underneath. One son of the owner was killed by the attack. After the bomb attack, the house was uninhabitable and waiting to be demolished and rebuilt.

The first thing Teeuwen did was dig out the soil under the first floor; she removed one and a half meter of sand. Then she opened up the floors of the second floor by cutting open three sides of the floor; the fourth side remained intact. As a result, the floors folded downward due to their weight. Subsequently most of the floors were hanging vertically, some of them supported by props preventing a completely vertical hanging. Thus, they replaced the walls that the bomb had blown away. By means of opening up the floors and digging out the soil beneath the ground floor, all the spaces in the house became visually connected and new perspectives were created. This intervention created depth, height, distance, and, as a result, vistas/views in an architectural space formerly consisting of two closed-off floors connected by a staircase. Whereas in the original building one could see only the room in which one found oneself, after these interventions one had visual access to all the house's spaces at the same time. The illusion of an endless space was created, with new spaces behind those nearest, reminiscent of the images of the eighteen-century artist Piranesi.

Debris and used materials from the house were reused for the construction of five new walls and two enormous piles, a black one and a white one, reaching from the ground to almost the roof of the building. Windows and other openings in the outer walls were closed with rubbish. These constructions are not creations ex nihilo but reorderings of what was already there. This reordering evoked archival organizations, of which memory is a prime instance. By closing off all openings to the space outside the house, Teeuwen transformed the house into an inner space. The suggestion of being inside an inner space was also evoked by the two enormous piles, because they looked like the spines of bodies. Not realistically, but symbolically functionally; they were like the nerve centers of this inner space. The black nerve center referred to the black spots and traces on walls and floors left by the bomb that had hit the house. The white nerve center referred to the original white color of the walls. The five walls covering the open

Figure 23.1 Marjan Teeuwen, Destroyed House Gaza #1 (2018).

Practical Aesthetics

Figure 23.2 Marjan Teeuwen, Destroyed House Gaza #3 (2018).

architectural structure created out of debris filtered the light into a very fine grid of white dots. This grid of light did not illuminate the inner space; it did not produce lightened areas, but became part of the reordered structuring Teeuwen's interventions brought about. Light was not used to enable vision but was dealt with as one of the materials that constituted the inner space. The grid of light and stone closing off the openings in the walls were like a new skin to the house.

On top of a low pile of ordered stones, Teeuwen showed the fragmented remains of the bomb that had destroyed the house and killed one of its inhabitants. All other material used was insignificant as such; its reuse evoked the ordering process and activity of memory, but not specific memories. The remains of the bomb, however, distinguished themselves from the other materials through signifying a specific memory: the moment in the forty-five years history of the building that the house was destroyed by being hit by bombs and grenades. The briefest moment in time definitively modified the spatial structure. The small display of remains of bombs and grenade shards could easily be overlooked because it was much less overwhelming and impressive than the obsessively structured space in which it was placed. But one could also claim that this modest exhibit *is* the center of Teeuwen's *Destroyed House*, because it is here that memory is not evoked as an ordering, archival process, but through a specific object of memory. It is here, in these traces of that intensely loaded moment, that the location of the *Destroyed House*, Gaza, is doing practical aesthetics.

Teeuwen has also transformed the bombed, ruined house into a "site of memory." This term was introduced by French historian Pierre Nora (Nora 1989 and 1996). These sites are places, objects, or other phenomena which have become of symbolic significance to a particular group of people when the continuity between past and present is broken. Monuments and memorials, as well as specific days of the year during which a loss or event is commemorated, can function as sites of memory. Although houses, olive trees, and pine trees already have symbolic significance in Palestine and Israel, this significance is general and not tied to specific houses or trees. Teeuwen's interventions in *Destroyed House Gaza* have intensified the symbolical significance of the house and turned it into a site of memory.

After it was finished in December 2016, people from Gaza visited the house, not just to admire the artistic project, but also to reflect on and to commemorate the broken bond between their land and their people. The space that a house is, and demarcates, commemorates the time that the bond between land and people was not yet broken; it commemorates the house and the family that was rooted in that house. But how is it possible that the spatial dimension of a ruined house can effectuate the reestablishment of memory of the past, of a dimension that is temporal? This is possible because the bombed house is more than a ruined, artistic architectural construction. The materiality of the spatial ruin already embodies time; the holes and wounds caused by the bomb attack embody the temporality of trauma. The chaos and damage caused by the bomb attack is not only material damage, but also a temporal havoc. It was an event, a historical moment, which could not be experienced when it happened. The event, literally a bomb attack, was unimaginable, too enormous in its devastating and killing effects, for the people to experience and work through. The traces of that event could be recognized all over the space of the house.[5] They are the symptoms of a failed experience, in other words of trauma. This failed experience makes it impossible to remember the events voluntarily. In order to do so, the conditions for memory first had to be developed and made available affectively. This is precisely what Teeuwen's *Destroyed House Gaza* has done.

This implies that Teeuwen's aesthetic interventions in *Destroyed House Gaza* did not just transform a discarded space into an artistic statement and an embodiment of memory. Rather, she transformed the blocked temporality of trauma into the temporality of memory. An event that because of its "explosive" nature could not be worked through is transformed into a memory by setting up the conditions for commemoration. Transforming chaos into order and transforming a ruin into an architectural sculpture, Teeuwen transforms trauma into memory. That is Teeuwen's contribution to the restoration of the cultural, social health of a people confined in reiterated traumatogenic situations. It is clear that her aesthetic interventions are "practical" because they were informed by the practical, real-world encounters, namely the Palestinian-Israeli conflict. It is also clear that this practical aesthetics is sense- and affect-based; the archival ordering is not a conventional signification of memory, but embodies memory on the basis of unconventional affective processes. My perception was affect- and sense-based but it was also a form of thinking. I have been *thinking with* Teeuwen's art, which created practical-aesthetically a world in which the temporality of trauma was transformed in the temporality of memory.

Practical Aesthetics

Figure 23.3 Marjan Teeuwen, Destryed House Gaza #6 (2018).

Notes

1. For more elaborate discussion of Damisch's thinking, see the chapter "Thinking About Art in History," in my book *Art In Mind: How Contemporary Images Shape Thought* (2005).
2. This reading of Marjan Teeuwen's work is based on a more extensive analysis in *Marjan Teeuwen. Destroyed House* (van Alphen and Doorman 2017).
3. See for an analysis of the principles that determine archival organizations my book *Staging the Archive: Art and Photography in Times of New Media* (2015).
4. See Carol Bardenstein, "Trees, Forests, and the Shaping of Palestinian and Israeli Collective Memory" (1999).
5. For an analysis of trauma, and its relation to memory, see my publications "Symptoms of Discursivity: Experience, Memory, and Trauma" (1999), "Caught By Images," (2005), and *Caught By History: Holocaust Effects in Art, Literature, and Theory* (1998).

References

Alphen, E. v. (1998), *Caught By History: Holocaust Effects in Art, Literature, and Theory*, Stanford: Stanford University Press.
Alphen, E. v. (1999), "Symptoms of Discursivity: Experience, Memory, and Trauma," in M. Bal, J. Crewe, and L. Spitzer (eds.), *Acts of Memory*, 24–38, Hanover: University Press of New England.

Alphen, E. v. (2005), "Caught By Images", in *Art In Mind: How Contemporary Images Shape Thought*, Chicago: The University of Chicago Press.

Alphen, E. v. (2015), *Staging the Archive: Art and Photography in Times of New Media*, London: Reaktion books.

Alphen, E. v., and M. Doorman (2017), *Marjan Teeuwen: Destroyed House*, Amsterdam: Valiz.

Bal, M. (2010), *Of What One Cannot Speak: Doris Salcedo's Political Art*, Chicago: University of Chicago Press.

Bardenstein, C. (1999), "Trees, Forests, and the Shaping of Palestinian and Israeli Collective Memory," in M. Bal, J. Crewe, and L. Spitzer (eds.), *Acts of Memory*, 148–68, Hanover: University Press of New England.

Bennett, J. (2012), Practical Aesthetics. Events, Affect and Art after 9/11, London & New York: Tauris.

Bois, Y.-A., D. Hollier, R. Krauss, and H. Damisch (1998), "A Conversation with Hubert Damisch", *October*, 85: 3–17.

Braverman, I. (2007), "Powers of Illegality: House Demolitions and Resistance in East Jeruzalem," *Law and Social Inquiry*, 32 (2): 333–72.

Braverman, I. (2009), *Planted Flags. Trees, Land and Law in Israeli/Palestine*, Cambridge: Cambridge University Press.

Gelder, L. v. (2016), "Performing Rootedness in a Landscape of War: Trees as Sites of Israeli and Palestinian Cultural Memory", MA thesis, Leiden University.

Nora, P. (1989), "Between Memory and History: Les Lieux de Mémoire," *Representations*, 26: 7–24.

Nora, P. (1996), *Realms of Memory: Rethinking the French Past*, vols 1–4, New York: Columbia University Press.

CONTRIBUTORS

John Luther Adams is a composer whose life and work are deeply rooted in the natural world.

Adams was awarded the 2014 Pulitzer Prize for Music for his symphonic work *Become Ocean*, as well as a Grammy Award for "Best Contemporary Classical Composition" (2014). *Inuksuit*, his outdoor work for up to ninety-nine percussionists, is regularly performed all over the world.

Columbia University has honored Adams with the William Schuman Award "to recognize the lifetime achievement of an American composer whose works have been widely performed and generally acknowledged to be of lasting significance."

A recipient of the Heinz Award for his contributions to raising environmental awareness, JLA has also been honored with the Nemmers Prize from Northwestern University "for melding the physical and musical worlds into a unique artistic vision that transcends stylistic boundaries."

Born in 1953, JLA grew up in the South and in the suburbs of New York City. He studied composition with James Tenney at the California Institute of the Arts, where he was in the first graduating class (in 1973). In the mid-1970s, he became active in the campaign for the Alaska National Interest Lands Conservation Act, and subsequently served as executive director of the Northern Alaska Environmental Center.

Adams has taught at Harvard University, the Oberlin Conservatory, Bennington College, and the University of Alaska. He has also served as composer in residence with the Anchorage Symphony, Anchorage Opera, Fairbanks Symphony, Arctic Chamber Orchestra, and the Alaska Public Radio Network.

The music of John Luther Adams is recorded on Cantaloupe, Cold Blue, New World, Mode, and New Albion, and his books are published by Wesleyan University Press.

Mieke Bal is a cultural theorist, critic, video artist, and occasional curator. She works on gender, migratory culture, psychoanalysis, and the critique of capitalism. Her thirty-eight books include a trilogy on political art: *Endless Andness* (on abstraction), *Thinking in Film* (on video installation), both 2013, and *Of What One Cannot Speak* (on sculpture, 2010). Her work comes together in *A Mieke Bal Reader* (2006). In 2016, appeared *In Medias Res: Inside Nalini Malani's Shadow Plays* (Hatje Cantz), and in Spanish, *Tiempos Trastornados* on the politics of visuality (AKAL). Her video project *Madame B*, with Michelle Williams Gamaker, is widely exhibited, in 2017 in Museum Aboa Vetus and Ars Nova in Turku, and combined with paintings by Edvard Munch in the Munch Museum in Oslo. Her most recent film is *Reasonable Doubt*, on René Descartes and

Contributors

Queen Kristina (2016). The installation of that project has been shown in Kraków, and in 2017 in Amsterdam and Warsaw.
www.miekebal.org

Jill Bennett is an Australian Research Council Laureate Fellow and Director of the National Institute for Experimental Arts at the University of New South Wales, Sydney. She is Founding Director of The Big Anxiety: festival of arts + science + people and has curated/produced many art projects relating to trauma, memory, and mental health. Her practice combines the development of 3D immersive environments with participatory exhibition design and the theoretical study of arts and mental health. Her books include *Empathic Vision: Affect, Trauma and Contemporary Art*, and *Practical Aesthetics: Events, Affects and Art After 9/11*, as well as monographs on contemporary art and curatorial practice. Her research involves a number of collaborations with neuropsychologists (on memory loss), psychosocial researchers (on public engagement), mental health researchers, and those with lived experience of neurodiversity and mental health.

Johannes Binotto is a lecturer for media studies and film theory at the Universities of Zurich and Basel and at the Lucerne School of Art and Design. Apart from that, he is continuously teaching on film and psychoanalysis at the Zurich Lacan-Seminar and at the Psychiatric Hospital Burghölzli. His research is specifically devoted to the intersections of psychoanalytical theory, philosophy of technology, film, and literature with a particular interest in cinematic and literary techniques as "affective effects." He has published extensively and on such diverse topics such as the gaze, abject bodies, male hysteria, medias of paranoia, or on spaces of anxiety in film, literature, and popular culture. Johannes Binotto's dissertation on the Freudian uncanny and its spatial representation in art, literature, and cinema was awarded in 2011 with the annual prize of the Faculty of Arts at Zurich University and was published in 2013 by Diaphanes under the title *TAT/ORT: Das Unheimliche und sein Raum in der Kultur*. Johannes Binotto is currently working on an habilitation project on "Disfigurations: Towards a Poetics of Cinematic Devices" in which he examines traditional cinematic devices such as rear projection, matte painting, or split screen for their subversive potential. Personal homepage: www.schnittstellen.me.

François J. Bonnet is a Franco-Swiss composer, writer, and theoretician. Based in Paris, he is the artistic director of the prestigious Ina GRM, an institute founded in 1958 and the birthplace of musique concrète, and also the curator of the Recollection *GRM* series on Editions Mego label. He has published several books (*The Order of Sounds, A Sonorous Archipelago*, and *The Infra-World* have been published in English by Urbanomic). His last work to date, *Après la mort*, was published in 2017 by éditions de l'Eclat. Under the moniker Kassel Jaeger, Bonnet has also been releasing acclaimed works on CD and vinyl.

Marcus Boon is a writer and professor of English at York University in Toronto. He is the author of *The Road of Excess: A History of Writers on Drugs* (2002) and *In Praise of*

Contributors

Copying (2010) and is coauthor with Timothy Morton and Eric Cazdyn of *Nothing: Three Inquiries in Buddhism* (2015). He coedited a collection of writings on *Practice* in the Visual Arts with Gabriel Levine (MIT/Whitechapel Documents of Contemporary Arts series, 2018) and is working on a new edition of William Burroughs and Brion Gysin's *The Third Mind* with Davis Schneiderman. He recently finished work on a book on the ontology of music called *The Politics of Vibration* and is working on a monograph on Catherine Christer Hennix. He writes about music for *The Wire*. www.marcusboon.com

Eugenie Brinkema is Associate Professor of Contemporary Literature and Media at the Massachusetts Institute of Technology. She holds a PhD in Modern Culture and Media from Brown University in 2010. Her research in film and media studies focuses on violence, affect, sexuality, aesthetics, and ethics in texts ranging from the horror film to gonzo pornography, from structuralist film to the visual and temporal forms of terror. Articles have appeared in the journals *Angelaki*, *Camera Obscura*, *Criticism*, *Differences*, *Discourse*, *The Journal of Speculative Philosophy*, *The Journal of Visual Culture*, *Polygraph*, *Qui Parle*, and *World Picture*. Her first book, *The Forms of the Affects*, was published with Duke University Press in 2014. Recent work includes an article on love and negative space in *Blue Is the Warmest Color*.

Christoph Ernst is a research assistant for Media Studies at the University of Bonn. Main research interests in diagrammatic thinking, interface theory, media theory and imagination; theories of tacit knowledge in the context of digital media; aesthetics of audiovisual media (film, television, photography). Last publications: *Zukünftige Medien. Eine Einführung*, Wiesbaden (with Jens Schröter, forthcoming 2020), *Diagramme zwischen Metapher und Explikation. Studien zur Medien- und Filmtheorie der Diagrammatik* (forthcoming 2020)

Michael N. Goddard is a reader in Film at Winchester University, England. He has been teaching and researching in the United Kingdom since 2007; prior to this he had a number of positions in Poland, Australia, and France. During this time, I have organized several international conferences on The Fall, Subcultures and Lifestyles in Eastern Europe, Polish Cinema, and Noise as well as numerous seminar series. He was involved with the foundation of the journal *Studies in Eastern European Cinema* and worked as both reviews editor and coeditor and am now serving on the editorial board. He was also a founding member of the Network for European Cinema and Media Studies (NECS) and served for three years on the publications committee working toward the successful establishment of the *NECSUS* journal among other activities. As well as actively developing an international research and teaching profile, Michael has been active in numerous conferences and other events in the United Kingdom and Europe, North America, Latin America, and the Antipodes and has delivered invited presentations in many of these locations. Recently, he was awarded the CAPES/Science without Borders Special Visiting Researcher Fellowship, valued at 46,000£, for a three-year project with researchers from UNISINOS, Brazil on Cites, Creative Industries and Popular Music

Contributors

Scenes (2014–16). Michael is the course leader of the Film, Television and Moving Image MA at Westminster. Prior to this he was PGR Director of the School of Arts and Media at the University of Salford. He has also been a visiting professor at the University of Łódź, Poland (2004–7), and before that held numerous positions including lecturer in Television at the Australian Film, Television and Radio School (AFTRS) and Lecteur d'anglais at the Charles V Institute, of the University of Paris 7.

Julius Greve is a lecturer and research associate at the Institute for English and American Studies, University of Oldenburg, Germany. He is the author of *Shreds of Matter: Cormac McCarthy and the Concept of Nature* (Dartmouth College Press, 2018), and he has published numerous essays on McCarthy, Mark Z. Danielewski, François Laruelle, and critical theory. Greve has co-edited *America and the Musical Unconscious* (Atropos, 2015), *Superpositions: Laruelle and the Humanities* (Rowman & Littlefield International, 2017), "Cormac McCarthy Between Worlds" (*EJAS*-special issue, 2017), and *Spaces and Fictions of the Weird and the Fantastic: Ecologies, Geographies, Oddities* (Palgrave Macmillan, 2019). He is currently working on a manuscript that delineates the relation between modern poetics and ventriloquism.

Sanne Krogh Groth is Associate Professor in Musicology at the Department of Arts and Cultural Sciences, Lund University, Sweden, and is since 2011 editor-in-chief of the Danish online journal *Seismograf.org*. She has previously been affiliated as researcher at the National Library of Denmark and as assistant professor at Performance-design, Roskilde University. In 2010, she achieved her PhD from the University of Copenhagen. Her present field of research includes postcolonial and performative aspects of electronic music and sound art. She is author of the book *Politics and Aesthetics in Electronic Music* (2014), publishes continuously in international academic journals, and has occasionally co-curated events and exhibitions.

Bernd Herzogenrath is Professor of American Literature and Culture at Goethe University of Frankfurt am Main, Germany. He is the author of *An Art of Desire: Reading Paul Auster* and *An American Body/Politic: A Deleuzian Approach*, and is editor of a.o. *The Farthest Place: The Music of John Luther Adams* and *Deleuze/Guattari & Ecology*. At the moment, he is planning a project, *cinapses: thinking/film*, which brings together scholars from film studies, philosophy, and the neurosciences (members include António Damasio and Alva Noë). His latest publications include the collections *The Films of Bill Morrison. Aesthetics of the Archive* (2017) and *Film as Philosophy* (2017). He is also (together with Patricia Pisters) the main editor of the media-philosophical book series *thinking|media* with Bloomsbury.

Tim Ingold is Professor of Social Anthropology at the University of Aberdeen, and a Fellow of the British Academy and the Royal Society of Edinburgh. Following twenty-five years at the University of Manchester, Ingold moved in 1999 to Aberdeen, where he established the UK's newest Department of Anthropology. Ingold has carried out

Contributors

ethnographic fieldwork among Saami and Finnish people in Lapland, and has written on environment, technology, and social organization in the circumpolar North, the role of animals in human society, issues in human ecology, and evolutionary theory in anthropology, biology, and history. In his more recent work, he has explored the links between environmental perception and skilled practice. Ingold is currently writing and teaching on issues on the interface between anthropology, archaeology, art, and architecture. He is the author of *The Perception of the Environment* (2000), *Lines* (2007), *Being Alive* (2011), *Making* (2013), *The Life of Lines* (2015), and *Anthropology and/as Education* (2017).

jan jagodzinski is a professor of Visual art and Media Education in the Department of Secondary Education, University of Alberta in Edmonton, Alberta, Canada. He is a coeditor with Mark Bracher of the book series *Pedagogy, Psychoanalysis, Transformation*. He is also a series editor for *Educational Futures*. Book credits: *The Anamorphic I/i* (1996); *Postmodern Dilemmas: Outrageous Essays in Art&Art Education* (1997); *Pun(k) Deconstruction: Experifigural Writings in Art&Art Education* (1997); editor of *Pedagogical Desire: Transference, Seduction and the Question of Ethics* (2002); *Youth Fantasies: The Perverse Landscape of the Media* (2004); *Musical Fantasies: A Lacanian Approach* (2005); *Television and Youth: Televised Paranoia* (2008); *The Deconstruction of the Oral Eye: Art and Its Education in an Era of Designer Capitalism* (2010), *Misreading Postmodern Antigone: Marco Bellocchio's Devil in the Flesh (Diavolo in Corpo)* (2011), editor of *Psychoanalyzing Cinema: A Productive Encounter of Lacan, Deleuze, and Žižek* (2012); *Arts Based Research: A Critique and Proposal* (with Jason Wallin) (2013). Editor: *The Precarious Future of Education* (2017). Editor: *What is Art Education? After Deleuze and Guattari* (2017). Editor: *Athropocene, Ecology, Pedagogy: The Future in Question* (2018), Schizoanalytic Ventures At the End of the World: Film, Video, Art and Pedagogical Challenges (2019), Pedagogical Explorations in a Posthuman Age: Essays on Designer Capitalism, Eco-Aestheticism, Visual and Popular Culture as West-East Meet (2020).

Tomáš Jirsa is a postdoctoral researcher and lecturer in comparative literature and media studies at Palacký University, Olomouc, Czech Republic. His work traces the relations between modern literature and visual arts; affect studies, media theory, and contemporary music video. After pursuing his doctoral studies at the University of California, Los Angeles, and Paris-Sorbonne University, he holds a PhD in 2012 from Charles University, where he subsequently taught at the Institute of Comparative Literature until 2017. In 2015 and 2017, he was awarded a junior fellowship from IKKM (Das Internationale Kolleg für Kulturtechnikforschung und Medienphilosophie) at Bauhaus University, Weimar. He is the author of two books in Czech, *Physiognomy of Writing: In the Folds of Literary Ornament* (2012) and *Facing the Formless: Affective and Visual Figures in Modern Literature* (2016), and numerous articles published in English (*Central Europe, Zeitschrift für Medien—und Kulturtechnik, Iluminace*). Currently, he is coediting (with Ernst van Alphen) the collected volume *How to Do Things with Affects: Affective Operations in Art, Literature, and New Media*, to be published by Brill in 2018.

Contributors

Along with translations from French in the fields of philosophy, cultural theory, and film history, he also translates French films.

Katerina Krtilova is a researcher and coordinator of the PhD program "Epistemologies of Aesthetic Practices," a collaborative project of ETH Zurich, University of Zurich, and the Zurich University of the Arts. In 2017, she defended her dissertation on Vilém Flusser's media philosophy at Bauhaus-Universität Weimar. In her research, she focuses on media philosophy, German media theory, and the relations between reflexivity, performativity, and materiality in twentieth-century philosophy. She initiated a number of German-Czech projects in the field of media theory and philosophy, and founded in 2016 together with Kateřina Svatoňová the research group Teorie/filosofie médií (Media theory/philosophy) at the Faculty of Arts, Charles University, Prague. Recent publications: *Mizení: Fenomény, mediální praktiky a techniky na prahu zjevného*, Praha: Karolinum 2017 (ed. together with Kateřina Svatoňová), Praha: Academia 2016; "Technisches Begreifen. Von ‚undinglichen Informationen'zu tangible interfaces," in: Jörg Sternagel, Fabian Goppelsröder (Hg.), Techniken des Leibes, Weilerswist-Metternich: Velbrück, 2016; "Can We Think Computation in Images or Numbers? Critical Remarks on Vilém Flusser's Philosophy of Digital Technologies," in: Flusser Studies 22/ 2016, www.flusserstudies.net.

Christoph Menke is Professor of Practical Philosophy at Goethe Universität Frankfurt am Main. Ph.D. 1987: University of Konstanz, Philosophy; "Habilitation" 1995: Freie Universität Berlin, Philosophy. 1997–9: Associate Professor, New School for Social Research, New York; 1999–2008: Full Professor, University of Potsdam.

Book publications in English: *The Sovereignty of Art: Aesthetic Negativity after Adorno and Derrida*, MIT Press 1998; *Reflections of Equality*, Stanford UP 2006; *Tragic Play: Tragedy. Irony and Theater from Sophocles to Beckett*, Columbia UP 2009; *Force: A Fundamental Concept of Aesthetic Anthropology*, Fordham UP 2012; *Law and Violence: Christoph Menke in Dialogue*, Manchester UP 2018.

Bill Morrison's films often combine rare archival material set to contemporary music. His work was recently honored with a mid-career retrospective at the Museum of Modern Art, New York, from October 2014 to March 2015.

Morrison is a Guggenheim fellow and has received the Alpert Award for the Arts, an NEA Creativity Grant, Creative Capital, and a fellowship from the Foundation for Contemporary Arts. His theatrical projection design has been recognized with two Bessie awards and an Obie Award. "Decasia" (67 min, 2002), a collaboration with the composer Michael Gordon, was selected to the US Library of Congress' 2013 National Film Registry.

"Spark of Being" (68 min, 2010), a collaboration with trumpeter/composer Dave Douglas, won the Los Angeles Film Critics Award for Best Independent Film of 2011.

"The Miners' Hymns" (52 min, 2011), a collaboration with the composer Jóhann Jóhannsson, was described as one of "the best and most beautiful films of the year" by the *Huffington Post*.

"The Great Flood" (78 min, 2013), a collaboration with guitarist/composer Bill Frisell, won the Smithsonian Ingenuity Award of 2014 for historical scholarship.

Morrison has collaborated with some of the most influential composers and performers of our time, including John Adams, Maya Beiser, Gavin Bryars, Dave Douglas, Richard Einhorn, Erik Friedlander, Bill Frisell, Philip Glass, Michael Gordon, Michael Harrison, Ted Hearne, Vijay Iyer, Jóhann Jóhannsson, Kronos Quartet, David Lang, David T. Little, Michael Montes, Steve Reich, Todd Reynolds, Aleksandra Vrebalov, and Julia Wolfe, among many others. His work is distributed by Icarus Films in North America, and by the British Film Institute in the United Kingdom.

Kristine Samson is Associate Professor in Performance Design at the Department of Communication and Arts, Roskilde University in Denmark. She holds a PhD in performative aesthetics in urban spaces from 2010, and has worked with performative aesthetics, affect. and emergence in relation to urbanism, urban design. and art in public. She is currently working on a national research project on urban affects and events, and has published extensively on topics on urbanism, sound, participatory. and performative aesthetics and art in public.

Allen C. Shelton was born in 1955 in Alabama. He is an associate professor of sociology. His work is in the field of social theory, culture, and ethnographic reportage. He arrived in Buffalo in 1998 in a Toyota one-ton pickup with 233,000 miles on the engine. The truck was stolen, which left him with a pair of R. M. Williams boots, a transparent Pelikan, Xenophon's *Anabasis*, cuffed Momotaro's, Rhodia paper, a creek named Cottaquila in another life, a Wetterling ax, an Ikaria disk, an abacus, a flower shirt that had never been washed, and Auburn, the color of the plains. Sometimes afterward he wrote *Dreamworlds of Alabama*, from University of Minnesota Press, 2007. He keeps time with a Bauman & Mercier mechanical. His latest book is *Where the North Sea Touches Alabama* (University of Chicago Press, 2013). His website is http://www.softarcades.com/.

Craig Shepard, a composer and member of the Wandelweiser group, creates music related to stillness, often outside. He studied trombone and composition at Northwestern University and the University of the Arts Zurich, and has worked closely with Frank Crisafulli, Michael Pisaro, Manfred Werder, Jürg Frey, and Christian Wolff. He has participated in Robert Fripp's Guitar Craft courses and Pauline Olvieros's Deep Listening. He has taken the Tomatis Listening Training.

Current projects include Creating Music Together workshops and retreats, On Foot, Trumpet City and Silent Walks. Scores and CDs published by Edition Wandelweiser. He lives in Brooklyn New York, where he directs Music for Contemplation.

Ernst van Alphen is Professor of Literary Studies at Leiden University in the Netherlands. His publications include *Francis Bacon and The Loss of Self* (1992), *Caught By History: Holocaust Effects in Contemporary Art, Literature, and Theory* (1998), *Armando: Shaping Memory* (2000), *Art in Mind: How Contemporary Images Shape Thought* (2005), *Staging*

Contributors

the Archive: Art and Photography in Times of New Media (2014), and *Failed Images: Photography and its Counter-Practices* (2018).

Elizabeth Waterhouse was a guest dancer with Ballet Frankfurt and founding member of The Forsythe Company, where she performed from 2005 to 2012. She worked as a freelance dancer and dramaturg from 2012 to 2016. Raised in upstate New York, Waterhouse studied Physics at Harvard University and received her MfA in Dance from The Ohio State University. Since 2015, she is a student in the Graduate School of the Arts at the Universität Bern/Hochschule der Künst Bern, where her dissertation is supported by the Swiss National Science Foundation. From 2016 to 2018, she was project director of the interdisciplinary research project "Motion Together" at the Institut für Theaterwissenschaft at the Freie Universität Berlin, supported by an "Arts and Science in Motion Grant" from the Volkswagen Stiftung. Having given lectures and master classes internationally, from 2015 to 2016 Waterhouse taught dance practice at the Institut Ästhetische Praxis und Theorie at the Fachhochschule Nordwestschweiz FHNW. Since 2016, she is a member of the artist group HOOD, supported by PACT Zollverein. http://www.dancelikething.org.

INDEX

aesthesis   2, 20, 215, 216
aesthetic episode   11, 45, 50, 52, 55, 57
aesthetic freedom   10, 25, 27–9
affect   2, 3, 17, 23, 51, 53, 64, 65, 105–15, 117–21, 160–9, 190, 191, 205, 217, 237, 238, 244, 248, 249, 255
affective   3, 5, 7, 12–15, 17, 21, 52, 57, 61, 66, 80, 90, 105, 110, 112–15, 119, 120, 159–69, 216, 227, 247, 248, 252, 255
agency   110, 172, 239
American Poetry   215, 218, 222
anachronism   14, 105–14, 243
Anderson, Wes   73–81
artwork   1, 2, 8, 10, 18, 19, 22, 25, 28, 50, 51–3, 178, 184, 193, 231, 233, 240, 241, 243, 247, 249
attunement   17, 160–8, 189, 190, 234
audio paper   9, 17, 159–69
audiovision   172, 173
audiovisual essay   8, 9, 23, 83, 91

Baumgarten, Alexander Gottlieb   1, 2, 23, 27, 47, 48, 215, 216, 218
Benjamin, Walter   8, 9, 19, 78, 79, 87, 198, 200, 205, 213
Bense, Max   20, 205–14
Berkman, Alexander   100
bioart   12, 63–71
buffering   84

Cage, John   15, 16, 121, 126, 133, 144, 156
choreography   18, 19, 85, 183–90
color   13, 47, 49, 52, 53, 68, 73–81, 84, 132, 133, 166, 253
Conrad, Joseph   199
contamination   21, 69, 237–9
contingence   86
Cowell, Henry   132

Damisch, Hubert   114, 247, 248
dance   18, 19, 106, 134, 183–94
Dawson City, Yukon Territory   14, 95–103
Deleuze, Gilles   1–7, 9, 12, 15, 17, 22–4, 61, 63–8, 80–2, 118–23, 157, 159, 161–4, 174, 180, 198, 205, 217, 244
depressive/depression   73, 231, 234
Dewey, John   12, 56, 57, 61, 70, 212

digital humanities   35, 37
Duo   18–19, 183–94

embodied   5, 120, 160, 161, 163, 166, 177, 178, 188, 206, 227, 230, 251, 252
empirical aesthetics   11–12, 45–60
essay   9, 13, 19–21, 23, 46, 55, 56, 60, 78, 80, 83–5, 89–91, 117, 118, 122, 123, 196, 198–202, 205–14, 216, 218
Expanded Cinema   18, 173, 175, 176
experience   2, 3, 9–12, 14, 16–21, 25–9, 32, 42, 45–6, 48–61, 64, 85–6, 97, 113, 117, 118, 120–2, 136, 138, 139, 143, 145, 155, 160, 164, 167, 173–4, 177–80, 184, 185, 190–2, 207, 211, 215, 216, 218, 220–4, 227–34, 255
experiment   8, 10, 12, 20, 25–33, 52, 56, 67, 69, 70, 207–12, 238, 244

force   13–15, 28, 30–4, 37, 59, 65–8, 75, 76, 79, 81, 90, 105, 110, 113, 120, 126, 137, 138, 190, 215–18, 220, 222, 224, 232
form   2, 8, 9, 12, 13, 20–3, 25–9, 31, 32, 35, 38, 50, 56, 60, 63, 64, 67–70, 73–6, 78–81, 83, 84, 86, 89, 105, 110, 118, 120, 121, 126, 127, 131, 136, 138, 139, 152, 156, 157, 159, 161, 165, 172–5, 177, 178, 180, 183, 189, 192, 193, 201, 205–7, 209, 211–14, 218–23, 230, 237, 239, 240–3, 247, 250, 255
Forsythe, William   19, 184, 187–92

Geballe, Tony   146
genealogy   88, 213
gesture   36–9, 127, 189, 219
Guattari, Félix   2–4, 6, 23, 61, 63, 65–7, 89, 119, 120, 174, 198, 205, 217

Harrison, Lou   132
heart   19–20, 36, 45, 48, 69, 74, 186, 195–203
Hennix, Catherine Christer   16–17, 149–57
Hoëné-Wronski, József   117

imagination   20, 21, 27, 28, 36, 42, 48, 63, 137, 165, 176, 200, 205, 207, 209–11, 213, 237
immersion   162–73, 177, 179, 238, 239
Israeli/Palestinian conflict   251–2, 255–6

Jonas, Hans   118–19

Index

Kant, Immanuel   11, 26–8, 47–8, 64, 174, 211
Kula, Sam   95

Lanyon, Peter   46, 59
'a life'   59, 66–8
life   2, 3, 10, 12, 13, 18, 21–3, 25, 28–30, 32–4, 55–60, 63, 65–70, 75, 106, 122, 136, 151, 156, 165–6, 179, 183, 195, 196, 199, 201, 217, 222, 227, 232, 238, 239, 242, 248
Lopez, Barry   131, 137
Ludlow Massacre   99
Lyotard, Jean-François   67, 127–9

media philosophy   7–11, 35, 36, 38, 39, 41, 42, 206, 212
media technology   10, 12, 13, 35, 36, 40, 42, 84, 88–90, 161, 171
media theory   10–11, 14, 35–8, 41–3, 84, 205, 207
memories   103, 189, 195, 196, 201, 203, 251, 254
mental health   21, 227, 232–3
Milner, Victor   99
modal ontology   17, 156
modernism   63, 222
movement   7, 11, 12, 14, 17, 19, 54, 57, 59, 67, 76, 84, 85, 102, 105, 111, 112, 121, 161, 167, 172, 173, 175, 183, 186, 188–93
Murai, Hiro   14, 105–8, 112
music   9, 12, 14–16, 19, 25, 29, 48, 57, 65, 106, 108, 111–13, 117–19, 121–3, 126–9, 131–9, 141, 142, 144–6, 149–58, 183, 189, 193, 230
music video   14–15, 105–6, 110–15, 179

new materialism   160, 161
Nietzsche, Friedrich   7, 27–9, 31–4, 84, 85, 117–19, 248
Noë, Alva   120

Olson, Charles   20, 215–25
organs   18, 19, 58, 67, 195–9

parapraxis   13, 83–91
performativity   239, 243
poor image   88
post-Kantian   63

Pound, Ezra   20, 215–24
practice   1, 2, 4, 7, 9–13, 15–22, 25, 27, 33, 35–42, 65, 67, 84–6, 89–91, 117, 118, 120, 122, 125, 128, 138, 139, 141, 142, 144, 146, 150, 155, 156, 159, 161, 164, 166, 183–5, 189, 192, 193, 206, 208, 209, 211–13, 215–24, 227–8, 232–3, 235, 237, 238, 243, 249, 250
psychoanalysis   64, 237

Ray, Dev   146
Rilke, Rainer Maria   117–18

Schaeffer, Pierre   127
sound   1, 8, 9, 14–18, 30, 48, 52, 58, 59, 60, 66, 73, 74, 90, 91, 96, 105, 106, 109–14, 117–23, 125–9, 132–8, 141–6, 150–6, 159–61, 163–8, 172–4, 179, 186, 189–91, 205, 230
sound thinking   15, 117–22
space   7, 16, 18, 19, 22, 34, 48, 59, 64, 69, 76, 125, 126, 131–9, 145, 149, 151–5, 167, 172, 176, 179, 183–6, 188–90, 201–3, 209, 210, 218, 227, 230–4, 238, 239, 241, 248, 253–5
style   14, 50, 53, 55, 56, 74, 188, 189, 220
symptomologist   12, 66

theoretical object   111, 243, 248
thinking in film   239, 244
Thoreau, Henry David   121–2, 131
Tomatis, Alfred   16, 144
topos   17, 153–6
transforming trauma into memory   22, 252, 255
transhuman   70–1, 177, 178

Varèse, Edgar   15, 117, 121
violence   13–15, 21, 59, 67, 73, 75, 76, 78, 80–1, 105, 106, 109, 113, 133, 190, 201, 202, 237, 239–41
virtual reality (VR)   18, 171–80

Wagner, Richard   29–34
Wolff, Christian   16, 144

Zielinski, Siegfried   18, 23, 172

www.ingramcontent.com/pod-product-compliance
Lightning Source LLC
Chambersburg PA
CBHW072130290426
44111CB00012B/1849